Contested Rituals

Contested Rituals

Circumcision,
Kosher Butchering,
and Jewish Political Life
in Germany, 1843–1933

✝✝✝✝✝✝✝✝✝✝✝✝✝✝

ROBIN JUDD

CORNELL UNIVERSITY PRESS

Ithaca and London

First published 2007 by Cornell University Press

Printed in the United States of America

Library of Congress Cataloging-in-Publication Data

Judd, Robin.
    Contested rituals : circumcision, kosher butchering, and Jewish political life in Germany, 1843–1933 / Robin Judd.
        p. cm.
    Includes bibliographical references and index.
    ISBN 978-0-8014-4545-3 (cloth : alk. paper)
    1. Jews—Germany—History—1800–1933. 2. Judaism—Germany—Customs and practices. 3. Circumcision—Religious aspects—Judaism. 4. Shehitah. I. Title.

    DS134.25.J83 2007
    305.892'404309034—dc22

                                                    2007010666

Cornell University Press strives to use environmentally responsible suppliers and materials to the fullest extent possible in the publishing of its books. Such materials include vegetable-based, low-VOC inks and acid-free papers that are recycled, totally chlorine-free, or partly composed of nonwood fibers. For further information, visit our website at www.cornellpress.cornell.edu.

Cloth printing   10 9 8 7 6 5 4 3 2 1

For My Parents

Contents

Acknowledgments

It is a pleasure to have the opportunity to publicly acknowledge the many people who have enabled me to complete this project. My doctoral advisers at the University of Michigan, Todd Endelman and Kathleen Canning, provided me with advice, criticism, and support. From them, I learned much about scholarly inquiry, engaged teaching, and persuasive writing. They have consistently offered sophisticated and passionate models of scholarly engagement. Professors Geoff Eley, Scott Spector, Anita Norich, and Laura Lee Downs also were crucial to this book. Alongside my Michigan colleagues and friends—Carolyn Comiskey, Rebecca Friedman, Caitlin Adams, Don LaCoss, Eric Goldstein, Nadia Malinovich, Deborah Starr, Ian McNeely, Jeff Wilson, Ellen Willow, Andy Donson, Ed Mathews, Julie Stubbs, Michael Sherman, and Tim Kaiser—they offered their ideas and assistance generously.

I arrived at The Ohio State University with three chapters of my dissertation in hand and limited teaching experience. Members of the "first book club": Judy Wu, Nicholas Breyfogle, Leslie Alexander, and Lucy Murphy helped me navigate the transition from graduate student to faculty member. They patiently read my first articles, conference papers, and grant proposals. Other colleagues offered liberal advice and friendship. I am particularly grateful to Ken Andrien, Gail Summerhill, Saul Cornell, Susan Hartman, Alan Beyerchen, Manse Blackford, Peter Hahn, David Cressy, David Hoffman, Geoffrey Parker, Dale van Kley, Tamar Rudavsky, Stephanie Smith, Brian Feltman, David Dennis, and David Lincove for their assistance. My mentor Carole Fink assisted me at every turn; she is a tireless advocate and generous friend. Matt Goldish served as an informal mentor, sounding board, and supporter. Donna Guy offered me a comfortable chair in which I could write. Yossi Galron tracked down strange bibliographic references and pamphlets, while David Staley and Chris Aldridge coaxed scanners to work and images to download. Finally, I am deeply grateful to my friends Paul Reitter, Birgitte Soland, Nicholas Breyfogle, Kevin Boyle, Alice Conklin, Carole Fink, and Steve Conn who kindly read countless versions of the manuscript.

During the past decade, many institutions have offered generous support, including the National Endowment for the Humanities, the National Foundation for Jewish Culture, the Memorial Foundation for Jewish Culture, the DAAD-German Academic Exchange Service, the Littauer Foundation, the American Historical Association, and the Wexner Foundation. I also am grateful to the Frankel Center for Jewish Studies, the Rackham Graduate School, the History Department at the University of Michigan, the Melton Center for Jewish Studies, and the History Department at The Ohio State University. My thanks to Marshall Weinberg whose graduate fellowship allowed me a summer of research and to Steven Poppel whose precious book gift arrived at a decisive point in my writing.

Archivists, librarians, and scholars throughout the world aided me with their knowledge and expertise. My special thanks to Hadassah Assouline (Central Archives for the History of the Jewish People) who first helped me think through the research process. In England, Germany, and Israel, I benefited tremendously from Shelley Harten, Till van Rahden, Andreas Gotzmann, Christian Weise, David Rechter, Jonathan Frankel, Michael Silber, Yosef Yuval, and Oded Heilbronner. In the United States and Canada, I received wonderful pointed advice from Adam Rubin, David Myers, Shaye Cohen, Jon Efron, Paula Hyman, Dorothee Brantz, Sander Gilman, Deborah Lipstadt, Ken Koltun-Frumm, Michael A. Meyer, Jim Retallack, Richard Levy, Mitchell Hart, Alain Corbin, Marsha Rozenblitt, Harriet Friedenreich, Peter Hayes, David Biale, Ben Baader, Paul Lerner, Sharon Gillerman, and Jonathan Sarna. Hasia Diner and Alan Steinweiss kindly read my book abstract and provided strategic guidance. My conversations with Marion Kaplan encouraged me to pursue new paths within German and Jewish history. This book also benefited from the suggestions offered by Cornell University Press's two anonymous readers and from Alison Kalett's stewardship.

There are other professional influences that I wish to acknowledge. Many years ago, Judy Arian, Devorah Heckelman, and Richard Robelloto introduced me to the historians' craft. At Wellesley College I had the fortune of studying with Marilyn Halter, Susan Reverby, Babara Geller, Alan Schechter, and Jacqueline Jones. I still think of them when I walk into the classroom. Frances Malino has been reading drafts of my work ever since she first walked into her office in Founders Hall; she is the

Introduction: Rituals, Identities, and Politics

In early April 1881, just five weeks after his circumcision, the son of Benjamin Hoffman of Huffenhardt (Baden) developed ulcers on his penis. The boy's concerned mother brought him to a local physician who, after observing the sick infant and his healthy twin sister, referred the case to the state medical examiner, E. Sausheim. Influenced by developing trends in public health research and by a growing concern with syphilis, Sausheim already had begun tracking similar cases. He had launched a formal investigation one month earlier when a third child developed symptoms analogous to those later exhibited by Hoffman. Now, after examining the fourth boy in Baden to be stricken by syphilis-like conditions, Sausheim issued a report to Baden's minister of interior. In his investigation, he discovered that the same circumciser (*mohel*), Simon Marx, had treated the four boys and that he had practiced the traditional form of oral suction (*metsitsah be'peh*) when he removed impurities from their incisions.[1] Sausheim requested that the *mohel* be suspended and that the allegedly risky practice of oral suction be outlawed by the state.[2] Moreover, he insisted that the government

[1] Marx's use of oral suction may explain why he attracted a number of eastern European–born clients. The controversy over oral suction recently resurfaced in New York. "Mayor Balances Hasidic Ritual Against Fears for Babies' Health," *New York Times* (6 January 2006), A1+; Benjamin Gesundheit et. al, "Neonatal Genital Herpes Simplex Virus Type 1 Infection After Jewish Ritual Circumcision: Modern Medicine and Religious Tradition," *Pediatrics* 114.2 (August 2004): e259–e263; www.nytimes.com/2005/08/26/nyregion/26/circumcise.html. An excellent study of the debates over *metsitsah* is found in Jacob Katz, "The Conflict over Metsitsah," *Jewish Law in Conflict* (Hebrew), ed. Jacob Katz (Jerusalem: Magnes Press, 1992), pp. 150–183.

[2] The medical examiner and the local physician, Geiger, disagreed over whether the act of oral suction or the use of the *mohel*'s fingernail endangered the children. 10 March

of Baden—and not the Jewish community—now assume the responsibility for regulating Jewish ritual behavior. Baden's Jewish community and the minister of interior both claimed ultimate jurisdiction. Their dispute over the right to adjudicate in these matters soon attracted the attention of health officials, pediatricians, and rabbis from across Germany.[3]

A second Jewish rite also attracted attention in the German states in 1881.[4] Just a few months after Sausheim issued his report on circumcision practices in Baden, the magistrate of Kattowitz (Silesia, Prussia) launched an investigation into the Jewish ritual of kosher butchering. The magistrate's public inquiry into the character and jurisdiction of the rite took place after several of the city's butchers and animal protectionists had complained that the Jewish method of slaughtering animals for food was unusually cruel. The magistrate reacted to this campaign by scrutinizing the rite and its impact.[5] One year later, a veterinarian and animal protectionist in Kaiserlautern (Palatinate) sparked an analogous conversation when he published a damning study of kosher butchering. His work prompted responses from animal protectionists and Jewish

---

1881 report of the medical examiner Neue Synagoge Berlin Centrum Judaicum Archiv (CJA) 75BKa124 2; April 6 1881 letter to the minister of interior from the medical examiner CJA 75BKa124 6; 7 April 1881 letter from the minister of interior to the Jewish community council of Baden CJA 75BKa124 1.

[3] 25 April 1881 letter from the minister of interior to the Rabbinate of Heidelberg CJA 75BKa124 13; 23 September 1882 letter from the Jewish community council of Baden to the minister of interior CJA 75BKa124 51; 28 October 1882 letter from the minister of interior to the Jewish community council of Baden CJA 75BKa124 52; 11 December 1882 statement from the Jewish community council CJA 75BKa124 55; 20 December 1883 letter from the minister of interior CJA 75BKa124 60; 10 January 1883 regulations CJA 75BKa1 24 62–3; 7 February 1883 letter from the minister of interior to the Jewish community council of Baden CJA 75BKa1 24 64. 1881 marked the outbreak of exclusionary violence in Pomerania and West Prussia. Christhard Hoffmann, "Political Culture and Violence Against Minorities: The Antisemitic Riots in Pomerania and West Prussia," trans. A. D. Moses, in *Exclusionary Violence: Antisemitic Riots in Modern German History,* ed. Christhard Hoffmann, Werner Bergmann, and Helmut Walser Smith (Ann Arbor: University of Michigan Press, 2002), pp. 67–92.

[4] I use the terms *rite* and *ritual* interchangeably, in part to ease the narrative flow of the project and because I think both terms are appropriate. Scholars often use "rite" to refer to the actions people undertake and "ritual" as the understanding of those actions. Catherine Bell, *Ritual: Perspectives and Dimensions* (Oxford: Oxford University Press, 1997), pp. 93–137.

[5] 1 December 1881 letter to Cohn from the magistrate of Kattowitz and response CJA 75DCo127 12–14. A similar but unrelated discussion took place in Weilburg. 20 September 1881 letter from Loeb to Goldschmidt CJA 75BWe12430.

communal leaders from across the country.[6] Like those who participated in the contemporaneous discussions about circumcision, animal advocates and Jewish community representatives debated the virtues of kosher butchering while each simultaneously maintained the exclusive authority to opine in such matters.

Between 1843 and 1933, four generations of Jews and non-Jews and several different political regimes in the German lands paid similar attention to Jewish ritual behavior. These participants came from disparate geographic areas and professional, political, and religious orientations. Many of them became interested in the rites of circumcision and kosher butchering because the ritual questions (*Ritualfragen*) offered them ways to welcome, resist, or reconcile themselves to change. During this era, German-speaking populations faced wars and political revolutions, reorganization and consolidation. In the face of German nation building, industrialization, and accelerated economic growth and downturns, contributors to the debates offered formulations concerning Jewish and German self-definition; the order of social relationships; and the appropriate responses to rapid social, political, and cultural transformations.

This book analyzes those ritualized markings of difference that became a focal point of political struggles among Jews and gentiles within Germany. Beginning with the concomitant movements for German unification and Jewish emancipation and ending with the National Socialist Party's assumption of power, it argues that the debates about circumcision and kosher butchering offered German Jews and non-Jews one arena in which they could understand the complicated relationships among constructions of authority, power, and governance.[7]

Circumcision and Kosher Butchering

Circumcision and kosher butchering share a number of procedural, discursive, and historical similarities. Circumcision (*brit milah*) is a biblical injunction whose act of separation takes place on a male newborn's

[6]Carl Bauwerker, *Das Rituelle Schächten der Israeliten im Lichte der Wissenschaft. Ein Vortrag Gehalten im Wissenschaftlich-Literarischen Verein zu Kaiserslautern am. 5 Dezember 1881* (Kaiserslautern: Verlag von Aug. Gotthold's Buchhandlung, 1882).

[7]David E. Barclay, *Frederick William IV and the Prussian Monarchy, 1840–1861* (Oxford: Oxford University Press, 1995), p. xv.

body. This rite of passage requires cutting off a baby's foreskin on his eighth day of life and includes four necessary components that must be performed, even if a circumcision falls on a Sabbath. They are:

1. The removal of the foreskin (*milah*).
2. The removal of the mucous membrane in order to uncover the corona (*periah*).
3. The sucking of the wound by the circumciser (*mohel*) in order to draw out the wound's impurities and excess blood (*metsitsah*).
4. The application of a bandage after warm water has been trickled on the wound.

According to the Bible, circumcision is a process of initiation. It represents the introduction of all (male) children into the covenant made between God and Abraham for the latter's descendants. Genesis 17:11 commands of Abraham "You shall circumcise the flesh of your foreskin, and that shall be the sign of the covenant between me and you. And throughout the generations, every male among you shall be circumcised."[8] Because of this relationship between the covenant and the rite of circumcision, Jewish law historically has insisted on the centrality of the rite to Jewish tradition, interpreting it to be as important as all of the other commandments combined.[9] Religious law forbids the abandonment of circumcision and allows the rite to be breached only if two other brothers have died from the procedure. If a child is ill, circumcision is postponed until he is sufficiently healthy for the operation. If the child is from a poor family, the community is to cover the costs of the *mohel*. If a Jewish boy does not undergo circumcision, he is considered an *aral*, an uncircumcised Jew with restricted rights.

By the 1840s many European Jewish communities had imputed an additional meaning to the rite beyond the already significant introduction to the covenant. The German-Jewish communities studied here, like many other Jewish communities in Europe, only registered male children as members of their communities after their circumcisions. Circumcision, then, not only initiated a child into the covenant with

---

[8]This translation can be found in David L. Lieber, ed., *Etz Hayim Torah and Commentary* (New York: Jewish Publication Society, 2001), p. 91. Genesis 17:10–15 includes the commandment for circumcision, but the four components of circumcision are set out in the Talmud and Mishnah. The injunction of circumcision is unambiguously male centered: It is intended for male children only, and it is the father who is obligated to ensure that his son's circumcision takes place. Rabbinic scholars and anthropologists have therefore described circumcision as a rite of gender differentiation. It separates the boy from his mother at an early age; juxtaposes the blood boys lose during their circumcisions with the blood women lose during their menstruation; and differentiates Jewish men, those marked with the covenant, from Jewish women, who bear no marking.

[9]On circumcision's importance, see Nedarim 32 a.

God but also into the local community in which he lived.[10] The timing of this practice made sense. The child's survival of his first week of life (and of his circumcision) suggested likelihood that he would endure infancy and could become a viable member of the community. Circumcision became necessary for entrance to the community's Jewish birth registry even though the ancient rabbis never envisioned the rite as *the single* standard for dictating one's Jewishness.[11]

Like circumcision, kosher butchering is also crucial to Jewish communal self-definition. The laws of kosher butchering (*shehitah*) are a subset of Judaism's dietary laws (*kashrut*), dictating the ways in which mammals and fowl must be slaughtered for the resulting meat to be permissible for consumption. Kosher butchering requires the presence of a pious and qualified practitioner (*shohet*) well versed in the laws of kosher butchering. The *shohet* must use a sharp and perfectly smooth knife to rapidly sever the trachea and esophagus of the animal and to cut the carotid arteries and jugular vein.[12] After he slaughters the animal, he must examine its carcass to verify that it has no blemishes or flaws. If the animal is free of these, the *shohet* hangs it upside down to encourage the rapid blood drainage mandated by the Jewish dietary laws. These regulations concerning meat preparation reinforce Jewish separateness. Judaism allows Jews to consume only meat prepared by kosher butchering.

In addition to these strictures, Jewish law mandates that the incision of *shehitah* be smooth and uninterrupted and prohibits the ritual practitioner from performing any other kind of cut.[13] Because Jewish law

---

[10]Because of its role in communal affiliation, circumcision often is performed publicly, witnessed by community members in a synagogue, home, or hospital room. One memoirist recalled that everyone in his late-nineteenth-century German village attended these community events. *Memories of weddings and a brit-milah: 1885–1909* Central Archives for the History of the Jewish People (CAHJP) File 963, p. 34.

[11]According to traditional Jewish law, matrilineal lineage determines Jewish affiliation. A child born to a Jewish mother is Jewish whether or not he is circumcised. See the different perspectives in Shaye Cohen, *Why Aren't Jewish Women Circumcised? Gender and Covenant in Judaism* (Berkeley: University of California Press, 2005); Howard Eilberg-Schwartz, *The Savage in Judaism: An Anthropology of Israelite Religion and Ancient Judaism* (Bloomington: Indiana University Press, 1990); Lawrence A. Hoffman, *Covenant of Blood: Circumcision and Gender in Rabbinic Judaism* (Chicago: University of Chicago Press, 1996).

[12]The laws of *kashrut* can be found in the Bible (Leviticus 11, Deuteronomy 14:4–21), the *Talmud* (tractate *Hullin*), and in the code of Jewish law, the *Shulhan Arukh* (*Yoreh Deah*). The *shohet* requires a license (*kabbalah*) from a recognized scholar in order to practice. While women are not forbidden to practice *shehitah*, almost all *shohetim* are (and were) male.

[13]There are five movements that are to be avoided: *Shehiyah* (pausing or delay), *Derasah* (pressing), *Haladah* (burrowing), *Hagramah* (deviating), and *'Aquirah* (tearing out).

insists on an even and continuous incision, *shohetim* (kosher butchers) utilize a variety of devices that restrict animal movement before and during slaughter. Moreover, kosher slaughterers do not stun animals into a state of unconsciousness before slaughter. Rabbinic authorities have warned that stunning an animal might bruise it in some way or cause it to experience involuntary muscle spasms. This might result in a jagged cut and could possibly injure the animal as well. Therefore, for kosher butchering to be valid, an animal must be conscious when killed for food.

This book does not equate the two rituals; nor does it suggest that the participants considered here invoked the two rites simultaneously. However, circumcision and kosher butchering do share several important similarities, all of which were at the core of the German ritual questions of the nineteenth and early twentieth centuries. Both rites erect social, cultural, and political barriers between Jews and their non-Jewish neighbors. One of the rituals seals difference on the flesh of Jewish men's genitalia; the other prescribes difference at the act of consumption. Circumcision and kosher butchering also lay emphasis on the incision, mandating that circumcisers and kosher slaughters use knives that are sharp, smooth, and in proper condition.[14] The laws of both rites stipulate some kind of blood loss. The *mohel* must shed at least two drops of the child's blood, even if the child is born without a foreskin, and use suction to rid the wound of excess blood. *Shohetim* are required to drain animals of their blood after slaughter is complete. Finally, because religious law places ultimate authority in the hands of religious overseers, the rituals reinforce Jewish political distinction. Ritual practitioners can practice only if they receive some sort of license from their rabbinic authority. It is that authority that can determine whether or not the rite was properly executed and, if not, what the punishment might be.[15] These political distinctions encouraged power to remain in the hands of Jewish communal authorities long after municipal and state governments had begun to incorporate the formerly autonomous Jewish communities within their realm.

The centrality of difference, blood, and knives to the two rites became issues of serious concern in parts of Europe after 1750, when various groups identified a conflict between rituals and the historical

---

[14]Because circumcision and kosher butchering shared the commonalties described here, I limited my exploration to these two rites. A study of the laws of family purity (*niddah*) would complement this project, but German debates about *niddah* never reached a public audience with the same intensity as the deliberations concerning *shehitah* and circumcision. Nor do they share the same commonalties.

[15]The two rites share another procedural similarity; both require inspection after their completion.

shifts changing society. Ritual observance lay at the center of debates concerning medicalization, Jewish emancipation, and religious reform. During much of the nineteenth century, opponents of Jewish integration argued that Jewry's dogged observance of religious rituals precluded acculturation and preserved Jewish separateness. Proponents agreed, demanding that Jewry abandon or reform its rites before governments accepted Jews as citizens. As European nation states slowly underwent their own consolidation and reorganization, the discussions about Jewish rites shifted and radicalized. Critics of circumcision and kosher butchering increasingly invoked radical antisemitic discourses concerning the Jews' alleged deviant sexuality and blood thirst. Supporters gradually relied on languages of toleration and humanitarianism to defend Jewish ritual behavior. These discussions recurred throughout Europe, in France, England, Switzerland, Denmark, Sweden, Austria, Russia, Hungary, and Germany.[16]

While German historical specificity has been an uncomfortable and highly contested theme within historical scholarship, an analysis of these disputes in the German-speaking states suggests that the controversies over the rites resonated especially there.[17] Unlike in many other European countries, the German-speaking states experienced active, continuous discussions concerning both rites over a long period of time. They began in earnest in the early 1840s when a few German-Jewish fathers refused to allow their sons' circumcisions, and when a group of physicians, governmental officials, and academics simultaneously considered the medical character of the rite. Public controversies concerning circumcision continued through the unification period and intensified in the 1890s. They then quieted somewhat in the political arena but remained a topic of interest in written disputes. The debates concerning kosher butchering began in the 1850s when German animal protectionists first called for slaughterhouse laws that interfered with kosher butchering practices. Like the conflicts concerning circumcision, these disputes continued through the unification period and escalated in the 1890s. Unlike the circumcision disputes, those concerning animal slaughter per-

[16]They also took place in the United States. See P. C. Remondino, *History of Circumcision from the Earliest Times to the Present: Moral and Physical Reasons for Its Performance, with a History of Eunuchism, Hermaphrodism, Etc., and of the Different Operations Practiced Upon the Prepuce* (Philadelphia: F.A. Davis, 1891).

[17]On the German so-called special path (*Sonderweg*), see David Blackbourn and Geoff Eley, *The Peculiarities of German History, Bourgeois Society, and Politics in Nineteenth Century Germany* (Oxford: Oxford University Press, 1984); Richard J. Evans, "Introduction: Wilhelm II's Germany and the Historians," in *Society and Politics in Wilhelmine Germany*, ed. Richard J. Evans (London: Barnes and Noble, 1978), pp. 11–39.

sisted in written and spoken form until the Nazi assumption of power in 1933.[18]

Between 1843 and 1933, the German debates over circumcision and kosher butchering had a significant impact on the formation of German state and Jewish communal policies and political strategies. Ritualized markings of difference served as guideposts to discussions concerning Jewish acculturation and state growth. In town council meetings, national parliamentary *(Reichstag)* debates, the press, and personal interactions, diverse German interest groups, governments, and Jewish communal leaders often looked to Jewish rites when they debated the nature and limits of religious and social tolerance and Jewish communal self-character. As participants in the ritual questions, they disputed the boundaries between German Jews and gentiles and considered the extent to which German municipal, regional, and state governments ought to protect the civic rights of religious entities or strip groups of those privileges. A study of these discussions, then, offers a new way to interpret the history of German-speaking Jews and their interactions with gentile populations.

Why Rituals Matter

Scholarly investigations of the modern Jewish experience often assume that the path from traditional to modern communities was accompanied by the abandonment, or at least the absence, of Jewish

[18]On the Swiss kosher butchering debates, see Pascal Krauthammer, *Das Schächtverbotin der Schweiz 1854–2000: Die Schächtfrage zwischen Tierschutz, Politik, und Fremdenfeindlichkeit* (Zürich: Schulthess, 2000). On the French circumcision debates (which were mostly limited to the 1840s), see Jay R. Berkovitz, *Rites and Passages: The Beginnings of Modern Jewish Culture in France, 1650–1860* (Philadelphia: University of Pennsylvania Press, 2004), pp. 154–155, 200–201; Joseph Grutzhaendler, *De la Milah (Circoncision) son Histoire, son Importance Hygiénique sa Technique Opératoire* (Paris: M. Schifrine, 1914); H. M. G. Martin, *De La Circoncision avec Un Nouvel Appareil Inventé par L'auteur Pour Faire la Circoncision* (Paris: Adrien Delahaye, 1870); Scherbel, "Die *Mohel*frage im 'L'univers Israélite,'" *Allgemeine Zeitung des Judenthums* (AZDJ) 29 (1913): 345. On the British kosher butchering disputes, see Board of Jewish Deputies (London), Opinions of Foreign Experts on the Jewish Method of Slaughtering Animals American Jewish Archives (AJA): Dietary Laws—books, pamphlets, Nearprint, box 2; Geoffrey Alderman, "Power, Authority and Status in British Jewry: The Chief Rabbinate and Shechita," in *Outsiders and Outcasts: Essays in Honour of William J. Fishman*, ed. Geoffrey Alderman and Colin Holmes (London: Duckworth, 1993), pp. 12–31; Albert M Hyamson, *The London Board for Shechitah 1804–1954* (London: London Board for Shechita, 1954). On the British circumcision disputes, see Madge Dresser, "Minority Rites: The Strange History of Circumcision in English Thought." *Jewish Culture and History* 1.1 (1998): 72–87. Also see Robert Darby, *A Surgical Temptation: The Demonization of the Foreskin and the Rise of Circumcision in Britain* (Chicago: University of Chicago Press, 2005).

ritual. They tend to rely on the conceptual axes of emancipation, acculturation, and antisemitism to examine the shifts experienced by Jews
during the nineteenth and early twentieth centuries.[19] The historiography on German Jews, which in many ways has dominated the literature
on modernization, is emblematic of this pattern. With the significant
exception of the histories of religious reform and orthodox movements,
these narratives often neglect the fundamental role of practiced Judaism within the modern German-Jewish experience. They push Jewish
religious practices to the margins of Germany's tumultuous political
history and presume that the onset of secularization and modernization made religious Judaism and its practices "practically meaningless"
for most Jews living in western and central Europe.[20]

By placing Jewish religious practices at the center of its narrative,
this book uses Jewish rituals to examine Jewish acculturation and German political growth. Decades ago, a group of cultural anthropologists
first called for the study of rituals in order to better understand society
and culture.[21] They looked at rites associated with major life events such
as birth, marriage, and death, and noted how traditional communities
devised systems to clarify the world based on these rituals of passage.
Over the last forty years, sociologists, historians, philosophers, and so-
ciobiologists have joined anthropologists in this effort. Identifying rites
as cultural and historical constructions, they too have used rituals to
understand the cultural dynamics by which people "make and remake"

[19]Analyses of the historiographical trends within German-Jewish historical scholarship
can be found in Evyatar Friesel, "The German-Jewish Encounter as a Historical Problem:
A Reconsideration," *Leo Baeck Institute Yearbook (LBIYB)* 41 (1996): 263–275; Christhard
Hoffmann, "The German-Jewish Encounter and German Historical Culture," *LBIYB* 41
(1996): 277–290; Michael A. Meyer, "Recent Historiography on the Jewish Religion,"
LBIYB 35 (1990): 3–16; Michael A. Meyer, "Jews as Jews versus Jews as Germans: Two His-
torical Perspectives," *LBIYB* 36 (1991): xv–xxii; Paul Mendes-Flohr, *German Jews: A Dual
Identity* (New Haven: Yale University Press, 1999).

[20]Shulamit Volkov, "The Ambivalence of *Bildung*: Jews and Other Germans," in *The
German-Jewish Dialogue Reconsidered: A Symposium in Honor of George L. Mosse*, ed. Klaus
L. Berghahn (New York: Peter Lang, 1996), p. 96; Michael Brenner, *The Renaissance of
Jewish Culture in Weimar Germany* (New Haven: Yale University Press, 1996). Important
exceptions can be found in Jay R. Berkovitz, *Rites and Passages*; Andreas Gotzmann,
"Reconsidering Judaism as a Religion: The Religious Emancipation Period," *Jewish
Studies Quarterly (JSQ)* 7 (2000): 352–366; and Marion Kaplan, "Redefining Judaism in
Imperial Germany: Practices, Mentalities, and Community," *Jewish Social Studies (JSS)*
9.1 (2002): 1–33.

[21]Catherine Bell, *Ritual Theory, Ritual Practice* (New York: Oxford University Press,
1992); Bell, *Ritual*; Jack Goody, "Religion and Ritual: The Definitional Problem," *British Journal of Sociology* 12 (1961): 142–164; Victor Turner, *The Forest of Symbols: Aspects of
Ndembu Ritual* (Ithaca: Cornell University Press, 1967) and *The Ritual Process: Structure and
Anti-Structure* (Ithaca: Cornell University Press, 1969).

their worlds.[22] By examining how historical actors performed rites and the values and attitudes that people associated with them, they have shown how a study of rituals provides a window onto the history of everyday life.

Cultural historians focus on the ways in which rituals offer entrée into varying ideological projects or intricacies of meaning. This book is concerned with how people imagined Jewish rituals. I do not look to whether individuals held religious beliefs or practiced Jewish rites.[23] I assume that many did not. Rather I examine the special attention that Jews and gentiles paid to Jewish ritual behavior.[24] Even as the observance of Jewish rites among German Jews seemed to be declining, circumcision and kosher butchering continued to serve as signposts within the story of German integration and politics. Because the two rites invoked power relationships and images that were salient and familiar to many German Jews and gentiles, the question of Jewish rituals remained part of the maelstrom of German culture and politics.[25]

Discussants did not imagine or experience symbols of circumcision and kosher butchering uniformly. Instead, members of shared associations, communities, and governments sharply disagreed with one another over the meaning, merits, and appropriate oversight of the two Jewish rituals. An analysis of the changing deliberations concerning Jewish rites, then, suggests deep divisions within and between individual groups.

[22]Bell, *Ritual Theory*, p. 3. Also see Berkovitz, *Rites and Passages*; Ivan G. Marcus, *Rituals of Childhood* (New Haven: Yale University Press, 1996); Edward Muir, *Ritual in Early Modern Europe* (Cambridge: Cambridge University Press, 1997).

[23]This project, then, engages with Arnold Eisen's contention that what mattered was practice and not belief. Arnold M. Eisen, *Rethinking Modern Judaism: Ritual, Commandment, Community* (Chicago: University of Chicago Press, 1998), esp. p. 11. Many German-speaking Jews continued to practice these rites, albeit with some significant changes, but many others followed eclectic patterns of observance or had abandoned the rites over time. A fascinating study of orthodoxy's response to nonobservance can be found in Adam S. Ferziger, *Exclusion and Hierarchy: Orthodoxy, Nonobservance, and the Emergence of Modern Jewish Identity* (Philadelphia: University of Pennsylvania Press, 2005).

[24]The centrality of these rites within Jewish tradition certainly encouraged some people to engage in the disputes; however, the diminution in observance levels during the period under review suggests that issues other than a respect for Jewish law or tradition drew people to the deliberations. On why individuals practice rites, see Emile Durkheim, *The Elementary Forms of the Religious Life*, trans. Joseph Ward Swain (New York: Free Press, 1965); Mordechai M. Kaplan, *Judaism as a Civilization: Towards a Reconstruction of American-Jewish Life* (New York: Macmillan, 1934); Mordechai M. Kaplan, *The Meaning of God in Modern Jewish Religion* (New York: Reconstructionist Press, 1962).

[25]Mary Louise Roberts, *Civilization Without Sexes: Reconstructing Gender in Postwar France, 1917–1927* (Chicago: University of Chicago Press, 1994), p. 5.

By looking to the *Ritualfragen* as a way to understand German-Jewish history, this book complicates and de-exceptionalizes the Jewish experience in Germany.[26] Between 1843 and 1933, the discussions about Jewish rites were part of larger patterns and processes of German history. They served as arenas in which Jews and gentiles engaged in political dialogue and laid the groundwork for the creation of diverse public spheres. In varying ways, discussants used and interacted with diverse political structures including town councils, parliaments, ministries, political and extraparliamentary associations, and the press. Their publications in newspapers and journals created communities of readers who understood their imagery and language.[27] They helped to create networks of political activity and encouraged generations of new political actors.

The disputes over kosher butchering and circumcision offered participants opportunities to wrestle over the nature of German governance and the corresponding boundaries between states/provinces and their minority communities. Between 1843 and 1933, the German states underwent profound changes. Participants looked to the conflicts over Jewish rites to address the appropriate limits to government especially as the national state was formed and expanded its reach. Some participants emphasized the regulatory powers of government; others called for controls over outside intervention. This would have serious policy implications. The ways in which German municipal, state, and national administrative agencies interpreted their regulatory power had a significant impact on whether they passed laws supervising ritual practitioners or banning aspects of the rites.

The ritual questions also offered an opportunity to consider the character and governance of Jewish communal life. In the debates, German Jews and gentiles weighed the extent to which Jewish law and custom mattered in the daily governance of Jewish communal life. Some individuals imagined Jewry as a community differentiated by religion only and devoid of any political authority. Others envisioned it as a separate economic, political, and cultural society that regulated itself. Jewish discussants similarly questioned the appropriate relationships among Jewish agencies and institutions across Germany, and disputed the extent to which collaboration among them was possible in Jewish self-defense. A wide range of discourses and concerns influenced these paradigms, which shifted over the course of the ninety-year period under discussion here.

[26]I am grateful to one of the anonymous readers for his observation concerning this point.

[27]On the place of newspapers and journals in the formation of national identity, see Benedict Anderson, *Imagined Communities: Reflections on the Origin and Spread of Nationalism*, rev. ed. (London: Verso, 1991).

These disparate portraits of Jewish community and German government not only delineated boundaries of power but also established possible trajectories for minority inclusion. Until unification in 1871, Jews and non-Jews often looked to Jewish rites when arguing for or against Jewish emancipation. Even after the extension of civic rights in 1871, they continued to invoke Jewish ritual behavior when discussing the successes, limits, and failures of Jewish political and social integration. To make sense of Jewish social and civic possibilities, participants in the ritual questions drew from several discourses, including the growing importance of medicine and science.[28] Increasingly, some of these gentile discussants also incorporated anti-Jewish sentiment and linked Jewish ritual behavior with charges of Jewish brutality, bloodthirst, and social unworthiness.[29]

As Jewish and non-Jewish contributors to the debates considered the possibility of Jewish integration, they simultaneously contemplated the type of culture into which Jews and other minorities were to assimilate. Discussants again drew from a wide array of attitudes and beliefs, including, the liberal embrace of technology, anticlericalism, education, and humanitarianism. They considered the ways in which Jewish rituals intersected or clashed with their understandings of toleration and cruelty, and questioned who had the jurisdiction to establish the standards for cultural mixing. Within the debates concerning Jewish rites, these discussants considered the extent to which German culture would or should invite Jewish integration and what Jewish communities were willing to concede for that acculturation to take place.

The ritual questions also affected the complex relationships among German ethnic and religious groups. Discussions about Jewish rites offered other minorities an opportunity to collaborate and advance their own political causes. Catholics and Jews, for example, often imagined themselves as political enemies, yet the German (Catholic) Center Party

---

[28]This book complements existing scholarship by historians of medicine and science who have made significant inroads into the study of the ritual questions by examining the published responses by Jewish and non-Jewish physicians to the debates. John M. Efron, *Medicine and the German Jews: A History* (New Haven: Yale University Press, 2001); Eberhard Wolff, "Medizinische Kompetenz und talmudische Autorität: jüdische Ärzte und Rabbiner als ungleiche Partner in der Debatte um die Beschneidungsreform zwischen 1830 und 1850," in *Judentum und Aufklärung; jüdisches Selbstverständnis in der bürgerlichen Öffentlichkeit,* ed. Arno Herzig, Hans-Otto Horch, and Robert Jütte (Göttingen: Vandenhoeck & Ruprecht, 2002), 119–149. I also have benefited from studies on the history of circumcision, including David L. Gollaher, *Circumcision: A History of the World's Most Controversial Surgery* (New York: Basic Books, 2000); Leonard B. Glick, *Marked in Your Flesh: Circumcision from Ancient Judea to Modern America* (Oxford: Oxford University Press, 2005).

[29]This project has been shaped by Sander Gilman's argument that the campaigns against Jewish rites influenced and were shaped by the sexualized and gendered nature

was the Jewish community's most important ally in its defense of ko-sher butchering.[30] Likewise, the deliberations concerning Jewish rites served as a forum in which Jewish leaders could comment on the social and political integration of other groups, thus positioning themselves as the appropriate arbiters of German culture. This was evident in the Jewish leadership's use of the ritual questions to comment on the Ger-man state's 1870s campaign against its Catholic minority. At times, then, Jewish supporters deployed the anti-Catholic rhetoric card to promote their program; at other times they forged a shared front with their Catho-lic compatriots to advance their shared agenda.

While these themes envisioned some kind of exchange between Jews and gentiles, the debates about Jewish rites also offered space for the consideration of issues that, at least theoretically, pertained to Jewish communities and to German governments separately. The deliberations reveal the complicated relations among different levels of German gov-ernment during periods of significant structural change. The local and regional management of Jewish religious practices not only provided precedents for state and national governments in their dealings with other religious and national minorities. They also presented an area of competition between local and regional authorities. Between 1843 and 1933, dozens of local magistrates and town councils insisted on their own authority to regulate religious minorities and public institutions, disagreeing on whether the supposedly offensive nature of circumci-sion or kosher butchering outweighed the slowly evolving tradition of religious tolerance. As German administrative bodies took part in the disputes, so too did a number of non-Jewish interest groups who used the conflicts as way to participate in the political arena and to create coalitions with like-minded organizations.

Finally, understandings of Jewish rites had significant implications for the development of modern German-Jewish political behavior. Between 1843 and 1933, the disputes offered Jewish leaders an opportunity to

---

of anti-Jewish animus. It was his studies of the published discourses concerning the rite that prompted my interest in this topic. Sander L. Gilman, *Franz Kafka: The Jewish Patient* (New York: Routledge, 1996); *The Jew's Body* (New York: Routledge, 1991); "The Indel-ibility of Circumcision," *Koroth* 9.11–12 (1991): 806–817; *Freud, Race, and Gender* (Prince-ton: Princeton University Press, 1993); *The Case of Sigmund Freud: Medicine and Identity at the Fin de Siècle* (Baltimore: Johns Hopkins University Press, 1993). Jay Geller's work on Freud and circumcision also has helped me better understand the field. Jay Geller, "(G)Nos(E)Ology: The Cultural Construction of the Other," in *People of the Body: Jews and Judaism from an Embodied Perspective*, ed. Howard Eilberg-Schwartz (New York: State Uni-versity of New York Press, 1992), pp. 243–282; "A Paleontological View of Freud's Study of Religion: Unearthing the Leitfossil Circumcision," *Modern Judaism* 13 (1993): 49–70.

[30]Chapter 5 will consider the German Center Party's interest in kosher butchering.

craft and test models of modern political behavior. German-Jewish leaders used the disputes to develop a language and set of strategies to counter the opposition of non-Jewish special interest groups and German authorities. Over this ninety-year period, Jewish leaders, whether or not they observed Jewish religious law, increasingly embraced a new form of politics that emphasized Jewish difference. Their participation and diverse strategies in these confessionally oriented politics suggest that Jewish political behavior underwent change before the event frequently identified as the birth of modern German-Jewish politics—namely, the creation of the Berlin-based Central Association of German Citizens of the Jewish Faith (Centralverein) in 1893. Moreover, because Jewish participation in the ritual questions involved a broad generation of activists who took part in varying associations, a study of the *Ritualfragen* revises our understanding of modern Jewish politics.

†††††

My introduction of Jewish practices into the mainstream of German and Jewish history is based on extensive archival evidence as well as published materials from Germany, Israel, the United States, England, and France. I look at documentation produced by Jews and gentiles across generational, class, and geographic divides, including medical reports, cartoons, letters, memoirs, liturgical texts, court documents, organizational records, newspaper accounts, and joke-books. My heavy reliance on archival sources moves away from a traditional dependence on texts written by members of the German-Jewish intelligentsia. It also drives the project's interest in Jewish and German politics and shapes the book's chronological format.

I have organized this book chronologically beginning with the 1843 discussions concerning circumcision and ending with the Nazi prohibition of kosher butchering in 1933. This framework allows me to examine the local, regional, and national variations of these debates across a ninety-year span while also emphasizing the nonlinear nature of public discourse. It also offers a way to integrate intersecting questions of Jewish communal transformation into the broader narrative of German political and societal change. Certain chapters, then, consider the conflicts over both rites while others focus exclusively on only one ritual question.

Chapter 1 explores only the disputes concerning circumcision. It analyzes the period between 1843 and 1857 when the Jewish rite of circumcision first attracted a wide audience of German speakers. Diverse Jewish leaders, German bureaucrats, philosophers, physicians, and governmental authorities expressed interest in the Jewish ritual during this time because the rite summoned compelling power relationships. Despite significant variations, participants used the deliberations to wrestle with important historical developments and their transformative impact on Jewish life and governance. They considered the consolidation of power within the different German states, the possibility of Jewish emancipation, the rise of religious reform, and medicalization. They proposed new boundaries of Jewish communal and state authority and introduced innovative definitions of Jewish and German membership. As they presented this complicated picture of Jewish leadership and integration, they embraced novel strategies for interacting with one another and with their governments. This chapter delves into the rich available scholarship on the 1843 Frankfurt circumcision disputes and goes considerably beyond it.[31] Archival material from places outside of Frankfurt and concerning years other than the mid-1840s proves that the midcentury circumcision disputes were issues of importance for the Jewish community everywhere and were central to the internal functioning of German cities and states.

Over time, the debates about the significance and danger of circumcision shifted in character, rhetoric, and impact. Chapter 2 explores the reemergence of the disputes over circumcision in the late 1860s and 1870s as well as the contemporaneous discussions concerning kosher butchering.[32] Part of a scholarly trend that interrogates the relationship of religion, nation building, and national identity, this chapter examines the dynamic interplay among Jewish rites and German nationhood,

[31]Interested in the confessional question, these scholars examined the circumcision disputes of 1843–1845 and 1869–1871. Lawrence A. Hoffman, *Covenant of Blood: Circumcision and Gender in Rabbinic Judaism* (Chicago: University of Chicago Press, 1996); Jacob Katz, "Die Halacha unter dem Druck der modernen Verhältnisse," in *Judentum im deutschen Sprachraum*, ed. Karl E. Grözinger (Frankfurt am Main: Suhrkamp, 1991), 309–324; Robert Liberles, *Religious Conflict in Social Context: The Resurgence of Orthodox Judaism in Frankfurt Am Main, 1838–1877* (Westport, CT: Greenwood Press, 1985); Michael A. Meyer, "Alienated Intellectuals in the Camp of Religious Reform: The Frankfurt Reformfreunde, 1842–1845," *AJS Review* 6 (1981): 61–86; Andreas Gotzmann, *Jüdisches Recht im kulturellen Prozess: Die Wahrnehmung der Halacha im Deutschland des 19. Jahrhunderts* (Tübingen: M. Siebeck, 1997). While Katz casts his gaze a bit more broadly, he tends to hold the Frankfurt case as paradigmatic.

[32]Helmut Walser Smith, *German Nationalism and Religious Conflict: Culture, Ideology, Politics, 1870–1914* (Princeton: Princeton University Press, 1995); Margaret Lavinia Andersen, "Piety and Politics: Recent Works on German Catholicism," *Journal of Modern History* (JMH) 63 (1991): 681–716; Ronald J. Ross, "The Kulturkampf and the Limitations of Power in Bismarck's Germany," *Journal of Ecclesiastical History* 46.4 (1995): 669–688; Michael B. Gross, *The War Against Catholicism: Liberalism and the Anti-Catholic Imagination in Nineteenth-Century Germany* (Ann Arbor: University of Michigan Press, 2004).

politics, and culture. During the years immediately preceding and following unification, contributors to the debates about circumcision and kosher butchering invoked concepts that were central to the concomitant deliberations regarding the newly proposed definitions of German character. Discussants raised concerns regarding the place of Catholics and Jews in the newly unified state. They interrogated the relationship of circumcision and kosher butchering with technology and German education. They cited the supposed German antipathy toward cruelty and its alleged belief in toleration. Jewish advocates also periodically deployed anti-Catholicism to advance their agenda, however, as later chapters show, they also found themselves on the same side of the divide as Catholics and in need of shared political programs. These discourses of cruelty, tolerance, culture, and anticlericalism would continue to be crucial in the relationships between the Jewish minority and the German state long after this set of deliberations concluded.

German controversies concerning kosher butchering and circumcision underwent a radicalization in the 1880s and 1890s. Chapters 3, 4, and 5 consider the ritual questions of 1880–1916, with the latter two focusing almost exclusively on the kosher butchering conflicts. Chapter 3 examines the ritual questions of this period and their escalation. During this era, the disputes concerning Jewish rites occurred with greater frequency in a wider range of public forums. As its participatory base broadened considerably, its content also changed. Mimicking the political trends within and outside of associations and extraparliamentary groups, many participants increasingly cloaked their contributions within a veil of apoliticism or the languages of biology and science. Others increasingly invoked the new antisemitic ideology. These charges of Jewish difference articulated four concerns: Jewish brutality, blood-centeredness, economic noxiousness, and health risks. This chapter's analysis of the many different ritual debates highlights their variations. It suggests that while antisemitism was significant to the debates, it alone did not propel the opposition to either rite.

Chapter 4 questions the relationship between ideology and action. In its exploration of the influence of the ritual questions on German law and extraparliamentary activism, it demonstrates that a second frame of reference existed alongside antisemitism, namely, that of religious toleration. Both ideologies were at the core of local, regional, and national disputes over kosher butchering. Both deeply influenced the politicization of the debates' participants and the shifting relations among the different levels of German government. Neither antisemitic ideology nor issues of tolerance consistently permeated everyday life. Instead, an analysis of the *Ritualfragen* suggests that antisemitism translated into policy more effectively at the local level but only within

was not supposed to complicate matters. Religion, according to the rabbi, "should make life comprehensible."[34] This project certainly does not suggest that Judaism made life simpler. However, it does argue that people used discussions about religious rites in a variety of ways to do exactly what Landau desired—to make sense of their everyday life.

[34]Wolff Landau, "Beschneidung," *Referat über die der ersten israelitischen Synode zu Leipzig überreichten Anträge* (Berlin: Louis Gerschel Verlagsbuchhandlung, 1871), p. 196.

CHAPTER 1

The Circumcision Questions in the German-Speaking Lands, 1843–1857

Before 1850, Joachim (Hayum) Schwarz, a small-town rabbi in Hürben, Bavaria, had limited interactions with the local non-Jewish community and authorities. He devoted most of his time to fulfilling his rabbinic obligations, tending to the needs of his congregants and teaching their children. He led services in the town's synagogue and oversaw some of the philanthropic endeavors of local Jewish communal institutions. Yet, from the middle of the century, Schwarz began to engage more frequently with his town's municipal leadership. After one of his congregants refused to circumcise his son, the rabbi became increasingly visible within the larger public sphere.[1]

The congregant, the physician Ignatz Landauer, renounced circumcision out of concern that the rite might harm his child, Robert. Despite his rejection of the ritual, however, the physician did not abdicate his own or his son's Jewishness. Instead, he requested that his uncircumcised child be included in Hürben's Jewish communal registry. This appeal presented a challenge to Rabbi Schwarz. Most Jewish parents registered their boys as Jews after their sons' circumcisions, while the majority of Christians baptized their sons and listed them as Christians.[2] Landauer broke ranks. He declined to circumcise his son and then petitioned the Jewish community to acknowledge the uncircumcised boy

---

[1]On Schwarz, see Herbert Auer, "Hayum Schwarz, der letzte Rabbiner in Hürben," in *Geschichte und Kultur der Juden in Schwaben* II, ed. Peter Fassl (Stuttgart: Jan Thorbecke Verlag, 2000), pp. 65–81.

[2]2 May 1850 letter from Traumbach to Bavarian authorities CAHJP Inv 6941; 5 December 1851 statement to authorities in Neuberg and Upper Bavaria Staatsarchiv München (SM) RA 33902; 25 December 1851 police order SM RA 33902; 5 January 1852 ruling

as its member. Schwarz refused to accept the child as a Jew because he believed that circumcision was a prerequisite for communal admission. According to the rabbi, the rite was "the acceptance on which the entrance into the [Jewish] community rests....Circumcision is for the Jews as baptism is for the Christians."[3] Moreover, the rabbi called for the total exclusion of the Landauer family, beseeching that "the Jewish community should not care for them [Robert and his father], but turn away from them."[4]

Schwarz may have refused to register the child as a member of his Jewish community, but he knew the Jewish law pertaining to this case. According to Jewish law, matrilineal descent and not circumcision determines Jewishness. Robert was Jewish because his mother was Jewish. The boy should have been listed as an *aral*, an uncircumcised Jew with limited religious rights and obligations. Schwarz's insistence that Judaism and its institutions exclude the Landauer family was obviously flawed.

Unwilling to choose either baptism or circumcision for his son, Landauer appealed to the local magistrate who demanded Robert's inclusion on the Jewish birth registry. For the next two years, Schwarz rebuffed local and regional governmental orders that he recognize the boy as a member of the Jewish community. After years of negotiations, arguments, and threats, a frustrated Landauer left Hürben. Rather than continue his battle with the local Jewish community, the physician moved to Speyer, where he set up his medical practice and petitioned its Jewish community to register his son.[5]

Schwarz remained furious at his ex-congregant. For more than twelve months after the physician's departure from Hürben, the rabbi fervently informed others of Landauer's failure to circumcise his son.

(#11651) from the judicial authorities in Krunsbach SM RA 33902; "Augsburg" *AZDJ* 7 (1855): 81–82. An 1838 Munich police act dictated that all inhabitants be registered with the religious community in which they presided. 5 December 1851 statement from the authorities in Neuberg and Upper Bavaria SM RA 33902.

[3] 19 March 1852 letter to the Hürben magistrate from Schwarz CAHJP Inv 6941.

[4] 3 June 1853 letter Jewish community of Speyer (no. 2119) CAHJP Inv 6941.

[5] 2 May 1850 letter to Traumbach; 7 November 1851 letter from the regional court to the Rabbinate of Hürben CAHJP Inv 6841; 5 December 1851 statement; 5 January 1852 ruling issued by the regional court in Augsburg SM RA 33902; 18 October 1852 statement by the Bavarian authorities Bayerisches Hauptstaatsarchiv (BH) Staatsrat 6511; 11 January 1852 letter from the Neuberg authorities to the Upper Bavarian authorities SM RA 33902; 19 March 1852 letter from Schwarz; 20 June 1852 order from the minister of religion and education CAHJP Inv 6941; 7 October 1852 letter from the magistrate to Schwarz CAHJP Inv 6941; 30 November 1852 report (no. 31) issued by the town council BH Staatsrat 6511.

"In order to prevent 'the spread of uncircumcised (*arelim*) among Israel,'" proclaimed one letter to a nearby Jewish community, "I declare that Dr. Ignatz Landauer, now living in Speyer, did not carry out the circumcision of his son."[6] In an even harsher tone, he urged neighboring Jewish leaders to exclude the Landauer family altogether.[7] Some rabbis supported Schwarz and promised to snub the Landauer family if such an opportunity presented itself.[8] Others called for a more sympathetic response. In contrast to Schwarz, they encouraged the inclusion of all male children born to Jewish parents regardless of whether a boy was circumcised.

When Landauer, Schwarz, and others doggedly fought over the status of the uncircumcised Robert, they were in actuality debating the appropriate models of Jewish communal organization, administration, and community membership in a new age. Their dramatic conflict was one of many contemporaneous struggles among a new generation of Jewish professionals, traditional rabbinic authorities, and local and regional governments. Landauer and other like-minded fathers disregarded traditional authority and desired social and political integration into non-Jewish society. As contributors to the circumcision debate, they championed the reformulation of the Jewish community into an entity that permitted Jewish integration, governmental intervention, and their own political participation. In contrast, Rabbi Schwarz and his supporters fervently called for Jewish society to retain its traditional character and, by extension, its extant authority. Their portraits of Jewish life reflected their response to modernity and conflicted with the formulations proposed by their opponents in these debates.

Between 1843, when a few fathers rejected circumcision for their sons, and 1857, when the circumcision disputes appeared to come to a close, two sets of deliberations concerning circumcision sharpened political struggles within and outside of the Jewish community. Discussions concerning circumcision's hygienic character and debates over the rite's relationship to standards of communal membership served as arenas in which participants helped to establish the boundaries of Jewish communal and German state authority and membership. The discussions and their contributors were influenced profoundly by the modernizing developments affecting German Jews and their relationships with the gentile communities among whom they lived.

[6] 19 May 1853 public letter issued by Schwarz CAHJP Inv 6941.

[7] 3 June 1853 letter Jewish community of Speyer (no. 2119) CAHJP Inv 6941; 3 June 1853 letter to the Jewish community of Kreigshaben (no. 2120) CAHJP Inv 6941; 3 June 1853 letter to the Jewish community of Durkheit (2121) CAHJP Inv 6941.

[8] 2 May 1850 letter to Traumbach; 30 April 1854 letter to Schwarz from the District Rabbi, Aaron Gugenheim CAHJP Inv. 6941.

Circumcision Disputes: 1843–1857

The so-called circumcision questions (*Circumcisionsfragen*) centered on the charge that the Jewish rite posed a risk to society's health. These disputes took place within written correspondence, conference meetings, and published medical and popular treatises. Its diverse contributors examined the training and licensing of ritual practitioners and investigated the ritual practices of using the fingernail for the separation of the corona (*periah*) and the mouth for removal of impurities from the wound.[9] Some of these participants encouraged state intervention or limited reform to improve these extant circumcision customs. Others wholly refuted the medical or hygienic critiques made against the rite. In all cases, they weighed the relevance of religious tradition against the alleged danger of Jewish practices and the power of medical authorities.[10]

Whereas these groups considered circumcision's medical benefits and shortcomings, others contemplated a second set of questions concerning the Jewish rite. The *Beschneidungsfragen* (ritual-circumcision questions) concerned the acts of over a dozen Jewish fathers who had spurned circumcision but affirmed their own and their sons' Jewish affiliations.[11] These men challenged traditional methods of recording Jewish membership, and while a few communities registered the uncircumcised boys, several others refused to do so. The result was a decade-long dispute in which certain Jewish community members, local and state governments, and religious authorities debated whether circumcision determined Jewish communal membership and who had the power to make that verdict.[12]

[9]Its participants included governmental authorities, physicians, academics, Jewish community members, and Jewish and non-Jewish reformers.

[10]Some examples of these published discussions include: Gustave Schilling (pseud. Ben Rabbi), *Die Lehre von der Beschneidung der Israeliten, in ihrer mosaischen Reinheit dargestellt und entwickelt* (Stuttgart: Hallberger'sche Verlagshandlung, 1844); Joseph Bergson, *Die Beschneidung vom Historischen, Kritischen und Medicinischen Standpunkt mit Bezug auf die neuesten Debatten und Reformvorschläge* (Berlin: Verlag von Th. Scherk, 1844); Gideon Brecher, *Die Beschneidung der Israeliten, von der historischen, praktisch-operativen und ritualen seite zunächst für den Selbstunterricht* (Wien: Gedruckt bei Franz Edl. v. Schmid und J.J. Busch, 1845) and "Die Beschneidung vor dem arztlichen Forum," *AZDJ* 52 (1857): 709–710; Klein, "Die rituelle Circumcision: eine sanitätspolizeiliche Frage," *Allgemeine Medicinische Central Zeitung* (11 June 1853): 365–366; M. Salomon, *Die Beschneidung: historisch und medizinisch Beleuchtet* (Braunschweig: Friedrich Vieweg und Sohn, 1844). Efron, *Medicine and the German Jews,* and Wolff, "Medizinische Kompetenz und talmudische Autorität" provide an excellent study of the published medical debates.

[11]The disputes also concerned the possibility of burying uncircumcised children.

[12]Some scholars have paid attention to the published *Beschneidungsfragen*, particularly those that took place in Frankfurt, the site of a vitriolic debate among reformers and

The two sets of discussions shared important commonalties, despite their different emphases. Several local *Beschneidungsfragen* followed municipal *Circumcisionsfragen* (circumcision questions), and the debates frequently referenced one another.[13] They also shared participants. Landauer rejected the rite after hearing rumors that circumcision had caused a local cholera epidemic; the Austrian physician Eugen Levit similarly abdicated the ritual after witnessing cases of disfigurement caused by sloppy practitioners. Unlike Landauer, Levit was an active participant in both disputes. He spearheaded a *Beschneidungsfrage* in his hometown of Horic, Austria, and later authored a widely read treatise on circumcision's medical character.[14] Like Levit, Hirsch B. Fassel, a rabbi in Prossnitz, Moravia, and Nagykanizsa, Hungary, also took part in the two deliberations. He published articles in the Jewish press on the *Beschneidungsfragen* and wrote the foreword to an important medical study of the rite.[15]

—————

traditionalists. Most examine these debates as an example of the reform/traditionalist divide or as a conflict concerning emancipatory hopes. See Hoffman, *Covenant of Blood*; Katz, "Die Halacha"; Liberles, *Religious Conflict*, pp. 34–38; Meyer, "Alienated Intellectuals"; Michael A. Meyer, *A Response to Modernity: A History of the Reform Movement in Judaism* (New York: Oxford University Press, 1988), pp. 311–313; Michael A. Meyer, "*Berit Mila* Within the History of the Reform Movement," in *Berit Mila in the Reform Context*, ed. Lewis M. Barth (United States of America: Berit Mila Board of Reform Judaism, 1990), pp. 141–151. This chapter does not dismiss these historical explanations. Drawing on published and unpublished sources, it analyzes the impact of the debates on Jewish and non-Jewish politics.

[13]"Dresden," *AZDJ* 49 (1844): 701–702; Zacharias Frankel, "Ueber manch durch den Fortschritt der Medicin im Judenthum bedingte Reformen," *Zeitschrift für die religiösen Interessen des Judenthums* 2 (1845): 300–301. Also see the Hürben anecdote with which this narrative began.

[14]Eugen Levit, *Die Circumcision der Israeliten beleuchtet vom ärztlichen und humanen Standpunkte von einem alten Arzte* (Vienna: Druck und Commissions-Verlag von Carl Gerold's Sohn, 1874), p. 3. On the use of Levit, see "Protokoll Der Sitzung Vom 2 November 1874," *Mittheilungen des Aertzlichen Vereines in Wien* 3.13 (1874): 169–72; "Rundschau," *Jüdische Volkszeitung* (*JV*) 19 (7 May 1873): 148. On Landauer's medical concerns, see M. W. Heicht to Rabbi Lobrecht CJA 75B Schw2 54 22. Others similarly invoked both deliberations when discussing the medical nature of the rite. See Ludwig Philippson, "Die Beschneidung Von Sanitäts-Polizeilichen Standpunkte," *AZDJ* 19 (1855): 240–243; "Die Beschneidung Vor Dem Ärztlichen Forum." *AZDJ* 52 (1857): 709–710; Ludwig Philippson, "Der Abfall Und Die Beschneidung." *AZDJ* 39 (1857): 525–528; Ludwig Philippson, "Beschneidung in Oesterreich," *AZDJ* 38 and 49 (1857): 512–514 and (1857): 667. Participants often relied on similar texts, frequently Bergson's *Die Beschneidung*.

[15]Brecher, *Die Beschneidung*; Hirsch B. Fassel, "Gr. Kanischa, im Mai: zur Beschneidung," *AZDJ* 23 (1855): 292–293; Hirsch B. Fassel, "Magdeburg, 31 August: Die Beschneidung in Oesterreich," *AZDJ* 37 (1857): 497–499.

The participation of men such as Levit, Landauer, and Fassel high-lights another common factor in these debates. After decades of sub-dued interest in the rite, circumcision now attracted attention from a wide spectrum of participants. Earlier *Beschneidungsfragen* had taken place, but they had failed to capture the interest of Jews and non-Jews outside of the communities where local conflicts had occurred. Like-wise, circumcision had been one of many rituals examined by medical professionals during the late eighteenth and early nineteenth centuries, but had not occupied a particular focal point. Now, as interest in other rites waned, attention to circumcision peaked. This was particularly true in the 1840s and, to a lesser degree, in the 1850s.[16]

Circumcision's religious significance only partially explains its sa-lience during the mid-nineteenth century. If it had been otherwise, more individuals would have expressed interest in the rite earlier. Instead, the midcentury discussions gained a national audience because the deliberations lent themselves to the contemporaneous developments affecting Jews. During the 1840s, the Jewish communities of western and central Europe were on the cusp of significant change. Premod-ern Jewish communities of the German-speaking world had been su-pralocal, semiautonomous, and defined by their religion. Now, internal and external historical phenomena threatened to dramatically change Jewish communal life and in some cases already had transformed it.[17] Despite considerable local and regional variations, the *Circumcisions-* and *Beschneidungsfragen* served as forums in which Jews and gentiles wrestled with these important developments or, as the contemporary physician Joseph Bergson termed it, "life's fundamental questions (*Lebensfragen*)."[18] Within the disputes, contributors offered their vision for the appropriate character of the changing Jewish community and its shifting relationship with the non-Jewish world.

[16]On the medical interest in Jewish ritual behavior, see Efron, *Medicine and the German Jews*; Gotzmann, *Jüdisches Recht*; Jacob Katz, *Out of the Ghetto: The Social Back-ground of Jewish Emancipation, 1770–1870* (Cambridge: Harvard University Press, 1977), pp. 143–144; Thomas Schlich, "Medicalization and Secularization: The Jewish Ritual Bath as a Problem of Hygiene (Germany 1820s–1840s)," *Social History of Medicine* 8.3 (1995): 423–442.

[17]The literature on these phenomena is extensive. Classic studies include Katz, *Out of the Ghetto*; Meyer, *Response to Modernity*; David Sorkin, *The Transformation of German Jewry 1780–1840* (New York: Oxford University Press, 1987). This chapter does not suggest that the 1848 revolution affected the deliberations in any way. The archival evidence does not show a significant change in the circumcision disputes immediately preceding or follow-ing the 1848 revolution.

[18]Bergson, *Die Beschneidung*. Also see Philippson, "Der Abfall"; Salomon, *Die Beschneidung*, pp. 75–78. The debates concerning circumcision tended to take place in communities

"Life's Fundamental Questions"

During the first half of the nineteenth century, several historical phenomena served as catalysts of Jewish communal change and, in turn, provoked interest in the boundaries of communal and state authority as well as in the Jewish rite of circumcision. One such catalyst was the consolidation of power within the different German states. By the 1840s, the thirty-eight German states had embarked on a process of modern state building. They incorporated the territories they had acquired through the Congress of Vienna, created or revised their judicial systems, and established their administrative offices.[19] The German territorial states, manorial demesnes, and free imperial cities also abolished, to varying degrees, some of the corporate privileges that their semiautonomous communities had enjoyed. All of these shifts affected the partially sovereign Jewish communities of the German-speaking world who now experienced interventions in Jewish educational, religious, and administrative spheres.

The governmental intrusions, which were designed to solidify state power and to hasten or prevent Jewish acculturation, included the reorganization of Jewish communal structures.[20] The proposed models of Jewish communal organization differed widely, shaped by the mores and cultures of the administrative institutions creating them. The states examined throughout this book demonstrate these wide-ranging differences. Württemberg and Baden refashioned their Jewish community councils to mirror their Protestant equivalents. The Jewish communities there reported directly to the government but had regulatory powers over their own religious and communal affairs. In contrast, the Prussian and Bavarian governments treated their

---

that were divided deeply over how to manage historical change, including Breslau and Frankfurt.

[19]On restoration in the aftermath of 1815, see Michael Broers, *Europe after Napoleon: Revolution, Reaction, and Romanticism, 1814–1848* (Manchester: Manchester University Press, 1996); John Breuilly, *Austria, Prussia, and Germany, 1806–1871* (London: Longman, 2002); Paul W. Schroeder, *The Transformation of European Politics, 1763–1848* (New York: Oxford University Press, 1994), pp. 517–636. An excellent synopsis can be found in David Blackbourn, *The Long Nineteenth Century: A History of Germany, 1780–1918* (New York: Oxford University Press, 1998), pp. 57–137.

[20]The intervention of government into previously autonomous religious societies was not limited to the German-speaking world, as illuminated by the French consistory. Phyllis Cohen Albert, *The Modernization of French Jewry: Consistory and Community in the Nineteenth Century* (Hanover, NH: Brandeis University Press/University Press of New England, 1977).

Jewish communities as private organizations whom they declined to financially support.[21] Elsewhere, state governments formally recognized Jews for the first time. In the 1830s, for example, the kingdom of Saxony allowed Jews to form a community (*Gemeinde*) with a public synagogue. Similarly, Vienna permitted the Jewish community to organize officially for the first time in the aftermath of the 1848 revolution.[22]

German state governments also encouraged dramatic Jewish communal change when they began to consider the political integration of their inhabitants.[23] Until unification in 1871, the thirty-eight German states independently determined varying standards for membership and political participation. As such, they each treated Jewish political integration differently. Some governments granted Jews full civic rights, incorporating Jews politically into the state and never revoking Jewish emancipatory privileges. Other states extended certain rights during periods of openness, only to repeal them during conservative phases, while a third group continuously resisted yielding to Jews any civic freedoms.[24]

Emancipation, much like other state intrusions, gradually changed the character of German-Jewish communities. Not only did some states encourage transformation as a prerequisite for civic rights, but German-speaking Jews also responded to emancipation's erratic nature on their own. Those who desired political integration attempted to meet

[21]They also refused to acknowledge the public status of rabbis. The status of these Jewish communities often shifted, as evidenced in Prussia. In 1841 the Prussian king, Frederick William IV, renounced Jewish assimilation and demanded that Jews organize into corporations that pursued only Jewish communal interests. He abandoned this formulation six years later.

[22]Simone Lässig, "Emancipation and Embourgeoisement: The Jews, the State, and the Middle Classes in Saxony and Anhalt-Dessau," in *Saxony in German History: Culture, Society, and Politics, 1830–1933*, ed. James Retallack (Ann Arbor: University of Michigan Press, 2000), p. 107.

[23]A state, explains Brubaker, is a nation state in that "it claims (and is understood) to be a nation's state." Rogers Brubaker, *Citizenship and Nationhood in France and Germany* (Cambridge: Harvard University Press, 1992), p. 28.

[24]See Arno Herzig, "The Process of Emancipation from the Congress of Vienna to the Revolution of 1848/1849," *LBIYB* 37 (1992): 61–69; Werner E. Mosse, "From 'Schutzjuden' to 'Deutsche Staatsbürger Jüdischen Glaubens': The Long and Bumpy Road of Jewish Emancipation in Germany," in *Paths of Emancipation: Jews, States, and Citizenship*, ed. Pierre Birnbaum and Ira Katznelson (Princeton: Princeton University Press, 1995), 59–93; Reinhard Rürup, "Emancipation and Crisis: The 'Jewish Question' in Germany, 1850–1890," *LBIYB* 20 (1975): 13–25; Hans D. Schmidt, "The Terms of Emancipation: The Public Debate in Germany and Its Effects on the Mentality and Ideas of German Jewry," *LBIYB* 1 (1956): 28–45.

emancipation's demands.[25] Across geographic, generational, religious, and gender divides, they shed some of their external religious and physical particularities. These Jews entered what professions were available to them and mimicked the cultural mores of the growing German middle class. Embracing notions of German self-improvement, many investigated the charge launched by opponents that Jewish religious particularities precluded their political and social integration.

This interest in Jewish religious difference was one component of the Jewish religious reform movement, a transformative historical shift that took place alongside emancipation and state growth. Until the middle of the nineteenth century, most German-speaking Jews embraced the practices, beliefs, and priorities of premodern Jewry. These traditional Jews continued to follow the Jewish calendar. They observed the Sabbath and educated their children in Jewish texts and languages.[26] Yet, by midcentury increasing numbers of Jews—particularly those in urban centers—slowly began to embrace change. They stopped attending synagogue regularly, increasingly violated the Sabbath, and ignored Jewish dietary laws. Some embraced modifications with little self-reflection. Others consciously articulated a desire for a reassessment of their religious practices and ideologies.[27]

The religious reform movement gradually changed the character of German Jewries. Over the course of the mid-nineteenth century, increasing numbers of German-Jewish communities slowly appointed rabbis who identified with the reform movement and implemented its liturgy, aesthetic changes, and religious reforms. The realization of reform was frequently preceded and followed by internal debates over communal control. Traditional rabbis warred with reformers over their jurisdiction as well as the kinds of adaptations permissible.[28] Within

[25]Steven Lowenstein's work reminds us that these transformations were protracted and inconsistent. Steven Lowenstein, *The Mechanics of Change: Essays in the Social History of German Jewry* (Atlanta: Scholars Press, 1992).

[26]Stefi-Jersch Wenzel, "Population Shifts and Occupational Structure," in Michael A. Meyer, ed., *German-Jewish History in Modern Times Volume 2: Emancipation and Acculturation 1780–1871* (New York: Columbia University Press, 1997), pp. 50–59.

[27]The movement for religious reform pushed first for aesthetic changes in order to create a modernized religious service that mimicked those of the Christian world. By the 1830s and 1840s, the movement had taken on ideological and administrative demands as well. Michael A. Meyer, "Jewish Communities in Transition," in Meyer, ed., *German-Jewish History in Modern Times*, vol. 2, pp. 119–127; Meyer, *Response to Modernity*; Sorkin, *Transformation of German Jewry*.

[28]See the comments made by the Frankfurt rabbi Trier concerning the reform movement. Salomon Abraham Trier, *Rabbinische Gutachten über die Beschneidung* (Frankfurt am Main: Druck der J.F. Bach'schen Buch- und Stenidruckerei, 1844), p. xviii.

the reform movement itself, moderate reformers often scrutinized the far-reaching changes advocated by their radical brethren. Radicals too expressed frustration with their coreligionists, complaining about the limited progress of reform and the leadership styles of their colleagues. These internal clashes were exacerbated by what was at stake. During the midcentury, state and city governments within the German-speaking world frequently demanded that only one officially recognized local Jewish synagogue community serve as an intermediary with non-Jewish governments. It alone collected taxes and established Jewish communal policies.

Like reform impulses, medicalization also contributed to the transformation of early nineteenth century Jewish communal life. The complex process of medicalization had begun in the late eighteenth century in parts of Europe and was marked by an extension and improvement of medical services and health institutions. By midcentury, physicians had begun to identify several Jewish customs, including circumcision, which allegedly risked the public's health. Jewish and non-Jewish physicians encouraged governmental intrusion into the previously autonomous spheres of religious behavior in order to protect the public good. Medicalization thus introduced a justification for governmental intervention. Moreover it encouraged change from within the Jewish community. As John Efron has shown in his study of Jews and medicine in Germany, Jewish physicians of the late eighteenth and nineteenth centuries increasingly drew from the discourses of medicalization to position themselves in places of leadership. They argued for the right to intercede with non-Jewish authorities and society and often invoked medical fears to encourage certain kinds of reforms within Jewish life.[29]

The historical changes wrought by medicalization, the reform movement, emancipation, and state growth were neither rapid nor seamless. The resulting divisive Jewish communities were hybrid creatures, what Heinrich Heine described in another context as "neither flesh nor fowl."[30] By the 1840s, German-Jewish communities were often uncomfortably dependent on governmental largesse and increasingly fragmented over questions of allegiance and religiosity. As communities experienced governmental interventions and confessional divides in varying contexts and speeds, Jewish leaders and state administrators questioned the definition of the Jewish community in this new age. Was it, they asked, a social entity that ought to encourage or discourage

---

[29]Efron, *Medicine and the German Jews*. In addition to the texts cited in note 15 above, also see Ute Frevert, *Krankheit als politisches Problem 1770–1880: Soziale Unterschichten in Preußen zwischen medizinischer Polizei und staatlicher Sozialversicherung* (Göttingen: Vandenhoeck & Ruprecht, 1984).

[30]Cited by Blackbourn, *Long Nineteenth Century*, p. 91.

integration into the changing, modernizing world? Was it a religious community whose governance should be subsumed by state authorities or a separate economic, political, and cultural entity that would regulate itself? This interrogation of Jewish communal character invariably considered whether ritual behavior and particular models of political authority allowed for the possibility of Jewish inclusion into civil society.

The deliberations concerning circumcision thus served as one forum in which German-speaking Jews and gentiles considered the transformations wrought by historical change. As they reflected on Jewries' potential for social and political integration, the political character of contemporary Jewish communities, and the appropriateness of governmental intervention in Jewish affairs, discussants often failed to offer consistent formulations. However, their contributions suggest that many Jews and gentiles viewed ritual markings of difference as a focal point of political struggle and understanding.

An "Irreversible" Divide?

In an 1857 article concerning circumcision, rabbi and editor Ludwig Philippson called on his readers to reflect on circumcision's relationship to social integration, governmental intervention, and Judaism's essence. For Philippson, German-speaking Jews had social and political integration within their grasp, and circumcision—as it then was practiced and understood—posed a challenge to this inclusion. His article did not repudiate the rite. Instead, it simultaneously championed regeneration, social integration, and the preservation and recasting of a few religious particularities, including circumcision, to reinforce Jewish stability and worthiness.[31]

Philippson was not alone. During the 1840s and 1850s, dozens of German-speaking Jews and gentiles suggested that circumcision, if practiced correctly, furthered inclusion. In so doing, they simultaneously embraced emancipation's demands and certain aspects of Jewish uniqueness. A number of Jewish physicians and reformers championed this position by promoting the rite's supposed medical benefits.[32] These participants inferred that the Jewish rite advanced Jewish inclusion because it resulted in something everyone desired, namely, healthier lives. They alleged that the rite prevented phimosis and paraphimosis,

[31]Philippson, "Der Abfall und die Beschneidung."
[32]Efron, *Medicine and the German Jews.*

conditions that restrict the penis opening, deform its shape, and make it more susceptible to infections. They also suggested that circumcision lowered infant mortality rates and resulted in cleaner newborns, possibly even healthier adult males.[33] Dr. Josef Hirschfeld, a physician and *mohel* in Vienna, was one of a number of authors who statistically showed that fewer Jewish newborns died in infancy than their non-Jewish counterparts supposedly because they had undergone circumcision. For him and other like-minded participants, circumcision was both a "religious and prophylactic duty."[34]

Whereas Hirschfeld advanced Jewish integration by touting circumcision's medical benefits, other proponents made similar claims by arguing that the rite reinforced the rational and moral character of Judaism. In their opinion, circumcision was one factor that allowed Jewish communities to integrate easily into a multireligious state. Gideon Brecher, a hospital physician in Prossnitz, articulated this view when he insisted that the ritual strengthened Judaism's moral and ethical foundation because it enabled Jews to create a permanent relationship with a higher power.[35] His readers could infer that Jews would therefore serve as strong moral participants in the society in which they lived. A second champion of emancipation and circumcision, Dresden chief rabbi, Zacharias Frankel, similarly linked the rite with morality. In his exchange with Saxon local and regional authorities, Frankel articulated an explicit relationship between the rite and social participation by juxtaposing the civic worthiness of circumcised Jews to the unassimilability of uncircumcised children born to Jewish parents. For Frankel, the implied religious observance of the former assured their morality. Uncircumcised Jews, however, posed a danger to state and society

[33]Bergson, *Die Beschneidung*, pp. 124–125; Brecher, *Die Beschneidung*, p. 44; Ben Rabbi, *Die Lehre von der Beschneidung*, p. 19; "Die Beschneidung von sanitäts-polizeilichen Standpunkte," *AZDJ* 19 (1855): 241; "Die Beschneidung," *AZDJ* 10 (1858): 129.

[34]"Die Beschneidung vor dem ärztlichen Forum," *AZDJ* 52 (1857): 709. Hirschfeld compared German-, Hungarian-, and Croatian-speaking Jews and non-Jews. Also see Mehrbach, "Dresden, 18 November," *AZDJ* 49 (1844): 701–702; "Leipzig, 2 Dec.," *Der Orient* 50 (1844): 388–389; "Die Beschneidung," *AZDJ* 10 (1858): 129; Vorsteher Kollegium der deutsch-israelitische Gemeinde, "Instruktion für die Mohelim der deutsch-israelitisch Geimeinde Hamburg," in *Die Beschneidung: Eine populäre Darstellung ihrer Bedeutung und Vollziehung*, ed. Simon Bamberger (Wandsbek: Verlag von A. Goldschmidt, 1852), pp. 28–30.

[35]Brecher, *Die Beschneidung*, pp. 21–23. Brecher also touted the rite's medical advantages. Also see "Hamburg, Eingangs Oktober" *AZDJ* 43 (1847): 640; Leopold Zunz, "4 May 1845 letter to Geiger," in *Nachgelassene Schriften*, ed. Abraham Geiger, vol. 5 (Berlin: Louis Gerschel, 1878), p. 184; Leopold Zunz, *Gutachten über die Beschneidung* (Frankfurt am Main: Druck der J.J. Bach'schen Buch- und Steindruckerei, 1844).

because they were part of neither the Jewish nor Christian communities; they could not be trusted because they were responsible to no one. "If these [uncircumcised] were citizens," Frankel warned, "who could guarantee them?"[36] Like Frankel, Rabbi Schwarz also contrasted the civic worthiness of circumcised Jews against the weaknesses of the uncircumcised. "Those who do not belong to a recognized religious community," suggested Schwarz, "do not, by nature, have the prerequisites for belonging to a state system."[37] In the words of another contributor, the absence of circumcision led to "shady" behavior; its presence, the anonymous author implied, guaranteed a vibrant, moral life.[38]

Archival evidence fails to suggest whether these participants genuinely believed that circumcision reinforced social integration and civic worthiness, yet their embrace of this view served as a good strategy for negotiating with non-Jewish authorities. First, this justification, similar to that concerning the medical benefits of the rite, offered circumcision's proponents a way to reconcile their conflicting desires. Many of them championed Jewish emancipation while also safeguarding a rite whose mission had once been the preservation of Jewish difference. The utilization of hygiene and ethics as a rationalization for protecting the rite cast the Jewish community and these specific leaders as entities that could be integrated and trusted. Moreover, this strategy of linking religious observance with ethical behavior would have been familiar to other German-speaking political actors at this time. During midcentury, German-speaking philosophers and civil servants from across the political and religious spectrums emphasized ethics and hygiene as crucial to the underpinning of society. The embrace of a respectable Jewish religiosity thus made good political sense.

Nonetheless, several participants in these deliberations expressed discomfort with this portrait. In their view, circumcision hindered social and political inclusion and therefore posed a dangerous challenge to emancipation. For Eugen Levit and other like-minded critics, the rite thwarted Jewish emancipatory aspirations because it maintained a physical difference between Jews and non-Jews. The embodiment of a covenant that only Jews shared with God, this "sign of the Bund" reinforced Jewish social isolation.[39] When he disallowed his son's circumcision, the

---

[36]27 January 1852 letter from Frankel to the minister of culture Sächsischen Hauptstaatsarchiv (SHD) MDI I sec III 16 6.

[37]19 March 1852 letter from Schwarz to the Mayor of Hürben CAHJP Inv 6941.

[38]"Aus Hinterpommern," *AZDJ* 2 (1852): 17–18. Also see "Königsberg," *AZDJ* 23 (1855): 296–297.

[39]Bergson, *Die Beschneidung*, p. 1; Ben Rabbi, *Die Lehre von der Beschneidung der Israeliten*, p. 18.

German-Jewish writer Berthold Auerbach relied on this kind of thinking and insisted that Jews were humans first and Jews second.[40] In his medical treatise on circumcision, M. G. Salomon similarly chided Jews for their "intolerant" embrace of circumcision's physical and "irreversible divide."[41] The Frankfurt-based teacher Josef Johlson concurred. Writing under the pseudonym Bar-Amithai, he asserted that circumcision had been established to promote national Jewish identity. Its origins, Johlson explained, lay in the "creation of the Israelites," not in promoting a religiously meaningful relationship among Jews or between Jews and God.[42] Johlson's fellow radical reformers in Frankfurt had issued a similar declaration. While the radical "Friends of Reform" later omitted any public censure of the rite, their earlier ideological platform had criticized circumcision as exclusionary.[43]

According to these writers, circumcision was also incompatible with social and political inclusion because the rite suggested the stability of Jewish political authority and, in so doing, clashed with emancipatory hopes. Circumcision encouraged a "fictive theocratic-national impulse," wrote the radical Jewish thinker, Samuel Holdheim.[44] Its laws supposedly

[40]27 January 1852 letter from Frankel to the Saxon minister of culture SHD MDI I sec. III 16, 6; 11 June 1852 police memo SHD MDI I sec. III 16, 11 r.s.; 26 February 1852 memo of the minister of culture SHD MDI I 839, 1–4; 26 February 1852 letter from the minister of culture SHD MDI I sec. III; 23 February 1853 letter between the minister of interior and the minister of culture SHD MDI I sec. III 16, 18. Other fathers gave similar reasoning. 23 April 1852 report issued by the police authorities of Munich SM RA 33902 and 22 June 1852 report issued by the State Ministry of Interior for Religious and Educational Affairs SM RA 33902; Sobernheim, "Bingen," *AZDJ* 23 (1847): 348–349.

[41]Salomon, *Die Beschneidung*, pp. 79–80, 89. Salomon did not encourage the rite's abandonment but hoped that physicians could eliminate its dangers. Also see Bergson, *Die Beschneidung*, p. 1; Ben Rabbi, *Die Lehre von der Beschneidung*, p. 18.

[42]Josef Johlson, *Ueber die Beschneidung in historischer und dogmatischer Hinsicht: ein Wort zu seiner Zeit. Den Denkenden in Israel zur Prüfung vorgelegt von Bar Amithai* (Frankfurt am Main: J.E. Hermann'sche Buchandlung, 1843), p. 18. Also see Salomon, *Die Beschneidung*, p. 79.

[43]The earlier statement also described the rite as barbaric and dangerous. Their final platform renounced the existence of the Messiah and of Zion and dismissed the importance of the Talmud. Meyer, *Response to Modernity*, p. 122; Meyer, "Alienated Intellectuals in the Camp of Religious Reform," p. 62.

[44]Samuel Holdheim, *Ueber die Beschneidung zunächst in religiös-dogmatischer Beziehung* (Schwerin: Verlag der E. Kürschner'schen Buchhandlung [M. Marcus], 1844). Holdheim also refuted the claim that circumcision was more significant than other Jewish rites. In his view, Judaism did not endorse one set of laws as more important than another. On different interpretations of Holdheim's interrogation of circumcision, see Andreas Gotzmann, *Jüdisches Recht im kulturellen Prozess: die Wahrnehmung der Halacha im Deutschland des 19. Jahrhunderts* (Tübingen: M. Siebeck, 1997); Robin Judd, "Samuel Holdheim and the German Circumcision Debates," in *Re-Defining Judaism in an Age of*

bolstered Jewish sovereignty by encouraging Jewish communities to punish the fathers who abdicated the rite and to enforce the ritual against parental wishes. Other discussants were also bothered by the decades-old fear that circumcision encouraged Jews to arrange themselves as sovereign units; they similarly saw such assumptions as threats to emancipation. In his 1844 study, Gustave Schilling (writing under the pseudonym Ben Rabbi) warned against the belief that circumcision reinforced Jewry's character as a "state." Warning of the rite's incompatibility with the emancipatory impulses of the time, he insisted that the rite belonged in the past. "The laws of circumcision are remnants from the period of Moses. Then it was sanctioned for the whole Volk."[45] In a book published the same year, Salomon reminded his readers that acculturation and emancipation had been most successful where Jews had cast off vestiges of their former political selves, including circumcision and its oversight.[46]

For Salomon, circumcision threatened emancipation because it highlighted Jewish political authority and caused significant health risks. "It is a bloody and not always harmless operation, he wrote."[47] Other contributors expressed analogous concerns. Poor cleanliness among ritual practitioners, the use of the fingernail for *periah*, and the practice of oral suction allegedly resulted in medical mishaps and in Jews being looked upon with suspicion.[48] Some critics, such as Joseph Bergson, called for Jews to abandon these specific practices.[49] Others insisted that the rite's medical danger and exclusionary character demanded the abandonment of the ritual altogether. For Levit, the rite threatened to "torture and disfigure thousands of innocent creatures." It was a "barbaric custom of our nation."[50]

Emancipation: Comparative Perspectives on Samuel Holdheim (1806–1860), ed. Christian Weise (Leiden: Brill, 2007), pp. 127–142.

[45]Ben Rabbi, *Die Lehre*, pp. 7–8.

[46]Salomon, *Die Beschneidung*, pp. 72 and 79.

[47]Ibid., p. 80.

[48]Jacob Katz has authored an important article on the *metsitsah* controversy of the first half of the nineteenth century. Katz, "The Conflict over Metsitsah (Hebrew)," 150–183. Also see Shabbat 133; Maimonides, *Mishnah Torah, Hilkhot Milah* 2:2; Karo, *Shulhan Arukh, Yoreh Deah, Hilkhot Milah* 264:3. Also see Judith Bleich, "Jacob Ettlinger, His Life and Works: The Emergence of Modern Orthodoxy in Germany," Ph.D. diss., New York University, 1974, pp. 116–117; Bernard Homa, *Metzitzah* (London: n.p., 1960); H. J. Zimmels, *Magicians, Theologians, and Doctors: Studies in Folk-medicine and Folk-lore as reflected in the Rabbinical Responsa (12th–19th Centuries)* (London: Edward Goldston & Son, 1952), pp. 158–168.

[49]Bergson, *Die Beschneidung*, pp. 101–102 and 108.

[50]Levit, *Die Circumcision*, p. 3.

While many of these participants distanced themselves from the Jewish rite, they did not necessarily reject Jewish communal life. Instead, they used the deliberations concerning circumcision to make claims for Jewish communal affiliation. In his treatise on the Jewish rite, Johlson designed a new initiation ceremony for boys and girls. His ceremony was supposed to introduce Jewish children into a covenant with God and the Jewish people. In their rejections of circumcision, Auerbach, Landauer, and Jacob Ehrenbaum also welcomed their communal links with other Jews. To assure their Jewish affiliation, they made significant personal sacrifices. Ehrenbaum succumbed to rabbinic pressure and, in order to preserve his and his son's membership in Munich's Jewish community, he ultimately allowed for the circumcision of his son.[51] In contrast, Auerbach and Landauer both left their homes and fled to Jewish communities that accepted their uncircumcised children as members. These men promoted a vision of Jewish communal character that did not enforce religious observance. Their idealized Jewish community centered on the "virtues" of the Israelites, not a physical mark on the body.[52]

When Auerbach and Landauer criticized the rite, they also were adopting an emancipatory strategy that made good political sense. Circumcision had been and was increasingly becoming an issue of municipal and state concern. By calling for the ritual's abandonment or for a rethinking of its centrality to Jewish communal life, these fathers implied that the Jewish community was readying itself for integration on their respective governments' terms.

Regulation and Reform

Governmental intervention in circumcision practices had begun with the earlier processes of state building and emancipation and intensified during the 1840s.[53] The intrusions were twofold. Influenced

[51]23 April 1852 report issued by the police authorities of Munich SM RA 33902; 22 June 1852 report issued by the State Ministry of Interior for Religious and Educational Affairs SM RA 33902.

[52]"Teterow," *AZDJ* (1849): 583.

[53]During the late eighteenth- and early nineteenth centuries, several governmental authorities and advisers had warned that Jewish rites prevented social integration. In 1831, the Reform Diet of Baden explicitly demanded religious regeneration as a quid pro quo for emancipation. According to the Diet, the Jewish practices of circumcision, among other rites, preserved Jewish social and political separateness. Other governments issued contemporaneous promulgations that explicitly targeted *mohelim* as candidates for

by the medical community's criticism of the rite, one set of regulations dictated the licensing and training of ritual practitioners and governed specific circumcision practices. A second set of interventionist measures concerned the relationship between circumcision and the registration of Jews into their local religious communities. These intrusions and the responses they received reflected the varying hopes different gentile administrations had for Jewish communities and for governments during this time.

Between 1843 and 1857, a number of German authorities intensified their supervision of circumcisers and circumcision as part of state attempts to regulate public health and consolidate power. These regulations varied by state but generally mimicked contemporaneous anti-quackery laws. Much like the newly created supervisory programs for surgeons and midwives whose supposed ignorance posed a public risk, these interventions demanded the medical oversight of *mohelim* (circumcisers).[54] Administrations increasingly insisted that they, and not the Jewish communities, were responsible for training and licensing ritual practitioners and for generating a list of acceptable *mohelim* in each community.[55] The license issued to *mohel* Henry Minden of Hamburg demonstrated this regulatory shift. After acquiring the medical knowledge identified as crucial by the city of Hamburg, Minden passed an exam that had been approved by the city state. The *mohel* then signed

---

acculturation. These laws mandated that the ritual practitioners and Jewish communal registrars maintain their books using the German language and secular calendar. 1858 letter to the rabbinic authorities of Weilburg concerning law no. 31, 451 CJA 75B Wel U1 24 16; S., "Frankfurt am Main" *AZDJ* 12 (1843): 184–185; "Aus dem Großherzogthum Baden," *AZDJ* 36 (1863): 552–553; 5 November 1848 report no. 19589 CAHJP GA II 49; Order no. 28 (10 November 1848) CAHJP GA II 49; 16 November 1848 report issued by the mayoral authority of Wertheim (No 19589) CAHJP GA II 49; 9 April 1837 order from the minister of interior SM RA 33902; M. G. Salomon, *Die Beschneidung*, pp. 58–59.

[54]Barbara Duden, *The Woman Beneath the Skin: A Doctor's Patients in Eighteenth-Century Germany*, trans. Thomas Dunlap (Cambridge: Harvard University Press, 1991); Edward Shorter, *A History of Women's Bodies* (New York: Basic Books, 1982), pp. 35–47, 140–145.

[55]These laws did not yet concern *shohetim*. In Bavaria and Prussia, neither of which recognized Jewish practitioners as public figures, *shohetim* were determined to be religious practitioners and therefore not to be supervised directly by the state. This would change slowly. "Die Anstellung Jüdischer Schächter betreffend: Resolution der Königl. Ministerien der Geistlichen-, Unterrichts- und Medizinal-Angelegenheiten, so wie des Innern an die israelitischen Handelsleute N.N.," in *Sammlung der die religiöse und bürgerliche Verfassung der Juden in den Königl. Preuß. Staaten betreffenden Gesetze, Verordnungen, Gutachten, Berichte und Erkenntnisse*, ed. Jeremias Heinemann (Hildesheim: Verlag Dr. H. A. Gerstenberg, 1976), pp. 407–408; 5 January 1845 police report SM RA 33907; 8 February 1843 ruling from the regional authorities of Upper Bavaria SM RA 33907; 16 November 1848 report issued by magistrate of Wertheim (No. 19589) CAHJP GA II 49.

a document agreeing that he would comply with the *city*'s circumcision laws. The Jewish community secretary stamped his license and returned it to the Hamburg authorities, which then issued the final stamp of approval.[56]

In addition to regulating *mohelim*, state and local administrators also specifically addressed circumcision practices. Some of these interventions did not have a major impact on the way in which Jews performed or experienced circumcision.[57] Promulgations that *mohelim* refrain from circumcising newborns in synagogues or delay the rite if a child was ill did not change Jewish practice in any significant way. Jewish law mandates that a circumciser postpone the rite if a baby is sick, and the place of the *brit milah* has no considerable impact on the ritual itself.[58] Like the laws that governed the supervision and licensing of *mohelim*, these reforms only proved significant because they positioned government as the regulatory power and depicted contemporaneous practices as unhealthy. Other reforms, however, had long-lasting implications and changed the way in which people practiced the rite. These regulations included the prohibition of oral suction and the ban on the use of one's fingernail for *periah*. When regional authorities in Pfalz mandated that the Jewish community "find another way of cleaning the wound [other than orally]," for example, they forced local *mohelim* to alter their practices. Circumcisers in Pfalz therefore had to contradict their contemporary understandings of Jewish law and abandon *metsitsah be'peh* or defy government demands.[59] Similar prohibitions in Vienna, Stuttgart, and Württemburg also changed the ways in which *mohelim* were expected to conduct the rite.[60]

[56] 28 March 1860 instructions and examination for *mohel* Henry Minden CAHJP AHW 563 165; 19 September 1860 License for *mohel* Henry Minden signed by Haarbleicher CAHJP AHW 563 166.

[57] 3 July 1847 regulation by the Pfalz government concerning circumcision SM RA 33902; 19 July 1845 letter from the Unterfranken government to its Jewish community SM RA 33902. Similar justifications could be found in 11 January 1852 letter from the Government of Schwabia and Neuberg to the Government of Oberbayern SM RA 33902.

[58] 20 November 1846 ministerial letter from the minister of culture and education to the minister of interior SHD MDI 3514 no. 13; 13 July 1847 regulation by the Bavarian regional government of Pfalz SM RA 33902; "Zeitungsnachrichten, Deutschland, Aus Württemberg," *AZDJ* 14 (1857): 182–185; A. C., "Aus Württemberg," *AZDJ* 6 (1857): 69; Altmannm, "Aus dem Großherzogthum Baden," *AZDJ* 36 (1863): 552–553; "1856 Rabbinic Ruling" in Simon Bamberger, *Die Beschneidung*, pp. 32–34. Bergson commented that extant state and regional laws had little impact on the ways in which circumcision was being practiced. Bergson, *Die Beschneidung*, p. 39.

[59] 13 July 1847 regulations by the Bavarian regional authorities in Pfalz SM RA 33902.

[60] A. C., "Aus Württemberg," p. 69; "Die Beschneidung vor dem ärztlichen Forum." Also see Katz, "The Conflict over Metsitsah."

These intrusions received mixed reactions from other gentile authorities, thus signaling the diverse aspirations that different non-Jewish administrations had for Jewish communities and for governments during this time. Some officials articulated the belief that modernity had transformed Jewry into an integrated confessional unit that lacked political oversight. Others conversely insisted that the Jewish community was entitled to maintain some of its past authority. Local and state administrators in Pfalz embraced the former view when they avowed that their offices held jurisdiction over all religious entities. They, and not the Jewish community, "assured public safety and effectiveness."[61] "We must legislate effectiveness," wrote one Munich magistrate and insisted on his jurisdiction despite past legislation that had assured the Jewish community oversight over its circumcision practices.[62]

Other participating gentile authorities expressed the contrary view. They envisioned the Jewish community as retaining some jurisdiction despite the political changes of the time. Frequently, they insisted that extant circumcision regulations interfered with a realm that ought to remain autonomous, namely, confession. In 1844, Dresden's medical officers articulated such a view when they criticized the kingdom's health department for issuing new regulations over local circumcisers. Arguing for the sanctity of religious rites, the medical officers refused to implement the state law and even permitted two ritual practitioners with little medical training to continue practicing the Jewish rite.[63] In their view, circumcision was a religious custom and needed to remain "free and untouched."[64] Four years later, health officials in Adelsheim (Baden) similarly reinforced the Jewish community's oversight despite complaints from local physicians concerning contemporary circumcision practices. As in Dresden, officials in Adelsheim permitted the Jewish community to retain supervisory oversight. The non-Jewish authorities introduced only one new demand: that municipal health officials occasionally observe the ritual to assure that "necessary precautions are taken."[65]

Local and regional authorities also considered the possibilities of Jewish communal oversight when they participated in the ongoing debates concerning the nature and standards of Jewish communal membership.

[61] 13 July 1847 regulation by the government of Pfalz concerning the circumcision of children SM RA 33902.

[62] 19 July 1845 letter and memo from the magistrate to the government of Lower Franconia SM RA 33902.

[63] "Leipzig, 2 Dec." *Der Orient* 50 (1844): 388–389; "Dresden," *AZDJ* 49 (1844): 701–702; Frankel, "Ueber manch durch den Fortschritt der Medicin," pp. 300–301.

[64] October 28 1844 policy established by Mehrbach.

[65] Order no. 28 (10 November 1848) CAHJP GA II 49.

In these conversations, most officials insisted on limiting Jewish authority in some way. They upheld the right of governments to oversee Jewish and Christian birth registries because state law mandated that all individuals affiliate with a religious community. In 1845, the Hamburg senate formally embraced this position, maintaining that the registry "was not a religious document, but one of civil significance."[66] Six years later, the Bavarian regional courts echoed this sentiment. In their ruling in the Landauer case, they determined that the "civil laws of the land" governed Jewish birth records.[67] Envisioning membership as a civic matter, these governments, as well as those in Wertheim and Baden, insisted on supervising Jewish birth registries, often dictating new language, format, and calendar-type for local Jewish records.[68]

While they may have agreed on their right to oversee Jewish birth registries, German authorities differed widely over the appropriateness of their establishing standards for Jewish communal membership. After requests for intervention from fathers or Jewish communal leaders, some gentile officials stripped Jewish communities and their rabbinate of the right to exclude individuals from religious society. Transferring that power from the Jewish community to the city or state, they insisted that local Jewish communities register all children born to Jewish mothers. In Dresden, where medical officers had preserved the Jewish community's right to supervise its *mohelim*, the city's magistrate demanded that Rabbi Zacharias Frankel formally acknowledge the uncircumcised son of Berthold Auerbach as a Jew. Despite

[66]21 October 1845 petition, November 1845 response, and October and November 1847 Senate reconsiderations in CAHJP AHW 563 48–58, 60–75; The case was reported in "Hamburg, Eingangs Oktober," *AZDJ* 43 (1847): 642; "Hamburg, 6 November," *AZDJ* 48 (1847): 705; "Hamburg, 13 November," *AZDJ* 49 (1847): 715–717.

[67]7 November 1851 letter to the rabbinate of Hürben from the royal Bavarian court CAHJP Inv 6941. It reiterated this sentiment in its 5 January 1852 ruling SM RA 33902. Similar sentiments can be found in the collection of reports and letters concerning circumcision CAHJP AHW 563, 1–58; 3 February 1853 letter from the minister of culture to the minister of the interior SHD MDI I sec III 16 18; "Breslau," *AZDJ* 41 (1845): 624; "Aus Württemberg," *AZDJ* 35 (1858): 478–479; "Vom Rhein," *AZDJ* 13 (1858): 175–176; 15 January 1852 letter and report from councilman Müller SHD MDI I sec III 16 10; 17 January 1852 letter from Steubert to Frankel SHD MDI I sec III 16 5; 27 January 1852 letter from Frankel SHD MDI I sec III 16 6; 26 February memo from the minister of culture SHD MDI 839 1–4; 11 June 1852 memo (police) SHD MDI I sec III 16 11 r.s.; 23 February 1853 report from the minister of culture SHD MDI I sec III 16 18.

[68]1858 letter to the rabbinic authorities of Weilburg CJA 75B Wel U1 24 16; Salomon, *Die Beschneidung*, pp. 58–59; S., "Frankfurt am Main"; "Aus dem Großherzogthum Baden"; 5 November 1848 report no. 19589 CAHJP GA II 49; Order no. 28 CAHJP GA II 49; 16 November 1848 report issued by the mayor of Wertheim (no. 19589) CAHJP GA II 49.

picture in which the Jewish community preserved its authority only in the religious realm.[83] Others made larger claims for Jewish semiautonomy. They rejected any kind of intervention and insisted on their own control over the rite.[84] When the health department of Frankfurt issued circumcision regulations in 1842, the city's chief rabbi, Rabbi Salomon Trier, immediately argued for the Jewish community's right to regulate its rituals. He requested that the Frankfurt senate declare the health department's wording a misunderstanding. On March 10th of that year, the senate stated that it did not wish to call Jewish law into question; Rabbi Trier, concerned that this was inadequate still, appealed again to the senate but did not gain any concessions from the secular administration.[85] Other Jewish communities voiced similar concerns. In an 1845 letter to a local official, 382 members of the Jewish community of Hamburg harshly criticized the magistrate's assumption that the municipal government could determine the standards for Jewish communal membership. The letter-writers demanded that Hamburg Jewry have a say in its self-regulation. "The Jewish community council," they argued, "should not only be welcomed [in the decision-making process], but also viewed as necessary."[86] Twelve years later, a group of twenty-eight Jews in Hamburg again complained that the city had interfered in Jewish communal affairs. Pointing to an 1850 statement issued by the Hamburg senate that defined the Jewish community as a "religious cooperative" (*Religionsgenossenschaft*), the petitioners renounced governmental interference in a religious practice.[87] Ironically, even when governments sided with traditional authorities, some Jewish leaders expressed frustration that secular officials had participated in confessional conflicts in the first place. After the Austrian government concurred with local rabbis over a circumcision dispute, Rabbi Hirsch B. Fassel criticized the state for presuming that it had jurisdiction over Jewish law. According to Fassel, religious authorities had sole jurisdiction over communal membership, and the state should have not entered into the discussions at all.[88]

[83]Fassel, "Magdeburg, 31 August"; Levit, *Die Circumcision*; M. W. Heicht to Rabbi Lobrecht CJA 75B Schw2 54 22. Despite their calls, many of these discussants still expressed inconsistent views about what constituted the religious realm.

[84]See, e.g., notes 1–5 above.

[85]S. "Frankfurt Am Main"; Trier, *Rabbinische Gutachten*, pp. ix–x. Also see Liberles, *Religious Conflict in Social Context*.

[86]1845 report from the Hamburg Jewish community CAHJP AHW 563 48–58. Frankel made a similar argument in his 27 January 1852 letter SHD MDI I sec II 16 6.

[87]Hamburg's senate had permitted the burial of uncircumcised [Jewish] infants in the Jewish cemetery, something forbidden by Jewish law. September 30 1857 report from the Jewish community CAHJP AHW 563.

[88]Fassel, "Magdeburg, 31 August."

When these discussants called for a curb on governmental intervention, they offered a model of Jewish leadership that safeguarded traditional Jewish authority. This authority was already under attack. Over the course of the early nineteenth century, the image and responsibility of the rabbi had shifted as his influence faced challenges from non-Jewish administrators and emerging reform leaders. In the circumcision disputes, traditional Jewish leaders insisted that they, and not their competitors, served as the spokesmen for and adjudicators of Jewish communal life. In 1852, Rabbi Schwarz publicly rejected the assumption that the rabbi was subservient to the state. Refusing to fulfill a magisterial order that he register the uncircumcised Landauer child, Schwarz admonished that the "rabbi is not a civil servant but a person chosen to guide Judaism."[89] Rabbi Trier of Frankfurt also used the circumcision deliberations to distance himself from his competitors. Juxtaposing his "beloved brothers of faith" with those who were "ignorant and frivolous," he called for the preservation of traditional Jewish authority in Frankfurt.[90]

Participants such as Schwarz often faced a strategic difficulty when they cast their communities simultaneously as political entities and as units worthy of social or political integration. Embracing the same strategy they used when arguing against the assumption that circumcision thwarted emancipation, many insisted that the preservation of religious autonomy was good for communal stability and civic worth. In their view, the loss of Jewish communal authority over matters of religion could pose a serious danger. When he maintained that religion "was the pier that supports the state," Rabbi Schwarz implied that state intrusion in religious affairs could damage the Bavarian state.[91] Ludwig Philippson similarly warned that if Jewish communities lost the right to self-govern in matters of religious affairs, there could be negative implications for society at large. Commenting on a series of decisions by local governments to override Jewish communities in circumcision disputes, Philippson bemoaned the loss of Jewish authority. According to the reform editor and rabbi, governmental intrusion threatened Christian communal- and middle-class associational life. Without the

---

[89] 19 March 1852 letter from the Jewish Community of Hürben CAHJP Inv 6941. Similar views could be found in 1845 report from the Hamburg Jewish community CAHJP AHW 563 48–58; September 30 1857 report from the Jewish community CAHJP AHW 563.

[90] Trier, *Rabbinische Gutachten*, p. xviii.

[91] 19 March 1852 letter to the Mayor Inv 6941. Also see 27 January 1852 letter from Frankel SHD MDI I sec II 16 6; Fassel, "Magdeburg;" Zevi Hirsch Kalischer, "Einiges zur Widerlegung der Ansichten des Herrn Dr. Samuel Holdheim in seinem Werkchen: 'Ueber die Bescheidung' enthaltend," *Der Orient* 1 (1845): 3.

order ensured by Jewish communal control, there could be "no church, no synagogue, no community, no society, and no *Verein* [association]."[92]

These Jewish communal leaders embraced a number of other political strategies as well. Some ironically appealed to their governments to enact laws that would safeguard religious authority. Soon after Berthold Auerbach refused to circumcise his son, Zacharias Frankel lobbied for the passage of a new law that would prohibit city councils from interfering with Jewish law.[93] Frankel was unsuccessful in lobbying for the new legislation, but the ministry did side with him in his struggle against the Dresden municipality. Like Frankel, Fassel also hoped that governments would create laws preventing authorities from interfering with the religious lives of Jews. Despite his criticism of the Austrian government for issuing the ultimate ruling in the circumcision conflict in Horic, the Hungarian rabbi allowed for this kind of governmental intervention to protect Jewish religious authority.[94]

Other Jewish communities responded to the possibility of state interference by proactively instituting Jewish communal regulations. Soon after the Hamburg government began to investigate whether circumcision posed a public health risk, the Jewish community quickly created a commission that supervised the rite and developed strict instructions for its circumcisers. Consisting of the city's chief rabbi, community council members, and three *mohelim*, the commission mimicked other state- and municipally sponsored circumcision reforms. It required the licensing and apprenticeship of a *mohel*, and also established laws concerning the tools *mohelim* could use.[95] At their national synods, reform rabbis weighed similar changes. As early as 1846, they suggested that every circumciser take a course from a competent physician, pass an exam, and obtain a license.[96]

---

[92]Philippson, "Jährliche Rabbinerversamlungen": 120 and "Die Beschneidung in Oesterreich," *AZDJ* 38 (1857): 512–514. Also see Moritz Steinschneider, *Die Beschneidung: der Araber und Muhamedaner mit Rücksicht auf die neueste Beschneidungsliteratur* (Vienna: Gedruckt bei Franz Edlen von Schmid und J. J. Busch, 1845), pp. 4–5. Many participants at the reform synods agreed with this view.

[93]27 January 1852 letter from Frankel SHD MDI I sec II 16 6.

[94]On Frankel's understanding of civil and religious law, see Ismar Schorsch, "Historical Consciousness in Modern Judaism," *From Text to Context: The Turn to History in Modern Judaism* (Hanover, NH: Brandeis University Press/University Press of New England, 2003), pp. 177–204.

[95]"Reglement für die Mohelim", pp. 26–28. Karlsruhe, Wiesbaden, and Vienna passed similar laws. The early regulations are described in the 1883 circumcision regulations of Karlsruhe CJA 75Bka124 62–63; Bamberger, *Die Beschneidung*, pp. 34–35.

[96]As quoted in Philippson, *Reform Movement in Judaism*, pp. 216–217. On the Breslau conference, see Meyer, *Response to Modernity*, pp. 138–141. When the Parisian consistory

While some communities created their own laws, others simply chose to ignore state or municipal reforms. This prompted governmental redress, which is one reason for its inclusion in the archival record. Throughout the 1840s, authorities in Würzburg, for example, consistently complained that *mohelim* conducted circumcisions without the required proper medical supervision.[97] In 1848, the regional government in Mannheim similarly protested that Jews ignored its 1803 stipulation concerning the education of circumcisers.[98] Jewish communal leaders also resisted intrusion in the *Beschneidungsfragen*. Rabbis Schwarz, Trier, and Frankel repeatedly refused to register uncircumcised boys in their communal registries despite municipal orders to do so.

Circumcision and Jewish Membership

The reactions of Rabbis Schwarz, Trier, and Frankel were significant because they illuminated another way in which participants in the "circumcision questions" wrestled with the relationship between the Jewish community and the state. Between 1843 and 1857, discussants reflected on the membership standards upon which their ideal communities rested. Participants offered several interpretations of Jewish communal membership, each illuminating different formulations of the boundaries of Jewish communal power and of governmental authority. Their conflicting sense of Jewish membership suggested that even when participants advanced a depiction of Jewish life that was devoid of political authority, they still attempted to carve out a place for themselves on the German historical stage.

Radical reformers, some Jewish fathers, and several physicians insisted on descent as the only necessary requirement for Jewish affiliation.

---

passed analogous laws in 1855, one German-Jewish commentator suggested that the French regulations drew from these kinds of German-Jewish influences. "Die Beschneidung durch jüdische Aerzte," *AZDJ* 12 (1855): 149.

[97]Order no. 10237 (12 July 1848) CAHJP D/Wu2/283. Early legislation could be found in 6 June 1844 memo between the Jewish community of Würzburg and the city authorities CAHJP D/Wu2/283. While the early legislation had ruled that physicians or surgeons needed to accompany the *mohelim*, the government now ruled that all circumcisions had to be done by Jewish physicians or surgeons. 31 August 1835 statement issued by the Bavarian minister of interior SM RA 33907; 19 July 1845 report from the magistrate to the government of Lower Franconia SM RA 33902; 12 July 1848 Ruling 10237 issued by the government of Lower Franconia CAHJP D/Wu2/283.

[98]Adelsheim regulation no. 28 (10 November 1848) CAHJP GA II 49.

the deliberations over the rite to carve out a space for their political participation. This process of self-definition would shift once again two decades later with the introduction of new historical variables. Unification, its resulting emancipation of German Jews, and the rise of an animal protection movement encouraged new understandings of the Jewish community and its appropriate relationship with the non-Jewish world.

CHAPTER 2

German Unification, Emancipation, and the "Ritual Questions"

Less than two decades after the physician Ignatz Landauer, Rabbi Schwarz, and local municipal officials had struggled over the changing character of Hürben Jewry, the majority of Jewish communities in the German states had experienced some kind of political and social transformation. By 1871, many of these communities had encountered the historical changes that had been central to the mid-nineteenth-century circumcision disputes.

Unification and emancipation in 1871 signaled significant political shifts within German-Jewish life.[1] Upon unification, Liberal Prussian political leaders extended civic rights to all property-holding men within the Empire, including Jews. Emancipation reinforced the trend among many Jewish men to participate actively in German civic life and even to serve in government.[2] Unification and emancipation changed the political landscape in which Jews interacted with non-Jewish authorities and other minority and majority groups. As such, during this decade,

[1]Scholars of German Jewry similarly consider German unification in 1871 a marker for German-Jewish periodization. See Michael A. Meyer, ed. *German-Jewish History in Modern Times*, vol. 3 (New York: Columbia University Press, 1997); Marion A. Kaplan, ed. *Jewish Daily Life in Germany, 1618–1945* (Oxford: Oxford University Press, 2005).

[2]States such as Hamburg and Baden extended rights to Jews earlier; the 1871 legislation extended the emancipation promulgated two years earlier by the Reichstag of the North German Confederation. Arno Herzig, "The Process of Emancipation from the Congress of Vienna to the Revolution of 1848/1849"; Werner E. Mosse, "From 'Schutzjuden' to 'Deutsche Staatsbürger Jüdischen Glaubens'"; Reinhard Rürup, "Emancipation and Crisis: The 'Jewish Question' in Germany, 1850–1890." A similar emancipation process took place in the Hapsburg monarchy.

Jewish and gentile leaders both were occupied with devising new strategies to negotiate those varying relationships.

By 1871, German-speaking Jews had experienced pervasive social changes as well. Many had acculturated and adopted the mores of the German middle class, moving to the cities, joining the liberal and medical professions, and marrying at a later age.[3] Many also adapted their religious lives to accommodate the world around them. Some Jews abandoned the laws governing dietary habits as well as Sabbath and holiday observance; others maintained Jewish religious traditions and customs but, like their more liberal coreligionists, integrated personally and professionally into German life. The denominational character of Jewish communities also shifted significantly. By 1871, most German-Jewish communities supported Reform Judaism (at that time referred to as Liberal Judaism). Jews who continued to adhere to Jewish law and prescription now comprised a minority of only approximately 20 percent. Rabbi Trier's earlier admonition that the reform movement would prove to be short-lived had proved false;[4] Jewish community councils were now overwhelmingly Liberal.

Just as historical shifts of the 1840s and 1850s sparked contemporaneous debates concerning circumcision, the rapid political and social changes of the late 1860s and 1870s also precipitated discussions concerning Jewish ritual behavior. After almost a decade of disinterest in Jewish ritual behavior, circumcision once again appeared as a focus of political and social struggles within the Jewish community as diverse community members revisited questions concerning the ritual's relationship with Jewish membership. As these conversations about circumcision took place within the Jewish community, some animal protectionists and municipal administrators began to pay attention to another Jewish rite. Interested in kosher butchering, these discussants paid no heed to issues concerning Jewish communal membership. Instead, their conversations, which originated outside the Jewish community, regarded the possibility of state intervention into religious affairs. These disputes often began as more specific deliberations concerning abattoir practices and evolved into broader discussions concerning Jewish rites. Sometimes they made no reference to Jewish rituals but they nonetheless influenced Jewish ritual behavior.

Both discussions were influenced by the significant historical shifts of this era. Between 1867 and 1876, Germans witnessed war, unification, emancipation, and economic booms and failures. They lived in a nation state that was under construction and whose constituents were diverse.

[3]On Jewish demographics during this time period, see Monika Richarz, "Demographic Developments," in Meyer, ed., *German-Jewish History in Modern Times*, vol. 3, pp. 7–34.
[4]Trier, *Rabbinische Gutachten*, p. xviii.

Similar to the circumcision debates that preceded them, the conflicts concerning Jewish rites that occurred during the unification period offered discussants an opportunity to contemplate the changes taking place around them. In the disputes, participants considered the new political realities of German religious minorities and statehood; they pondered the expectations of the recently bestowed civic rights and questioned whether emancipation necessitated the abandonment of Jewish religious particularities. They also explored the process of integration, questioning what elements of Jewish communal character and administration should be sacrificed for social acceptance and incorporation. In contrast to earlier deliberations concerning Jewish rites, participants from across the continuum of religious observance and political affiliation now recognized Jewish emancipation as a reality. They accepted that some form of governmental intrusion into community life would take place; however they disagreed over the boundaries of intervention and over the character of the community that would experience these intrusions.

To formulate their vision of state and Jewish community in the post-unification age, the discussants in the ritual questions (*Ritualfragen*) turned to the concepts used within the contemporaneous conversations regarding the definition of German character. German political leaders recognized that the success of the new Germany depended on discovering a strategy for developing an integrative culture. The cultural forms embraced by them were hardly inclusive but contributors to the ritual questions drew from these attitudes and beliefs to make an argument regarding the place of Jewish rites in the new German state. They interrogated the relationship of circumcision and kosher butchering to technology, anticlericalism, and German education. They contemplated the association of Jewish rituals with the alleged German tradition of opposing cruelty and supporting toleration. These discourses of culture, cruelty, and tolerance would continue to be crucial in the relationships between the Jewish minority and the German state long after this set of ritual questions concluded.

The *Ritualfragen* of the unification era highlight the intersections between the search for a national German identity for all Germans and the German-Jewish experience.[5] At certain moments, the deliberations

[5]Several historians of modern Germany have analyzed the centrality of confessional identity to German nation building and to German culture. Few of them have extended their analyses to the German-Jewish communities of this era, a gap that Helmut Walser Smith acknowledged in his first monograph and has worked to remedy. Smith, *German Nationalism and Religious Conflict*, p. 22; Andersen, "Piety and Politics"; Ross, "The Kulturkampf and the Limitations of Power in Bismarck's Germany"; Gross, *War Against Catholicism*, p. 241.

concerning Jewish rites sharpened understandings of Jewish integration and citizenship. At other times, they invoked anxieties regarding the place of Catholics in the newly unified state, thus illustrating the dynamic relationship among Judaism and German nation building, politics, and culture.

The Circumcision Questions

Between 1867 and 1876, two discrete sets of deliberations took place concerning Jewish ritual behavior.[6] One set of discussions paid attention to the rite's role in establishing Jewish communal affiliation; the second concerned the rite of kosher butchering and the possibility of governmental interference in religious affairs.

The circumcision deliberations of the unification period differed from earlier debates. The conflicts of the 1860s and 1870s took place almost exclusively within the Jewish community: in its press, contemporary mohel guides, and at the national meetings of German reform rabbis. In contrast to the midcentury discussions, the quarrels of this period were not consumed by medical and scientific considerations, a trend that would change dramatically a decade later.[7] Health concerns certainly motivated many contributors to take part in the discussion, but there was no major movement among physicians or health commissioners to regulate circumcision. Instead, these disputes almost solely concerned issues regarding Jewish communal membership.

During this period four types of circumcision conflicts were common. As in previous years, the most common deliberation concerned the Jewish identities of uncircumcised male infants born to Jewish parents. Widespread interest in this issue resurged in 1869 after the Viennese Jewish community refused to register two uncircumcised boys as Jews. For the next two years the German reform rabbinic synods and press contemplated this and other similar cases, questioning whether circumcision ought to be a standard for Jewish membership and angrily debating who had the authority to make such a determination in the modern age.[8] No Jewish communal resolution ended this dispute.

[6]Because the circumcision disputes of the unification period share some commonalities with those that preceded them, their analysis here will be brief.

[7]An exception can be found in "Protokoll der Sitzung vom II November 1874," *Mittheilungen des Aertzlichen Vereines in Wien* (November 1874): 169–172.

[8]The Viennese magistrate and Austrian minister of interior demanded the newborn's registration. The latter ruling contradicted past adjudications in the circumcision

Instead, the 1876 decision by the German government to allow Jews to withdraw from their congregations without repercussion discouraged future conflicts over circumcision's relationship to communal membership. The German promulgation essentially allowed a father to refuse to circumcise his child and to still register that boy as a Jew even if his community disapproved. This shift originated in the May laws of 1873, which permitted liberal Catholics to repudiate their affiliation with the Catholic community but still be registered by the state as Christian.

Other models of the *Beschneidungsfragen* raised analogous questions. Between 1869 and 1876, the rite attracted notice when a few local rabbis considered the permissibility of circumcising infants born to women who converted to reform Judaism or boys born to Jewish fathers and non-Jewish mothers. Fifteen years after its previous circumcision conflict, Hamburg's religious authorities sparked such a dispute when they refused to permit the circumcision of a boy born to a mother who had converted to Judaism under the auspices of a reform rabbi. In 1872 the orthodox rabbinate ruled that the woman's conversion was not sufficient to transform her or her child into a Jew and they therefore considered the child to be outside of the Jewish community.[9] That same year, Hannover's Jewish benevolent society embarked on another type of dispute when it interred the body of an uncircumcised child outside of the Jewish cemetery walls. The decision, albeit in accordance with Jewish law, sparked strong objections from several factions within and

---

disputes. "Wien, 12 April," *AZDJ* 17 (1869): 332–333; "Wien, 19 Juli," *AZDJ* 31 (1869): 623; "Wien, 28 September," *AZDJ* 42 (1869): 845–846; "Zur Beschneidungsfrage I und II," *AZDJ* 39 and 1 (1869 and 1870): 779–780 and 8; *Verhandlungen der ersten israelitischen Synode zu Leipzig vom 29. Juni bis. 4 Juli 1869* (Berlin: Louis Gerschel's Verlagsbuchhandlung, 1869); "Über die zweite Synode I and II" *AZDJ* 20 and 25 (1871): 591–594; "Bericht über die zweite Synode I," *AZDJ* (1871): 612–614; "Die sogenannte zweite Israel. Synode I, II, III," *Der Israelit* 28, 29, and 31 (1871): 547–551; 583–585; "Referate über die der ersten Israelitischen Synode zu Leipzig überreichten Anträge," *AZDJ* 17 (1871): 333–335; Freunde der Wahrheit, "Einige Worte des Aufschlusses über die Beabsichtigte sogenannte 'Israelitische Synode' zu Augsburg," *Der Israelit* 27 (1871): 511–514; Hermann Wassertrillung, *Torat Ha'brit* (Militsch: self-published, 1869); "Zur Synode," *Der Israelit* 28 (1871).

[9] "Hamburg im März," *AZDJ* (1872): 330–331; "Hamburg," *Jüdische Volkszeitung* (*JV*) 7 (1875): 4–5. On the third type of dispute, see "Hannover," *AZDJ* 24 (1870): 473–474; 23 May 1870 letter from the government of Lower Franconia to the government of Upper Bavaria SM RA 33902; David Ellenson, "Accommodation, Resistance, and the Halakhic Process: A Case Study of Two Responsa by Rabbi Marcus Horovitz," in *Jewish Civilization: Essays and Studies*, Robert A. Brauner, ed. (Philadelphia: Reconstructionist Rabbinical College, 1981), pp. 83–100; Ferziger, *Exclusion and Hierarchy*, pp. 97–98; 144–146; 160–162; 197–199.

outside of the community.[10] Each of these cases raised similar questions concerning the place of Jewish rituals in the modern age and the right of extant Jewish communal leaders to differentiate members from outsiders.[11]

This alleged contradiction between religious custom and modernity simultaneously appeared in a second set of deliberations concerning Jewish rites. Beginning in the 1860s, increasing numbers of German animal protectionists and civil servants expressed interest in the Jewish ritual of kosher butchering. In contrast to the circumcision disputes, the deliberations regarding animal slaughter originated from concerns outside of the Jewish community and made no mention of Jewish communal membership.

The Kosher Butchering Questions

The debates concerning kosher butchering grew out of mid-nineteenth-century animal protectionist attempts to improve Europe's slaughterhouses. Influenced by a number of sentimentalist causes such as temperance reform, these reformers worried that the culture and practices within the slaughterhouse encouraged brutal behavior among men.[12] To protect the public's moral and physical health, animal advocates sought a variety of correctives. They called for the licensing of slaughterers, the implementation of stricter inspection procedures, and the restriction of the abattoir to men only. They also expressed concern that

[10]"Hannover," *AZDJ* 18, 24, 29 (1870): 353–354, 473–474, 577–578; "Hannover, 8 April," *AZDJ* 17 (1872): 332–333; "Der Vorgang in Hannover" *AZDJ* 19 (1873): 307–308; "Rundschau," *JV* 19 (1873): 148. Jewish law dictates that Jews who commit suicide and non-Jews must be buried outside the cemetery gates. Vienna's Jewish community witnessed a similar dispute. "Wien," *AZDJ* 1 and 6 (1872): 5–6 and 103.

[11]Participants now tended to agree that the rite had no bearing on one's individual Jewishness. In almost no case during the 1870s did a mainstream rabbi suggest that boys born to a Jewish woman had to be circumcised to be Jewish. An exception can be found in A. Sulzbach, "Ein Rabbiner (!) über die Beschneidung," *Der Israelit* 24–27 (1871): 456–457, 497–498, 472–473; A. Sulzbach, "Noch einmal zur Synode," *Der Israelit* 29 (1871): 555–557. Majority views can be found in Ludwig Philippson "Ueber die Beschneidung vom biblischen Standpunkte," *AZDJ* 35 (1869): 696; Julius Dessauer, *Brit Olam der Ewige Bund: Die Beschneidung, vom Ritualen, Operativen und Sanitären Standpunkte nach den besten Quellen dargestellt* (Budapest: self-published, 1879); Landau, "Beschneidung," p. 196.

[12]Dorothee Ingeborg Brantz, "Slaughter in the City: The Establishment of Public Abattoirs in Paris and Berlin, 1780–1914 (France, Germany)," Ph.D. diss., University of Chicago, 2003.

existing abattoir practices caused animals pain and fear. Consequently, they championed laws that would mandate the stunning of animals into a state of unconsciousness before slaughter.

The midcentury coexistence of the viewpoints that existing abattoir practices encouraged human violence and pained animals revealed a shift in European animal advocacy. For much of the nineteenth century, activists had embraced an anthropocentric tradition, which argued that animals were to be protected not for their own sake but because man's cruelty to animals encouraged him to act out against other human beings.[13] Concerned that the targets for such brutality would be those individuals who could not defend themselves, animal protectionists made parallels between animals and society's "vulnerable," namely, women and children. By the mid-nineteenth century, advocates also increasingly argued that animals warranted protection because they had their own intrinsic value. Reformers continued to admonish that cruel abattoir practices could lead to domestic violence, verbal abuse, and drunken scuffles, but they also expressed anxiety over the anguish and agony animals experienced during slaughter.[14]

The early reforms championed by animal protectionists did not necessarily target European Jewry. At midcentury, most butchers slaughtered conscious animals with sharp knives, and licensing procedures were uneven. However, animal protectionist's call for the stunning of an animal before its slaughter conflicted with Jewish law. The laws of kosher butchering dictate that an animal must be conscious when slaughtered. Thus, if a government implemented these reforms, Jewish communities would have to request an exemption, flout Jewish tradition, or import kosher meat from another source. Animal advocacy's new interest in slaughterhouse procedures therefore had the potential to affect Jews significantly.

During much of the nineteenth century, most German animal protection societies expressed little interest in kosher butchering and

---

[13]Immanuel Kant articulated this view. He denied that animals had rights of their own because they allegedly lacked the facility to reason, but he worried that an individual who mistreated an animal without any ramification would be encouraged to act similarly with humans. Kant, "Grundlegung zur Metaphysik der Sitten (1785)," in *Kant's gesammelte Schriften*, vol. 4., ed. Georg Reimer (Berlin: Georg Reimer, 1902–1903), pp. 385–464. Also see Andreas Holger Maehle and Ulrich Tröhler, "Animal Experimentation from Antiquity to the End of the Eighteenth Century: Attitudes and Arguments," in *Vivisection in Historical Perspective*, ed. Nicolaas A. Rupke (London and New York: Routledge, 1987), pp. 36–37; Richard Sorabji, *Animal Minds and Human Morals: The Origins of the Western Debate* (Ithaca: Cornell University Press, 1993).

[14]I use the terms *brutality* and *cruelty* interchangeably here.

instead embraced a variety of sentimentalist calls.[15] The movement pushed animal cruelty laws and promoted kindness toward animals. It advocated the prohibition of cockfights and bull-baiting and encouraged women and children to stay away from sites of animal cruelty. It was only during the 1860s that German animal advocates became interested in kosher butchering. Their attention to the Jewish rite coincided with German unification and with anti–kosher butchering campaigns in Switzerland and England.

Swiss and British animal protectionists had launched their crusades against kosher butchering in the mid-1850s, soon after their respective governments enacted new animal cruelty laws. These reforms echoed other regulations being passed across the continent, which made it illegal to mistreat, strike, overwork, or torture animals or to allow for such abuse to occur.[16] After their implementation in England and Switzerland, local animal advocates accused their Jewish communities of being in breach of these promulgations because of the supposedly gruesome nature of the Jewish method of animal slaughter.[17] These activists pushed their governments to pursue one of two options: to punish Jewish communities for defying animal cruelty laws or to promulgate new regulations that would explicitly mandate the stunning of an animal before its slaughter.

The government of Aargau, Switzerland, pursued the latter, passing these "stunning laws" in 1855. While at first the canton permitted its

[15]One exception was in Munich whose animal protection movement during the 1840s described Jewish animal slaughter as "gruesome" and "cruel." J. J. Zagler, *Pflichten gegen der Thiere* (Munich: self-published 1844); J. J. Zagler, *Bericht des Münchener Vereins gegen Thierquälerei für das Jahr 1843* BH MA 59906; 1852 report of the Tierschutzverein (German Animal Protection Society, TSV) of Munich BH MA 59906. Later annual reports and calendars did not mention *Schächten* again until after unification. Annual reports issued by the secretary of the Munich TSV BH MA 59906.

[16]On European animal protection advocacy at this time, see Gerald Carson, *Men, Beasts, and Gods: A History of Cruelty and Kindness to Animals* (New York: Scribner, 1972); Moira Ferguson, *Animal Advocacy and Englishwomen, 1780–1900* (Ann Arbor: University of Michigan Press, 1998); Robert Garner, *Political Animals: Animal Protection Politics in Britain and the United States* (New York: St. Martins Press, 1998); Harriet Ritvo, *The Animal Estate: The English and Other Creatures in the Victorian Age* (Cambridge: Harvard University Press, 1987); Laurent Sueur, "Rever du Paradis sur Terre: La Morale de la Societe Protectrice des Animaux de Paris au XIXe Siecle," *Revue Historique* 293.1 (1995): 133–155; Miriam Zerbel, *Tierschutz im Kaiserreich: Ein Beitrag zur Geschichte des Vereinswesens* (Frankfurt am Main: Peter Lang, 1993). Also see "Prevention of Cruelty to Animals," *The Times* 19922 (22 July 1848): 6; "Cruelty to Animals" *The Times* 21749 (24 May 1854): 11.

[17]"Die Anklage der jüdischen Schächter von London durch die Gesellschaft gegen Thierquälerei," *AZDJ* 47 (1855): 599–600; "Police," *The Times* 22187 (17 October 1855): 9; Krauthammer, *Das Schächtverbot in der Schweiz*.

Jewish community to continue practicing kosher butchering, it revoked this exclusion in 1867.[18] The British government pursued the former option. In 1855, the same year that the anti–kosher butchering campaign in Aargau began, the London police charged a local Jewish butcher with being in breach of parliament's animal protection law. According to prosecutor Henry Rumsey Forster, the butcher Yankoff Cohen, "did unlawfully and cruelly ill-treat and torture a certain ox by improperly cutting its throat."[19] In the course of the ensuing trial, witnesses painted a horrific picture of the Jewish rite, arguing that animals slaughtered according to the Jewish method survived longer and felt more pain. One animal supposedly lay in chains for thirteen minutes waiting for slaughter and, once his throat was cut, remained alive for nine minutes more. Despite this colorful testimony, a number of British physicians and scientists defended kosher butchering on its own merits. The court ruled that this method of slaughter was no more brutal than any other form of killing animals for food and permitted British Jews to continue practicing *shehitah*.[20]

The events in Switzerland and England had a significant impact on German animal advocacy. German animal protection groups pointed to the Swiss and British debates as sources of influence; the prolific German veterinarian and animal protectionist Carl Bauwerker conceded that the Swiss ban on kosher butchering (*Schächtverbot*) had provided the precedent for his activism.[21] Within a few years after the British and Swiss debates, German animal protection societies began

[18]Hermann Engelbert, "Die Anklage und das Verbot des Schächtens der Thiere nach jüdischem Ritus in der Schweiz," *AZDJ* 3 (1867): 44–47 and *Das Schächten und die Bouterole* (St. Gallen: Zollilofer'sche Buchdruckerei, 1876). Also see "Literarischer Wochenbericht," *AZDJ* 49 (1867): 335–336; "Aus der Schweiz," *JV* 5 (1875): 37; "Ueber das Schächten," *AZDJ* 12 (1876): 191–193.

[19]"Police," *The Times* 22187 (17 October 1855): 9; Krauthammer, *Das Schächtverbot in der Schweiz*, pp. 29–94.

[20]"Police," *The Times* 22187 (17 October 1855): 9. The 1855 case did not end the *shehitah* debates in England. Instead, British animal protectionists continued to express concern over slaughtering methods. On the British debates, see Alderman, "Power, Authority and Status in British Jewry."

[21]Bauwerker, *Das Rituelle Schächten*; 14 July 1886 letter from the police authorities to the Jewish community of Händen CJA 75Aer1 97 10; Verband der Thierschutzvereine des deutschen Reiches, *Die Thierschutzgesetzgebung im Deutschen Reich und in anderen Kulturstaaten* (undated) CJA 75 A Ar1 48; "Zur Schlachtreform," *Ibis* 10/12 (October/December 1893): 53; "Eine rege Agitation gegen das Schächten," *Dresdener Neueste Nachrichten* (DNN) 20 September 1912 CJA 75CVe1341 no. 60. Also see A. Keller, *Das Schächten der Israeliten, Referat gehalten an einer Versammlung von Thierschutzfreunden am 2 April 1890* (Aargau: Ph. Wirz-Schriften, 1890); Meier Danziger, *Der theoretische und praktische Schächter nach dem Ohel Jisrael des Rabbi J. Weil*, 5th ed. (Brilon: Druck u. Verlag der M. Friedländer'schen Buchdruckerei u. Buchhandlung, 1858), p. 3.

to push for slaughterhouse reforms that mirrored those demanded by their European colleagues.[22] They called for the creation of better restraining pens for animals and for the stunning of animals before their slaughter.

While animal advocacy groups desired modifications that could have impinged on kosher butchering, many of these German reformers did not explicitly identify the Jewish rite as an issue of concern. German animal protectionists tended to criticize butchers more generally and not specifically target Jewish kosher slaughterers. Moreover, many reformers of this era did not yet support the stunning of animals before slaughter. Stunning practices were still rudimentary, and some animal advocacy groups believed in the humanity of slaughtering conscious animals with a sharp knife. The wide continuum of opinions concerning animal slaughter was illustrated clearly at the 1869 international meeting of animal protection congresses. Challenged by a member to identify the "best, most painless form of slaughter," representatives from more than thirty cities spent two days debating the merits and detriments of all forms of killing animals for food. At the meeting's conclusion the majority accepted an opaque proposal, which said little about kosher butchering and instead requested further scientific guidance.[23] Such a view would change dramatically over the course of the 1880s. By the turn of the century, most German animal protection societies demanded some kind of legislation that enforced the stunning of animals before slaughter.

Whether or not German animal protectionists identified the Jewish method of animal slaughter as particularly cruel, animal advocacy of the unification period proved influential. It led to regulations that, similar to the circumcision reforms of the 1840s and 1850s, shifted the locus of power from the Jewish community to the state. German states and municipalities passed new laws concerning the oversight of animal slaughterers. These regulations, which modified the training, licensing, and supervision of butchers, as well the availability of other professions to them, included kosher animal slaughterers under their

[22]During the decades following unification, animal protectionists often expressed an interest in vivisection, but it was not the focus of their programs. Ulrich Tröhler and Andreas-Holger Maehle, "Anti-Vivisection in Nineteenth-Century Germany and Switzerland: Motives and Methods," in *Vivisection in Historical Perspective*, ed. Nicolaas A. Rupke (London: Routledge, 1987), pp. 161–162; Konrad Alt, "Etwas vom "Weltbund zur Bekämpfung der Vivisection"," *Die Irrenpflege: Monatsblatt zur Hebung, Belehrung und Unterhaltung des Irrenpflegepersonals* 6 (1899): 133–136.

[23]Sondermann, *Bericht über die Verhandlungen des fünften internationalen Thierschutz-Congresses in Zürich vom 2. bis 6. August 1869* (Zurich: Druck von J. Herzog, 1870), 72–106. Quote from p. 73.

purview.[24] These laws stripped the Jewish community of its traditional jurisdiction over its ritual employees. New directives concerning general animal slaughter produced a similar outcome. These promulgations dictated when and where slaughter could take place and the appropriate taxes on meat. They not only influenced when kosher butchering was practiced but also diminished Jewish communal control over ritual behavior.[25]

In addition to expressing interest in the jurisdiction over Jewish ritual acts, the German animal protection campaigns also demonstrated a heightened interest in the boundaries of permitted deviance. During the late 1860s and 1870s, animal advocates increasingly focused on the ways in which kosher butchering was outside the norm. Such interest was timely. During this period, a wide spectrum of German Jews and gentiles considered the expectations that would follow German unification, the ensuing emancipation of German Jewry, and the initiation of a Prussian-state campaign against Germany's Catholic minority.

Ritual Behavior and German "Projects of Homogeneity"

German unification raised questions about difference and the limits of communal and state authority, considerations that were central to that period's *Ritualfragen*. German statehood was accomplished in January 1871, just months after the French government declared war on the North German Confederation and launched the third of the wars of German unification. The German empire now contained a radically diverse citizenry within a fixed set of external borders. At its formation, Germany incorporated the Poles of Eastern and Western Prussia, the

[24]Levi, "Gießen, im November: Ueber die Verbindung des Schächterdienstes mit dem Lehreramte," *AZDJ* 48 (1855): 614–616; December 1857 regulations issued by the Government of Billigheim CAHJP PFV6; Ludwig Philippson, "Die Schächtfrage," *AZDJ* 4 (1875): 49–50; *Denkschrift betreffend die von der Israelitischen Religions-Gesellschaft in Offenbach gewünschte Anstellung eines zweiten Schächters sowie auch das Verhältniß dieser Gesellschaft zur Israelitischen Religions-Gemeinde im Allgemeinen* (Offenbach a.M.: Druck von Kohler & Teller, 1864).

[25]1 October 1862 slaughterhouse and meat-selling regulations of Munich Stadtarchiv München (StM) Schlacht und Viehhof (SUV) 7; 9 February 1863 slaughterhouse laws and tax rates for Karlsruhe CAHJP S153/17; 14 May 1869 Munich slaughterhouse regulations StM SUV 7; 1875 Contract of Service issued by the city of Bayreuth CAHJP D/BA28/28; 9 August 1878 Munich slaughterhouse and stockyard regulations StM SUV 7; "Zum Kapitel die Ungebundenheit der Kälber," *Süddeutsche Presse und Münchener Nachrichten* (22 September 1878) StM SUV 7.

Danes in Schleswig-Holstein, the French of Alsace-Lorraine, and other minority groups. The Reich included Protestants, Catholics, and Jews, with many of the Reich's new inhabitants identifying as Catholic. In Alsace-Lorraine, for example, the territory's 1,200,000 Catholics greatly outnumbered its 250,000 Protestants.[26] Other differences existed as well. Germany "inherited" individuals who had campaigned vigorously for a nation to be organized by Austria as well as those who envisioned a Germany with Prussia at its head. Moreover, at its formation, the empire permitted individual states to retain a significant portion of their pre 1871 powers. The newly formed Germany was, in the words of Theodor Schieder, an "unfinished nation."[27]

Upon unification, German political leaders did not revoke the extant rights that some citizens already had obtained in their states or municipalities.[28] Rather, the new empire emancipated all property-holding men, including Jews, although the legal status of Jewish communities varied considerably by state.[29] Recognizing that emancipation would not necessarily bring about social or political inclusion German leaders embarked on a process of integrating these groups into the German state. They did not promote a vision of German multiethnicity. Instead, they strategized over how to develop an integrative culture that could forcefully unite its people. The German state, suggested the German liberal historian Heinrich von Treitschke in 1879, was a "cultural power" whose institutions could advance a national Protestant culture (*Kulturprotestantismus*) that would connect its residents.[30]

---

[26]Gross, *War Against Catholicism*. On Alsace-Lorraine, see Dan Silverman, *Reluctant Union: Alsace-Lorraine and Imperial Germany, 1871–1918* (University Park: Pennsylvania State University Press, 1972). Also see Vicki Caron, *Between France and Germany: The Jews of Alsace-Lorraine, 1871–1918* (Stanford, CA: Stanford University Press, 1981).

[27]Theodor Schieder, *Das deutsche Kaiserreich von 1871 als Nationalstaat* (Cologne: Westdeutscher Verlag, 1961). Also see John Breuilly, "Nation and Nationalism in Modern German History," *The Historical Journal* 33.3 (1990): 659–675; Geoff Eley, "State Formation, Nationalism, and Political Culture: Some Thoughts on the Unification of Germany," in *From Unification to Nazism: Reinterpreting the German Past* (Boston: Unwin Hyman, 1986), pp. 61–84.

[28]Liberal support of emancipation has encouraged scholars to describe German liberalism as fundamentally embracing individual freedoms, toleration, and rights. See Hajo Holborn, *A History of Modern Germany*, vol. 2 (Princeton: Princeton University Press, 1982); Gordon A. Craig, *Germany, 1866–1945* (New York: Oxford University Press, 1978).

[29]On the authority of the German states, see Michael John, "Constitution, Administration, and the Law," in *Imperial Germany: A Historiographical Companion*, ed. Roger Chickering (Westport, CT: Greenwood Press, 1996), pp. 185–214.

[30]As cited by Smith, *German Nationalism and Religious Conflict*, p. 37. Also see Frank Trommler, "The Creation of a Culture of *Sachlichkeit*," in *Society, Culture, and the State in*

The German cultural forms promoted by liberal leaders invoked middle-class values, such as bourgeois civic pride, a confidence in education, and an appreciation of associational life and the written word. *Kulturprotestantismus* was also deeply nationalistic, embracing a historical connection to the struggle for German unity although that nationalism was Prussian, Protestant, and deeply anticlerical. This proposed German cultural identity predictably clashed with other customs, traditions, and ways of life.[31] Emblematic of the larger liberal program that expressed suspicion of the masses, *Kulturprotestantismus* was not the culture of all people even if it was put forward in the name of all. Historian Helmut Walser Smith explains it was "not the amicable union of popular and elite culture, the world of folklore with the world of print, but rather an ideology of elites propounded in the name of the people."[32] The clash between the project of cultural homogeneity and the reality of different cultural forms would prompt several promoters of this national Protestant culture to cast a suspicious light on minority integrative possibilities.

The clearest manifestation of suspicion was the state-sponsored campaign against Germany's Catholic minority (*Kulturkampf*). The *Kulturkampf* was justified as a means to defend national identity and middle-class values. German liberals had long dedicated themselves to warring against the Roman Catholic Church in order to consolidate Germany. Soon after the German defeat of France and the Vatican Council's proclamation of papal infallibility, Bismarck launched an assault against the Catholic Church in the name of German unity. One year after unification, the German parliament authorized legislation that was intended to unite Germany around a homogeneous social and moral code. The 1872 laws allowed the state to inspect all public and private schools and restrict the citizenship rights of individual German Jesuits. They also permitted the state to dissolve monastic orders and expel some of their members from Germany. Subsequent laws extended state control over

---

Germany 1870–1930, ed. Geoff Eley (Ann Arbor: University of Michigan Press, 1996), esp. p. 468; Celia Applegate, *A Nation of Provincials: The German Idea of Heimat* (Berkeley: University of California Press, 1990).

[31]Zygmunt Bauman has called these "the practical heterogeneity of cultural forms." Bauman, *Modernity and Ambivalence* (Cambridge: Polity Press, 1991). Also see Uriel Tal, *Christians and Jews in Germany: Religion, Politics, and Ideology in the Second Reich, 1870–1914*, trans. Noah Jonathan Jacobs (Ithaca: Cornell University Press, 1975), pp. 32–80; Fritz Stern, *The Politics of Cultural Despair*, paperback ed. (Berkeley: University of California Press, 1961); Michael Walzer, *On Toleration* (New Haven: Yale University Press, 1997), p. 27.

[32]Smith, *German Nationalism and Religious Conflict*, p. 21.

previously autonomous realms, including those of civil marriages, civil registries, and the education and selection of priests. By the end of the *Kulturkampf* in 1878, the government had exiled or punished 1,800 priests and seized 16 million marks of property.[33] According to recent historical studies, the *Kulturkampf* was a carefully planned campaign by Liberals who did not believe they were contradicting the precepts of liberalism. Instead, "the attack on the Catholic church was...consonant with liberal beliefs."[34]

State obsession with Catholic deviance did not provide German-speaking Jews with relief. Rather, during this period groups of diverse Jewish and gentile thinkers and activists commented on Jewish integration. The deliberations concerning Jewish rites offered some of these observers a forum in which they could express their frustration over Jewry's slow acculturation; they provided others with an opportunity to laud Jewish accomplishments vis-à-vis Catholics. Using the same language being invoked by the *Kulturkampf*, this latter group argued that circumcision and kosher butchering reflected high standards of German-Jewish morals and ethics (*Sittlichkeit*), which allegedly distanced Jewish religious customs—and Jews—from the "religious fanaticism" of Catholics.

Supporters and detractors of Jewish rites relied on the *Kulturkampf*'s standards for cultural integration to articulate these positions. They contemplated the ways in which kosher butchering and circumcision reinforced or clashed with the alleged German antipathy toward cruelty and its supposed embrace of tolerance. They also examined the relationship of the two rites to the endorsement of German education, technology, and anticlericalism. These conversations did not result in dramatic legislative shifts, but they laid the foundation for future disputes.

Cruelty and *Kultur*

The discussions about cruelty, which were central to the *Ritualfragen* of the unification period, had a long-standing history within European tradition. Early modern philosophers had imagined cruelty as a nonhuman form of violence or as a type of human aggression characterized by its excessiveness. In their view, both appearances of brutality were

---

[33]Ibid., pp. 1–113.; Sheehan, *German Liberalism in the Nineteenth Century*, pp. 137–140.

[34]Gross, *War Against Catholicism*, p. 245. Also see Dieter Langewiesche, *Liberalismus in Deutschland* (Frankfurt am Main: Suhrkamp Verlag, 1988), pp. 68–69, 180–186.

components within God's schema for the world.[35] By German unification in 1871, philosophical treatments of cruelty had been divorced from this religious context. From the Enlightenment on, Europeans had increasingly defined brutality as a choice made by man, not by God. The authors of treatises on cruelty worried that violence encouraged men to become increasingly spiteful to others, especially society's "innocents," namely, women and children. Over the course of the nineteenth century, commentators on German life increasingly characterized cruelty by its impact and by its lack of compassion, what James Steingardner has referred to as "moral monstrosity."[36] They also gradually came to understand it as a self-conscious decision. During the years immediately preceding and following unification, a significant characteristic of cruelty, according to German commentators, was the awareness people supposedly had when they committed cruel acts.

German writers and political leaders became interested in human brutality during the unification period in part because their social experiences had been characterized by violence. Germany had just emerged from three wars of unification and was undergoing, to varying degrees, the social trauma from these conflicts and from Germany's relatively rapid industrialization and urbanization.[37] Certainly, the late 1860s and early 1870s saw the rise of a number of sentimentalist movements that articulated a concern with the increasing presence of violence in society, particularly in current forms of discipline and punishment, domestic violence, intemperance, animal cruelty, and dueling.[38] In each case, reformers called for government involvement and wide-ranging change. Understandings of cruelty offered these reformers a strategy to contend with the anxieties of everyday life and increasingly served as a way to think about social integration.

[35]Daniel Baraz, *Medieval Cruelty: Changing Perceptions, Late Antiquity to the Early Modern Period* (Ithaca: Cornell University Press, 2003); Richard J. Evans, *Rituals of Retribution: Capital Punishment in Germany 1600–1987* (Oxford: Oxford University Press, 1996).

[36]James A. Steintrager, *Cruel Delight: Enlightenment Culture and the Inhuman* (Bloomington: Indiana University Press, 2004).

[37]Evans, *Rituals of Retribution*; Isabel V. Hull, *Absolute Destruction: Military Culture and the Practices of War in Imperial Germany* (Ithaca: Cornell University Press, 2005).

[38]The popular concern with brutality also can be explained by the theory of the "civilizing process," a premise first articulated by Nobert Elias. Elias found that the adoption of new mannerisms and values took place simultaneously with the creation of new states. In his schema, new emphases on restraining physical urges and public displays of emotion originated with the decision by governments to take on increased responsibility for their inhabitants and for disciplining wrongdoing. It was at this historical moment that the upper class, and later the middle and working classes, articulated concerns that an inability to restrain oneself could have harmful effects on society at large. It is possible that a similar phenomenon occurred at the moment of

Interest in brutality offered political leaders and reformers a means to determine varying people's potential for assimilation, a task that held tremendous salience during the unification period. Understandings of cruelty facilitated the classification of individuals and groups by their social and ethical habits (their generosity or temperance, for example) and by their potential for acculturation. This may explain the fascination of the German liberal press during the 1860s and 1870s with anecdotes concerning the alleged brutality of Catholics. One occurrence that garnered significant attention was the 1869 "Ubryk affair," in which a Carmelite order in Kraków supposedly detained and tortured a Catholic nun for breaking her vow of celibacy. Over the next few months, the press provided detailed accounts of Sister Barbara Ubryk's torture and reported on other gruesome "convent atrocity stories."[39] The press was similarly occupied with the possibility of Polish Catholic subversion, as evidenced by the scaremongering that followed the arrest of Emil Westerville, who allegedly plotted to assassinate Bismarck.[40]

These stories of Catholic cruelty served as cautionary tales for bourgeois society. Westerville's distant relationship with the private secretary and archbishop of Gnesen-Posen, and the torture narratives supposedly emerging from the Polish convent seemed to reinforce German liberal accusations that Poles were disloyal, aggressive, and mean-spirited. Furthermore, in their admonishment of what would occur to women if they abdicated their traditional responsibilities as wives and mothers and became nuns, these popular narratives validated fears concerning unregulated female behavior and contested the emerging German women's movement. The antimonastic attacks in the press and on the streets advanced an image of Catholics as untrustworthy, sexually brutal, and offensive to the liberal vision of the modern nation.[41]

Similar conversations took place concerning Jewish ritual behavior. During the unification period, increasing numbers of Jews and gentiles

---

unification. Nobert Elias, *The Civilizing Process,* trans. Edmund Jephcott (New York: Urizen Books, 1978). On German associational life, see Thomas Nipperdey, "Verein als soziale Struktur in Deutschland im späten 18. und frühen 19. Jahrhundert. Eine Fallstudie zur Modernisierung I," in *Gesellschaft, Kultur, Theorie: Gesammelte Aufsätze zur neueren Geschichte,* ed. Thomas Nipperdey (Göttingen: Vandenhoeck und Ruprecht, 1976), pp. 174–205.

[39]Gross, *War Against Catholicism,* pp. 157–170.

[40]See Lech Trzeciakoskki, *The Kulturkampf in Prussian Poland,* trans. Katarzyna Kretkowska (New York: Columbia University Press, 1990); Ronald J. Ross, *The Failure of Bismarck's Kulturkampf: Catholicism and State Power in Imperial Germany, 1871–1887* (Washington, DC: Catholic University of America Press, 1998), esp. pp. 22–23.

[41]Gross, *War Against Catholicism.*

looked to the ways in which kosher butchering and circumcision encouraged or discouraged brutality toward animals and children. Discussants in the *Ritualfragen* paid attention to the pain animals and children experienced at the hands of ritual practitioners, the uneven power relationships inherent within the rites, and the rituals' influences on society more generally. Their resulting claims justified arguments concerning Jewish preparedness for full integration and the appropriateness of governmental intervention into previously autonomous realms.

Participants tried to understand how animals and children experienced kosher butchering and circumcision. Influenced by theriocentric impulses taking shape within the animal advocacy movement, these discussants labeled kosher butchering and other forms of slaughter that killed conscious animals as cruel. In their view, these animals suffered panic, muscle cramping, and intense pain when killed.[42] Moreover, because conscious animals supposedly remained alive longer than those stunned before death, it was likely that conscious cattle experienced this agony longer than animals stunned before slaughter.[43] A reporter for the *Neue Freie Volks-Zeitung* articulated this charge in his 1878 article. "The *shochet* [*sic*] comes with his knife the length of his arm and cuts the sword into and through the neck of the animal; that [knife] however goes right through his shaking bellow.... Such barbaric animal cruelty still takes place today... With this kind of animal cruelty, all others [kinds of animal cruelty] are kids' play."[44] Animal advocates offered analogous complaints over the ways in which slaughterers shackled steer before killing them (*Niederlegen*). The devices that chained animals into pens, held them on their sides, and tipped them upside down purportedly inspired tremendous fear and also left wounds or burns on the animals, causing them much anguish.[45]

---

[42]20 June 1879 from Munich TSV to Perles Leo Baeck Institute Archives (LBA) RSC AR 2112 (B 30/7); Vereins gegen Thierquälerei zu Königsberg, *4 & 5 Bericht uber die Thätigkeit des Vereins gegen Thierqualerei zu Königsberg in den Jahren 1873 und 1874* (Königsberg: Ostpreußische Zeitungs- und Verlags-Druckerei, 1875); 1 December 1881 letter to Jacob Cohn from the magistrate of Kattowitz CJA 75Dco127 12; July 15 1879 letter from Perles to the Munich TSV LBA RSC AR 2112 (B 30/7).

[43]Bauwerker, *Das Rituelle Schächten*, p. 11.

[44]"Was gibt es neues: Jüdische Thierquälerei im neuen Schlachthaus," *Neue Freie Volks-Zeitung* 22 (28 September 1878). Also see Bauwerker, *Das Rituelle Schächten*, p. 37; 20 June 1879 letter from the Munich TSV to the magistrat StM SUV 84. The Jewish community responded to this charge. 15 July 1879 letter from Perles to the TSV LBA RSC AR 2112 (B 30/7).

[45]Not all animal protectionists singled out the Jewish community as the perpetrators of this misdeed (or named the Jewish community at all). Vereins gegen Thierquälerei

While it was less common, participants in the deliberations concerning circumcision similarly objected to the pain infants suffered during the rite and to the uneven power relationship between children and adults. A few critics censured circumcision for exposing children to mutilation, discomfort, and illness. In his 1874 study, the physician Eugen Levit complained that the ritual brutally exposed infants to pain and disease; according to the doctor, it forced children to begin their lives in fear and agony.[46] Moreover, circumcision was the choice of parents and communities, not of infants. Newborns, wrote another commentator, "do not know into what they entered."[47] They had no choice in whether they would undergo the ritual; that was a decision to be made by their fathers and communal leaders. Critics of the rite similarly held up the events in Hannover as an example of deliberate cruelty. There, the religious community buried an uncircumcised child outside of the cemetery walls despite the Jewish lineage of the parents and despite parental pleas that the child be given a Jewish burial. Jewish opponents of circumcision pointed to the stubborn and deliberate acts of the Jewish community council as an example of brutality. Even though they took no knife to the Jewish child, the Jewish community council had monstrously decided to inter the child outside of the cemetery walls.[48]

In these portraits of Jewish brutality, critics complained that Jewish communities valued tradition and law over technological improvement. According to these opponents, German Jews self-consciously rejected the machinery that could lessen the pain animals or children experienced. Jewry's intentional choosing of technologically inferior methods supposedly indicated the "unnecessarily" cruel nature of their rites,[49] an assertion that grew out of contemporary understandings of brutality as

zu Königsberg, *4 & 5 Bericht; Bericht über die Verhandlungen des fünften internationalen Thierschutz-Congresses in Zürich vom 2. bis 6. August 1869* (Zurich: Druck von J. Herzog, 1870); "Zum Kapitel 'die Ungebundenheit der Kälber" *Süddeutsche Presse und Münchener Nachrichten* (22 September 1878). Also see Rothschild, "Die rituelle Schlachtweise der Juden," *JV* 13 (30 March 1875): 97–99.

[46]Levit, *Die Circumcision der Israeliten*; Salomon Alexander Wolff, *Dreinundzwanzig Sätze über die Beschneidung und den jüdisch-confessionell Charakter, Mischnalese oder Talmudtexte* (Leipzig: Albert Fritsch, 1869).

[47]Wolff, *Dreinundzwanzig Sätze über die Beschneidung*, p. 7.

[48]"Der Vorgang in Hannover" *AZDJ* 19 (1873): 307–308; "Rundschau," *JV* 19 (1873): 148.

[49]Wilhelm Landsberg, *Das Rituelle Schächten der israeliten im Lichte der Wahrheit* (Kaiserlautern: Verlag von Eugen Crufins, 1882); 20 June 1879 letter from the Munich TSV to the Jewish community of Munich, LBA RSC AR 2112 (B 30/7); "Munich, 29 September," *Augsburger Abendzeitung* 272 (2 October 1878): 4; 18 September 1878 letter to the magistrate of Munich StM SUV 84.

something deliberate. Moreover, such a belief cast Jews as indifferent to social integration. It raised questions concerning the civic worthiness of a people who disrespected the middle-class embrace of technology and who, more significantly, chose to preserve their separateness by removing an infants' foreskin or cutting the throat of a conscious animal.[50] "Act as citizens," one discussant ordered.[51]

Whether or not participants explicitly raised questions concerning Jewish violence, several contributors to the debates articulated a worry that the cruelty of these rites would negatively affect society as a whole. Anxious that witnessing the brutality of animal slaughter could cause someone emotional harm, animal protection advocates demanded that local and state governments remove kosher butchering from the eyes of gentile and Jewish women and children. The magistrate of Kattowitz, for example, articulated concern that the public nature of *shehitah* allowed society's innocents to observe a "dreadful process." "We need to limit the number of people who see it," he wrote to the city's chief rabbi. "It should not be done near a window. Nor should it take place in a house where children live or have access.[52] Two decades earlier, the governments of Prussia, Hesse, and Austria had begun to design legislation to protect school children from the brutality of the slaughterhouse. Some authorities forbade teachers from working simultaneously as *shohetim*;[53] others dictated that teachers who wished to serve as ritual slaughterers had to apply to their municipal governments for permission and pay additional taxes.[54] Authorities justified these laws by explaining that no teacher should participate in activities that would expose his charges to the horrors of inhumanity.

Defenders of Jewish rituals disputed this characterization of brutality and, in so doing, allowed their critics to set the terms of the debate. Supporters of Jewish rites inversely argued that Jewish rituals were humane, thus implying that Jews indeed were worthy of full social integration.

[50]1879 letter from the Association of Animal Protection Societies of the German Reich (TSV) to the slaughterhouse authorities of Berlin CJA 75CVe1341 75.

[51]Bauwerker, *Das Rituelle Schächten*, p. 3. Also see "Was gibt es neues: Jüdische Thierquälerei im neuen Schlachthaus," *Neue Freie Volks-Zeitung* 22 (28 September 1878). Such a view sometimes foreshadowed a rhetorical turn that would be crucial during the 1890s and early 1900s.

[52]1 December 1881 letter to Jacob Cohn from the magistrate of Kattowitz CJA 75Dco127 12. Also see 5 March 1878 minutes of the Jewish community of Kattowitz CJA 75Co1 27; 8 March 1878 letter from the Jewish community concerning *shehitah* CJA 75Dco1 27. For Baden, see 9 February 1863 regulation concerning *shehitah* tariffs no 91. CAHJ S153/17.

[53]Levi, "Gießen, im November."

[54]December 1857 request and governmental decision (Billigheim) CAHJP PFV6; Philippson, "Die Schächtfrage," *AZDJ* 4 (1875): 49–50.

They reasoned that the rite compassionately killed animals for food; in their view, the ritual had been fashioned deliberately as a response to the barbaric ways in which ancient peoples had treated animals. "Judaism," argued one proponent "created this method on the principles of humanitarianism."[55] Kosher butchering, wrote another, was intended to be different than other methods of slaughter in which "people practiced the greatest forms of cruelty."[56] Proponents also juxtaposed the ritual with the contemporary method of stunning the animal before slaughter. In their defenses of the rite, they described the stunning of animals, and not kosher butchering, as cruel. Stunning an animal with iron stakes or bullets allegedly only resulted in unconsciousness because the stunning mechanisms destroyed the animal's brain and, nervous system. According to these studies, animals sometimes awoke from their state of unconsciousness during slaughter, experienced more pain from the stunning than the beheading itself, and experienced tremendous agony.[57]

In contrast to their critics, defenders of circumcision cast the rite as deliberately kind and moral. They dismissed the notion that male infants experienced trauma from their circumcisions and reminded readers that the wine given to newborns before the circumcision served as an anesthetic. Moreover, like their predecessors of the 1840s and 1850s, they touted the health benefits of the rite, insisting that the ritual was designed for the public good. One enthusiastic physician so lauded the prophylactic and hygienic benefits of the rite for newborns that he recommended that all German male newborns—whether they were born to Jewish parents or not—undergo the surgery.[58]

[55]"Die rituelle Schlachtweise der Juden vom Standpunkte der Humanität," *JV* 13 (1875): 99.

[56]Israel Michel Rabbinowicz, *Die thalmudischen Prinicipien des Schächtens und die Medicin des Thalmuds,* trans. S. Trier (Paris: self-published, 1881), 1–4; "Die rituelle Schlachtweise der Juden vom Standpunkte der Humanität," *JV* 13 (1875): 97–99; S. Pucher, *Tza'ar Ba'alei Hayim De'orytah [H] Mitgefühl mit den Thieren eine heilige Pflicht der jüdischen Religion: Ein Wort an seine Glaubensgenossen* (Mitau: J. F. Steffenhagen und Sohn, 1876).

[57]Hermann Engelbert, *Das Schächten und die Bouterole: Denkschrift für den hohen Großen Rath des Kantons St. Gallen zur Beleuchtung des diesbezüglichen regierungsräthlichen Antrags und mit Zugrundlegung der neuesten mitagedruckten Gutachten* (St. Gallen: Zollikofer'sche Buchdruckerei, 1876); Gerlach, "Ueber das "Schächten," vom physiologischen Standpunkte," *Monatsschrift für Geschichte und Wissenschaft des Judenthums,* vol. 16 (Breslau: Verlag der Schletter'scen Buchhandlung, 1867), pp. 93–100.

[58]David Rosenzweig, *Die Beschneidung: ein Beitrag zur öffentlichen Gesundheitspflege* (Schweidnitz: Verlag von C. F. Weigmann, 1889); "Zur Beschneidungsfrage," *AZDJ* 17 (1878): 259–260. Also see Dessauer, *Brit Olam.*

As these defenders of Jewish rites lauded their humane character, other proponents taunted their critics' use of cruelty to censure Jewish ritual behavior. They unmasked these rhetorical flourishes for what they often were; namely, veiled attempts to portray Jews as outside the social norms. Rabbi Meyer Kayserling of Aargau wryly condemned his critics for ignoring their own brutality and chauvinism. "Man protects animals and torments men; he abolishes the death penalty and plots new ways of killing; he improves prisons [while] making the whole world into a prison."[59] Ten years later, Rabbi Hermann Engelbert argued "this is not the first time that an inhumane act is practiced against the Jewish community in the name of humanitarianism."[60] For these two German-born Swiss rabbis, this use of humanitarianism to condemn ritual behavior represented a dangerous turn in the non-Jewish world. Perhaps as a response, they advanced a second strategy in their defenses of Jewish rituals. They promoted toleration and, in so doing, reclaimed the upper hand in setting the terms of the debate.

Tolerating Jewish Rites

As some participants looked to cruelty as a justification for Jewish segregation or regeneration, other discussants invoked understandings of tolerance as a means to downplay Jewish difference. Toleration, like cruelty, had served as an important theme in Enlightenment discourses, when toleration and freedom of the religious conscience came to be seen as natural rights of man.[61] Over the course of the late eighteenth

---

[59]Kayserling, "Das Verbot des Schächtens der Thiere nach jüdischem Ritus in der Schweiz," *AZDJ* 8 (1867): 150. Kayserling's colleague, Engelbert, similarly reproached animal protectionists ten years later.

[60]Engelbert, *Das Schächten und die Bouterole*, p. 4.

[61]Perez Zagorin, *How the Idea of Religious Toleration Came to the West* (Princeton: Princeton University Press, 2003), pp. 292–293. Contemporary and historical treatments of religious tolerance (the attitude) and toleration (the practice) are extensive, but most examine its usage in early modern Europe, particularly in reformation England. Recent studies have pushed for a study of toleration outside of England. Ole Peter Grell and Roy Porter, "Toleration in Enlightenment Europe," in *Toleration in Enlightenment Europe*, ed. Ole Peter Grell and Roy Porter (Cambridge: Cambridge University Press, 2000), pp. 1–22; Martin Fitzpatrick, "Toleration and the Enlightenment Movement," in *Toleration in Enlightenment Europe*, ed. Grell and Porter, pp. 213–230; Hugh Trevor-Roper, "Toleration and Religion after 1688," in *From Persecution to Toleration: The Glorious Revolution and Religion in England* (Oxford: Clarendon Press, 1991), pp. 389–408.

and early nineteenth centuries, some German philosophers and political leaders had advanced toleration as a state strategy for regeneration. Under the label of "tolerance," this pre-emancipatory model called for the state to acknowledge religious diversity within its borders and on occasion to grant civic rights to religious minorities. The Austrian Toleration Edict (1781) recognized Jewish religious difference and extended social and educational privileges to Jews living in the Austrian empire.[62] Before German unification in 1871, several other central European decrees similarly categorized Jews as "tolerated" inhabitants, permitting Jewish residences and sometimes granting certain political, educational, or social rights. Toleration, however, did not ensure protection. The Prussian edict of 1812 differentiated Judaism, a "publicly tolerated religion," from the Reform churches, Lutheran churches, and Roman Catholic churches that would receive formal protection from the state.[63]

Unification complicated this pre-emancipatory model and influenced the ways in which participants used toleration in the *Ritualfragen*. Upon unification, toleration was increasingly understood as the acknowledgment of religious difference and as the justification for removing restrictions based on religion.[64] As was the case in other parts of Europe, this understanding of toleration did not extend to permitting a minority religion the right to interfere with social integration or the governance of the state. With unification, the German state was responsible for considering the extent to which it would accommodate the beliefs and practices of its religious minorities. The German constitution enshrined this model of toleration but it left no blueprint for how it could be implemented. Instead, the constitution left political leaders with a significant paradox. Article 12 of the constitution granted legal equality to religious minorities and eliminated "all remaining restrictions in civil and political rights based on differences of religion." Nevertheless, Article 14 secured the privileged status of the Christian religion "in

[62]In addition, the 1782 decree forbade clandestine baptism of Jewish children under the age of seven but permitted it for those between the ages of seven and fourteen if those children were in mortal danger. In 1787, the government made baptism dependent on the permission of the civil authorities.

[63]It left the meaning of this "publicly tolerated religion" unclear and postponed defining the legal status of the Jewish religion until an undisclosed date.

[64]Advocates of toleration did not necessarily call for the unprejudicial embrace of equal freedom, something that would be invoked by participants in the *Ritualfragen* later in the century. On this distinction, see David C. Itzkowitz, "The Jews of Europe and the Limits of Religious Freedom," in *Freedom and Religion in the Nineteenth Century*, ed. Richard Helmstadter (Stanford, CA: Stanford University Press, 1997), pp. 150–171.

those state institutions that are connected to the practice of religion."[65] This contradiction not only allowed for considerable discrimination against Jews in the judiciary, military, and educational professions but also raised questions about the place of Jewish ritual behavior in the German state. Participants in the ritual questions considered whether the constitution's promise of civic equality protected Jewish religious freedoms. They also pondered whether Jewish rituals' alleged clash with social integration could be accommodated by state and society.

Echoing the anti-emancipatory rhetoric of an earlier era, late-nineteenth-century critics of Jewish rites argued that Jewish ritual behavior reinforced Jewish social isolation and posed an obstacle to integration. They described circumcision and kosher butchering as fundamentally intolerant practices. In his 1869 *Twenty-Three Thoughts About Circumcision and Its Jewish-Confessional Character*, the Jewish author Salomon Alexander Wolff articulated such a position, maintaining that circumcision represented the willing separation from others. Mimicking the platforms presented by critics during the 1840s and 1850s, he and other participants questioned the place of Jewish rites in the emancipatory period.[66] Levit's medically oriented treatment of the rite came to similar conclusions. He emphasized that external signs of religio-nationality were unnecessary during the modern age and criticized the Jewish rite for being socially exclusive and, more important, medically dangerous.[67] A few critics of kosher butchering crafted comparable critiques, arguing that the existence of kosher butchering was troubling because it encouraged Jews to preserve their separate dietary habits and illustrated that Jewish particularism trumped morality. These discussants may have been influenced by simultaneous liberal claims against Catholicism. During the *Kulturkampf*, liberals censured Catholics for interpreting toleration to mean that Catholics had the freedom to suppress the freedom of others. German Liberal politicians described Catholic rites in ways similar to critics of Jewish rites: as customs that deliberately sacrificed the good of the state and populace for the ideological desires of a few.[68]

As detractors pointed to the purportedly intolerant character of Jewish rites, proponents used toleration to defend their religious particularities and to call for state sanction of Jewish difference. This group compared toleration to other fundamental rights of the modern period,

[65]Werner E. Mosse, "From Schutzjuden to Deutsche Staatsbürber Jüdischen Glaubens," p. 87; Peter Pulzer, "Legal Equality and Public Life," *German-Jewish History in Modern Times*, vol. 3, p. 155.

[66]Wolff, *Dreinundzwanzig Sätze*, p. 4.

[67]Levit, *Die Circumcision*.

[68]On this see, Gross, *War Against Catholicism*, pp. 258–259.

particularly freedom of religion and speech. According to one writer, toleration was akin to the "elevated principles of the uninjured freedom of belief and speech." In his view, these rights were due to anyone, without "distinction of position and rank of birth and of religion."[69] Such a comparison was intriguing because toleration in the *Ritualfragen* did not call for the protection of beliefs but of actions that were predicated upon a belief system and appeared antithetical to German cultural forms.

Despite the fact that ritual behavior increasingly was seen as a departure from societal norms (and in some cases state or local law), these supporters of ritual difference justified their expansive view of religious toleration on the grounds that Jewish rites were deeply meaningful and that toleration provided an underpinning for state stability.[70] When Rabbi Jacob Cohn appealed to his magistrate to permit the Jewish community to continue practicing kosher butchering, he argued that the rite, while humane, should be tolerated by the city primarily because of its ritual significance. In his view, *shehitah* was one of the most basic religious customs, without which the Jewish community would dissolve.[71] Rabbi Julius Dessauer defended circumcision on similar grounds. For him, the state should safeguard the rite because it reinforced Jewish morality and was central to Judaism and the Jewish people. Circumcision, he wrote, was a "mark in which the community expresses its societal beliefs, families bond themselves with the community."[72]

Like midcentury assurances that circumcision guaranteed civic worthiness, these defenses suggested that the absence of tolerance posed a risk to the state. Similar rhetoric could be found in the *Kulturkampf.* Despite the irony of embracing toleration in order to eliminate the freedoms of others, German Liberal leaders argued that toleration was essential to the German state. In his vote in favor of the anti-Jesuit

---

[69]Engelbert, *Das Schächten und die Bouterole*, p. 1. Also see Meyer Kayserling, *Die rituelle Schlachtfrage oder ist Schächten Thierquäelerei?* (Aargau: Druck und Verlag von H. R. Sauerländer, 1867), pp. 1–2; Ludwig Philippson, "Ueber die Beschneidung vom biblischen Standpunkte," *AZDJ* 35 (1869): 693–696, esp. p. 694.

[70]Philosophers and scholars have identified six motivations that encouraged such a broad usage of tolerance and toleration: (1) an acquiescence of difference adopted for the sake of peace; (2) an indifference to diversity; (3) an openness to others; (4) an enthusiastic embrace of difference; a (5) a moral acknowledgment that minority groups have rights even if they practice those rights distastefully; and (6) the legal necessities that were inherent to the establishment of the state. Walzer, *On Toleration*, pp. 10–11.

[71]December 1881 response from Jacob Cohn to the magistrate of Kattowitz CJA 75Dco127 12. Also see Kayserling, *Die rituelle Schlachtfrage* and Danziger, *Der theoretische und praktische Schächter.*

[72]Dessauer, *Brit Olam*, p. 9. Also see *Verhandlungen der ersten Isr. Synode*, p. 93; "Die Synode und der Gemeindetag II," *AZDJ* 28 (1869): 549–551.

laws, the Catholic Progressive Eduard Windthorst described Germany as "the land of the Reformation, the land of free science, the land of tolerance and enlightenment."[73] The German-born Rabbi Meyer Kayserling viewed the *Kulturstaat* (culturally defined state) similarly. In his study of kosher butchering, he linked toleration with political maturation and warned that its absence could lead to extremism and prejudice. In the new *Kulturstaat* "man is valued by his learning, one is no longer interested in the religious affiliation of citizens; one no longer asks another whether he belongs to a church or synagogue...the times for fanaticism, intolerance, and religious persecution are over."[74] His colleague Hermann Engelbert described toleration as a "republican ideal." Paradoxically while some animal protectionists at this time championed the Swiss example because of their animal cruelty laws, Engelbert warned that the elimination of tolerance could lead Germany to a state of religious fanaticism. In Switzerland, he claimed, citizens were witnessing a "shrinking of freedom...it [Switzerland] is following the ways of religious intolerance and religious fanaticism."[75]

Whether or not he intended to invoke this rhetoric, Engelbert's warning against religious fanaticism echoed contemporaneous warnings against Catholic extremism and, in so doing, juxtaposed Jewish rituals with Catholic ones. Like Engelbert, a few participants, perhaps motivated by political opportunism and by what many Jews saw as Catholic anti-Jewish policies and behavior, referred to the *Kulturkampf* in their defenses of Jewish rituals. They portrayed Judaism as a religion that promoted German cultural values and encouraged integration; they implied the opposite about Catholicism. In his 1875 defense of kosher butchering, for example, editor and rabbi Ludwig Philippson called for the toleration of Jewish rites while simultaneously endorsing the Prussian state's campaign against the Catholic Church. Contrasting Judaism's historical "authenticity" with Catholicism's "invented" rites and practice, he made Jews and Protestants equal partners in the struggle against Catholics and hence in the leadership and organization of the new German state. His article praised the state's defending itself against Catholicism "without harming the *real* interests of religion."[76] Another Jewish supporter of the *Kulturkampf* also juxtaposed Jewish and Catholic behavior. In his anonymous defense of kosher butchering, he looked to its prohibition in Switzerland to show that Catholic rule could lead to the downfall of the *Kulturstaat*, the creation of anti-Jewish policies,

---

[73]Windthorst as cited by Gross, *War Against Catholicism*, p. 258.
[74]Kayserling, *Die rituelle Schlachtfrage*. Also see Dessauer, *Brit Olam*, p. 9.
[75]Engelbert, *Das Schächten*, p. 1.
[76]Philippson, "Die Schächtfrage," *AZDJ* 4 (1875): 50.

In Moritz Oppenheim's portrait of a ritual circumcision, he placed the circumcision rite in the synagogue, thus reinforcing its religious character. *Source:* "Der Gevatter Erwartet das Kind," Moritz Oppenheim 1868 (reproduction), Courtesy of the Leo Baeck Institute, New York, ND 588–562 B54 and F 1591 1358089.

and a ban on Jewish religious observances. The animal protectionist campaign against kosher butchering, then, provided this writer with the ideal opportunity to replace Catholic rites and behavior with the ritual scorned by animal protectionists.[77] In this way, he could fashion an argument for Jewish social worth while remaining true to Liberal ideals.

✝✝✝✝✝

In his 1874 critique of circumcision, Eugen Levit bemoaned his failures in combating the ritual's alleged evils and in limiting its significance to the German-speaking Jewish world. Realizing he could not fight circumcision alone, the Austrian doctor called for the creation of an association whose members opposed the Jewish rite. "Just as there is an animal protection society so too there should be a benevolent association against

[77]"Aus der Schweiz," *JV* 5 (1875): 37. Also see "Rundschau," *JV* 19 (1873): 148; Ludwig Philippson, "Zur Beschneidungsfrage," *AZDJ* 22 (1870): 429–431; Josef Ruff, "Die rituelle Beschneidung," *AZDJ* 2 (1879): 19–21.

cruelty to children."[78] His solution to the circumcision question was compatible with German middle-class life. Over the course of the nineteenth century the German-speaking bourgeoisie organized a dense network of voluntary associations, and, as a physician, Levit would have taken part in a number of different clubs and associations. No child protection society was ever formed in Germany to fight circumcision, but the 1867–1880 deliberations about circumcision and kosher butchering occurred within the framework of organizational life.

The *Ritualfragen* of 1867–1880 were inventions of the middle class. The participants tended to be physicians, rabbis, journalists, veterinarians, and municipal employees. The deliberations took place in the public sphere: in the press, at society meetings, and at Jewish community- and municipal council meetings. There, discussants drew on discourses that mattered to the German bourgeoisie. Contributors looked to the meaning of the rights extended by the modern state. They embraced diverse technologies and encouraged education. They championed toleration and censured cruelty. They filtered their discussions through the lenses of German patriotism. These discussions about Jewish rites were specific to the post-unification period, for discussants now evaluated the place of Jewish rites in the new German state.

Unification changed the *Ritualfragen*, which were influenced by the contemporaneous attempts by German leaders to use the state to further their idealized cultural projects. As Liberal leaders launched a campaign against Germany's Catholic minorities, members of animal protection societies and internal critics within the Jewish community also raised questions about the possibility of minority integration. To offer their idealized formulation of Jewish communal character, participants in the ritual conflicts invoked a wide array of attitudes and beliefs implicit in the liberal notion of German culture. Often, when they did so, these supporters of Jewish rites juxtaposed their "tolerant" customs with the "intolerant" and "fanatic" rites of Catholics. In so doing, they drew on the languages and ideologies of the *Kulturkampf* to portray Jews as more respectable.

The *Ritualfragen* of the 1860s and 1870s reinforced the dynamic relationship among Judaism and German nation building, politics, and culture. Whether or not they explicitly named the German-Jewish communities as outside the norm, the deliberations publicly raised questions concerning the nature and compatibility of Jewish and German culture. They provided opportunities for Jews and Gentiles to articulate their idealized projects of integration into the new state. They also encouraged observers to classify minority groups in the aftermath of unification.

[78]Levit, *Die Circumcision*, p. 18.

This clash between different cultural forms and projects of integration would prove increasingly important over the next few decades. When the circumcision and kosher butchering disputes would reemerge in the 1880s, questions concerning the rites' relationship to toleration, cruelty, and culture would remain crucial. What shifted, however, were how these themes and the rites themselves were understood. During the three decades preceding World War I, the disputes concerning kosher butchering and circumcision radicalized. The participants in these deliberations and the issues, images, and power relationships they found compelling are the subjects of the following chapter.

CHAPTER 3

The Radicalization of the Ritual
Questions, 1880–1916

In 1892 the kingdom of Saxony promulgated a set of slaughterhouse regulations that had been championed by German animal protectionists for decades. These edicts prohibited women and children from entering the slaughterhouse and mandated stricter inspection and licensing procedures. As such, they resembled contemporary laws in all but one significant component. In contrast to other state regulations, the Saxon reforms required the rendering of *all* animals into a state of unconsciousness before their slaughter. Throughout the kingdom, it was illegal to conduct any form of slaughter that did not include the stunning of animals before killing them. Saxon Jews appealed for an exemption from these reforms, citing the kingdom's supposed history of religious toleration, but the state government rejected their pleas.[1] The debates concerning the right of Saxon Jews to practice kosher butchering continued for decades, even after the minister of interior exempted the Jewish practice in 1910.[2]

[1]Das Schächtverbot in Sachsen," *Die Laubhütte* 16 (1892): 152–153; "In Bezug auf das Betäuben der Schlachtthiere," *Ibis: Deutsche Thierschutz-Zeitung* (*Ibis*) 5/6 (1892): 29; O. Hartmann, "Aus dem Rechenschaftsbericht für 1889/92." *Ibis* 9/10 (1892): 49–51; "3 August Polizeiverordnung betreffend das Verfahren beim Viehschlachten," *Ibis* 11/12 (1892): 66; J. Auerbach II, "Das Schächtverbot in Sachsen." *AZDJ* 6 (1894).

[2]1910 minister of interior order SHD MDI 16178 12; 1910 response of the Association of Slaughterhouse Veterinarians of the Rhine-provinces SHD MDI I 16178 18; March 1910 minutes of the Federation of Saxon German Jewish communities (Saxon Jewish Federation) CJA 75CVe1 340 250–255; 22 April 1910 letter from the Saxon Jewish Federation to the Verband CJA 75CVe1 243; "Das Schächten in Sachsen weider erlaubt!" *Leipziger Neueste Nachrichten* (*LNN*) (23 December 1910) CJA 75CVe1344 432; "Nachtrag Aufhebung des Schächtverbots in Sachsen," *Im Deutschen Reich* (*IDR*) 12 (1910): 831–832; Y., "Das aufgehobene Schächtverbot," *Lehrerheim* 52 (1910): 516–517.

Saxony was the only state in imperial Germany to allow for a statewide ban on kosher butchering, yet the events there were not unique. Over the course of the imperial period, the earlier small-scale campaigns concerning animal slaughter began to come to fruition in Saxony and elsewhere. Many German towns and states gradually engaged in some form of debate concerning animal stunning and kosher butchering, regardless of the size of their Jewish population. Just as before, some discussions focused solely on Jewish ritual behavior while many others originated within larger campaigns for slaughterhouse reform and then transformed into disputes concerning the Jewish rite. No matter their origins, these deliberations attracted the attention of a wide range of participants who contemplated the character of Jewish rituals, the rights of religious minorities, and the possibilities for state or local control over religious customs and by extension, religious minorities.

As dozens of cities, villages, towns, and states considered the permissibility of kosher butchering, several German Jews and gentiles revived the circumcision question. Similar to the contemporary discussions concerning kosher slaughter, these disputes intensified in the late nineteenth century and correspondingly changed in character. Unlike the quarrels of the previous decade, these conflicts frequently originated outside the Jewish community and overlooked the rite's relationship to communal identity. Focusing instead on the ritual's medical and ethical character, the turn-of-the-century *Circumcisionsfragen* typically followed one of two events. Some deliberations took place after local children fell ill or died as a result of complications stemming from their circumcisions. In these cases, the rite's critics, usually physicians and health professionals, lay the blame with the continued presence of oral suction among *mohelim* and with the allegedly poor training of ritual practitioners. Other disputes accompanied antisemitic episodes. Participants in these conversations invoked the supposed centrality of blood and knives to Jewish culture and blamed circumcision for preserving Jewish separateness and encouraging Jewish brutality.

Like the historical phenomena of the 1860s and 1870s that transformed the ritual questions of the unification period, the political, social, and economic rearrangements of the late nineteenth and early twentieth centuries fundamentally changed the disputes of fin-de-siècle Germany. Participants continued to question the nature of German culture, the responsibilities of government, and the viability of minority communities in the newly created state. By the turn of the century, however, the debates concerning circumcision and kosher butchering had intensified. They occurred with greater frequency in a wide range of public forums: in a broad spectrum of published media, in the Reichstag, in state parliaments, in town council meetings, in court proceedings, and in association meetings. No longer limited to a group of governmental administrators, physicians, animal protectionists, and extant and emerging Jewish leaders, they now attracted attention from individuals across the German middle class. Five contemporaneous historical impulses helped to shape these increasingly popular debates: (1) technological progress, (2) dramatic changes in the economy, (3) the rise of the social question, (4) the growing reliance on antisemitic imagery and rhetoric, and (5) an embrace of apoliticism.[3]

Rituals in Print and Politics, 1881–1916

Between 1881, when the municipal governments of Kattowitz and Karlsruhe launched local investigations into Jewish ritual practices, and 1916, when animal protectionists in Munich and a few other cities spearheaded campaigns to ban kosher butchering, the deliberations concerning the two rites intensified.[4] As in the discussions of the previous decades, the imperial *Ritualfragen* featured prominently in medical tracts, political essays, and works of biblical criticism. They also appeared

[3]Some historians have examined the antisemitic images generated by the kosher butchering and circumcision debates. Several have utilized European printed disputes and medical texts to study the nature of modern antisemitism and the sexualized and medicalized character of antisemitic rhetoric. Others have looked at medical and scientific tracts to examine the place of Jewish rites in the history of Jews and medicine. Peter Pulzer, "The Return of Old Hatreds," in Meyer, ed., *German Jewish History in Modern Times*, vol. 3, p. 225; Gilman, *Franz Kafka: The Jewish Patient*; Richard S. Levy, *The Downfall of the Anti-Semitic Political Parties in Imperial Germany* (New Haven: Yale University Press, 1975). A departure can be seen in Dorothee Brantz's study. While I think her gloss is too positive, due perhaps to her limited examination to the Reichstag debates only, it is a welcome addition to the existing literature. Dorothee Brantz, "Stunning Bodies: Animal Slaughter, Judaism, and the Meaning of Humanity in Imperial Germany," *Central European History* 35 (June 2002): 167–194.

[4]See notes 2, 3, and 5 in the introduction. On the 1916 debates, see Mölter, "Im Münchener Schlachthaus," *Sudd. Monatshefte* (April 1916) pp. 125+; April 1916 Recommendations and Memo issued by the Munich slaughterhouse commission StM SUV 90; Büro für Schächtschutz, *Mitteilungen des Büros für Schächtschutz: zur Frage der Verwendbarkeit des Blutes geschächteter Tiere für die Volkswirtschaft* CAHJP D/Ba28/212, 19 June 1916 letter to the Jewish community of Hüttenbach from its magistrate; "Protokoll der Sitzung vom II November 1874," *Mittheilungen des Aertzlichen Vereines in Wien* 3.13 (1874): 169–172; Alexander, *Die hygienische Bedeutung der Beschneidung*; Richard Andree, *Zur Volkskunde der Juden* (Bielefeld: Verlag von Velhagen & Klasing, 1881); Wilhelm Ebstein, *Die Medizin im Alten Testament* (Stuttgart: Verlag von Ferdinand Enke, 1901); Großherzoglich Badischen Oberrat der Israeliten Baden, *Dienstvorschriften für Mohelim* (Karlsruhe: Buchdruckerei

in media as disparate as antisemitic publications, Jewish joke books, psychoanalytic journals, and calendars.[5] This extensive coverage of Jewish rites extended to German-Jewish and non-Jewish newspapers, whose treatment of the debates brought ritual behavior to an even broader reading public. During this period, *Im Deutschen Reich*, a journal sponsored by the German-Jewish Centralverein, published at least ninety-three articles concerning local and statewide kosher butchering debates, while in a single year the Dresden-based non-Jewish newspaper, *Dresdener Nachrichten* published over a dozen articles concerning local debates over kosher butchering. Circumcision prompted fewer publications, but still attracted significant attention, particularly in medical and anthropological journals and in works of biblical scholarship.

Kosher butchering and, to a lesser extent, circumcision figured notably in spoken debates as well. Governmental officials regularly weighed the character of these Jewish rites and the ability of their administration to regulate them. Most of these conversations took place locally. Between 1880 and 1890, eleven German municipalities considered kosher butchering, but that number grew exponentially after 1890. A handful also investigated local circumcision practices. Interest in Jewish rituals, however, was not limited to the city, village, or town. State institutions and national agencies also paid attention to Jewish rites. The Bundesrat and Reichstag debated the possibility of a ban on kosher butchering three times during the decades preceding World War I.[6] Seven state parliaments and ministries also contemplated the possibility of regulating kosher butchering, while three state governments examined the dangers of circumcision and the need for its reform.[7]

---

von Malsch & Vogel, 1897); Josef Grünwald, *Die rituelle Circumcision (Beschneidung) operativ und rituell bearbeitet von Dr. Josef Grünwald* (Frankfurt, a.M.: Verlag von J. Kauffmann, 1892). Similar charges later appeared in "Bei Gefahren der Beschneidung," *Zeitschrift für Sexualwissenschaft* (*ZFS*) 5 (1922): 153; "Zur Geschichte und Bedeutung der Beschneidung bei den Juden," *ZFS* 3 (1922): 89; Maurice Ascher, *Sexuelle Fragen vom Standpunkte des Judentums* (Frankfurt a.M.: A.J. Hofmann, Verlag 1922); Julie Bender, "Zur Geschichte und Bedeutung der Beschneidung bei den Juden," *ZFS* 8 (1922): 229–230; Berndt Götz, "Das Zweigeschlechterwesen und die Beschneidung der Knaben und Mädchen," *Archiv für Frauenkunde und Konstitutionsforschung* 17 (1931): 60–69.

[5]See, e.g., Hermann Blumental, "Die Lehre vom Schächten," in *Die beste jüdischen Anekdoten: Perlen des Humors* (Vienna: Rudolf Lechner und Sohn, 1924), 26; "Die Dewaldschen Ansichtspostkarten," *IDR* 9 (1901): 457–463; Julius Preuss, *Biblical and Talmudic Medicine*, trans. Fred Rosner (Norvale, NJ: Jason Aronson, 1993); Lorenz Curtius, *Der politische Antisemitismus vom 1907–1911* (Munich: Kommissions-Verlag des National-Vereins für das liberale Deutschland, 1911); Verein zur Abwehr des Antisemitismus, "Schächten" in *Abwehr ABC* (Berlin, Verein zur Abwehr des Antisemitismus, 1920), pp. 105–106.

[6]Neither body ever formally considered circumcision.

[7]An examination of Jewish communal responses can be found in chapter 5.

By the turn of the century, the *Schächtfragen* outpaced the circumcision questions, but both sets of debates experienced a dramatic growth in their audience. This rising popularity can be explained in part by the ways in which the disputes' tone and content increasingly found salience among a widening group of participants in German political life.[8]

The Participants

Contributors to the kosher butchering and circumcision debates at the turn of the century represented a broad cross-section of German middle-class society. Discussants now included members of Germany's mainstream political parties, veterinarians, Catholic leaders, biblical literary critics, bird-watchers, scientists, anthropologists, Christian missionaries, dentists, and professors. While some participants limited themselves to one form of involvement, many took part in both the written and spoken debates. In published letters and essays and in speeches on the Reichstag floor, for example, the well-known pathologist Rudolf Virchow championed the toleration of kosher butchering. His ideological opponent, the animal rights crusader Otto Hartmann (pseudo. O. von Tegernsee) similarly took part in both the spoken and written deliberations. In town council, state parliament, and Reichstag debates, as well as in dozens of publications, he censured the allegedly inhumane nature of kosher butchering. As the secretary of the largest animal rights organization in Germany, he stamped his influence on the ritual questions of the era.[9]

The largest single group of participants included members of voluntary associations concerned with issues of animal advocacy, much like the organizations in which Hartmann took part. Animal protectionist groups had grown significantly after unification, partially because of their successful campaigns to pass slaughterhouse reforms. Their efforts brought diverse animal advocacy associations together, and they

[8]There are a number of reasons why the kosher butchering debates outpaced those concerning circumcision. Several Jewish communities no longer permitted *mohelim* to conduct oral *metsisah*. Moreover, because the *Circumcisionfrage* preceded the *Schächtfrage* by several years, many German states and cities had been regulating circumcision far longer than they had overseen kosher butchering.

[9]On Virchow, see Christian Andree, *Rudolf Virchow als Prähistoriker* (Cologne: Böhlau, 1976). On Hartmann, see Leopold Hamburger, *Herr Otto Hartmann in Cöln und sein Kampf gegen die Schlachtweise der Israeliten* (Frankfurt a.M.: Buchdruckerei von M. Slobotzky, 1889).

gradually interacted with one another at national meetings and in smaller settings to share resources, programs, and strategies. By 1882, over 150 associations in Germany publicly endorsed the promulgation of animal protection laws. Of these organizations, two types expressed interest in kosher butchering: animal protectionists who were interested in general slaughterhouse reform and animal rights advocates who specifically focused on the Jewish rite.[10]

The Association against Animal Cruelty in Königsberg was emblematic of the former category. Beginning in the early 1870s, the Association against Animal Cruelty in Königsberg began supplementing its work on behalf of domesticated and hunted animals by promoting slaughterhouse reform. Under the leadership of police deputy August Müller, members of the Königsberg society pushed for abattoir improvements. They encouraged the introduction of new stunning techniques, better fastening mechanisms, and superior methods of transporting animals to the abattoir. Despite its animal advocacy, the association never championed a ban on kosher butchering and instead supported the Jewish community's right to practice its ritual. The association's stance on the *Schächtfrage* was well known. The tireless advocate of kosher butchering, Hirsch Hildesheimer, described Königsberg as one of the few cities that would remain free from a ban on kosher butchering because its animal protection association permitted Jewish exceptionalism. In his words, Königsberg was a city that was "won."[11]

The Jewish leader never would have offered a similar portrait of Berlin's animal protection society, whose anti–kosher butchering campaign drove its animal advocacy.[12] Unlike the Königsberg society, Berlin's association pushed for laws that universally mandated the stunning of animals into a state of unconsciousness, with no regard for religious tradition or custom. It spearheaded national and local campaigns in which it embraced exclusionary and radical rhetoric. Group members

[10]1887 Pamphlet concerning *shehitah* issued by the Association of Animal Protection Societies of the German Reich CAHJP GA II/166; H. Ehrmann, *Thier-Schutz und Menschen-Trutz: Sämmtliche für und gegen das Schächten geltend gemachten Momente kritisch beleuchtet nebst einer Sammlung aller älteren und neueren Gutachten hervorragender Fachgelehrten* (Frankfurt a.M.: Verlag von J. Kauffmann, 1885); Vereins gegen Thierqüalerei zu Königsberg, *4 & 5 Bericht*. On German animal protectionism, see Zerbel, *Tierschutz im Kaiserreich*.

[11]1906 organizational letter by Hirsch Hildesheimer CJA 75CVe1344 81; "29 Deutscher Fleischer-Verbandstag," *Königsberger Hartungsche Zeitung* CJA 75DCo128 111. While the Königsberg society voted against a *Schächtverbot* during the 1890s, it later changed its view. 1906 Minutes of the Association of Animal Protection Societies of the German Reich (TSV) CJA 75Cve1 344 154.

[12]Hans Beringer headed the Berlin association.

highlighted the supposedly cruel, violent, and bloody nature of kosher butchering and its practitioners; they emphasized the alleged financial gains Jews made by conducting Jewish rites; and they cast doubts on Jewry's political and social integrative possibilities. They also articulated a deep yearning for an establishment of social order. While fanciful, their petitions and pamphlets suggested that a law mandating universal stunning could help preserve Germany's character as a "civilized, Christian Volk."[13]

Other associations participated in the *Ritualfragen* as well. Professional associations, such as societies of butchers, meat sellers, and abattoir equipment vendors participated in the debates, positioning themselves on both sides of the spectrum. So too did merchants who specialized in circumcision equipment or medical bags.[14] In addition, as increasing numbers of doctors, anthropologists, and scientists published studies of both rites, medical and veterinary societies met to discuss their publications. By the late 1890s, antiquackery associations and anthropological societies were meeting to do the same.[15]

The ritual questions also witnessed the involvement of associations seemingly unconnected to the issues at hand. In 1912, for example, members of the German Congress for Women's Suffrage (CWS) debated the merits of kosher butchering after its chapter in Munich

[13]"Mit der Schlachtmethode," *Norddeutschen Allgemeinen Zeitung* (*NAZ*) (22 April 1909); "Aufruf und Bitte," *Berliner Tierschutzverein* (*BTV*) 39 (1888–1892): 1–2; "Die unnöthigen Thierquälerein beim Schlachten des Kleinviehes," *BTV* 2 (1888/9?): 2; "Zur Schächtfrage," *BTV* 72 (189?): 1–2; 1901 Berlin TSV petition CJA 75AEr1 96 68; Hans Albrecht, "Kunst, Wissenschaft und Leben: Tierschutzbestrebungen der Gegenwart." (1925) CAHJP AHW 568 a 157; H. Beringer, ed., *Lesebüchlein des Berliner Tierschutz-Vereins (Zur Bekämpfung Der Tierquälereien Im Deutschen Reich)*, 5 vols. (Berlin: Deutscher Verlag, 1910).

[14]Meat sellers association of Hannover, "Einladung" (1899) CAHJP BII 3; 3 December 1910 letter to the Jewish community of Geisa from the meat sellers association there CJA 75AGe229 57; 12 June 1901 observations of Vienna slaughterhouses by Adolf Chotzen CAHJP A/W 1388; Michael Cahn, *Die Einrichtungen des Koscher Fleisch Verkaufs unter besonderer Berücksichtigung der Zeichnungs und Stempelungs-Methoden* (Frankfurt: A.J. Hofmann, 1901); 11 July 1911 letter to minister of culture and education no. 721 SHD III L MDI 16178 24; "Der Alte Tierschutzverein" *Dresdner Nachrichten* (*DN*) (30 November 1911) CJA 75Cve1 341 no. 43. Often authorities mentioned their receipt of such letters. See 18 February 1891 letter to the Jewish community council from the police authorities CJA 75aEr1 96 24.

[15]31 May 1888 memo from Landmann to the Bavarian minister of the interior BH MA 76592; "Korrespondenzen, Schwerin i.M." *IDR* (1899); "Dänemark: Der 16. Internationale Tierschutz-Congreß in Kopenhagen," *Der Israelit* (24 August 1911) CJA 75DCo1 29 22; 20 April 1912 letter from slaughterhouse authorities to the magistrate of Munich StM Suv 43; Rabbinat der jüdischen Gemeinde, "Hochgeehrter Herr!" (Berlin, 1900) CJA 75Dco128 32; 5 November 1907 minutes of the *shehitah* commission meeting CJA 75Dco128 233; March 1910 minutes of the Saxon Jewish Federation CJA 75Ve1 340

supported the city's animal advocacy campaign for a *Schächtverbot*.[16] The deliberations similarly attracted attention from dentist groups, hiking clubs, and circles of biblical critics. As was the case with the CWS, some of these associations had Jewish and gentile members. Other participating groups, including a number of self-proclaimed antisemitic organizations, maintained a non-Jewish membership only.

As a broad range of different associations took part in the ritual questions, diverse bureaucratic administrators and political party representatives also became involved in the disputes. In towns across Germany, magistrates, health commissioners, slaughterhouse directors, and local police commissioners weighed in on the conflicts concerning Jewish ritual behavior. The many animal protection campaigns in Munich at the turn of the century, for example, encouraged the participation of local slaughterhouse commission members, town council representatives, and the magistrate, as well as officials at various levels of state and regional governance.[17] Similarly, as an anecdote from the book's introduction revealed, an 1881 syphilis scare in Baden encouraged the involvement of a local magistrate, police deputies, state medical examiners, and eventually Baden's ministers of interior and education and culture.[18]

Finally, representatives from Germany's political parties also participated in these deliberations within their professional capacities. In 1886–1887, 1898–1899, and 1908–1910, Reichstag deputies formally considered implementing new animal cruelty laws that would have

---

250–255; "Gegen das Schächten," *Staatsbürger Zeitung* (21 July 1911) CJA 75CVe1 340 329; "Zur Aufhebung des Schächtverbotes in Sachsen." Also see "Zur Schächtfrage," DN (2 August 1911) CJA 75CVe1340. Studies of the published writings concerning these medical and scientific debates include Efron, *Medicine and the German Jews;* Gilman, *Freud, Race, and Gender;* Gilman, *Franz Kafka;* Gilman, "The Indelibility of Circumcision."

[16]"Ein neuer Vorstoß der Schächtgegner," *Mitteilungen aus dem Verein zur Abwehr des Antisemitismus* 26 (1912): 217–219; "Frauenstimmrecht und Shechitah," *Jüdische Rundschau (JR)* 43 (1912) CJA 75CVe1341 92; "München (Die Schächtresolution des Frauenstimmrechtskongresses)," *Israelitisches Familienblatt (IF)* 48(1912): 28; "Nochmals Frauenstimmrecht und Shechita," *JR* 49 (1912) CJA 75CVe1341 106; "Zum Vortrage des Herrn Dr. Weigl in München," *Deutsche Israelitische Zeitung (DIZ)* 51 (1912): 4–5; Y. "Frauenstimmrecht und rituelle Schächtmethode," *Israelitisches Gemeindblatt (IG)* 51 (1912): 549–550; "Nochmals die Schächtfrage im Verein für Frauenstimmrecht," *IG* 4 (24 January 1913): 39–40.

[17]See 1896 Munich regulations StM SUV 7; 1896 slaughterhouse regulations StM SUV 7; 15 August 1898 letter from Arthur Stoff to the Bavarian minister of foreign affairs BH MA 76592; 15 December 1898 petition BH MA 76592; 1898 letter from the Munich chapter of the TSV to Munich senate and response BH MA 76598.

[18]See notes 2 and 3 in the introduction.

made the killing of conscious animals illegal. As chapter 4 reveals, only the representatives of Germany's antisemitic and Catholic center parties voted consistently in these parliamentary discussions. The former approved of mandatory stunning laws; the latter unswervingly pushed for German Jewry's right to practice its rituals without interference. Other party representatives were less consistent. Members of the progressive and moderate Liberal parties tended to vote against the mandatory stunning laws but often disapproved of any amendment designed to protect Jewish rites. Conservatives were similarly inconsistent, although they almost never approved of regulations that would have supported Jewry's right to free religious practice. Analogous discrepancies could be witnessed in state or town parliamentary debates where members of regionally based parties, such as the right-leaning Bavarian Volkspartei, joined representatives of the mainstream national parties.

Whether they entered the disputes as governmental representatives, defenders of Jewish rites, or advocates for society's vulnerable, participants frequently shifted their position as the disputes unfolded and evolved. When it met in 1894, for example, the Royal Delegation for Medical Affairs approved a strong statement in support of kosher butchering. Six years later, it articulated a preference for methods that stunned animals into states of unconsciousness before slaughter. The faculty at the Veterinary School in Dresden underwent a similar transformation. It once had supported the Saxon Jewish Federation's campaign to overturn Saxony's statewide ban on kosher butchering. By 1911 it spoke out in favor of mandatory stunning laws.[19] These shifts in view moved in the opposite direction as well. During the early 1890s, the Conservative representative Johannes Hoeffel articulated a support for a ban on the slaughter of conscious animals. In 1899 he modified his earlier position. The conservative deputy continued to serve as an outspoken enthusiast of slaughterhouse reform, but he would no longer champion what he envisioned to be specifically anti-Jewish legislation.[20]

Varying impulses motivated contributors like Hoeffel to change views or to become involved in the disputes. Technological advances encouraged

[19]On the former, see "Hochgeehrter Herr!"; 5 November 1907 minutes of the *shehitah* commission CJA 75Dco128 233; March 1910 minutes of the Saxon Jewish Federation CJA 75Ve1 340 250–255. On the Dresden statements, see "Gegen das Schächten," *Staatsbürger Zeitung*; "Zur Schächtfrage," *DN* (2 August 1911) CJA 75CVe1340; "Zur Aufhebung des Schächtverbotes in Sachsen." Baden's medical examiner expressed an analogous shift. 6 April 1881 letter from the medical examiner to the minister of the interior (no. 122) CJA 75Ka124 6.

[20]1899 Reichstag Transcript CAHJP TD 475, p. 7.

the Royal Delegation and the Dresden veterinary faculty to embrace new slaughterhouse reforms, while a concern with the antisemitic implications of the animal protectionist petition moved Hoeffel to reject a proposal whose essence he supported. Their changes in view highlight the ways in which the issues and images central to the ritual questions shifted over time. Discussants now expressed interest in developments in technology, the economy, society, science, and medicine. As they did so, they relied on the languages of antisemitism and apoliticism to present their views. The presence of these ideologies and issues within the *Ritualfragen* lent the deliberations a sense of purpose and immediacy; it also partially explains why growing numbers of people expressed interest in Jewish ritual behavior.

Technology and the Ritual Questions

The second industrial revolution, which took place throughout western and central Europe after 1871, shaped the ritual questions of the imperial period. As European industry found new uses for steel, chemicals, electricity, and petroleum, inventors created new technological devices for ritual practices. By the 1890s Germany's industrial superiority lay in areas of manufacturing such as organic chemicals, electric equipment, and medical apparatuses. These diverse industries produced novel devices that changed the ways in which practitioners executed Jewish rites and people conversed about them.

Innovative stunning mechanisms and constraining devices transformed the ways in which butchers slaughtered animals and encouraged some individuals, such as members of the Dresden veterinary college, to become more sympathetic to certain animal protectionist demands. Earlier stunning mechanisms had simply pummeled animals into a state of unconsciousness. By the early 1880s, these devices covered the animal's head and left a space through which butchers could stun them with mallets, spikes, or revolvers. Gradually, veterinary labs began to use the technologies of the second industrial revolution; namely, organic chemicals and electricity. They developed the use of anesthesia and high voltage electrotherapy as a stunning technique, which several animal protection advocates welcomed as humane.[21]

---

[21]Early stunning mechanisms included the bouterole, which covered the animal's head but left a space through which butchers could stun animals with heavy mallets; the Bruneau's mask, which allowed for a slaughterer to drive a bolt or spike through an animal's skull; and the Sigmund's mask, which was like the Bruneau's mask but was connected to a revolver. "Was giebts denn Neues (Nachdruck nur mit

Technological innovations similarly changed traditional circumcision techniques. By the 1890s, medical professionals and many Jewish leaders encouraged *mohelim* to use the glass tube for *metsitsah*. Patented by Michael Cahn of Fulda, the tube was a small stick of glass with openings at either side that was large enough to cover the newborn's penis. Instead of sucking on the wound's surface, the circumciser would suck on the mouthpiece in such a way as to cleanse the wound without getting any blood in his mouth or any of his saliva on the child's penis.[22] Other new technologies included a chemical mix that would numb the child's penis, clamps for *periah*, and medical bags with the appropriate tools needed for circumcision.

These technologies offered participants issues around which they could discuss the character of Jewry and the role of government. Now that new methods for kosher butchering or circumcision were more widely available and ostensibly improved, several contributors sharply condemned Jewish communities if they failed to adopt them. In an 1888 memo to the Bavarian minister of interior, the Munich animal protection society questioned why Bavarian Jews would reject the new mechanisms given their vast improvement over past methods. The association now requested that the state intervene and enforce the technologies' use. Conceding that earlier stunning mechanisms had been primitive, it asserted that the sophistication of the current advancements demanded governmental intrusion.[23] One Bavarian administrator agreed that "abuses occur with the slaughter of animals, for which

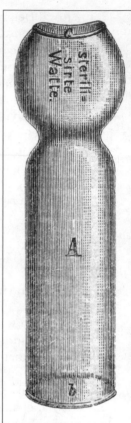

This glass tube was invented as a substitution for direct oral suction. *Source:* "Das Mezizah-Glasröhrchen," Central Archives for the History of the Jewish People Inv/855.

---

voller Quellenangabe gestattet)—Den recht mißlungenen Versuch," *Allgemeinen Fleischer Zeitung* (*AFZ*) 59, 138, 151 (1906): 2, 2, 2; "Tierbetäubungsversuche mittels Elektrizität," *LNN* 28 (1912) CJA 75CVe1341 88; Meyer, "Der Kopfschlag oder der Genickstich nach dem Schächten," *DIZ* 2 (1912): 1–2. Also see Brantz, "Slaughter in the City."

[22]"Das Metsitsah-Glasrohrchen" CAHJP Inv. 855; Freie Vereinigung, *Mitheilungen an die Vereinsmitglieder*, vol. 15 (Frankfurt am Main: Buchdruckerei Louis Golde, 1902); Frankfurt Chewrath Mohalim *Statuten* (Frankfurt a.M.: self-published, 1907. Cahn also invented devices for kosher butchering. Cahn, *Die Einrichtungen des Koscher-Feleisch-Verkaufs*. Also see Katz, "The Metsitsah Controversy."

[23]31 May 1888 memo from the Munich TSV to the Bavarian minister of interior BH MA 76592. Also see July 1886 letter to the Jewish community from the police authorities

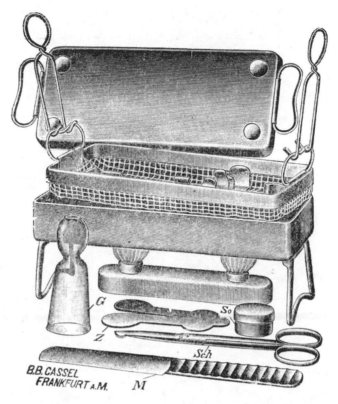

These circumcision instruments from the early twentieth century
include a knife, glass tube, shield, and sterilization and holding
device. *Source:* Simon Bamberger, *Die Beschneidung: Eine populäre
Darstellung ihrer Bedeutung und Vollziehung* (Wandsbek: Verlag von
A. Goldschmidt-Hamburg, 1913), p. 15.

a remedy is necessary...." While he rebuffed the "police measures
recommended by the animal protectionist movement," he similarly
encouraged the Jewish community to support the technical advancements of the time.[24]

Yet, it was not technology alone that transformed the *Ritualfragen.*
Instead, the deliberations concerning Jewish rites increasingly relied on
new developments in the economy, science, and medicine and incorporated sharper attacks against the Jewish populace. It was a combination
of these issues and images, along with the shifts in technology, which

of Händen CJA 75Aer1 97 10; 1901 memo from Landmann and Beringer (Berlin TSV)
CJA 75AEr1 96 68.

[24]31 May 1888 memo from Landmann to the Bavarian minister of interior BH MA
76592.

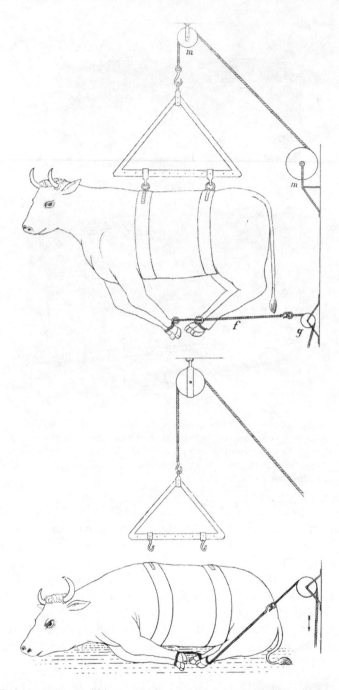

In 1893, R. Stern promoted his new mechanisms for *Niederlegen* (shackling) in a short pamphlet entitled, "A New Method of *Niederlegen*." *Source:* R. Stern, *Eine neue Methode zum Niederlegen des zum Schächten bestimmten Rindviehes* (Fulda: self-published, 1893), kindly reproduced by the Central Archives for the History of the Jewish People, Jerusalem.

offered sufficient conditions for the emergence of a popular set of deliberations concerning the Jewish rites.

Economic Concerns and the Ritual Questions

Like the innovations in technology, Germany's dramatic economic rearrangements also influenced the disputes over Jewish rites. During the Great Depression of 1873–1896 and the economic boom that followed, the ritual questions increasingly concerned the economic relationships among Jews, their ritual practitioners, and their gentile neighbors.[25]

As Europeans experienced fluctuations in prices, wages, and agricultural and industrial profits, critics of Jewish rites increasingly charged that Jewish rituals posed a pecuniary risk. Participants in earlier conflicts had expressed little interest in the finances of the Jewish rites; by the 1890s, however, contributors increasingly identified Jewish economic spite as a serious worry. Influenced by the economic uncertainty and by traditional images of the "Jewish usurer," they linked Jewish rites with Jewish avarice.[26] In jokes and cartoons, radical antisemites suggested that greed drove *mohelim* to circumcise larger numbers of children and to execute these rites quickly. Exchanging the words *penis*, *jewelry*, and *jewels*, these texts suggested that a financial noxiousness drove the rite. One Austrian cartoon depicted an observant Jewish *mohel*, large scissors in hand, with piles of gold. Grotesque, with a large bulbous nose, unseemly teeth, tattered clothes, and sidelocks flying in the wind, the *mohel*'s caption read, "It makes a profit: that is why the Jews practice it."[27] Carl Sedlaßek, the editor of the antisemitic *Generalanzeiger*, similarly accused Jews of profiting from kosher butchering. According to Sedlaßek, Jews intentionally sold infected or damaged meat, which Jewish law prohibited them from consuming themselves. Supposedly when a *shohet* found a diseased animal, he would gleefully and greedily announce, "This is for the goyim!"[28]

---

[25]Some historians locate the explosion of antisemitism in this moment. Hans Rosenberg, *Grosse Depression und Bismarckzeit: Wirtschaftsablauf, Gesellschaft und Politik in Mitteleuropa* (Berlin: de Gruyter, 1967).

[26]On this cliché, see Derek Penslar, *Shylock's Children: Economics and Jewish Identity in Modern Europe* (Berkeley: University of California Press, 2001), pp. 11–49; Stefan Rohrbacher and Michael Schmidt, "*Judenbilder: Kulturgeschichte antijüdicher Mythen und antisemitischer vorurteile* (Reinbeck bei Hamburg: Rowohlt Taschenbuch Verlag, 1991), pp. 43–147.

[27]Eduard Fuchs, *Die Juden in der Karikatur: Ein Beitrag zur Kulturgeschichte* (Munich: Albert Langen, 1921), p. 194.

[28]The Centralverein later successfully sued Sedlaßek for libel. "Fleischbesudelungs-Prozesse (Referat und Diskussion in der ordentlichen Versammlung des Central-Vereins deutscher Staatsbürger jüdischen Glaubens am 12. Oktober 1896," *IDR* 10 (1896): 465–495.

In this Austrian antisemitic cartoon, the caption reads, "It makes a profit: that is why the Jews practice it." *Source:* Eduard Fuchs, *Die Juden in der Karikatur: Ein Beitrag zur Kulturgeschichte* (Munich: Albert Langen, 1921), p. 194.

Sedlaßek's concern that Jews profited from the sale of kosher meat to non-Jews intersected with contemporary anxieties over Jewish war profiteering, a concern that had its origins in the Thirty Years War and emerged again during the wars of unification and the battles for imperial lands. The German military was one sphere, along with the judiciary, diplomatic corps, and the higher reaches of the civil service, in which Jews were historically unable to achieve positions of influence.[29] Ironically, some of the meat that the military purchased came from cattle that were slaughtered without previously being stunned. No evidence suggests that the meat was kosher. Nevertheless, members of the radical Berlin animal rights movement expressed outrage when they discovered that the German army served meat from cattle that had been "slaughtered ritually."[30] Worried that Jews had chosen this sphere of influence as a method of revenge, one antisemitic reporter bitterly complained that "Jews have received their wish that German soldiers must eat kosher meat."[31] Anxieties over Jewish profiteering skyrocketed again during World War I when German authorities worried that Jewish communities slaughtered more cattle than rationed.[32]

Participants in local deliberations concerning kosher butchering invoked similar concerns over Jewish financial practices, although their accusations were not as sharp as those lodged by the antisemitic publications of the time. During a period of tremendous price and wage fluctuation, critics in varying locations across Germany accused Jews of inflating the price of meat and of depleting the availability of cattle. This charge was grounded in some reality. By the late nineteenth century, it had become clear that several Jewish communities butchered animals in disproportionate numbers to their non-Jewish neighbors.[33] In the Rhine town of Rheydt, for example, Jews consti-

[29]Werner T. Angress, "Prussia's Army and the Jewish Reserve Officer Controversy Before World War I," *LBIYB* 27 (1972): 19–42.

[30]Its source was the army cannery in Haselhorst. Some military spokesmen insisted that the meat from animals that had been conscious when slaughtered stayed fresher for longer periods of time; others denied that such meat had been purchased. "Schächten in den Kaiserlichen Konservenfabriken," *Rundschau auf dem Gebiete der Fleischbeschau und Trichinenbeschau (RDG)* 15 (1903): 161; "Zur Schächtfrage," *Das Recht der Tiere* 2 (1905): 10–12.

[31]"Zur Schächtfrage," *Das Recht der Tiere*. Also see the report of the comments of Berlin-based Dr. E. Biberfeld in "Dänemark."

[32]Perhaps worried that the practice went unregulated or that Jewish communities might employ illegal slaughterers to avoid rations, the Bundesrat demanded an investigation. Bundesrat Session, 2 March 1917 SHD MDI 16178 33; 19 June 1916 letter to the Jewish community of Hüttenbach CAHJP N 13/24.

[33]There were several reasons for the high number of cattle slaughtered according to the Jewish method. Some non-Jewish butchers continued to slaughter animals

tuted only 0.8 percent of the total population, but slaughterhouse records there revealed that more than 50 percent of all cattle were slaughtered by the *Schächten* method.[34] In Bütow, allegedly 95 percent of the meat slaughtered in the public slaughterhouses was killed by kosher slaughterers, even though Jews composed less than 1 percent of the population.[35] Critics agonized over this disproportionate rate of slaughter. They worried that Jews enjoyed the act of animal slaughter, sold the excess meat to Christians for a profit, or simply ate more meat than non-Jews.[36] In response, they encouraged government to set restrictions on Jewish kosher butchering practices. They hoped local or state administrators would enact high tariffs on kosher butchering or limit the amount of cattle Jews could slaughter. Other contributors championed the prohibition of the sale of kosher meat to

---

without stunning them first (*Schächten*), believing that the slaughter of conscious animals produced a higher quality of meat that remained fresher longer. Furthermore, the high percentage of animals slaughtered by *shehitah* had its roots in Jewish law. Judaism's dietary laws prohibit Jews from ingesting the sciatic nerve or the fatty portions of the animal carcass, as well as animals who, on further inspection, are found to have blemishes or lesions. To produce a sufficient amount of kosher meat for their customers, *shohetim* had to slaughter more cattle than non-Jewish butchers. 14 November 1907 letter from H. Hildesheimer to J. Cohen CJA 75D Co129 237–238; 29 October 1907 report of the Bremen senate CJA 75CVe1 344 199–200; "Butow, i.P." *IDR* 5 (1898): 270–271; "Das Schächten: Gießen," *Jüdische Presse* (*JP*) 96 (1909): CJA 75CVe1344 417.

[34]The *Schächten* method referred to slaughtering an animal by cutting his throat without stunning the animal first.

[35]Bütow, i.P," *IDR* 5 (1898): 270–271; "Schächten," *Deutsche Tageszeitung* (*DT*) (6 May 1898); "Die Schächtfrage in Rheydt," *Der Israelit* 6 May (1897): 691–692; "Die ortsstatutarischen Bestimmungen der Stadt Rheydt über die Einschränkung des Schächtens auf dem gemeinsamen öffentlichen Schlachthofe von Rheydt und Odenkirchen: I, II, & III," *IDR* 8, 9, & 10 (1898): 363–370; 438–445; 504–505; "Korrespondenzen, Soest," *IDR* 4 (1898): 222–223; "Doppelte Schlachtgebühr fürs Schächten," *RDG* 14 (1902): 137. In 1898 alone, three town councils in Prussia—Soest (Westphalia), Rheydt (Rhineland), and Bütow (Pomerania)—passed restrictions on *shehitah* because the majority of cattle slaughtered in their abattoirs were killed without previous stunning, allegedly for Jewish consumption. Future debates saw similar complaints. 18 February 1914 letter from Werner to the Centralverein CJA 75Dco1 68; "Korrespondenzen, Aachen," *IDR* 1 (1899): 45; "Ueber das Verbot des Schächtens," *RDG* 14 (1903): 146.

[36]Animal sentimentalists voiced this charge with greater frequency during and after the Reichstag debates of 1898–1899. 1899 Reichstag transcript, CAHJP TD 475, pp. 1–2; W. Back *Schächten oder Betäuben? Ein Bedürfnisefrage: Ein Beitrag zur Erlaß eines Reischsschlachtgesetzes* (Straßburg: Akademische Buchhandlung, 1911); "Ein Vorschlag zur Schächtfrage," *DT* (25 January 1911); 16 January 1911 letter to Verband from the Jewish community council of Straßburg CJA 75CVe1344 461.

non-Jews.[37] While this charge of Jewish avarice tended to be employed mostly at the local level, some participants voiced this concern in the Reichstag deliberations as well.

While accusations of Jewish greed influenced these fiscal considerations of Jewish rites, other economic interest in the rituals seemed to be devoid of antisemitic rhetoric or content. As local and state commissions moved toward regulating meat tariffs, finance reform, and trade treaties, increasing numbers of them also expressed interest in the taxes for kosher meat within cities and across state lines. In Prussia, Bavaria, and Baden, state ministries began to regulate the transport of kosher meat just as they did the movement of other meat and meat products. These administrations intervened in the economics of Jewish ritual practices in other ways as well. They compared the pension and insurance expenditures of ritual practitioners with those of state and municipal employees; the cost of supervising *mohelim* and *shohetim* with that of regulating unlicensed healers; and the expenses of overseeing Jewish rituals with that of managing common surgeries and animal slaughter.[38] At the core of these comparisons was an anxiety over the economic and social risks ritual practitioners and rites posed.

Social Problems

As social anxieties worsened over Germany's rapid industrialization and urban growth, activists across local and regional divides looked to kosher butchering and circumcision as two potentially problematic practices. In imperial Germany, social conditions had worsened as dramatically and as quickly as industrialization advanced. Concerned that the health of the nation depended on the health of the public (both physically and genetically), German reformers and activists proposed solutions to the so-called social problems. One important solution called for science and medicine to combine with the state to

[37]"Doppelte Schlachtgebühr fürs Schächten"; 12 May 1905 letter to the city council from I. Werner CAHJP BII3. Others punished Jews after a *Schächtverbot* was rescinded. After the Saxon government repealed the statewide ban on *shehitah*, the city of Leipzig doubled the original tariff. "Sitzung der Stadverordneten," *Leipziger Tagesblatt* (23 February 1911). Tariffs also were proposed and accepted in Vienna "Ein Attentat auf unsere Gewissensfreiheit" *JV* (27 February 1914).

[38]They questioned whether *mohelim* and *shohetim* should fall under the financial promulgations for physicians and butchers or for those concerning minority priests and rabbis.

help cure societal ills. Increasing numbers of doctors began to rely on the state to intervene within the spheres of sanitation, water supply, and infection control. Such a turn was evidenced in 1891–1892 when Hamburg experienced its cholera epidemic. Physicians, who previously had endorsed the separation of the state from day-to-day health care, slowly began to demand medically supervised state intervention to thwart the disease's impact on the city's population.[39] As a result of this prodding and of governmental concerns more generally, Hamburg's government tried to create social policies that allegedly improved conditions and constructed order within the social realm. These policies governed issues as diverse as prostitution, censorship, and the tutoring of the poor, as well as the medical interventions suggested by Hamburg's physicians.

It was in this milieu of social concern that officials and activists looked to Jewish ritual behavior. For some discussants, particularly physicians, veterinarians, and health commissioners, ritual practitioners posed a considerable danger to social order. Influenced by antiquackery impulses, these critics charged that *mohelim* and *shohetim* allegedly caused unnecessary pain to animals or infants and spread contagions. In 1905 veterinarians and slaughterhouse officials in Erfurt used this language of social oversight when they approached their magistrate with concerns that *shohetim* needed greater controls. Worried that ritual practitioners who deformed animals or spread illnesses went unpunished, the complainants called for increased governmental control.[40]

The antiquackery movement certainly helped to shape the formulations of these anxieties. During the late nineteenth century, increasing numbers of health commissioners and university-trained physicians called for greater governmental regulation over healers.[41] Just as they worried that unlicensed healers treated diseases incompetently, performed abortions, and stole from their patients, many critics of Jewish rites expressed anxiety over practitioners who supposedly botched circumcisions or animal slaughter. As antiquackery activists called for the national government to punish unlicensed medical professionals, contributors to the ritual questions championed the national policing of untrained *mohelim* or *shohetim*. A few were themselves active in the antiquackery movement.[42] Carl Alexander took part in both campaigns.

[39]Richard J. Evans, *Death in Hamburg* (Oxford: Oxford University Press, 1987).

[40]13 February 1905 letter (no. 2447) to the Jewish community of Erfurt from the city's magistrate CJA 75aEr1 96.

[41]They also pushed the national government to revoke its 1868 classification of medicine as a "free profession." Weindling, *Health, Race, and German Politics*, pp. 20–25.

[42]6 April 1881 letter from the medical examiner to the minister of the interior (no. 122) CJA 75Ka124 6; R[ichard?] Pott, "Ueber die Gefahren der Rituellen Beschneidung,"

A frequent contributor to the circumcision debate and the author of *The Hygienic Significance of Circumcision*, he helped to found the Society for the Suppression of Quackery.[43]

Like many of his colleagues, Alexander drew from an odd fusion of biology, bacteriology, eugenics, sexology, and social Darwinism to address contemporary medical concerns. Over the course of the imperial period, discussants increasingly linked Jewish rites with the illnesses typically associated with urbanization and moral deviancy. They envisioned a relationship between Jewish ritual behavior and syphilis, gonorrhea, and tuberculosis (TB), three diseases that historian Paul Weindling has described as "universally present."[44] In fin-de-siècle Germany, scientists assumed that over 90 percent of the German population had traces of TB, while 40 percent had syphilis.[45] They viewed these diseases as the result of overcrowding, poor working environments, unsatisfactory sanitary conditions, and poor moral and sexual health.

References to syphilis, TB, and gonorrhea sharpened the ritual debates. As in Baden, critics of circumcision accused *mohelim* of spreading sexual infections by sucking the baby's wound.[46] Opponents of kosher butchering offered similar reasoning, contending that the blood drained from kosher butchering was more likely to carry and spread diseases.[47] It was within this context that Jewish physicians inversed charges against the rites. Heinrich Loeb argued that German Jews avoided the "urban problem" of syphilis because of their circumcised status. His contemporary Max Rawitzki similarly claimed that circumcision prevented Jewish men from being stricken by the "evil smell" and "terrible itching and burning" of venereal diseases.[48] During a moment when increasing numbers of people drew parallels between the body of the nation state

---

Münchener medizinische Wochenschrift (25 January 1898): 100–113. A more supportive view could be found in Julius Winter, "Der Arzt als Mohel," *AZDJ* 40 (1910): 474–475.

[43]Carl Alexander, *Die Hygienische Bedeutung der Beschneidung* (Breslau: Druck von Th. Schatzky, 1902); "Fort mit den Mißbräuchen bei der Beschneidung," *AZDJ* 31 (1910): 366–368.

[44]Weindling, *Health, Race, and German Politics.*

[45]Ibid., 174, 181–184.

[46]See note 2 in introduction.

[47]Ernst Froelich, *Das Schächten—ein mosaischer Ritualgebrauch? Beitrag zur Lösung der Schächtfrage* (Potsdam: Selbstverlag des Verfassers, 1899), pp. 13–28; "Seid barmherzig—auch beim Schlachten der Thiere," *BTV* 35 (1888/9?): 1–2.

[48]Heinrich Loeb, "Circumcision und Syphilis-Prophylaxe," in *Sonderabdruck aus der "Monatsschrift für Harnkrankheiten und Sexuelle Hygiene"* (Leipzig: Verlag der Monatsschrift für Harnkrankheiten und Sexuelle Hygiene, W. Malende, 1904), 6; Max Rawitzki, "Ueber die Nützlichkeit des Vorhautschnittes (Posthetomie) bei Neugebornen vom

and a human corpus, the relationship of Jewish ritual behavior with diseases took on greater meaning.

Other concerns hovered here as well. During the late nineteenth and twentieth centuries, participants in the ritual questions invoked charges of Jewish deviant sexuality, among other antisemitic concerns regarding the Jewish presence in Germany. Antisemitic tropes appeared in the local, regional, and national debates, clearly influencing the disputes but never solely defining them.

Antisemitism

German Jews did not experience antisemitism consistently or universally, but a few generalizations can be made about antisemitism in Wilhelmine Germany. Modern antisemitism shared its popularity with the exponential rise of chauvinistic discourses and attitudes in the late nineteenth century. Both movements had their origins in the dramatic social, political, and economic rearrangements at this time. They both articulated a concern with the particularity of Germany's minority groups, championed the removal of deviance from society, and expressed a longing to return to a "utopian" past. They also manifested themselves in a variety of different ways.[49]

As a frame of reference, antisemitism provided one lens through which an individual could understand his/her world. According to historian Derek Penslar, this way of viewing the world produced a "double helix of intersecting paradigms."[50] On the one hand, anti-Jewish campaigns painted Jews as powerful manipulators who used their influence in cunning ways. On the other hand, they depicted Jews as social savages, unlearned in the ways of *Kultur* and unworthy

---

medizinischen Standpunkte aus betrachtet nebst zwei Abbildungen," in Abraham Glassberg, ed., *Die Beschneidung in ihrer geschichtlichen, ethnographischen, religiösen und medicinischen Bedeutung: Zum ersten Male umfassend dargestellt* (Berlin: Verlag C. Boas Nachf., 1896), p. xxvii.

[49]German states and municipalities frequently enshrined discrimination in their exclusion of Jews from certain judiciary, military, or university posts. Social clubs and informal social settings encouraged antisemitism by rejecting Jewish participation, while political parties and special interest groups increasingly adopted anti-Jewish rhetoric. Such a theory has been complicated by Marion Kaplan, "Friendship on the Margins: Jewish Social Relations in Imperial Germany" *Central European History* 34.4 (2001): 471–501; Till van Rahden, "Intermarriage, the New Woman, and the Situational Ethnicity of Breslau Jews, 1870s to 1920s," *LBIYB* 46 (2001): 125–150.

[50]Penslar, *Shylock's Children*, p. 13; also see pp. 11–49.

of integration. These clusters materialized in antisemitism's counter-intuitive claim that Jews were both unable to socially and politically integrate and that they had acculturated so successfully that they could disguise themselves among their German compatriots. These binary constellations took other forms as well: antisemitic literature simultaneously portrayed the Jew as dandy and as slovenly; as the supersexualized, violent male Jew and as the emasculated, feminized male-child; as the occidental sexualized Jewish temptress and as the desexualized materialistic Jewess.

As antisemitic ideology, rhetoric, and imagery developed over the course of the late nineteenth- and early twentieth centuries, so too did the coterminous campaigns against kosher butchering and circumcision. There were four key points of intersection: (1) the alleged brutality of Jewish rites, (2) their supposedly bloody nature, (3) their health risks, and (4) their economic noxiousness. By relying on these themes, critics of Jewish rites addressed the supposed problems lurking within Jewish ritual behavior. However, they disagreed over whether this behavior illustrated Jewry's malevolence. Some contributors elaborated on the evils of Jewish rites; others suggested that Jews were themselves evil.

Jewish Cruelty

In both print and spoken debates, participants in the ritual questions identified ways in which Jewish ritual behavior constituted some form of cruelty. Earlier discussants had made similar claims. However, the availability of new methods for practicing Jewish rites and the increased attention paid to the alleged relationship between Judaism and blood radicalized the ways in which discussants understood cruelty.

Similar to the previous campaigns, critics portrayed kosher butchering and circumcision as inherently brutal in part because they believed that Jews knowingly caused animals and infants pain. Yet now hundreds of petitions submitted to local town councils, regional parliaments, and the Reichstag described kosher butchering as cruel.[51] One advocate, who criticized the rite for its cruel treatment of animals, beseeched his

---

[51]Proposal to the Reichstag 1887 submitted by "die Kommission für Petitionen Freiherr" BH MA 76592; proceedings of the Bundesrath Session 26 May 1888 BH MA 76592. Also see 8 February 1913 letter from the regional government of Upper Bavaria to the magistrate of Munich ALM SUV 90; Otto Hartmann, ed. *Bericht über die neunte Versammlung des Verbandes der Tierschutz-Vereine des Deutschen Reiches in Leipzig* (Cologne: Tierschutzvereine des deutschen Reiches, 1904).

fellow activists to imagine the pain cattle experienced when they died fully aware of their surroundings. "When we cut our finger we feel the pain," he cried. "We can hardly even imagine what severe anguish the animal must feel."[52] While only a handful of animal protectionists had made analogous claims during the unification era, turn-of-the-century animal activists promoted these charges. According to animal protectionist literature, Germans heeded this call. Of 460 citizens questioned in a Saxon poll taken in 1893, 441 (99.5%) of them described kosher butchering as cruel to animals.[53]

Opponents of circumcision relayed similar complaints. Advocates of circumcision-reform had long expressed concern with the pain newborn boys experienced at the hands of their circumcisers. Influenced by medical advancements in the late nineteenth century, they expressed specific unease that circumcision could lead to the penis's permanent mutilation or nerve damage. In an article published in a Munich medical journal in 1898, physician R. Pott warned the medical public that the Jewish rite caused infants serious, long-lasting pain. The operation was "not the simple incision we believe it to be," but a practice that could lead to serious injuries, even death.[54] Four years earlier, Heidelberg's medical officer made a similar claim. After Moritz Benjamin died from complications of his circumcision, the medical examiner described the botched circumcision in sharp tones. In his view, the oral suction that had illegally accompanied Benjamin's circumcision led to the child's severe pain and anguish before his death.[55] Antisemitic opponents of the rite took this further, penning polemical poems and essays that depicted infants as the prey of malevolent *mohelim*. These portrayals emphasized the power imbalance between "innocent creatures" and their "cruel" tormentors, namely, the ritual practitioners.[56]

The campaigns against Jewish rituals advanced a second link between Jewish religious behavior and brutality. In pamphlets, public testimonies, and medical manuscripts, discussants engaged with the knife-centered character of Jewish ritual behavior and its implications

[52]Otto Hartmann, ed., *Bericht über die elfte Versammlung des Verbandes der Tierschutz-Vereine des Deutschen Reiches in Düsseldorf* (Cologne: Jacob Pohl, 1908), p. 67.

[53]Der Vorstand des Verbandes der Tierschutzvereine des Deutschen Reiches, *Eingabe an den Reichstag um Nichtannahme des Beschlusses der Kommission betr. Unzulässigkeit von Bestimmungen bezüglich der rituellen Schlachtungen* (Cologne: Jacob Pohl, 1910).

[54]Pott, "Ueber die Gefahren der Rituellen Beschneidung."

[55]4 September 1894 letter to rabbinate in Heidelberg from the medical authorities there CJA 75BKa124 191.

[56]Animal protection societies depicted cattle slaughtered by the Jewish method as "martyrs." See "Die unnöthigen Thierquälerein beim Schlachten des Kleinviehes," *BTV* 2 (1888–1892): 1–2; "Seid menschlich beim Tödten der Thiere," *BTV* 43 (1888/9): 1–2.

more generally. Both circumcision and kosher butchering rely on sharp knives and incisions for their executions. More moderate discussants questioned whether the knives used in Jewish rituals were too sharp or jagged or if ritual practitioners did not clean their knives thoroughly.[57] In its petition to the Reichstag in 1887, animal protectionists in Elmshorn articulated the concern that kosher butchers used knives whose unevenness or extremely sharp points caused the animals unnecessary anguish.[58] Five years earlier, a medical examiner in Karlsruhe similarly commented on the sharp and painful nature of the *mohel's* knife. In his investigation into local circumcision practices, he suggested that *mohelim* often exhibited a laziness, stubbornness, or carelessness regarding the care of their knives.[59]

Antisemitic critics emphasized these concerns and exaggerated the length and serration of knives used for Jewish ritual purposes. Several emphasized the length and sharpness of the knives. In an article in the antisemitic *Hammer*, journalist Hans Wehleid portrayed the *shohet* as a savage-like creature who was unable to stand erect but could cut the animal severely. "The shohet crouches near the animal whose body has been bounded. He takes a long, long, sharp knife to the motionless animal and cuts a single line across its throat. Out of this cut gushes a flow of blood. One does not need to be a weakling or a Jew-hater to be disgusted."[60] The radical antisemite Bernadin Freimut similarly identified the moment of incision as particularly dangerous. Like Wehleid's *shohet* who "had not raised a single finger" until the act of kosher butchering began, Freimut's rabbi [*mohel*] also suddenly "drew near" with his knife when the moment of incision arrived.[61] The antisemitic Reichstag deputies Otto Boeckel and Georg Wilhelm Vielhaben similarly maintained that Jewish law mandated the knife's centrality to Jewish traditions. In their view, the Talmud was simply a tract about "knives and ways to kill animals."[62]

[57]See, e.g., the testimony in Otto Hartmann, ed., *Bericht über die zwölfte Versammlung des Verbandes der Tierschutzvereine des Deutschen Reiches in Berlin* (Cologne: Jacob Pohl, 1910): 44; "Das Schächtritual und die Gutachen der Physiologen über das Schächten," *BTV* 86 (189?): 2; "Zum Schächtverbot," *Tages-Zeitung* (Potsdam) (10 May 1909) CJA 75ve1340 212; "Seid barmherzig—auch beim Schlachten der Thiere," *BTV* 35 (188/9?): 1.

[58]1886 petition from animal protectionists in Elmshorn to the Reichstag deputies CJA 75A El 5 24. Also see January 1887 petition from the Jewish Community of Elmshorn CJA 75 A El 5 24.

[59]1881 report of Dr. Hamburger CJA 75BKa124. Even a "supportive" defense of *shehitah* painted the rite as knife-centered. Willy Staerk, "Der Streit Ums "Schächten," *Der Protestant* 23 (10 June 1899): 419–421.

[60]Hans Wehleid, "Vom Schächten," *Hammer* (15 February 1911): 102.

[61]Bernadin Freimut, *Die Jüdischen Blutmorde von ihrem ersten Erscheinen der Geschichte bis auf unsere Zeit* (Münster: A. Russell's Verlag, 1895).

[62]1899 Reichstag transcript CAHJP TD 475, 1–2.

Anxieties over Jewry's alleged attraction to knives lay at the core of several related concerns. First, during the two decades preceding World War I, participants in the ritual questions increasingly identified Jewish itinerant slaughter as a cause for unease.[63] Both Jews and non-Jews practiced unregulated butchering, but animal protectionists, butchers, and public health officials seemed to express more concern with unlicensed *shohetim* than with non-Jewish butchers. In their view, itinerant kosher slaughterers, whom they called "*Wildschächter*," disregarded slaughter regulations, abstained from paying taxes, and sold infected meat. Moreover, *Wildschächten* suggested an image of knife-wielding Jews wandering the countryside, poised to attack innocent animals (if not innocent Germans).[64] In response, a number of German local governments inquired into the practice of *Wildschächten*, and in 1910 German slaughterhouse directors organized a national meeting to discuss the issue.[65] Although no national laws resulted from this meeting or from earlier inquiries, the participating slaughterhouse directors encouraged local communities to continue investigating this practice and, in some cases, to pass local regulations.[66]

Jewish Blood-Thirst and the *Ritualfragen*

Just as *Wildschächten* implied the existence of unregulated, knife-wielding Jews, it also validated popular concerns regarding Jews and blood-thirst. Common accusations of blood libel invoked this supposed

[63]Itinerant *shehitah* was common because of the absence of an abattoir in a specific area, because of a long-standing tradition within that community of individuals slaughtering their own meat, or because slaughterhouse reforms had forced slaughterers to slaughter their cattle outside of government controlled spaces.

[64]European discourse long had judged morality by one's productivity and stability. See 16 July letter to the German-Jewish League of Communities (DIGB) from J. Erchelbaum and 23 June 1903 letter from the Jewish community of Stuttgart to the DIGB CJA 75C Ge1 893 63–65 r.s. Also see "Hauschlächterei," *DIZ* 22 (1911): 7; Bundesrat Session on 2 March 1917.

[65]16 June 1903 letter from the Breslau Jewish community CJA 75Cge1 93 62; 23 June 1903 letter from Oldenburg Jewish community 75Cge1 93 66; 25 June 1903 letter from the Posen Jewish community 75Cge1 93 67; 1903 letter from the West Prussian Jewish community 75Cge1 93 72. Also see "Das Schächten auf dem städtischen Schlachthofe beschäftigte wider einmal das Kuratorium," *Vorwärts* (30 May 1911) CJA 75Cve1 340 316.

[66]Of the local laws passed, those that affected Jewish populations too small to support their own *shohet* had a significant impact. In Membressen, for example, when the town council prohibited *Wildschächten*, the community there could no longer rely on an

affinity of Jews with knives and added a new dimension concerning the bloody nature of Jewish ritual behavior.

The accusation of Jewish blood-thirst took place amidst a general preoccupation in central Europe with blood. During the late nineteenth and early twentieth centuries, German and Austrian scientists and pseudo-scientists devoted themselves to the study of blood and its pathogens.[67] At the same time, a strand of German nationalism and racism called for blood as the cornerstone for German national identity; and blood already served as the basis on which the state determined eligibility for German citizenship. In addition, vampirism occupied a new place of interest in European literature and folklore. The image of the human blood-sucker had been significant in early modern religious folk thought and reemerged as scientific advances were made in the study of blood and its pathogens.[68] Blood mattered in the late nineteenth- and early twentieth-century European imagination.

As the existence of human blood-suckers, race science, and blood-centered nationalism became more prominently accepted, radical antisemites increasingly made two distinct charges against their Jewish compatriots. Racial antisemitism warned that Jewry could injure Germandom through Jewish-Christian procreation. Arguing that Germany's "future lies in the blood," racial antisemites expressed concern that Jewish intermarriage would threaten Germany's viability and strength.[69] Similarly influenced by the preoccupation with blood, a second charge cautioned that Jews delighted in, if not depended on, the blood of other humans and/or animals. This accusation saw its expression in seventy-

---

itinerant *shohet* to serve their needs. 16 July letter to the DIGB from J. Erchelbaum and 23 June 1903 letter from the Jewish community of Stuttgart to the DIGB CJA 75C Ge1 893 63–65 r.s.; 1913 report of the meat-packers association CAHJP TD/942. In Berlin, a city that had several Jewish butchers, the animal protection society reported to the slaughterhouse commission that there were "a dozen or so *Wilde Schächter* who were not under the supervision of the Rabbis." "Das Schächten auf dem städtischen Schlachthofe beschäftigte wider einmal das Kuratorium," *Vorwärts* (Berlin) (30 May 1911) CJA 75CVE1 340 316.

[67]Weindling, *Health, Race, and German Politics.*

[68]David I. Kertzer, *The Popes Against the Jews: The Vatican's Role in the Rise of Modern Anti-Semitism* (New York: Alfred A. Knopf, 2001), pp. 152–165; Clemens Ruthner, "Vampirism as Political Theory: Voltaire to Alfred Rosenberg and Elfriede Jelinek," *Visions of the Fantastic: Selected Essays from the Fifteenth International Conference on the Fantastic in the Arts*, ed. Allienne R. Becker (Westport, CT: Greenwood Press, 1996), pp. 3–11.

[69]Ernst Hasse as cited and translated by Peter Pulzer, "The Return of Old Hatreds," p. 248.

nine blood libel charges against Jewish communities and in several novels, short stories, and antisemitic postcards.[70]

The campaigns against kosher butchering and circumcision also articulated and reinforced this supposed affinity between Jews and blood.[71] While many participants distanced themselves from specific charges of Jewish blood-thirst, others grossly distorted why and how Jews conducted their religious rituals.[72] Locating blood lust in the incision of kosher butchering and, to a lesser extent, circumcision, they described the bloody nature of both rituals. Animal protectionists described the "torrent of blood" that poured from the animal's neck and covered the floor of the abattoir. According to these critics, this "blood letting" was not only visually repulsive but also immoral. It caused the allegedly conscious creature tremendous fear and pain. It also covered the abattoir floor with blood, which, if contaminated, could infect other animals and butchers.[73] Critics of circumcision similarly emphasized the bloody wound of the innocent newborn. Worried that "hemophilia was particularly common among Jewish children," Pott warned that a child could bleed to death if his *mohel* accidentally cut an artery or vein.[74]

---

[70]Verein zur Abwehr des Antisemitismus, *Ergänzung zum Antisemiten-Spiegel: Die Antisemiten im Lichte des Christenthums, des Rechtes und der Wissenschaft* (Berlin: Hoffschläger Buchdruckerei u. Verlag (F. Sommer), 1903), p. 26.

[71]See, e.g., "Zum Schächtverbot," *Tages-Zeitung* (Potsdam) (10 May 1909): 24; December 1886 petition to the community of Elmshorth, CJA 75 A El 5; 1.1.87; Hans Wehleid, "Das Schächten."

[72]According to some antisemites, Jews practiced their rites only in order to receive the religious sanction to draw the blood of others. For the range of reception to the blood-thirst charge, see the 1899 Reichstag transcript CAHJP TD 475.

[73]Otto Seehaus, *Tierschutz und Tierquälerei* (Berlin: Otto Bremer, 1896), 27. Also see 1901 public statement issued by the Berlin TSV CJA 75AEr1 96 68; "Zur Schächtfrage," *Das Recht der Tiere* 15 October 1905 CJA 75DCo128 66; Alte Tierschutzverein in Dresden, "Volksgenossen hört!" *Deutsche Reform* (Dresden) (26 September 1912) CJA 75CVe1341 88; Carl Mittermaier, *Das Schlachten geschildert und erläutert auf Grund zahlreicher neuerer Gutachten* (Heidelberg: Carl Winter's Universitätsbuchhandlung, 1902); Mittermaier, "Die Schächtfrage," *BTV* 91 and 92 (1888–1892): 1; 1–2. Explicitly linking blood drainage with blood lust, the slaughterhouse director Ernst von Schwartz described this "old barbaric practice" as befitting the bloodthirstiness of Jews. Ernst von Schwartz "Das Schächten," *Süddeutsche Monatshefte* (April 1910): 523, 515; "29 deutscher Fleischer-Verbandstag," *Königsberger Hartungsche Zeitung* (9 August 1906) CJA 75DCo128 111. Even those who defended the Jewish community's right to practice this blood removal sometimes mentioned blood. In his refusal to mandate stunning, the slaughterhouse director of Bremen still associated Jews with blood, unnecessarily reminding readers that Jews could eat only the meat "from the warm-blooded animals." 29 October 1907 report to the Bremen senate CJA 75CVe1344 199–200.

[74]See, e.g., Pott, "Ueber die Gefahren."

Possibly influenced by discourses concerning vampirism, some critics expressed concern that Jews used the blood from infants or cattle once it had been removed. Describing Jewish rites and their practitioners as "blood-drinking,"[75] opponents of kosher butchering worried that Jews consumed the blood of animals, that they sold it to others, or that they intentionally allowed the blood to contaminate meat or the environment. These contributors demanded that slaughterhouse commissions promulgate laws forbidding Jews from ingesting the blood of animals. Radical opponents of circumcision expressed similar concerns, worrying that *mohelim* intentionally spread disease through oral suction, used the blood of circumcision for nefarious purposes, or drank the blood from the wound. For Freimut, circumcision involved the eating of Jewish and Christian blood. In his retelling of the ritual, the *mohel* fed the child a mixture of circumcision and innocent Christian blood.[76] Both of these charges were tainted with tremendous irony. Judaism forbids the ingestion of blood. Moreover, it was not uncommon for gentile Germans to consume blood sausage, a popular and economic food item.

Given the interest in the alleged blood-thirst of Jewish rites, it is not surprising that Freimut and other critics conflated Jewish rituals with the increasingly popular blood libel charge.[77] In their view, the two had much in common. Both allegedly required a sharp incision, a process of blood-letting, and the utilization of the blood after the rite's completion. Imagining the Jewish butcher or circumciser as a Jewish murderer, detractors used the libel charge to condemn Jewish rites while simultaneously pointing to Jewish ritual behavior as proof of the blood libel's existence. As such, when blood libel charges were laid, officials and townspeople often blamed local ritual practitioners. While few *mohelim* were arrested for ritual murder, butchers met a less fortunate fate.[78] In 1892, for example, police authorities arrested a local Jewish butcher after a child in Xanten (Rhineland) was found brutally murdered. The police suspected him because he was believed

[75]Von Schwarz, "Das Schächten." Also see 1901 public statement by the Berlin TSV; "Zur Schächtfrage," *Das Recht der Tiere: Zeitschrift des Verbandes westdeutscher Tierschtuzvereine* (15 October 1905) CJA 75DCo128 66; Alte Tierschutzverein in Dresden, "Volksgenossen hört!" As chapter 5 will discuss, Jewish defenses immediately reacted to this charge.

[76]Freimut, *Die Jüdischen Blutmorde*, p. 126.

[77]Many accused Jewish butchers of these crimes. See "Seid barmherzig—auch beim Schlachten der Thiere," *BTV* 35 and 38 (1888–1892): 1–2, 1–2; Back, *Schächten oder Betäuben*; Carl Klein, *Sind geschächtete Tiere sofort nach dem Schächtschnitt bewußtlos?* (Berlin: Berliner Tierschutz-Verein, 1927); Ernst von Schwartz, *Das betäubungslose Schächten der Israeliten: Vom Standpunkt des 20. Jahrhunderts auf Grund von Schächt-Tatsachen geschildert und erläutert* (Konstanz am Bodensee: Verlag von Ersnt Ackermann, 1905). For a study of this phenomenon, see Gilman, *Freud, Race, and Gender* and *Case of Sigmund Freud*.

[78]Freimut, *Die Jüdischen Blutmorde*, p. 126.

to be one of the few residents in Xanten who would be capable of decapitating and bleeding a human. A kosher butcher, they argued, would be called on to use brutal strength and constraining devices to hold down his victim; he would employ sharp knives to cut the victim; and he would know how to drain the victim's body of its blood. Eight years later, another Jewish butcher was indicted after a student was killed in the West Prussian town of Konitz. A popular postcard from the Konitz affair dramatized this link. The card depicted a man restrained in chains and surrounded by ten Jewish men (representing the quorum required by Jewish law for religious services). One man appeared to be decapitating the victim while another drained his blood into a bucket. The inscription read, "Remember 11 March 1900. On this day the student Winter was sacrificed in Konitz by the knife of a kosher butcher."[79] A postcard circulated after an 1899 ritual murder case (Hilsner affair) similarly portrayed a bound maiden surrounded by three unkempt Jewish butchers.[80]

Fin-de-siècle concerns with sexual deviance also influenced the Hilsner postcard, as well as the general campaigns concerning the Jewish rites.[81] As social fears concerning overpopulation, degeneracy, and criminality became fused with and articulated through sexual anxieties, the *Schächt-* and *Ritualfragen* conflated concerns of Jewish brutality with Jewish sexual difference. The campaigns hinted that ritual practitioners were violent, oversexed, and/or sexually different. Some participants in the *Schächtfragen* explicitly invoked the language of rape. Referring to the "throwing down" of cattle, they compared the binding of slaughtered animals with that of women.[82] Their illustrations of dewy-eyed calves and women bound with ropes and metal chains sent a clear message: Kosher butchering and the Jewish employees of the abattoir presented a significant danger to society at large.[83] The sexual connotations in oral suction were similarly worrisome. The sucking of a child's

---

[79]Peter Pulzer also refers to the postcard, although he overlooks the centrality of *she-hitah* to it. Pulzer, "The Response to Antisemitism," in Meyer, ed., *German-Jewish History in Modern Times*, vol. 3, pp. 252–280.

[80]The reader would have known that they were butchers because the card labeled them as such. Interestingly, the man indicted was not a butcher but a cobbler.

[81]On this, see Michel Foucault, *The History of Sexuality: An Introduction*, vol. 1, trans. Robert Hurley (New York: Vintage Books, 1990); John C. Fout, ed., *Forbidden History: The State, Society, and the Regulation of Sexuality in Modern Europe* (Chicago: University of Chicago Press, 1992); Jeffrey Weeks, *Sex, Politics, and Society: The Regulation of Sexuality since 1800*, 2nd ed. (London: Longman, 1989); Jeffrey Weeks, *Sexuality and Its Discontents: Meanings, Myths, and Modern Sexualities* (London: Routledge, 1989).

[82]See, e.g., Wehleid, "Vom Schächten."

[83]"Aufruf und Bitte," *BTV* 39 (1888–1892): 1–2; "Seid menschlich beim Tödten der Thiere," *BTV* 43 (1888–1892): 1–2; Wehleid, "Vom Schächten," 102.

penis was "ethically problematic."[84] These charges were the exact opposite of the common antisemitic belief that Jewish men were emasculated and weak, fears that would be articulated frequently with the charge that circumcision feminized Jewish men.

Postcard depicting the ritual murder of Ernst Winter by the Jews in Konitz. It reads "Remember 11 March 1900. On this day the student Winter was sacrificed in Konitz by the knife of a kosher butcher." *Source*: "Der Ritualmord zu Konitz," Stadtarchiv Nürnberg, E 39 "Stürmer"-Archiv 1420/34.

[84]See 11 May 1853 Hamburg Jewish community council minutes CAHJP AHW 563 30–32; May 1888 report filed by the Baden authorities CJA 75BKA1 24 159; "Das Mezizah-Glassröhrchen"; "Die Beschneidung durch jüdische Aerzte," *AZDJ* 12 (1855): 149; "Frankfreich," *AZDJ* 36 (1843): 542; "Haag," *AZDJ* 41 (1864): 644–645; "Hamburg," *AZDJ* 3 (1848): 39–40; "Hamburg, Eingangs Oktober," *AZDJ* 43 (1847): 640–641; "Protokoll der Sitzung vom II November 1874"; "Regierungs-Verfügung vom 22 Oktober 1885 I C 7414," in *Die Beschneidung: Eine populäre Darstellung ihrer Bedeutung und Vollziehung*, pp. 35–35; "Warschau," *AZDJ* 6 (1873): 90–91; "Wien, 20 Oct," *AZDJ* 45 November (1886): 715; A.C., "Aus Württemberg." *AZDJ* (1857): 69; Abraham Glassberg et al., "Die Beschneidung in ihrer geschichtlichen, ethnographischen, religiösen und medicinischen Bedeutung," In Glassberg, ed., *Die Beschneidung* (Berlin: Verlag von C. Boas Nachf., 1896), pp. 41–135; Naphtali Hirsch, *Die Freie Vereinigung für die Interessen des orthodoxen Judenthums: Eine Beleuchtung ihrer Aufgabe und seitherigen Wirksamkeit* (Frankfurt: Buchdruckerei Louis Golde, 1900).

In the published literature, physicians asserted that circumcision dulled the sensory organ, thus robbing Jewish boys of their manliness. This claim appeared in the antisemitic press and in the established medical literature as well.[85] A few physicians evoked images of castration in their claims that the removal of the foreskin caused Jewish men to experience severe sexual frustration. Such frustration allegedly would result either in abstention from any type of sexual contact or, on the contrary, excessively passionate behavior and sexual deviance. Others charged that circumcision led to masturbation, a powerful charge since nineteenth- and twentieth-century medicine and science considered masturbation antisocial—the cause of homosexuality, deviant sexual behavior, insanity, even death.[86] Impossibly categorizing the Jewish man as both undersexed and supersexual and his penis as both unresponsive and hyperactive, these medical writings suggested that there was indeed something abnormal about the Jewish man.[87]

The concerns with Jewish sexual deviance suggested that Jewish ritual behavior—and Jewish brutality more generally—could have a significant impact on the non-Jewish world.[88] Linking animal cruelty, sexual abuse, and child brutality, radical critics accused ritual practitioners of having violent urges toward their non-Jewish neighbors. More moderate critics also worried about the effect of Jewish ritual behavior on the non-Jewish populace. In their view, some of the greatest dangers of circumcision and kosher butchering lay in the economic and financial spheres. These critics—far more mainstream than those that envisioned Jewry as a malevolent violent force—worried that Jewish rites validated the existence of and furthered Jewish economic danger and political unworthiness.

---

[85]G. W. "Beschneidung an Deutschen?" *Hammer* 285 (1914): 248–249. Such a charge was discussed in "Protokoll der Sitzung vom II November 1874," *Mittheilungen des Aertzlichen Vereines in Wien* 3.13 (1874): 169–172; Alexander, *Die hygienische Bedeutung der Beschneidung*; Richard Andree, *Zur Volkskunde der Juden* (Bielefeld: Verlag von Velhagen & Klasing, 1881); Wilhelm Ebstein, *Die Medizin im Alten Testament* (Stuttgart: Verlag von Ferdinand Enke, 1901); Großherzoglich Badischen Oberrat der Israeliten Baden, *Dienstvorschriften für Mohelim* (Karlsruhe: Buchdruckerei von Malsch & Vogel, 1897); Josef Grünwald, *Die rituelle Circumcision (Beschneidung) operativ und rituell bearbeitet von Dr. Josef Grünwald* (Frankfurt, a.M.: Verlag von J. Kauffmann, 1892).

[86]David L. Gollaher, "From Ritual to Science: The Medical Transformation of Circumcision in America," *Journal of Social History* (JSH) 28 (1994): 5–36; R. P. Neuman, "Masturbation, Madness, and the Modern Concepts of Childhood and Adolescence," *JSH* 8 (1975): 1–27.

[87]See the refutation in Alexander, *Die hygienische Bedeutung der Beschneidung*.

[88]See, e.g., the opinions expressed by Magnus Schwantje, *Die Beziehungen der Tierschutzbewegung zu andern ethischen Bestrebungen* (Berlin: Gesellschaft zur Förderung der Tierschutzes und verwandter Bestrebungen, 1909). Most articulations of this view could be found in the kosher butchering debates.

Political Integration

Modern antisemitism professed that Jews were disproportionately represented in certain economic fields, that they were motivated by avarice and greed, and that they were incapable of full social integration. As a wide range of participants gradually questioned the relationship of Jewish ritual behavior with economic matters and with cruelty, increasing numbers concomitantly maintained that Jewish rites forced Jews to remain on the margins of public life. On the one hand, they pointed with alarm to the integration of Jews within German economic, social, and political settings. On the other hand, they maintained that Jewry's choice to preserve ritual behavior, despite the advances of the modern world, illustrated Jewish desires to remain on the borders of German political and social life.

Discussants invoked longstanding claims that Jewish ritual behavior encouraged Jewish marginalization. They continued to cite the physical manifestations of both rites as significant. Physicians and anthropologists, as well as antisemitic activists, expressed a deep interest in the ways in which circumcision distinguished Jewish bodies from those of their non-Jewish compatriots, an ironic charge since a person's circumcision generally remains hidden.[89] Despite the similarity of this campaign with past criticism, contributors now described Jewish physical difference by invoking a wide range of rhetoric and images. Participants tapped into concerns with the physical transformative powers of surgery and the interest in the corporeality of German workers. For some critics of circumcision, the physical marking of circumcision differentiated Jews from non-Jews because the rite altered the perfectibility of a man's body. As publisher Max Lieberman von Sonnenberg crudely remarked to a Jewish Socialist Reichstag deputy, "I do not want to go into the other characteristics distinguishing between Jews and other nations, but only to say to Herr Stadthagen: if he wants to become closely acquainted with these differences, then he should go to a Turkish bath and stand in front of the mirror."[90] While von Sonnenberg was content to leave the physical differences to the naked eye, other critics argued that circumcision had a metamorphosing effect. Supposedly the removal of the foreskin transformed the individual, a claim they emphasized in their use of the terms deform or disfigure (*verunstalten*) when describing the rite.

[89]These physicians were not the first to point out circumcision's relationship to Jewish difference, as discussed in chapter 1.

[90]Von Sonnenberg was the publisher of the *Deutsch-Sozialen Blatter*. Dietz Bering, *The Stigma of Names: Antisemitism in German Daily Life, 1812–1933*, trans. Neville Plaice (Ann Arbor: University of Michigan Press, 1992) p. 93.

German antisemite Friedrich Lange embraced this view; the statutes of his German League prohibited men who were born Jewish from joining the association. According to Lange, the association was to exclude these men because circumcision had "harbored his nature."[91]

Critics of kosher butchering similarly maintained that the rite preserved Jewish distance. Opponents held that the laws of *kashrut* forced Jews to remain separate from non-Jews because they were unable to dine together. In addition, they also charged that kosher butchering reinforced social isolation because *shohetim* chose to slaughter their animals in separate parts of the abattoir and affiliated with associations specifically for ritual practitioners and not the associations of German butchers. In Helmut Walser Smith's *The Butcher's Tale*, a non-Jewish butcher was responsible for framing a local kosher butcher for blood libel, while in Munich professional antagonism between Jewish and non-Jewish butchers remained a topic of interest for the city's slaughterhouse commission into the Weimar era.[92]

Ironically, as antisemitic critics demonstrated the ways in which Jewish rites preserved separateness, they also claimed that Jewish social integration had been far reaching. Opponents worried that Jews were so successful at acculturation that circumcision's mark of difference would be the only remaining way to identify a Jew. Similarly, in their campaigns to bring about mandatory animal stunning laws, animal protectionists and other critics of kosher butchering increasingly argued that German Jews gradually had abandoned Jewish dietary customs. By suggesting that large numbers of German-speaking Jews no longer needed to procure kosher meat, these critics rejected religious tolerance as a justification for granting Jews exemptions from slaughterhouse laws. If increasing numbers of Jews had abdicated kosher butchering, the state could prohibit the rite.

The issue of whether to protect Jewish rights under the rubric of free religious practice was a cornerstone of the discourses critical of kosher butchering and circumcision. Critics expressed frustration over Jewish communal requests for exemptions from city or state law.[93] Their

---

[91]Translated by Pulzer, *Rise of Political Anti-semitism*, p. 225.

[92]Helmut Walser Smith, *The Butcher's Tale: Murder and Anti-Semitism in a German Town* (New York: W.W. Norton, 2002); 22 January 1901 letter from the Munich TSV to the Munich magistrate Archiv der Landeshauptstadt München (ALM) SUV 91; February 1902 exchange of letters between the magistrates of Würzburg and Munich concerning local butchers ALM SUV 90.

[93]See, e.g., the antisemitic "Zur praktischen Lösung der Judenfrage" *Volks-Zeitung* (*VZ*) (22 December 1885) CJA 75CGe891 21; A. Keller *Das Schächten der Israeliten: Referat gehalten an einer Versammlung von Thierschutzfreunden am 2 April 1890* (Aargau: Ph Wirz-Schriften, 1890), 2; "Zur Schächtfrage," *BTV* 72 (189?): 1l; "Zur Betäubungs- und Schächtungsfrage," *DT* (4 August 1913): CJA 75Cve1341 187.

petitions, court appearances, and testimonies consistently argued that if emancipation had granted Jews citizenship than Jews were required to follow the law of the land. Between 1880 and 1916, opponents questioned the patriotism and civic worthiness of the dozens of Jewish communities that had called for their release from promulgations that affected their ritual practices.[94] When Saxony overturned its statewide ban on kosher butchering, the Dresden animal protection society publicly censured local and national German-Jewish associations, threatening that the push to safeguard Jewish rites could lead to the reconsideration of Jewish emancipation. Why, they asked, did the state continue to consider Jews citizens if Jews had no regard for its laws?[95] Earlier, in 1901, the radical Berlin animal protection society similarly had questioned Jewry's commitment to the German state. Its petition and letter-writing campaign juxtaposed German citizens with their Jewish neighbors. "All citizens *[Staatsbürger]*," they beseeched, "follow this [mandatory stunning] with the exception of the Jews."[96]

The Berlin animal protectionists considered the possibility of Jewish political integration within the public sphere, but they tried to distance themselves from the supposedly tainted world of politics. The society's newsletters made no mention of any political affiliation, and its members lobbied representatives from across the different parties within the Reichstag, Prussian parliament, and Berlin city leadership.[97] The organization consistently denied any political motivations. Instead, it alleged that its push for slaughterhouse reforms came from a deep belief in animal advocacy and the assumption that the protection of animals led to the creation of good policies concerning "the protection of men."[98]

[94]These laws licensed surgeons or butchers, prohibited oral suction, banned slaughter without stunning, and/or mandated the utilization of technologies and tools that would have voided Jewish ritual practice. See, e.g., September 23 1882 statement issued by the Jewish community of Karlsruhe CJA 75BKa124 37–8; "Die Politik: Versuchtes Schächtverbot," *Israelitische Wochenschrift (IW)* 11 (1899): 164.

[95]"Stimmen aus dem Publikum," *Dresdner Anzeiger (DA)* (29 December 1910) CJA 75CVe1344 166; "Die Israeliten und der Toleranzantrag des Zentrums" *Trierische Landes-Zeitung* (3 December 1908) CJA 75CVe1344 419. Also see Hermann Ramdohr, *Leipziger Flugschriften Sammlung zur Betäubungsfrage der Schlachttiere* CJA 75Cve1344 1–53.

[96]1901 public statement by the Berlin TSV. Also see the grossly misused letter by Rabbi Leopold Stein of Frankfurt, *Rabbinisch-theologisches Gutachten über das Schächten* CJA 75A Erl 97 68.

[97]"Die unnöthigen Thierquälerein beim Schlachten des Kleinviehes," *BTV* 2 (1888/9?): 2.

[98]"Seid barmherzig- auch beim Schlachten der Thiere," *BTV* 38 (1888/9?): 1; "Aufruf und Bitte," *BTV* 39 (1888/9?): 1–2.

Apoliticism

The Berlin animal protection society was not alone in its use of apoliticism to champion explicitly political goals. Whether or not they embraced the antisemitic rhetoric of the times, participants in the ritual questions expressed distrust of national politics and of large political party life. Such a manipulation of apoliticism was endemic to extraparliamentary politics in imperial Germany. As scholars of German political history have shown, apoliticism was essential to successful political gains. To attract members and to accomplish various goals, political and associational leaders of all kinds distanced themselves from what was seen as the inefficiency and radicalization of national party politics.[99]

By denying any political benefit from participating in the *Schächt-* or *Circumcisionsfragen*, the leaders of the associations described here partook in local, regional, and national debates without allying themselves either with one national party or with any kind of political gain. They pushed for political goals without seemingly sullying themselves by participating in the world of politics. Potsdam businessman and animal protectionist, Ernst Froelich, for example, enthusiastically denied any political motivation for his involvement in the *Schächtfragen* other than his desire to safeguard animals and German moral honor. In 1907, Munich butchers and meat sellers who endorsed a petition concerning local animal slaughtering practices similarly insisted that they acted alone, outside of any structured political party or debate.[100] Defenders of Jewish rites did the same. The vice president of the Centralverein, Eugene Fuchs, argued that the defense of kosher butchering was "not Liberals against Conservatives. It represents no party. Rather, it represents the interest of all German Jews."[101]

Despite their claims of apoliticism, the participating associations pushed an explicitly political agenda. Fuchs, Froelich, the Berlin animal protection society, and the Munich meat sellers made claims with significant political implications within the public sphere. Even though he claimed to be apolitical, Rabbi H. Hildesheimer took part in dozens of political debates concerning the rite of kosher butchering. He and his ideological opponents appeared at Reichstag committee and town

[99]Rudy Koshar, *Social Life, Local Politics, and Nazism: Marburg, 1880–1935* (Chapel Hill: University of North Carolina Press, 1986). Also see Jan Palmowksi, "The Politics of the 'Unpolitical German': Liberalism in German Local Government, 1860–1880," *The Historical Journal* 42.3 (1999): 675–705.

[100]Froelich, *Das Schächten*; 1907 petition by Munich butchers and meat sellers/handlers StM SUV 7.

[101]November 9 minutes of the *shehitah* commission meeting CJA 75Ve1340 263.

council meetings, and they argued as witnesses or lawyers in court cases. Similar to Hildesheimer, Fuchs may have fashioned his self-defense efforts as an apolitical act, but he did so by consistently trying to gain the support of sympathetic Liberal leaders and governmental administrators. Finally, while the Berlin animal protectionist leadership embraced apoliticism in spirit, it concomitantly encouraged its members to "raise their voices with their votes" to bring about change.[102] Discussants, then, did not use apoliticism reliably and in so doing echoed the rhetoric's use by other unrelated associations in the public sphere.

✝✝✝✝✝

As kosher butchering and circumcision increasingly became a focus of ongoing intense struggle, the content and form of the disputes changed significantly. Over the course of the late nineteenth- and early twentieth centuries, the ritual questions attracted the attention of growing numbers of Germans within the political arena. The disputes increasingly tapped into contemporary anxieties over the economy, industrialization, and social threats. As participants tried to make sense of these issues, they invoked the emerging discourses of apoliticism, antisemitism, and science.

Yet, the local, regional, and national debates, like the use of these ideologies as a frame of reference, were uneven and manifested themselves in varying ways. Most of the kosher butchering disputes took place at the local level; many of the circumcision conflicts occurred between state medical authorities and Jewish communal leaders. Variation could be seen in the participants' use of rhetoric as well. Much of the egregiously antisemitic language and imagery remained in the printed realm, while local participants were more likely to invoke economic or political concerns than they were the rituals' supposed affinity with blood libel. State and national debates consistently focused on issues concerning the political implications of ritual behavior and the limits of religious protection.

Interested in how disputes over Jewish rites served as a site of political struggles, the following chapter analyzes the ways in which ritual questions helped to shape the political functioning of certain public authorities and associations. In so doing, it questions antisemitism's influence on these disputes and their participants.

---

[102]"Die unnöthigen Thierquälerein beim Schlachten des Kleinviehes." *BTV* 2 (1888/9?): 2.

CHAPTER 4

"The Disgrace of Our Century!"
Circumcision, Kosher Butchering, and Modern German Politics

At the 1904 national meeting of the Association of Animal Protection Societies of the German Reich, one participant offered a disclaimer, which had been and would continue to be invoked with great frequency during the decades leading up to World War I. After Karl Krämer of Hilchenbach assumed the speaker's mantle to champion slaughterhouse reforms, he quickly separated himself from the antisemitic rhetoric and movements of the previous two decades. "I have nothing against the Jews," he said, "I like one man just as I would like another."[1] Dismissing antisemitism as a motivation for his involvement in the animal protection movement, the physician Storch also argued that his support for a national ban on kosher butchering lacked anti-Jewish animus. "If a Christian sect was doing this [practicing kosher butchering]," he rationalized, "I would be just as vehemently opposed.[2] Krämer and Storch did not want their campaign's message to be diminished because of any linkage between them and anti-Jewish rhetoric, imagery, or movements. They therefore appropriately distanced themselves from the radicalizing antisemitism of the era.

The contributions of Krämer and Storch to the ritual questions illuminate the messy nature of the disputes. As chapter 3 suggested, animal protectionism, a concern with health and hygiene, and antisemitism played a crucial role in the late nineteenth- and early twentieth-century

---

[1]Otto Hartmann, ed., *Bericht über die neunte Versammlung des Verbandes der Tierschutz-Vereine*, p. 59.

[2]"Stimmen zur Schächtfrage," *Deutsch-Soziale Blätter* (19 June 1907) CJA 75CVe1344 172–3. Similar statements can be found in Berlin TSV, *Was befiehlt das jüdische Religionsgesetz über das Schächten* (Berlin: Deutscher Verlag, 1906), p. 1; von Schwarz, "Das Schächten"; "Berlin 10 Januar" *Kölnische Zeitung* (11 January 1913) CJA 75CVe1341 113.

Ritualfragen. Yet, a further frame of reference drove the ritual questions; namely, an expansive understanding of toleration.[3] Just as one group of participants increasingly became attracted to the anti-Jewish rhetoric of the imperial period, another set of discussants crafted their involvement around an interpretation of toleration that was synonymous with religious protection. As their opponents warned against Jewish cruelty and bloodthirstiness in ever more radical terms, this set of contributors suggested that the safeguarding of religious values was more important than the prevention of other kinds of risk. They fused toleration with religious protection, while many of their critics tried to differentiate one ideology and practice from the other.

Changing views of toleration and antisemitism transformed these ideologies from the idealistic to the practical, and even partisan, realm. Between 1880 and 1916, these frames of reference resulted in different governmental policies. In addition, local, state, and national agencies used these emerging ideologies to determine the boundaries of their own intervention and to debate their right to oversee their local institutions. These frames of reference also encouraged parliamentary and extraparliamentary groups to adapt varying political strategies. Within the ritual questions, religious toleration, like antisemitism served as a "cultural code."[4] Both ideologies allowed participants to position themselves with other groups in the political arena and to insist on their own political prestige.

This chapter examines the place of these two ideologies and practices in the local, regional, and national disputes over kosher butchering.[5] As scholars of antisemitism have shown, the presence of ideologies alone does not necessarily impact everyday life. Rhetoric can filter down to everyday life or hover in the written or spoken world with little consequence. As such, it is imperative to understand the relationship between thought and action and to chart the disconnects that often exist between an ideology and its consequences.[6] A study of the different *Ritualfragen* and their influence on their participants reveals the various means through which antisemitic ideology and issues of tolerance did

[3] On the scientific interest in the debates, particularly in the national disputes, see Efron, *Medicine and the German Jews;* Brantz, "Stunning Bodies."

[4] Shulamit Volkov, "Antisemitism as a Cultural Code: Reflections on the History and Historiography of Antisemitism in Imperial Germany," *LBIYB* 23 (1978), esp. p. 36. Also see van Rahden, "Words and Actions" and "Ideologie und Gewalt."

[5] This chapter incorporates the conflicts over circumcision when relevant. However, because fewer political disputes concerning circumcision occurred at this time, the rite plays a secondary role here.

[6] See e.g., Oded Heilbronner, "From Antisemitic Peripheries to Antisemitic Centres: The Place of Antisemitism in Modern German History," *Journal of Contemporary History* 35.4 (2000): 559–576; Till van Rahden, "Words and Actions."

or did not permeate everyday life. It allows us to "see anti-Semitism at work" and at rest.[7]

Rethinking Religious Toleration

The available scholarship on the German campaigns against kosher butchering and circumcision focuses on their antisemitic and scientific elements.[8] There is sufficient evidence to read the movements in this way. Antisemitic depictions of both rites materialized in joke books, novels, cartoons, medical treatises, and pamphlets. Participants drew from antisemitic rhetoric, and antisemitic organizations and individuals frequently participated in the debates. When viewed through an antisemitic lens, anxieties over Jewish ritual behavior provided a foundation for central Europe's blood libel accusations and, for a brief time, for an ideological platform for national antisemitic political movements.

Alongside antisemitism, toleration also provided an ideological underpinning to the debates. Because the proposed slaughterhouse reforms necessitated the violation of Jewish law, the growing support of animal advocacy campaigns encouraged wide discussion of the meaning of toleration and its use in creating policy. Some participants defined toleration broadly to include religious protection. In their view, state and national law demanded the safeguarding of kosher butchering, even if such protection clashed with extant practices and norms. "The State constitution guarantees Jews our religious freedom," petitioned the Prussian Jewish Federation, whose responses to the debates will be considered in the following chapter. "And the Reichstag has repeatedly stated that *shehitah* will not be banned."[9] Other contributors furthered a narrow understanding of toleration. They encouraged their governments to force Jewish compliance with new laws and therefore transgress religious beliefs. For them, public health and humanitarianism outweighed religious practice.[10] A discussant's support of animal protection did not

[7]Walser Smith, *The Butcher's Tale*, p. 23. This chapter deviates from the little extant scholarship on the ritual questions in two ways. Historians have been far more interested in the *Ritualfragen*'s intellectual history than in how that history became translated into action. Moreover, the available scholarship has centered on the place of antisemitism in the debates rather than examining the centrality of religious tolerance to the disputes.

[8]See, e.g., Levy, *The Downfall of the Anti-Semitic Parties*; Pulzer, "The Return of Old Hatreds," p. 225.

[9]1902 petition (draft) from the Prussian Jewish Federation CJA 75CGe1893.

[10]This conversation was concomitant with a second conversation, namely, whether the proposed reforms themselves were appropriate for all of Germany.

necessarily dictate his endorsement of a narrow understanding of toleration. The Reichstag deputy Leonard Hoffmann, for example, embraced a broader view of toleration in 1898 when he rejected a proposal submitted to the Reichstag that would have universally mandated the stunning of animals into states of unconsciousness before their slaughter. Hoffmann would not condone legislation that forced German Jews to violate their religious law even though he was an outspoken advocate of the new stunning technologies.[11]

In their contributions to the *Ritualfragen*, Hoffmann and others built on earlier understandings of toleration. As chapter 2 suggested, previous incarnations of toleration believed in the acknowledgment of difference, not in the embrace of deviation. Nineteenth-century actors were unlikely to insist that toleration extended to forms of behavior that diverged from acceptable norms, as illustrated by the term's use during the *Kulturkampf*. Even when proponents had used toleration to justify the removal of restrictions based on religion, they did not often argue that minority behavior deserved safeguarding because of its particularistic nature. By the turn of the century, however, a group of participants in the *Ritualfragen* increasingly argued that religious protection was a fundamental right of citizenship, an interpretation some saw as being reinforced by Title II of the Prussian constitution. The statute, which had been amended in 1898, not only guaranteed residents full freedom of belief and conscience but also promised the freedom to exercise their religious customs and laws.[12]

A number of historical phenomena encouraged gentile and Jewish participants to begin championing the protection of customs and mores that conflicted with norms and extant laws. Improvements in animal slaughter technology encouraged such a shift. These innovations made it more difficult for supporters of Jewish rites to argue for the superiority of kosher butchering over those methods that utilized new scientific advancements. Greater numbers of advocates now contended that kosher butchering needed to be safeguarded because of its religious significance, not because of its advantage over other methods. For some, then, toleration provided a way to defend kosher butchering without trying to argue for the rite's benefits. In 1900, the Prussian Royal Commission for Medical Affairs presented this vision of toleration when

[11] 1899 Reichstag Transcript, CAHJP TD 475, 7–8.

[12] 9 April 1908 letter from the Jewish community of Munich to local police authorities SM Pol Dir. München 4644; 13 June 1912 letter (no. 16.6.12/3238) from the Jewish community of Dresden to the Verband der deutschen Juden (Verband) CJA 75CVe1 341 nr. 45. See, e.g., "Aufhebung des Schächtverbotes," *Rheydter Zeitung* 136 (3 June 1906); "Die Aufhebung des Schächtverbots in Rheydt," *IDR* 7/8 (1906): 451–453; "Die Ortsstatutarischen Bestimmungen der Stadt Rheydt."

it refused to publish a defense of kosher butchering, something it had done in the past. The commission's members no longer accepted that the rite offered a superior method of animal slaughter. However, the organization would not condone the prohibition of the ritual because it believed that the law protected the toleration of religious customs.[13] Six years later, twenty-five local animal protection societies voiced analogous concerns when they rejected a proposal from their national leadership to campaign for a German ban on the slaughter of conscious animals. These advocates agreed that kosher butchering constituted a cruel form of slaughter, but they maintained that the rite needed to be tolerated.[14]

Just as technological improvements encouraged discussants to consider a more expansive understanding of toleration, so too did the proliferation and radicalization of antisemitic rhetoric and sentiment. Ironically, as some critics disputed the growing German-Jewish presence in the body politic, defenders of Jewish ritual behavior were forced to insist on Jewry's right to take part in society and to do so on their own terms. The act of Jewish defense necessitated an admission of Jewish particularity: The new definition of toleration justified Jewish difference and provided the means for its protection. Opponents of kosher butchering also attempted to use the language of tolerance in their debates. Trying to distance themselves from the radicalism of antisemitism, they painted themselves as "tolerant" and argued against the state's "toleration" of fundamentally "intolerant" acts.[15]

Finally, the German constitution's puzzling formulation concerning the rights of religious minorities prompted discussion about the relationship between tolerance and protection. The constitution that united Germany in 1871 inconsistently stipulated that states dictated religious policy; that such guidelines could not be used to enshrine discrimination against religious minorities; and that Christianity constituted the normative religion of the German states. At various points during the Kaiserreich (German Empire, 1871–1918), this strange formulation encouraged national and state leaders to look to the Reichstag and Bundesrat—the parliamentary bodies enshrined with the responsibility of proposing new national regulations—to establish a single policy concerning religious tolerance. The ritual questions afforded these individuals the opportunity to clarify the constitution's position on religious

---

[13]"Hochgeehrter Herr!"; 5 November 1907 minutes of the *shehitah* commission meeting CJA 75Dco128 233.

[14]1906 minutes of the TSV Meeting CJA 75Cve1 344 154.

[15]"Zur Schächtfrage," *DT* (17 October 1911): CJA 75CVe1 nr 340. Also see "Einspruch gegen die Aufhebung des Schächtverbots," *DNN* (19 December 1910): CJA 75CVe1344 436; Alter Tierschutzverein Dresden, "Aufruf," *Dresdener Anzeiger* (*DA*) (21 July 1911): CJA 75 C Ve1 340; W. Back, *Schächten Oder Betäuben?* p. 23.

protection and toleration. Within the deliberations, contributors asked whether religious toleration should be defined narrowly or broadly and whether national policy on religious tolerance superseded state jurisdiction over religious institutions.

Between 1881 and 1916, the presence of conflicting visions of toleration and of antisemitism influenced more than the deliberations' rhetoric. They resulted in different policy implications at the national, state, and local levels and in the embrace of varying political strategies by extraparliamentary and parliamentary groups.

Toleration, Antisemitism, and the National *Ritualfragen*

Four national debates offered participants an opportunity to use the discourses of antisemitism and toleration when debating the acceptability of kosher butchering and the appropriate policies that would govern the rite. In 1886–1887 and in 1898–1899, Reichstag deputies considered petitions that, if passed, would have made the slaughter of conscious animals a punishable offense under animal cruelty laws. In 1905, dozens of animal protection societies launched a third national political dispute when they met in Nuremberg to plan a campaign to coordinate local prohibitions of kosher butchering. Soon after the campaign folded, the German Center Party (Deutsche Zentrumspartei) unleashed a fourth national debate when it proposed an amendment to the Reichstag to make it illegal to ban ritual behavior. Animal advocates responded by encouraging parliament to institute a higher financial penalty on animal cruelty, whose definition they hoped would extend to kosher butchering.

Anti-Jewish themes inevitably impacted each national dispute concerning kosher butchering. Several Reichstag deputies and lobbyists drew from the chauvinistic discourses of the time to coarsely promote the notion of a Jewish obsession with knives and blood and the belief that German Jews existed outside of political and social norms. A number of the individuals who championed the animal protectionist bills were self-identified antisemites.[16] In addition, local and national newspapers covered these charges and their campaigns, thus bringing the national debates to the attention of German readers nationwide. Despite the presence of antisemitic rhetoric, however, the national animal protection campaigns failed to result in a countrywide ban on or a dramatic restriction of kosher butchering. Instead, until

[16]1899 Reichstag transcript CAHJP TD 475, 1–2.

1933, the only national campaign concerning kosher butchering that materialized into a change in policy was the Center Party amendment designed to safeguard the rite.[17] Understandings of toleration, then, and not antisemitism, became translated directly into policy within the national disputes.

The Center Party's attempt to legislate toleration was a result of its encounter with almost two decades of anti-Catholic legislation and animus, as well as Germany's unclear constitutional formulation concerning the protection of religious difference. Center Party members wished to resolve this constitutional dilemma by enshrining a broader understanding of toleration into law. These deputies did not simply speak in favor or against the petitions concerning animal slaughter. Instead, they embraced one of three strategies, which called for the adaptation of the proposed animal advocacy bills, the promotion of a toleration amendment, or the embrace of legislation that would safeguard religious behavior.

In order to advance a more inclusive interpretation of toleration, Center Party leaders attempted to change the wording of the animal protectionist recommendations. Center Party leaders expressed concern that the animal advocacy amendments as currently framed would have long-lasting implications for all religious minorities. As such, they requested that the legislation be adapted to exempt Jewish communities from its purview. The bills therefore still would call for the stunning of animals before slaughter, but they would include an exception for German Jewry and thus recognize the sanctity of religious behavior. According to Center Party leader Ludwig Windthorst, the state had the responsibility to protect the rights of a religious minority and to "safeguard the ancient beliefs of the religion of our Jewish citizens from interference."[18] In successive *Ritualfragen* in 1886–1887 and 1898–1899, Windthorst and his successor, Ernst Phillip Lieber, championed adaptations to the proposed animal advocacy bills. If they had passed they would have established a legal precedent for an expansive application of tolerance throughout the Reich.[19]

Representatives from across party lines expressed unease with the legal implications of the proposed modifications and the expansive definition of tolerance put forth by the Center Party leadership. However they concomitantly invoked toleration to advance their position.

---

[17]This would be one way in which the imperial debates would differ from those of the Weimar era. During the latter period, national and state campaigns resulted in restrictions on the rite but not a national ban. On the Weimar debates, see chapter 6.

[18]*Aus den Verhandlungen des Deutschen Reichstags über das Schächten (18. Mai 1887, 25. April 1899, und 9. Mai 1899)* (Berlin: n.p., 1909), p. 3.

[19]*Aus den Verhandlungen des Deutschen Reichstags über das Schächten*, pp. 3–4.

The Reichstag's moderate and progressive Liberal deputies leaders rejected both the proposed animal protectionist bills and the Center Party's suggested modifications. Championing a narrower understanding of tolerance, the Liberal leadership distinguished tolerance from religious protection. In their view, toleration simply assured nondiscrimination, which is why they voted against the animal protectionist bill. They opposed legislating religious protection because it allowed for religious particularities to supersede state objectives. That is also why they opposed the Center Party modifications in 1887 and again in 1898. Liberal leader Johannes von Miquel warned his colleagues against the dangers of enshrining religious protection into law. In his view Germany's "principles of tolerance and reciprocal respect among German citizens" sufficiently protected Jewish communal practices; anything more would interfere with a state's ability to govern.[20] Ten years later, Liberal deputy Heinrich Rickert sidestepped any discussion about kosher butchering but insisted that religious protection "was not so simple" as Lieber had implied. Despite his position as one of the heads of the League to Combat Antisemitism, he similarly thwarted Center Party efforts to create a policy that would mandate religious protection.[21] The Liberal leadership's position on the kosher butchering question reflected its larger stance on issues of integration and nondiscrimination. The party acknowledged diversity and promised the absence of prejudice, but it hoped that minorities would abandon their particularities and embrace the cultural norm.

Conservative party members similarly opposed the Center Party's attempt to introduce and enforce a broader understanding of toleration. Like their more liberal colleagues, Conservative deputies also distinguished between religious protection—which they defined as the extension of particular treatment because of religious belief—and toleration. Their understanding of toleration differed from the portrait furthered by either the Liberal or Center Party leadership. Indicative of their unyielding position on issues of difference, the Conservatives did not envision toleration as an assurance of nondiscrimination but as an acknowledgment of difference. Not all Conservative leaders, however, supported a ban on kosher butchering. In fact, a few rejected the animal protectionist bill because they believed it would have singled out the Jewish minority or because they preferred the slaughter of conscious animals.[22] However, Conservative deputies unanimously opposed any bill that enshrined religious protection over state law. In

[20]Ibid., pp. 4–5, 7 (quote from 7).

[21]Ibid., p. 6.

[22]Ibid., p. 8. Christoph Willners von Tiedemann of the German Reich Party maintained that *shehitah* was humane and voted accordingly.

his public testimony on the Reichstag floor, the conservative deputy George Oertel strongly argued against the suggestion that religious protection ought to be legislated in some way. For Oertel, religious protection mocked the cultural values and institutions of the new Germany. It allegedly would make the execution of state objectives more difficult and elevate the needs of a religious minority over that of state and society.[23]

After the turn of the century, Catholic Center Party leaders adopted two new strategies to promote an expansive understanding of religious toleration. In 1900, they crafted a "Tolerance Bill," which they introduced at intervals over the next nineteen years. This proposed law enshrined a broad image of toleration by guaranteeing complete freedom of religious activity to all religious minorities. Toleration, then, would become synonymous with religious protection. Like its engagement with the slaughterhouse laws, the Center Party's drafting of the Tolerance Bill was not merely an altruistic maneuver. Indeed, had it passed, the bill would have also effectively repealed the remaining anti-Jesuit laws from the *Kulturkampf* and established a legal precedent for the protection of Catholic religious rights. It failed because most Reichstag deputies continued to be unwilling to enshrine toleration in the form of protection. Moreover, as historian Michael Gross has suggested, anti-Catholicism was absolutely central to Liberal ideology and identity. Even if, by the early 1900s, Liberals had supported the notion of religious protection, the freedoms that such a bill would have allotted to Catholics made the proposal unpalatable.[24]

By 1907, some members of the Center Party began to approach the topic of religious protection and toleration somewhat differently. When it became clear that the Tolerance Bill would fail on the Reichstag floor, Center Party deputy Adolf Gröber proposed another piece of legislation that would have similar ends. Unlike the more open-ended Tolerance Bill, Gröber's proposition (Absatz 3 §360) specifically targeted animal slaughter. Framed as a reform of the Reich's penal code, it outlawed "state regulations that interfere with the ritual prescriptions of any religious group in the matter of animal slaughtering."[25] Absatz 3 §360 did not enshrine religious protection in all cases. Instead, it limited its purview to the abattoir and, if expanded, to the creation of regulations that forced the transgression of religious dictates.

[23]Ibid. Also see Froelich, *Das Schächten*, p. 6.
[24]Gross, *War Against Catholicism.*
[25]Graef, 1911 Speech CJA 75Dco1 29 1–8. Also, see, "Die Strafgesetznovelle (Schächtparagraph)," *DIZ* 49 (1911): 19; "Zur Schächtdebatte im Reichstage," *DIZ* 3 (1911): 1–2; F. Rosenthal, "Zu dem Antrage Gröber," *Lehrerheim* 52 (1910): 515–516; Y., "Die Schächtfrage im Reichstag," *IG* 3 (1911): 23–24.

A group of National Liberals and Conservatives opposed Gröber's bill on three grounds. They maintained that toleration established an undesirable legal precedent; that kosher butchering was cruel; and that it made little sense for the state to protect kosher butchering at the expense of animals or the state's authority because the majority of Jews allegedly no longer practiced the rite. Opponents of the Jewish rite had uttered the latter justification with greater frequency.[26] Similar to critics who previously had held that Jewish rites lacked religious import, detractors now argued that the majority of Jews failed to maintain a level of observance. In their view, it was unnecessary for the state to create policies to protect the religious particularities of a small minority. Such a rationalization neatly justified their opposition to religious protection without seemingly appearing to harbor any anti-Jewish animus. Moreover, it contained an element of truth. Greater numbers of Jews no longer observed the dietary laws, an issue of tremendous concern for the traditional Jewish leadership.[27]

It was significant that the opposition to Absatz 3 §360 included National Liberals alongside Conservatives. By 1910, Liberals had demonstrated internal divisions over their support of the Jewish rite and over their stance on religious toleration. As a few Progressive Liberals called for enshrining religious protection into law, other National Liberals promoted legislation that would mandate the use of stunning technologies. Rejecting earlier Liberal utterances of nondiscrimination, they increasingly expressed concern with kosher butchering's allegedly cruel nature and small following. In his opposition to Gröber's bill, for example, Rudolf Karl Heinze, a National Liberal deputy from Dresden, emphasized the brutality of the Jewish rite and warned against creating a legal precedent in which religious beliefs trumped state objectives. W. Back, a National Liberal Reichstag candidate from Strassburg, voiced a similar concern. When he ran for a seat in the Reichstag, he spoke about his opposition to stunning-less slaughter and his discomfort with efforts to enshrine religious protection into law.[28]

This split among Liberal party members over kosher butchering was illustrative of larger historical phenomena, including the normalization of conservative platforms, the decline of liberal political power, and the

[26]Carl Mittermaier, *Das Schlachten geschildert und erläutert auf Grund zahlreicher neuerer Gutachten* (Heidelberg: Carl Winter's Universitätsbuchhandlung, 1902), p. 5; quote by Karl Kramer, in Hartmann, ed., *Bericht über die neunte Versammlung*, p. 60.

[27]On the place of this line of thinking in the Jewish self-defense campaigns, see chapter 5.

[28]Back envisioned restrictions that would allow Jewish communities some access to kosher butchering but that would reduce the total amount of kosher slaughter that took place. Back, *Schächten Oder Betäuben?*

disconnect between national movements and their local politicians. Liberal politicians, such as Back, may have felt more comfortable championing a ban on kosher butchering because right-leaning platforms and conservative measures had become increasingly accepted. In the 1880s most national politicians perceived *Schächtverbot* proposals as maneuvers of the antisemitic right. By the turn of the twentieth century, however, many Liberals interpreted the *Schächtfrage* as a valid political question. In addition, it is possible that some Liberal leaders may have seen a strong stance in the ritual questions as one antidote to the decline of liberal political power. Liberals experienced a slow decline after their parties were unable to ensure domestic stability and quickly seize the public's distaste for the political sphere. Now, with the additional threat of strengthening Socialist and Conservative power, these leaders may have envisioned a Liberal rejection of a Jewish religious rite as a means of demonstrating Liberal political viability. Finally, the split among liberal parties demonstrated the disjuncture between national movements and their local politicians and institutions. Unlike a number of national leaders, Back felt comfortable using kosher butchering as a stamp of his cultural identity, in part because of the conservative culture of his community of Strassburg.[29]

Despite the resistance to Gröber's bill, by 1910 there was sufficient representation within the Reichstag on the left to support it. A coalition of Socialist, Progressive Liberal, National Liberal, and Center Party deputies pushed the bill through with a small but adequate majority. Perhaps the bill passed because in the aftermath of repeated attempts by the Center Party to champion the Tolerance Bill, left-liberal deputies were willing to accept the protection of the Jewish community instead of the Catholic minority. It also is possible that now that the Tolerance Bill had failed, the Liberal leadership was less concerned over the legal precedent of Gröber's bill. Willing to grant some kind of exemption to the Jewish community, they approved the new legislation, which circumscribed exceptional treatment within strict boundaries. Finally, perhaps Absatz 3 §360 succeeded because municipalities, regional courts, and state governments already had issued similar promulgations. They had been debating the ritual question continuously during the previous three decades. Since the Reichstag previously had extended no clear mandate concerning religious protection and toleration, individual state governments and municipalities had been left to determine their own policies concerning toleration and the degree to which they wished to implement the period's anti-Jewish charges.

[29]Strassburg also was home to a significant-sized Jewish community. For an earlier discussion, see Paula E. Hyman, *The Emancipation of the Jews in Alsace: Acculturation and Tradition in the Nineteenth Century* (New Haven: Yale University Press, 1991).

The Municipal and State Debates

As the national parliament debated kosher butchering, German local, regional, and state governments simultaneously considered slaughterhouse reforms that, similar to the national bills, would have outlawed kosher butchering. The participants of these other deliberations similarly reflected on the meaning of religious protection and toleration, the objectives of government, and the period's antisemitic ideology and rhetoric.

There were significant differences between the national and local debates. First, municipalities engaged in a greater number of disputes concerning kosher butchering than the Reichstag did.[30] While the national parliament entertained four bills concerning the Jewish rite, dozens of German cities and villages considered similar proposals numerous times. Such frequency lay in the fact that German towns were responsible for their municipal institutions, such as the abattoir, and for their sanitation services. As municipal responsibilities and infrastructure grew with mobility, urban growth, and Germany's rapid industrialization, greater number of cities and towns expressed interest with their local slaughterhouses and with their Jewish population.[31] These dramatic changes pressured municipalities to expand their traditional responsibilities and to develop new regulatory and service agencies.[32] Of course, rural councils were not immune from these shifts. Towns and villages experienced similar, if less swift, bureaucratization in the late nineteenth and early twentieth century. Many of the municipalities examined here were quite small but expressed concern with the every day practices in their abattoirs.[33]

Second, until the Gröber amendment the national leadership passed neither the animal protectionist proposals nor the bills intended to protect the Jewish community. Because of this legislative absence,

[30] This is one of the points where Brantz and I diverge. Brantz, "Stunning Bodies."

[31] For an excellent study of this growth, see Horst Matzerath, "Städtwachstum und Eingemeindungen im 19. Jahrhundert," in *Die deutsche Stadt im Industriezeitalter*, pp. 67–89. Jews also experienced urbanization during the Kaiserreich. By 1918, over half of Germany's Jews lived in cities of more than one hundred thousand inhabitants, as opposed to only 20 percent of the larger population. Monika Richarz, "Demographic Developments," in *German-Jewish History in Modern Times*, vol. 3, pp. 7–34.

[32] Wolfgang Köllmann, "Von der Bürgerstadt zur Regional-'Stadt': Über einige Formwandlungen der Stadt in der deutschen Geschichte," in Jürgen Reulecke, ed., *Die deutsche Stadt im Industriezeitalter* (Wuppertal: Peter Hammer, 1978), pp. 15–30.

[33] In 1871 70 percent of Jews were living in villages and towns with less than 20,000 residents; by 1910 this percentage had shrunk to 32 percent. Richarz, "Demographic Developments," p. 24.

municipal and state leaders had the freedom and opportunity to translate into policy ideas concerning religious protection and Jewish cruelty. Few local communities banned or dramatically restricted kosher butchering during the 1880s but between 1890 and 1916, over twenty-two German municipalities and one German state prohibited kosher butchering altogether.[34] Over thirty other communities restricted the Jewish rite slightly, while dozens of other town councils instituted more drastic reforms.[35] Finally, larger numbers of communities rejected animal protectionist proposals and formally exempted Jewish customs from their municipal laws.[36]

As local and state participants considered these proposals and requests for exemptions, they simultaneously invoked religious protection and Jewish deviancy as frames of reference. Reichstag deputies tended to downplay the anti-Jewish rhetoric of the debates and focused instead on issues concerning religious protection, toleration, medicine, and hygiene. Participants in the local and state disputes were more likely to express and act on concerns with Jewish cruelty, economic greed, and political deviance as they concomitantly weighed the benefits and meaning of toleration. Their formulations were instrumental in constructing policies concerning minority integration and also allowed governmental agencies the opportunity to delineate the boundaries of their own authority and the limits on the jurisdiction of others.

Influenced by anxieties over animal mistreatment and Jewish cruelty, municipalities and state governments composed and passed bans on kosher butchering despite the clear interference with Jewish tradition. In drafting its 1894 *Schächtverbot*, Vienna's slaughterhouse commission justified its disregard of religious toleration in order to rid the local

[34]Although Braunschweig also mandated the stunning of animals before their slaughter, it allowed for local councils to exempt Jewish communities from the law's purview.

[35]These severe reforms dramatically reduced the number of cattle that Jewish communities could slaughter and the times when that slaughter could take place. Some also set exorbitant taxes on the rite and prohibited Jewish communities from hiring new *shohetim*. In smaller communities, the latter restriction was onerous because it meant that the affected Jewish community council could not replace the practitioner who had retired or fell ill. See, e.g., "Aufhebung des Schächtverbotes"; "Die Aufhebung des Schächtverbots in Rheydt"; "Die ortsstatutarischen Bestimmungen der Stadt Rheydt"; "Ueber das Schächt-Urtheil des Oberverwaltungsgerichts," *IDR* 3 (1901): 141–54.

[36]Whether these political debates resulted in a ban on the rite or its exemption, they proceeded with a familiar sequence of events. Slaughterhouse directors, either on their own or influenced by their local animal protection societies, proposed an abolition of or restriction on stunning-less slaughter. After the slaughterhouse commission approved such a law, it would go to the town council and to the magistrate for approval. The Jewish community would appeal, sometimes with favorable results.

abattoir of "extreme cruelty."[37] That commission members would embrace a ban on kosher butchering or that they would invoke charges of Jewish brutality was not surprising. During the last decades of the nineteenth century, Vienna, whose Jewish population was proportionately higher than in any other major German city, had become a center of militant antisemitism. An anti-Liberal, antisemitic presence now had increasingly influenced its associational life and its city politics, which once had been dominated by a Liberal oligarchy. Five years later, Potsdam's town council echoed the Vienna commission. Despite vehement claims from Jewish activists that the local ban on kosher butchering constituted a "rape of the [Jewish] beliefs,"[38] proponents cited the "unnecessary cruelty towards animals" as reason for its passage.[39] None of these officials referred to the Jews who practiced these rites as cruel, yet their utilization of the term "quälerei" (cruelty) to refer to kosher butchering's horrific nature portrayed the ritual as something demonic. Its brutality necessitated intervention.[40]

Other municipal promulgations similarly translated antisemitic rhetoric into policy and provided a clear rationalization for the violation of Jewish tradition. Despite the fact that Judaism itself prohibits the ingestion of blood, a number of cities specifically prohibited Jews

[37]2 April 1894 letter to the Jewish communities of Austria from the Jewish community of Vienna CAHJP A/W 1388 2. The commission's use of "cruelty" as a justification continued through the early twentieth century. "Ein Schächtverbot in Aussicht," *Ibis* (1899); *Antrag des Landeskulturausschusses, IX Wahlperiode, II. Session: 235/Praes/Lds. Kult. A. 22* CAHJP A/W 1388 14; "Eine Aktion gegen das rituelle Schächten," *Neue Freie Presse* (*NFP*) (8 November 1904): 3–4; 27 December 1905 letter from Karl Lueger to the Jewish community of Vienna CAHJP A/W 1389 and A/W 1388 14; "Das Schächtverbot des Wiener Gemeinderates," *Deutsches Volksblatt* (*DV*) (6 November 1907) CJA 75CVE1344 152; "Gemeinde-Angelegenheiten," *DV* (6 December 1907) CJA 75CVE1344 152. For other examples of cruelty's use, see 18 February 1891 statement by the mayor of Erfurt CJA 75aEr1 96 24; "Die Politik: Versuchtes Schächtverbot," *Israelitische Wochenschrift* (*IW*) 11 (March 1899): 164; "Korrespondenzen, Berlin," *IDR* 6/7(1901); "Das Schächtverbot in Angermünde," *DIZ* (June 9 1911) CJA 75CVe1 340; "Angermünde, Brdbg," *JR* 19 (May 1911) CJA 75CVe1 340 308; 8 February 1913 letter from the Royal Government of Upper Bavaria to the magistrate of Munich ALM SUV 90; 10 December 1912 letter from the Government of Middle Franconia ALM SUV 90.

[38]"Korrespondenzen, Berlin" *IDR* 1(1905): 34.

[39]Robert Kaelter, *Geschichte der Jüdischen Gemeinde zu Potsdam*, trans. Julius H. Schopes and Hermann Simon, reprint ed. (1903; repr., Berlin: Edition Hentrich, 1993), p. 100; "Ein Schächtverbot," *RDG* 10 (15 May 1901): 78; "Potsdam," *AZDJ* 26 (1901): 2–3; "Potsdam, 27 Februar (Agitation Gegen Das Schächten)," *IW* 9 (1899): 140; "Potsdam, 10 Februar," *IDR* 2(1905).

[40]Moreover, other participants would champion the passage of these rites as proof of Jewish cruelty. See, e.g., von Schwartz, *Das Betäubungslose Schächten*; "Der Alte Tierschutzverein" *DN* (30 November 1911) CJA 75Cve1 341 43.

from benefiting from the blood of slaughter. In Munich, Dresden, Halberstadt, and elsewhere, local authorities forbade Jews from eating or using the blood in any way, including the sale of blood for the purposes of making blood sausage.[41] Economic concerns that Jews profited from animal slaughter motivated other regulations. Several municipal councils in Saxony, Prussia, and Bavaria restricted the time, amount, and place of kosher butchering and also taxed it at a higher rate. This type of legislation became increasingly common in communities where participants had charged that Jews butchered animals in disproportionate numbers to non-Jews. The Bamberg, Dresden, and Leipzig town councils taxed kosher butchering at such a high rate that it became difficult to practice the rite; these municipalities also severely restricted the times when kosher butchering could take place.[42] The municipal government of the Rhine town of Rheydt extended this concern further when it banned the rite. According to some town council members, a combination of avarice and cruelty motivated Jews to butcher more animals than needed.[43]

As these municipal agencies justified their interventions on the supposed violence and economics of the practice, others promulgated measures that focused on the brutality of the practitioners themselves. Some communities passed laws, which, similar to the legislation of the unification period, refused to allow kosher butchers also to serve as teachers. According to this view, anyone who chose to butcher animals without previously stunning them posed a social and moral threat to his students.[44] Others used animal cruelty laws to penalize specific *shohetim* whom they believed to be particularly brutal. In January 1901, for example, the Munich police charged the kosher butcher Ruhland with animal cruelty, after local protectionists had alerted them of this specific butcher's supposed proclivity for brutality. Supposedly when Ruhland slaughtered an animal, "something would go so wrong" that the animal

[41] 12 May 1896 Munich regulations concerning the blood of slaughtered animals StM SUV 7; Halberstadt slaughterhouse regulations CJA 75Cge1893 32–4; 7 December 1910 police laws concerning the blood of animals CJA 75CVe1344 445; "Zur Schächtfrage" *Das Recht* (15 October 1905) CJA 75DCo128 66; "Eine neue Polizeiverordnung über das Schächten," *DT* 13 (December 1910), CJA 75CVe1344 423; "Mit der Schlachtmethode." *NAZ* April 22 (1909), CJA 75CVe1 nr. 159; "Ueber das Schächt-Urtheil des Oberverwaltungsgerichts," *IDR* 2 (1901): 141–154.

[42] 12 May 1905 letter to the city council from Werner CAHJP BII3; "Sitzung der Stadverordneten," *Leipziger Tageblatt* (23 February 1911). The Viennese government also passed high tariffs "Ein Attentat auf unsere Gewissensfreiheit" *JV* (27 February 1914).

[43] "Doppelte Schlachtgebühr fürs Schächten," *Rundschau für Fleischbeschau* (RF) 14 (15 July 1902): 137.

[44] 19 April 1914 Darmstadt letter from magistrate; also see, "Seid barmherzig—auch beim Schlachten der Thiere," *BTV* (188?) 1–2.

would remain conscious despite the fact that his trachea would be in many pieces all over the slaughterhouse floor.[45] Although the Munich law and a similar one like it in Berlin avoided any reference to kosher butchering as brutal, these animal cruelty promulgations depicted ritual practitioners in a negative light, thus reflecting poorly on Jewish ritual behavior and rationalizing governmental interference.[46]

In many of these cases, the municipalities (in and outside of Prussia) that prohibited or dramatically restricted kosher butchering justified their regulations by pointing to three Prussian statutes: (1) an 1889 law that mandated the prevention of animal cruelty; (2) a 1901 high court decision that granted local municipalities the jurisdiction to grant exemptions from normative slaughterhouse laws; and (3) the 1868 and 1881 slaughterhouse laws that granted local municipalities the authority to determine how slaughter would be done.[47] Yet, there were other links that bound them as well. Many of the turn-of-the-century ordinances examined here originated in cities and towns whose Jewish communities had grown exponentially during the late nineteenth century with the immigration of foreign-born Jews. Antisemitic agitation during this time had been directed against these Jews who had settled in communities with a large Jewish presence. By 1910 over 50 percent of the Jews living in Dresden, a city that witnessed several anti-kosher butchering initiatives, were foreign born; Munich, which also had issued regulations concerning *shehitah*, contained a Jewish community with 34.8 percent non-native German Jews.[48] Moreover, Prussian towns and cities, particularly those in the Rhine and Brandenburg provinces, tended to pass a greater number of bans and dramatic restrictions on kosher butchering than municipalities in Bavaria or Baden did, reflecting, perhaps, the hold and influence there of Christian antisemitism and of the strong presence and influence of small merchant and shopkeeper associations.

Yet, despite the existence of these municipalities that embraced restrictive legislation, other governmental agencies—sometimes within the same locality—offered contradictory views, rejecting any law that

[45] 18 September 1901 letter from the Munich TSV to the local magistrate ALM SUV 91. "Allgemeine Münchener Chronik," *Der Bayerische Metzgermeister* 46 (18 November 1902); January 1901 letter from the Munich TSV to the magistrate and his 29 January 1901 response ALM SUV 91.

[46] "Unter der Anklage der Tierquälerei," *Berliner Tageblatt* 175 (1910).

[47] A. Bundle, "Zur Schächtfrage," *RDG* (July 1 1901); "Die Politik: Versuchtes Schächtverbot" *IW* (March 17 1899); "Ein Schächtverbot" *RDG* (15 May 1901). Also see later references to this line of thinking in "Zum Schächtverbot," *Tages-Zeitung* (Potsdam) (10 May 1909) CJA 75ve1340 212; "Das Schächtverbot in Angermünde," *DIZ* (June 9 1911) CJA 75CVe1 340; 15 July 1912 letter from the Centralverein to Elb CJA 75CVe1 341 no 77–82. Also see 24 June 1912 letter from Loewenthal to Elb CJA 75CVe1341 74–5.

[48] Richarz, "Demographic Developments," pp. 20–21.

forced the violation of Jewish tradition and practices. Town councils in cities as geographically diverse as Düsseldorf, Kattowitz, and Bremen exempted Jewish communities from their abattoir reforms that otherwise would have compelled the transgression of kosher butchering.[49] Their exemptions explicitly engaged with the question of toleration and protection. In 1907, for example, Bremen's slaughterhouse commission eventually determined that religious freedom outweighed concerns over animal cruelty. After considerable debate, the majority of slaughterhouse commission members drafted a report in which they argued that the senate had to create an exception from its pending slaughterhouse laws for Jews because they only ate meat from ritually slaughtered animals. "Jews can only consume the meat from warm blooded animals when those animals are not stunned," they reported, "We need, then, to consider the spiritual health of the Jews."[50] That same year, Munich town council members expressed similar beliefs when they rejected a proposal that would have stricken the exclusion of kosher butchering from the city's abattoir laws. Local authorities not only preserved the exemption clause but also met with Jewish community leaders and butchers to discuss the new regulations and to assure them that the community could continue its practices without interference.[51]

To ensure religious protection, authorities in Munich and elsewhere looked to a number of different legal precedents, including Germany's alleged legacy of religious freedom and the Prussian constitution's 1853 mandate that public institutions be accessible to all citizens.[52] The magistrate of Rheydt invoked the former and latter when he overturned a local ban on kosher butchering. According to the magistrate, kosher

---

[49]Although Kattowitz and Düsseldorf exempted Jews immediately after the law's passage, Bremen and Munich witnessed considerable debate before they granted the exceptions. §7-§9 police regulations concerning the public slaughterhouse of Kattowitz CJA 75DCo128 6–8; "Kein Schächtverbot" *Ibis* 28 (June 1899): 71; 1885 Grünstadt slaughterhouse regulations CAHJP PF IV/29; 19 April 1893 minister of interior order no. 9940 CAHJP A/W 1388 #2; *Antrag des Landeskulturausschusses, IX Wahlperiode, II. Session: 235/Praes/Lds. Kult. A. 22* (1904) CAHJP A/W 1388 #14; May 1 1901 Halberstadt slaughterhouse regulations CJA 75CGe1893 41–47; "Mit der Schlachtmethode," *NAZ* (22 April 1909): CJA 75Ve1340 159; "Aus der Reichshauptstadt," *Tägliche Rundschau* (April 21 1909) CJA 75Ve1340 159; "Minutes of the town council meeting of 14 March 1907," *Münchener Gemeinde Zeitung (MGZ)* 22 (21 March 1907): 457–478; 27 November 1907 letter from the mayor of Würzburg to the magistrate of Munich ALM SUV 90.

[50]29 October 1907 report to the senate CJA 75CVe1344 199–200.

[51]"Minutes of the town council meeting of 14 March 1907"; 27 November 1907 letter from the magistrate of Würzburg to the magistrate of Munich ALM SUV 90. There are fewer shared characteristics among the cities and states that enacted toleration policies toward Jews.

[52]24 June 1912 letter from Loewenthal to Elb CJA 75CVe1341 74–5.

butchering "belonged to the rules of the recognized Jewish religion." As such, a prohibition of the rite "could not take place where Jews reside" particularly since the constitution assured citizens the right to participate in public institutions, including abattoirs. Saxony's minister of the interior similarly relied on an expansive understanding of religious freedoms when he repealed the two-decade-old ban in his state. Concerned that the ban on kosher butchering flew in the face of toleration as he defined it, the minister of interior assured the Jewish community that it now had the right to resume its practice of the Jewish ritual.[53]

The reversal of the Saxon ban on kosher butchering reflected the ways in which governments could translate the impulse for religious toleration into action. Yet, as the Saxon ministry promulgated the religious protection of kosher butchering, the Saxon city councils of Dresden and Leipzig passed local bans on kosher butchering, implementing much of the anti-Jewish rhetoric described above. Despite, or perhaps because of, the state's repeal of the 1894 prohibition, these town councils insisted on their jurisdiction to create policies that prevented cruelty and violated religious freedoms.[54] The Saxon *Schächtfrage* suggests that the ritual questions not only encouraged the formulation of policy concerning religious protection and Jewish cruelty but also offered an opportunity for local, regional, and state policies to delineate their authority vis-à-vis one another.

Governmental Struggles for Control

Sometimes the ritual questions served purposes other than an investigation into the behavior and rights of Jews. They encouraged town councils, magistrates, ministries, and regional parliaments to struggle for greater control. The *Ritualfragen* seemed to be most common in states, such as Saxony and Prussia, where governmental agencies commonly experienced internal debates over the right to oversee minorities and local institutions. In this way, the debates were less about

[53]20 December 1910 slaughterhouse order SHD MDI 16178 12; 11 July 1911 letter to the minister of culture no. 721 SHD MDI 16178 24. Also see March 1910 minutes of the Saxon Jewish Federation CJA 75Ve1 340 250–255.

[54]"Einspruch gegen die Aufhebung des Schächtverbots"; "Der Alte Tierschutzverein"; "Zur Schächtfrage," *DA* (3 June 1911P CJA 75CVe1 340 320; 15 September 1911 letter from Nathanson to the Verband CJA 75CVe1 341 24; January 1 1911 letter to Elb from Centralverein CJA 75CVe1344 437. In Dresden, the ban saw support from members of conservative parties, as well as local liberals and SPD representatives. Leipzig town council members and the Saxon ministers of interior and culture simultaneously entered into

toleration and deviance than over jurisdiction for determining the place of toleration and deviation in the city or state.

The multilayered and quickly developing character of German municipal and state governance encouraged these kinds of political struggles. German local governance was complicated. During the late nineteenth and early twentieth centuries, German towns were administered according to a system of representative government that had been established in Prussia in 1808. Local administrations were made up of an executive council (known as the *Magistrat* in East Prussia and Bavaria and elsewhere as the *Senat* or *Kollege*), the Mayor (or Mayors), and a town council. The executive council, which was chaired by the Mayor, carried out all imperial, state, and local laws. The representative town councils had the ability to pass laws, but only with the recommendation and approval of the executive.[55] German town councils ratified legislation, but magistrates executed or overturned them. Similarly while town councils had ultimate power in the spheres of finance, elections, the contracting of loans, and the use and disposal of public property, executive councils were responsible for all municipal institutions and enterprises. Cities and towns controlled their schools, parks, markets, savings banks, and water works; states could intervene in managing trade, licensing public employees, and crafting health regulations. Often states and local agencies differed over who could ensure the moral and physical well-being of its citizenries. Municipal practices were supposed to follow state policy; however, this did not always take place.

As mobility, urban growth, and Germany's rapid industrialization necessitated new services and regulations, competing governmental agencies laid claim to the right to control Jewish ritual behavior. Some disputes took place among local magistrates, town councils, and slaughterhouse commissions. Local abattoir reforms often originated

dialogue over the Jewish community's practice of restricting *shohetim* to Jewish slaughterers only. The Leipzig town council ironically identified this restriction as an act of discrimination against non-Jews and unsuccessfully attempted to open the practice to non-Jewish butchers. 11 July 1911 letter to the minister of culture no. 721 III L SHD MDI 16178 24.

[55]While each local administration was not identical in structure, scope, or character, they shared enough similarities that they can be examined as a group. See, e.g., the different systems described by Theodor Ilgen, "Organisation der staatlichen Verwaltung und der Selbstverwaltung," in *Die Rheinprovinz 1815–1915: Hundert Jahre preußischer Herrschaft am Rhein*, ed. Joseph Hansen, vol. 1. (Bonn: A. Marcus & E. Webers Verlag, 1917), pp. 87–148; Wolfgang Hofmann, "Preußische Stadtverordnetenversammlungen als Repräsentativ-Organe," in Jürgen Reulecke, ed., *Die deutsche Stadt im Industriezeitalter* (Wuppertal: Peter Hammer, 1978), pp. 31–55.

with the locally appointed slaughterhouse commissions, although in some exceptions it came out of recommendations by local police who were influenced by the their findings.[56] Although slaughterhouse commissions frequently represented the interests of the councils that appointed them, these local agencies might disagree with them over methods and goals. In 1903, for example, slaughterhouse commissions in Perleberg (Brandenburg, Prussia) and Quedlinburg (Sachsen, Prussia) individually proposed regulations that included provisions mandating the stunning of animals into a state of unconsciousness before their slaughter and rejected any exemptions. The town councils in both locales rebuffed these reforms, demanding an exemption for the Jews. Thus the councils held an expansive view of religious toleration, while the slaughterhouse commissions warned against the danger of weighing religious particularities more heavily than the implementation of social norms.[57]

A second debate took place between town councils and magistrates, each of which claimed jurisdiction over the regulation of Jewish ritual behavior. Here, however, there was no consistent argument. In some cases, executive councils promoted laws that required the stunning of animals before slaughter, while town councils protested such promulgations. In the small communities of Soest (Westphalia), Küstrin (Brandenburg), Sorau (Brandenburg), and Hanau (Nassau-Hesse), for example, local magistrates endorsed prohibitions on kosher butchering despite the disapproval of their town councils. In the view of these councils, the mandatory stunning laws not only interfered with Jewish religious freedom but also exaggerated the diminished authority of the local representative bodies. Insisting on their ultimate authority to execute local

[56]The Erfurt police and the Harburg police crafted such recommendations in 1885 and 1893. 31 May 1886 police statement concerning slaughterhouse recommendations CJA 75aEr1 97 1.

[57]"Korrespondenzen, Perleberg," *IDR* 12 (1903): 730; "Quedlinburg," *AZDJ* 2 (1904): 2; "Quedlinburg, 3 Januar," *IDR* 1 (1904): 38; 15 July 1912 letter from the Centralverein to Elb CJA 75CVe1 341 77–82. Similar disputes took place in Marienwerder and Danzig in 1894, Obschon Treptow in 1908, Hamburg and Stuttgart in 1909, Düsseldorf in 1910, and Hamburg again in 1913. "Amtliche Bekanntmachungen der Behörden," *Danziger Intelligenz-Blatt* 138 (25 May 1893): 1; "Marienwerder," *Der Jüdische Kantor Kultusbeamten-Zeitung* (*JK*) 16 (4 May 1894): 93; "Danzig," *JK* (22 June 1894): 130; June 30 1908 letter to Verband from Goldschmidt CJA 75CVe1344 379; "Hannover, Die Schächtgegner an Der Arbeit," *IF* (29 July 1909): 5; 22 May 1909 letter to Verband from Fränkel CJA 75CVe1344 414; "Stuttgart, 12 August," *Der Israelit* (19 August 1909) CJA 75Ve1340 208; Minutes of the 25 September 1913 meeting of the Verband CJA 75CVe1 341 11; "Hamburger Schlachthofsorger," *IF* (24 July 1913): CJA 75CVe1341 166. These do not include those more common conflicts when town councils and magistrates were divided over the *Schächtfrage*.

laws, magistrates validated council complaints when they paid them little heed.[58] In these cases, magistrates and mayors implemented the bans on kosher butchering. Elsewhere, however, town councils recommended mandatory stunning laws, which magistrates then overturned. Often town councils tried to reinstate these laws, either by passing them again or by appealing to state governments for permission to force the violation of Jewish religious custom. In 1899, 1903, and 1905, for example, Potsdam's town council repeatedly promulgated *Schächtverbote* after local magistrates rejected the newly passed abattoir regulations. The city's *Schächtverbot* controversies quieted somewhat after the magistrate finally approved the ban in 1905.[59]

Local disputes among magistrates and town councils tended to occur mostly in Prussia, where two-thirds of German Jewry resided. A number of factors may account for this. First, Prussian town councils had the least opportunity to be representative or proactive. Berlin, for example, should have had a council of 300 with its population of over 2 million, but it had only 144 members. The municipal ordinance for the Rhine province had an even lower ratio.[60] Perhaps town councils used the *Schächtfragen* as ways to buttress their power, while the executive bodies utilized the debates to maintain the power disadvantage of their local representative bodies. Second, unlike in other German states, members of the Center and Socialist parties could not serve in a Prussian executive council (or mayoral position). Center and Socialist parties tended to support some kind of religious freedom, and their absence from executive councils had a negative impact on some kosher butchering debates.[61] Third, the multiethnic and religious character

[58]They did pay greater attention when the town councils appealed to the Prussian state. See "Sorau," *IDR* 7/8 (1904): 427–428; "Cüstrin," *IDR* 12 (1906): 22; Hanau a.M," *IDR* 1 and 2 (1910): 32, 111.

[59]Potsdam finally justified the prohibition then because allegedly only 34 of the 442 of the city's Jewish families kept kosher. "Die Politik: Die Antisemiten über den Reichstag und der Schächtantrag der Antisemiten," *IW* 11 and 21 (1899): 164, 324; "Die Vorbereitungen zum Schächten," *AZDJ* 3 (1905): 21–22+; "Korrespondenzen, Berlin," *IDR* 1 (1905): 34; "Potsdam," *IDR* 2 (1905): 101–102; "Potsdam," *IDR* 2 (1910): 100–105; Froelich, *Das Schächten*. According to a list of members from 1902, however, there were only 127 voting members of the synagogue community in Potsdam, many of whom did keep kosher, as well as eastern European Jews who were not members but presumably followed Jewish dietary rules. Kaelter, *Geschichte der jüdischen Gemeinde zu Potsdam*, pp. 55–57.

[60]William Harbutt Dawson, *Municipal Life and Government in Germany* (London: Longmans, Green, 1916), pp. 52–53; Friedrich Lenger, "Bürgertum und Stadtverwaltung in Rheinischen Grossstädten des 19. Jahrhunderts: zu einem vernachlässigten Aspekt bürgerlicher Herrschaft," in *Stadt und Bürgertum im 19. Jahrhundert*, ed. Lothar Gall (Munich: R. Oldenbourg, 1990), pp. 97–169.

[61]Hofmann, "Preußische Stadtverordetenversammlungen," p. 31.

of Prussia and its high rate of internal migration during this period also could have contributed to the disproportionate number of internal governmental conflicts over kosher butchering. Despite the existence of an 1808 Prussian statute, which ordered that local imperatives could not contradict state orders, by the turn of the twentieth century Prussian law allowed for tremendous regional autonomy within certain areas.[62] Such jurisdiction could be seen in the Rheydt case, but it also meant that significant discrepancies existed in practice and in policy across Prussia.

It was common—in Prussia and elsewhere—for state agencies to intervene in local struggles for control over kosher butchering. Despite municipal attempts to insist on their jurisdiction over local Jewish ritual behavior, state governments frequently claimed sovereignty. When they did so, leaders drew from state trade laws, the 1808 Prussian law establishing the hegemony of state practice, and legal precedents concerning religious freedom. After Jewish communities petitioned the state for exemptions from two slaughterhouse regulations in Silesia, for example, the Prussian lower court overturned the local bans. Contradicting an earlier Rhine decision, the state's court argued on October 15, 1906, that kosher butchering was a form of trade and, as such, fell under the auspices of the state, not the local police, who regulated animal protection. Soon after the ruling, the Silesian district president in Bunzlau and Schweidnitz repealed the previous prohibitions.[63] In 1913, the Prussian minister of trade reaffirmed this opinion, thus forcing the community of Oppeln to revoke its newly passed set of restrictive slaughterhouse laws.[64]

Unlike in Prussia, where governmental agencies tended to use state commerce laws as a way to justify their claims for sovereignty, various leaders in Bavaria and Schaumburg-Lippe pointed to the violation of

---

[62]Dawson, *Municipal Life*, p. 32.

[63]Korrespondenzen, Berlin," *IDR* 6 and 12 (1906): 377–379, 718–720; Alphonse Levy, "Erlasse Von Schächtverboten," *IDR* 1 (1907): 48–49; "Schächtverbot, Bunzlau, 28 September," *DT* (29 September 1906): CJA 75CVe1344 118.

[64]21 February 1914 letter to Goldmann from the Centralverein CJA 75Dco1 29 69, 22 February 1914 letter from Goldmann to his rabbinical colleagues CJA 75Dco1 29 70; 1914 report of councilman Wiener CJA 75Dco1 29 78–80; April 1914 letter from Goldmann CJA 75Dco1 29 97; Oppeln Jewish Community petition CJA 75Dco1 29 84–89; 3 April 1914 letter to councilman Wiener CJA 75Dco1 29 92–96; "Aus Reich und Provinz, Bunzlau," *NAZ* (July 27 1906) CJA 75CVe1344 118; "Korrespondenzen, Bunzlau," *IDR* 12 (1906): 722–723; "Schächtverbot," *Schlesische Zeitung* (4 November 1906) CJA 75CVe1344 118; "Schächtverbot, Bunzlau, 28 September," *DT* (29 September 1906) CJA 75CVe1344 118; "Schweidnitz," *IDR* 7–8 and 11 (1907): 444, 651; "Verfügung zur Schächtfrage," *Breslauer Zeitung* 52 (21 February 1914). The Prussian minister of interior later upheld this ruling in 1914. 1914 minister of interior letter CJA 75Dco129 103.

religious freedoms as their motivation for intervention in the local disputes. While these authorities supported municipal attempts to regulate animal slaughter, they insisted on the state's right to interfere in these local attempts because the Jewish community's right to practice its religious traditions was at risk. In 1898, for example, Bavarian ministries used this reasoning to prohibit Bayreuth's slaughterhouse director and commission from enforcing a set of regulations that included the mandatory stunning of all animals into a state of unconsciousness before their slaughter. According to the ministers of interior and justice, the regulations violated the Jewish community's access to free religious practice.[65]

As state governments insisted on their right to overturn (or reinforce) local bans, they internally divided over which state agency had the jurisdiction over Jewish ritual behavior. In Bavaria, for example, the Bavarian ministers of Interior, Justice, and Commerce and Transportation each positioned his ministry as the suitable interventionist body.[66] A few right-leaning Bavarian members of the state parliament made similar claims as well. Frustrated that the ministries had made little progress in preventing alleged animal abuse, members of the Bavarian Volkspartei (Bavarian People's Party) proposed state bans on kosher butchering, which the state parliament debated during the *Kaiserreich* and again during the Weimar Republic.[67] Saxony, too, experienced dissension among its ministries and houses of parliament. The Saxon parliament intervened first in that state's *Schächtfrage*, approving a ban on kosher butchering in 1892. The kingdom's ministry of culture, unlike that of the interior, opposed the ban and spoke against it. Almost twenty years later, the same ministry, now under a different head, changed views and overturned the prohibition. In response, the second house of the state parliament requested the passage of a new law that would universally mandate the stunning of animals into a state of unconsciousness before

[65] 15 January 1909 memo of the Verband CAHJP DA/439.

[66] 1 August 1887 report from the minister of interior (Bavaria) sent to the minister of justice and the minister of justice's response BH MA 76592; 12 July 1889 minister of interior report on *Schächten* BH MA 76592; 31 May 1888 memo from Landmann to the Bavarian minister of interior BH MA 76592; 19 February 1890 letter from the Bavarian minister of interior BH: MA 76592; 5 June 1908 letter from the Bavarian minister of interior to that of foreign affairs BH MA 92570; 8 February 1913 letter from the governor of Upper Bavaria to the magistrate of Munich ALM Suv 90; 9 April 1908 letter and minutes of meeting of the Jewish community (Munich) concerning the new regulations over the sale of meat SM Pol Dir. München 4644.

[67] 20 May 1894 letter from the minister of justice to the minister of foreign affairs BH MA 76592; 1894 proposal BH MA 76592; Friedrich Frank, *Die Schächtfrage vor der Bayerischen Volksvertretung* (Würzburg: Buchdruckerei von Leo Woerl., 1894).

their slaughter. That state ban failed, but local cities then attempted to implement new prohibitions.[68]

The Bavarian, Saxon, and Prussian cases remind us of the differences in character among the state debates. All three states witnessed a struggle for control among diverse governmental bodies, but their actors, justifications, and location differed slightly. Prussia saw greater numbers of internal debates among local governing agencies and between cities and state. The outbreak of Prussian *Schächtfragen* in the 1890s and 1900s occurred across the Prussian provinces. Fewer Saxon and Bavarian cities attempted to implement mandatory stunning laws, but their state parliaments debated the possibility of creating statewide bans on kosher butchering. Saxony passed such a prohibition; Bavaria did not. Finally, Prussian state ministries were more likely to invoke trade and not the safeguarding of religious freedoms as a way to insist on state control. Ministries in Bavaria and Saxony justified their reversals of local or state bans by arguing for the safeguarding of religious customs.[69]

The states' debates contained some important commonalties as well. Across all three states, ministries tended to be more tolerant of religious difference than local municipalities, even if the latter were more effective at preserving liberal dominance at the local level than national leaders had been. In addition, in Bavaria, Saxony, and Prussia constant interplay among the participating governments characterized the *Ritualfragen*. Government officials constantly interacted with one another and with extraparliamentary groups in- and outside the geographic boundaries of the state. They read contemporary publications concerning Jewish rites and received dozens more from a variety of special interest groups.[70] Such a vibrant political atmosphere was reflective of the political culture of the time. They also suggest that the *Ritualfragen* involved participants other than government agencies. These nongovernmental groups also experienced a politicization process, which similarly revolved around questions concerning minority rights and the permissibility of deviation.

---

[68]21 October 1907 letter to Philippson from Elb CJA 75CVe1344 195; 1908 petition (draft) to the minister of culture from the Saxon Jewish Federation CJA 75CVe1344 321–322; March 1910 minutes of the Saxon Jewish Federation CJA 75Ve1 340 nr. 250–255; "Antrag: Eingegangen am 9 November 1911" SHD MDI 16178 29.

[69]Another important distinction could be made in the comparison of regional parliaments in Germany and Austria. *Antrag des Landeskulturausschusses, IX Wahlperiode, II. Session: 235/Praes/Lds. Kult. A. 22.*

[70]29 January 1884 memo to the minister of the interior about the publication of Damman's letter concerning kosher butchering BH MA 7659229; March 1910 letter from the Bavarian envoy to Saxony to the minister of foreign affairs.

Consequences and Cultural Codes: Antisemitism, Toleration, and Associational Life

Ultimately, the ritual questions would have a significant political impact on its participants, as well as its governing bodies. The deliberations provided a wide range of associations the opportunity to engage in political debates and to learn the lessons of mass politics when they did so. The discourses of contemporary political debate also stamped their influence on the participants. Both toleration and antisemitism served as important frames of reference, which lent varying groups the issues and language around which they could coalesce and insist on their own political prestige.

The deliberations afforded different associations the opportunity to take part in political debates. In 1899, for example, a local *Schächtfrage* helped to politicize the Bamberg society of meat sellers. Soon after slaughterhouse officials proposed reforms to its extant abattoir regulations, the Bamberg society began to discuss the potential *Schächtverbot* at its monthly meetings. It reached out to the city's Jewish community council to help reach a compromise, and its members began to communicate with slaughterhouse officials and town council members concerning the implications of the proposed reforms. When no compromise among the Jewish community, meat-sellers society, and municipal authorities was forthcoming, the meat sellers pushed their town council members for immediate action and even appeared at council meetings to express their support for a prohibition on kosher butchering.[71] Local debates in Schweinfurt similarly offered butchers an opportunity to be visible in the public sphere. They made recommendations to their town councils, magistrates, and police forces and appeared in front of these governmental bodies as expert witnesses.[72]

[71] 1899 minutes of the council of butchers in Bamberg CAHJP BII 3 and 1899 letter from the council of butchers in Bamberg to Bamberg's Jewish community CAHJP B II 3.

[72] 10 December 1910 letter from Hommel to Verband CJA 75CVe1344 269; "Korrespondenzen, Schweinfurt," *IDR* 8 (1900): 421. Another example can be found in Leipzig "Gegen die Tierquälerei auf den Schlachthofen," *Leipziger Volks-Zeitung* (6 January 1913) CJA 75CVe1341 121. Some directors even published supportive and critical articles concerning the debates in trade and popular journals. As slaughterhouse directors positioned themselves across a wide continuum of opinions on the *Schächtfrage*, they increasingly insisted on their autonomy and expertise. Negative opinions included: "Stimmen zur Schächtfrage," *Deutsch Soziale Blatter* (19 June 1907); von Schwartz, *Das Betäubungslose Schächten Der Israeliten*. More positive stances on kosher butchering can be found in 8 April 1909 letters from Leiger (Tübingen) and other professors of veterinary medicine and directors CJA 75Ve1340 nos. 144, 148, 153, and 157; "Unverhältnismäßig große Zahl der geschächteten Tiere," *RDG* 16 (15 August 1908): 247.

When these associations participated in the *Ritualfragen* they utilized the tactics of mass politics. As evidenced in the Schweinfurt and Bamberg cases, the meat sellers moved away from the judicious lobbying and discreet action they had embraced during earlier decades when they had desired changes in the abattoir. Instead, they now launched political discussions in a variety of different forums and actively lobbied a wide cross-section of governmental leaders. Other groups relied on the additional strategies being utilized by extraparliamentary groups at this time. They sent out mass mailings and published treatises. They increasingly aimed at gathering a mass membership, a professionally edited press, and a properly funded office. Such efforts were evident, for example, in the activities of the Leipzig-based Association for the Advancement of Humane Slaughter. In 1907, a year after it broke away from the mainstream animal rights movement in Germany, the Leipzig society actively began targeting cities outside of its base in Gotha and Leipzig to lure members away from other animal protection societies and to push aggressively for new laws requiring the stunning of animals before slaughter. Distributing their posters and pamphlets in Munich and Berlin, they issued a new publication, which ironically (and possibly intentionally) mimicked the anthologies produced by Jewish self-defense efforts. They also worked to raise funds in their base cities and in other municipalities with a strong animal protectionist presence.[73] Other groups acted similarly. Berlin's radical animal protection society self-published a wide range of texts, organized frequent fund-raising ventures, and tried to recruit members from cities outside of Berlin.

The ritual questions also provided participating groups with an opportunity to be influenced by and to use the discourses of contemporary political debate. Concerns over kosher butchering encouraged some participating organizations to become open to certain distasteful images, to ally themselves with right-leaning groups, and to move to the right within the political spectrum. Until 1903, for example, the Neu-Ruppin animal protection society consistently and unanimously supported its Jewish community's right to practice kosher butchering.

---

[73]Like the 1894 and 1904 publications of the Jewish community, this collection included several letters setting out the professional and educational expertise of the letter writers. Not all letters advocated the refusal of exemptions to Jews. The letter from Lissa, a veterinarian from Posen, did allow for the possibility of an exception. Hermann Ramdohr, ed., *Leipziger Flugschriften-Sammlung zur Betäubungsfrage der Schlachttiere*, 9 vols. (Leipzig: Haberland, 1907), p. 14. Also see Hermann Ramdohr, *Kritische Betrachtungen, Wünsche und Anregungen* (Leipzig: Franz Wagner, 1928) and Der Verein zur Förderung humanen Schlachtens, *Aufruf zum Beitritt in den Verein zur Förderung Humanen Schlachtens* SHD MDI 16178 4. H. Hildesheimer first warned about this organization in 1907. June 1907 letter from Hildesheimer CJA 75CVe1344 150.

However, over the course of the first decade of the nineteenth century, the group increasingly invoked the anti-Jewish charges being made by other animal advocates, including those of Jewish cruelty and avarice. Moreover, by 1906, they had politically allied themselves with a local antisemite.[74] This trend was clear in the evolution of the Bavarian animal protection society as well. For much of the nineteenth century, the state organization openly had supported kosher butchering and, more important, had distanced itself from its antisemitic local chapter in Munich. By the mid-1890s, however, the organization had begun to embrace a ban on kosher butchering. It now allied itself with the Munich group and with the antisemitic Volkspartei. Its literature utilized far stronger language and imagery than it had in the past.[75]

A few non–animal advocacy organizations also found a bridge between their cause, animal protection, and antisemitism, which allowed them to attract new members and to further their immediate goals within a variety of political arenas. In the case of the suffragists, the Munich CWS (German Congress for Women's Suffrage) chapter linked abattoir reform with women's rights and with demands for political and social hegemonic norms. According to Lida Gustava Heymann, the women's group protested all types of cruelty, whether toward animals or humans, and would not condone Jewish particularities simply because of their religious significance.[76]

Toleration similarly offered participating organizations the issues and language around which they could coalesce. CWS chapters in Kattowitz and Cologne broke away from their Bavarian counterparts over the kosher butchering disputes. The suffragists in Kattowitz and Cologne aligned themselves with local Jewish organizations rather than other feminist groups in order to thwart the national campaign against the

[74]3 February 1903 report of the magistrate concerning local animal slaughtering practices CJA 75CVe1350 9; 14 May 1906 letter from Levithal CJA 75CVe1350 1; 6 January 1907 to Pälegrimm from Verband CJA 75CVe1344 134, 1907; 21 April 1907 letter to Robert Drucker CJA 75CVe1350 14, 1907. Another example of such a coalition could be found in that created by the Saxon-based Alte Tierschutzverein and the Society for the Advancement of Humane Slaughter.

[75]"Die Thierschutzgesetzbung im deutschen Reich und in anderen Staaten," *National Zeitung* (15 May 1887) STM SUV 90; 31 May 1888 memo BH MA 76592; 1 December 1893 petition BH MA 76592; 15 December 1898 petition and accompanying letters BH MA 76592; S.Z.R, "Zur Schächtfrage," *Meissner Tageblatt* (March 1911) CJA 5CVe1340 283. This was true of the national animal protection organization more generally. In 1898, the national leadership failed to sway its local chapters to push for a ban on kosher butchering. By 1906 and certainly again by 1910, the majority of affiliated local chapters now championed the passage of new slaughterhouse laws that would transgress Jewish tradition.

[76]"Frauenstimmrecht und Schechita," *JR.*

Jewish rite. According to the former organizations, the implementation of policies to ensure toleration was more important than the creation of mandatory stunning laws.[77] Similarly, the local animal protectionist chapter in Offenbach diverged from the national German animal protectionist society when the latter launched its attempt in 1906 to push for new slaughterhouse reforms. Insisting on the importance of religious tolerance, the Offenbach group worked with its local Jewish community to defend kosher butchering. As animal protectionists, they petitioned, "we should direct our energies to protecting horses, hunted animals, etc. and not go after the rights of man and the followers of the ancient cultural religion of Judaism."[78]

As Shulamit Volkov has described of antisemitism more generally, the anti-Jewish tropes of the ritual questions provided organizations not only with an opportunity to create coalitions but also with the rhetoric to use when insisting on their own political prestige. Supporters of mandatory stunning laws tended to distance themselves from Progressives, Center-party Catholics, and Socialists and to insist on their Conservative credentials. Defenders of kosher butchering consistently swore their allegiance to Liberalism. In its propaganda literature, for example, the Leipzig Association for the Advancement of Humane Slaughter drew on the redemptionist language of the period to portray the ritual questions as a dispute between two camps: Conservatives and National Liberals against the Center Party, Freemasons, Poles, and Social Democrats. Belittling the progressive camp by aligning them with the much-feared Freemasons, Catholics, and Poles, the animal advocates glowingly identified their position as being in allegiance with respectable Conservatives and local National Liberals.[79] The Berlin animal protection society moved their camp even further to the political right. According to these activists, the passage of a ban on kosher butchering would demonstrate a victory in the fight against liberalism.

In contrast, animal protection societies in Kattowitz and Cologne not only interacted with progressive Liberal groups in order to safeguard the Jewish practice, but they also used antisemitism as a way

[77]"Ein neuer Vorstoß der Schächtgegner," *Mitteilungen aus dem Verein zur Abwehr des Antisemitismus* 26 (1912): 217–219; "Frauenstimmrecht und Shechitah," *JR* 43 (1912) CJA 75CVe1341 92; "München (Die Schächtresolution des Frauenstimmrechtskongresses)," *IF* 48(1912): 28; "Nochmals Frauenstimmrecht und Shechita," *JR* 49 (1912) CJA 75CVe1341 106; "Zum Vortrage des Herrn Dr. Weigl in München," *DIZ* 51 (1912): 4–5; Y. "Frauenstimmrecht und rituelle Schächtmethode," *IG* 51 (1912): 549–550.

[78]30 July 1906 letter to the national animal protectionist association from the TSV in Offenbach a.M. CJA 75 CVe1344 138.

[79]Verein zur Förderung humanen Schlachtens, *Aufruf zum Beitritt in den Verein zur Förderung humanen Schlachtens* (1910) SHD MDI 16178 4.

to politically de-legitimize their opponents. Rather than position the mandatory stunning laws within the politically Conservative camp, they emphasized its antisemitic character to disadvantage their opponents.[80] The Bavarian Center Party politician Friedrich Frank thus dismissed his state's animal protection campaign to implement mandatory stunning laws. Frank insisted that the majority of Bavarian animal advocates were not conservatives but belonged to the antisemitic Volkspartei, a political party that did "not simply oppose the Jewish method of slaughter, but all of Jewish existence; it does not only want to eliminate *Schächten*, but rather wishes to chase away all of Jewry from Germany."[81]

The ritual questions forced its participating organizations not only to embrace certain markers of self-definition but also to consider whether they were adherents to or disbelievers of the rhetoric concerning the character of Jewish rites and their practitioners. Now that their organizations were involved with the *Schächtfrage*, participants became familiar with Jewish ritual behavior and with the language and imagery used to describe it.[82] Whether or not they endorsed a ban on kosher butchering or a policy that exempted Jews from extant laws, discussants, by engaging in the ritual questions, allowed for discourses concerning Jewish difference to remain active within the public sphere.

Yet, despite this narrative, the choices of individual participants complicate our understanding of how discussants used toleration or antisemitic rhetoric as a cultural marker. Participants often acted in unexpected ways, deviating from the choices of the organizations with which they affiliated. A number of local animal protectionists, for example, voted against their chapters' petitions to endorse a ban on kosher butchering.[83] Others acted similarly, as evidenced by the decisions of Conservative Reichstag deputies Hoffmann and Johannes Hoeffel to reject the

[80]1906 minutes of the TSV Meeting CJA 75Cve1 344 154; 12 July 1906 letter from Cohn to the TSV of Kattowitz and their response 75DCo128.

[81]Frank, *Die Schächtfrage vor der Bayerischen Volksvertretung*, p. 6. Also see Alphonse Levy, "Umschau," *IDR* 1 (1898): 33–35.

[82]Interestingly, in a number of the Jewish newspapers, writers looked at the anti-Jewish stances of suffragists elsewhere. One writer, for example, criticized the London Suffragette Flora Drummond for lambasting Parliament deputies Rufus Isaacs and Herbert Samuel for not siding with her on the women's right to vote issue. "Frauenstimmrecht und Schechita," *JR* (25 October 1912) CJA 75CVe1341 92.

[83]The chapters that voted against a national prohibition in 1906 were AltGlienicke, Altona, Augsburg, Blankenburg, Bruanschweig, Breslau, Burgdorf, Cassel, Charlottenburg, Darmstadt, Fürth, Graudenz, Halberstadt, Hanau, Kattowitz, Landeshut, Laurahütte, Liegnitz, Lübeck, Ludwigshaffen, Nürnberg, Offenbach, Stuttgart, Wilmersdorf, and Zabern. 1906 minutes of the TSV. Also see "Korrespondenzen, Neu-Ruppin," *IDR* 1 (1899): 42; "Chemnitz," *IDR* 3 (1907): 188; "Nürnberg, 14 Januar," *IDR* 2 (1907): 127.

animal advocacy bills that their colleagues had endorsed.[84] There also was a small group of Jews who promoted the universal stunning laws.[85] These cases suggest an uneasy relationship between the ideologies of the ritual debates and practice.

††††††

In his campaign for the passage of mandatory stunning laws in Potsdam, the businessman Ernst Froelich criticized the Jewish community for consistently using "antisemitism" as a defense against animal protection societies. Asserting that his campaign was removed completely from the "Jewish-Question," Froelich described his motivations as grounded in the humane, Christian protection of animals. "We Christians," he insisted, "need to protect animals on behalf of humanity."[86] Twisting the Kaiser's claim that antisemitism brought shame to the modern period, Froelich described the Jewish method of slaughter in similar terms. "*Schächten*," he exclaimed, is "The Disgrace of the Century!"[87]

Like Froelich, most participants in the ritual questions distanced themselves from antisemitism whether or not they invoked its themes and images. For some discussants, the maneuver was fruitless. Despite Froelich's repeated claims that antisemitism bore no influence on him, his alliance with antisemitic politicians and use of antisemitic rhetoric suggested otherwise.[88] Yet the businessman's obvious embrace of antisemitic rhetoric should not suggest that the ritual questions in Potsdam or elsewhere resulted in the neat translation of ideology into practice. While the anti–kosher butchering campaigns in Potsdam led to a series of bans on kosher butchering and their reversals, other municipalities exempted the Jewish rite immediately. A few towns and cities expressed little interest in either the rite or in abattoir reform.

Discussions similar to those in Potsdam took place in the published arena and in political debates across Germany at different levels of governance. As in Potsdam, these ideologically rich campaigns sometimes resulted in policy change. When they did so, two competing discourses complemented animal protectionism to influence these processes: a radicalizing antisemitism and a changing understanding of toleration.

---

[84]1899 Reichstag Transcript, CAHJP TD 475, 7–8. Hoffman was a professor of veterinary medicine at the Hochschule in Stuttgart (1845–1921).

[85]See, e.g., the much contested Jacob Stern, *Das Schächten: Streitschrift gegen den jüdischen Schlachtritus, Ein Mahnwort an die deutschen Tierschutzvereine von einem Juden* (Leipzig: Guillermo Levien, 1891).

[86]Froelich, *Das Schächten*, pp. 4, 6–7.

[87]Ibid., p. 3.

[88]"Zum Schächtverbot des Wiener Gemeinderates," *Dr. Bloch's Oesterreichische Wochenschrift* 5 (May 1905).

The ways in which these frames of reference affected policy change shifted dramatically across place and time. National disputes over kosher butchering resulted only in an amendment that enshrined religious protection. This took place gradually, as Center Party, Progressive Liberal, and Socialist deputies increasingly articulated discomfort with the German constitution's awkward formulation concerning religious toleration and as Conservative parties gradually adopted the chauvinistic discourses of the antisemitic right. After the Center Party leadership failed to pass an amendment that broadly allowed for the safeguarding of all religious particularities, it eventually pushed through a bill that protected kosher butchering at the local and state level.

Local and state deliberations, however, resulted in the creation of varying types of laws. Influenced by a combination of animal protectionism, concerns over the social order, and antisemitism, one set of policies restricted or banned the rite. Another group of promulgations assured Jewish communities their right to practice kosher butchering without interference. When championing these exceptions, participants articulated a much broader understanding of toleration than their predecessors had in earlier debates. Here too, time and place mattered significantly. Local municipalities were most likely to promise non-discrimination during the 1880s and early 1890s than they were during the decade preceding World War I. During its disputes in the 1890s, for example, the Potsdam magistrate ensured its Jewish community the right to practice kosher butchering without interference; however, by 1905 it instituted a ban. Moreover, Prussian towns and cities, particularly those in the Rhine and Brandenburg provinces, tended to pass a greater number of bans and dramatic restrictions on kosher butchering than municipalities in Bavaria or Baden did. Differences across states were evident as well. Saxony and Braunschweig both passed statewide slaughterhouse reforms; however Braunschweig allowed for its municipalities to exempt Jewish communities because the reforms forced the transgression of Jewish tradition. Until 1910, the kingdom of Saxony refused to offer Jews an exception to their new laws and instead argued that religious toleration should not trump state objectives.

The debates in Saxony and Bavaria may have begun as discussions about the possibility of Jewish exceptionalism, but they often concluded as deliberations concerning the boundaries and limits of governmental authority. Between 1880 and 1916, local, state, and national agencies used the emerging ideologies of toleration, antisemitism, and animal protectionism to determine the possibilities for their own intervention. The *Schächtfrage* saw several kinds of internal disputes: conflicts among ministries, between ministries and national officials, among ministries and municipal officials, and among municipal agencies. In each case, these officials attempted both to buttress their own power and to shape and redefine policy.

These changes in policy did not occur in a vacuum. Instead, the *Ritualfragen* significantly shaped the functioning of several extraparliamentary groups. A wide range of groups became involved in the deliberations concerning Jewish rites. Their involvement not only offered them an opportunity to take part in public debate, but they also afforded them a chance to adopt the strategies of mass politics. The participating *Vereine* (societies) acted boldly in the public sphere, attempted to attract a wider base of support, created fund-raising networks, and relied on the press. They also began to rely on the discourses of mass politics. The *Schächtfrage* presented an issue around which right-wing organizations could coalesce, and that bolstered their presence in local and national political spheres.

Within the ritual questions, then, religious toleration and antisemitism served as a "cultural code."[89] Both ideologies allowed participants to position themselves with other groups in the political arena and to insist .on their own political prestige. Whether or not these groups began to adopt the chauvinistic or tolerant languages of the time, their mere participation in the ritual questions allowed for discourses concerning Jewish difference to remain active within the public sphere.

The continued presence in imperial Germany of these campaigns concerning Jewish rites encouraged Jewish communities to intensify their defense efforts. The shifts in animal protection crusades complicated strategies Jewish leaders previously had employed to defend their rites. Between 1880 and 1916, Jewish leaders bitterly debated what kinds of strategies and spokesmen were most appropriate when defending Jewish particularisms. As they did so, they offered new models for Jewish political behavior.

[89]Volkov, "Antisemitism as a Cultural Code," p. 36; van Rahden, "Words and Actions" and "Ideologie und Gewalt."

CHAPTER 5

The *Schächtfragen* and Jewish Political Behavior

During the late nineteenth century, the Federation of Saxon Jewish Communities helped to establish new norms of Jewish political behavior. Between 1892, when the kingdom of Saxony promulgated its *Schächtverbot* and 1910 when it repealed it, Saxony's Jewish leaders practiced the strategies of mass politics. They no longer quietly appealed to a few non-Jewish notables as they had done during past moments of conflict. Instead, they petitioned governmental authorities at all levels. They organized numerous letter-writing campaigns and garnered letters of support. They attended animal protection society meetings, spoke at city council meetings, and worked hard to identify allies inside and outside of Saxony. The federation's president, Max Elb, thrust himself into the political sphere. The Dresden businessman served on the executive board of a national kosher butchering–defense agency. He attended the national meetings of different Jewish organizations and consulted with Jewish institutions on the art of defense. Emphasizing his Jewish distinctiveness as well as his Saxon citizenry, he made no secret of his specifically "Jewish" agenda.[1]

In the late nineteenth and early twentieth centuries, new Jewish organizations and leaders such as Elb emerged across Germany. Regardless of their denominational or political affiliation, these Jewish leaders and associations demonstrated a form of political behavior that departed from the past. Before the late 1880s, German-Jewish communal leaders tended to discourage public defense efforts targeted at specifically

[1] 1892 letters between the Jewish community of Dresden and the minister of interior CJA 75CVE1 344 10–39; 21 October 1907 letter from Elb to Philippson CJA 75Cve1 344 195; 1908 petition of the Saxon Jewish Federation CJA 75Cve1 344 320; 22 April 1910 letter from the Saxon Jewish Federation to the Verband CJA 75Cve1 243.

religious themes. Many Jewish defensive efforts focused on the situation of Jews in other lands and supplicated for protection from non-Jewish notables and authorities. They supported the Liberals who promoted nondiscrimination. As evidenced in the earlier kosher butchering and circumcision disputes, Jewish community leaders reacted to real or perceived attacks by publishing apologetics, implementing religious reform, and maintaining a wall of silence. Now, whether or not they ate kosher meat at home, Jewish activists defended kosher butchering by demanding their civic and religious freedoms. Articulating an awareness of problems facing Jews inside—and not outside—of Germany, they aired their concerns within the public (non-Jewish) political sphere.

The *Schächtfragen* provide a useful case study for analyzing the rich texture of Jewish political life during the late nineteenth and early twentieth centuries.[2] A study of these ritual questions stresses the ways in which Jewish political life was deeply influenced by imperial German politics and by the paradoxes German Jews faced in everyday life. As German Jews participated in these disputes, they adopted some of the political strategies employed by their non-Jewish compatriots. They lobbied, utilized mass mailings, infiltrated their opponents' organizations, and developed publishing houses and fund-raising networks. They identified novel issues of concern. Reflecting common struggles between Jewish particularism and German universalism, Jewish defense strategies simultaneously advocated Jewish rights and downplayed Jewish difference. They petitioned for protection and defended Jewish privileges; they spoke for "all of German Jewry" while representing only particular interests. Their efforts to safeguard kosher butchering exhibited the paradoxical characteristics of confessionally oriented defense campaigns.

The movements to safeguard kosher butchering highlight the moments when German-Jewish politics shifted. The defense efforts underwent two significant changes, both of which paralleled variations within German politics more generally. Participating Jewish organizations first departed from previous forms of political activism in 1886 after German animal protection societies launched their national campaign to ban the slaughter of conscious animals. The Jewish activists involved in the ritual questions of the late 1880s and 1890s entered the debates as Jews, no matter their level of religious observance. They emphasized the religious value of kosher butchering and explicitly asked that religious tradition and custom supersede state or local laws. Thirteen years later, Jewish political behavior witnessed a second change marked by

[2]Because the interest in circumcision never fully materialized into a campaign, there were few political responses to it.

a dramatic polarity. On the one hand, defense activities proliferated. Organizations and individuals who previously had not taken part in public demonstrations of Jewish politics now participated in activities intended to safeguard kosher butchering. Jewish leaders also employed novel methods, including the creation of new defense organizations. Yet, on the other hand, deep fissures and debates also characterized the Jewish politics of this period and threatened to destabilize the already vulnerable Jewish agencies of Germany. As increasing numbers of Jews and their representative organizations participated in the safeguarding of Jewish religious behavior, they bitterly disputed how best to defend kosher butchering and represent the religious character of modern German-Jewry. Long-standing internal turf wars exaggerated these quarrels, and Liberal and Orthodox groups in- and outside Berlin wrestled over who had inherited the right to speak on behalf of German Jews.

This portrait of modern German-Jewish political life challenges extant understandings of Jewish political activism in an additional way.[3] Existing studies on German-Jewish politics tend to focus almost exclusively on the Central Association of German Citizens of the Jewish Faith (Centralverein) as the central force within the German-Jewish fight against antisemitism. They therefore pinpoint 1893, the year of the Centralverein's establishment, as the moment when Jewish politics changed decisively.[4] In contrast, an analysis of the efforts to safeguard kosher butchering begins the study of modern German-Jewish politics in 1886 and highlights the activities of political organizations other than the Centralverein. It similarly includes types of political behavior that were beyond the Centralverein's purview and physical locations that were untouched by the Centralverein's influence.[5]

[3]On the shift in Jewish politics, see Jacob Borut, *"Wehrt Euch!" Founding of the Centralverein deutscher Staatsbürger Jüdischen Glaubens* (Hebrew) (Jerusalem: Dinur Center, 1996); Marjorie Lamberti, *Jewish Activism in Imperial Germany: The Struggle for Civil Equality* (New Haven: Yale University Press, 1978); Jehuda Reinharz, *Fatherland or Promised Land: The Dilemma of the German Jew, 1893–1914* (Ann Arbor: University of Michigan Press, 1975); Ismar Schorsch, *Jewish Reactions to German Anti-Semitism* (New York: Columbia University Press, 1972). An excellent example of European Jewish intervention on behalf of Jews elsewhere in the world can be found in Carole Fink, *Defending the Rights of Others: The Great Powers, the Jews, and International Minority Protection, 1878–1938* (Cambridge: Cambridge University Press, 2004).

[4]Borut suggests that Jewish defense did not begin in Berlin in 1893 but outside of Berlin several years earlier. Jacob Borut, "The Rise of Jewish Defense Agitation in Germany, 1890–1895: A Pre-History of the C.V.?" *LBIYB* 36 (1991): 59–96.

[5]This reading of Jewish politics does not contest the significance of the Centralverein, an organization that urged Jews to openly acknowledge their Judaism and fight for it. Between its inception in 1893 and its dissolution by the Nazis, the Centralverein worked

This chapter reveals the politicization of Jewish organizational life in this period.[6] The voluntary and nonvoluntary organizations discussed here were at the center of Jewish political activities. Jews enthusiastically formed societies during the late nineteenth century, in part because they frequently were excluded from running for electoral office. No Jew sat in the Prussian parliament for over a decade after 1886, and when the last Jewish legislator of the founders' generation, Ludwig Bamberger, retired in 1893, the Reichstag contained no Jew outside the ranks of the Social Democratic Party (SPD) until 1912.[7] The political defenses of kosher butchering therefore tended to take place outside of traditional party politics.[8]

The discourse employed by these activist organizations was often deliberately deceptive, a strategic maneuver taken into consideration here. Participants in the *Schächtfragen* often hid their resistance behind declarations of apoliticism and patriotism. When the Saxon Jewish Federation claimed to be apolitical, however, it was not insinuating that it held no political opinions. Instead, much like their non-Jewish compatriots, Saxon Jewish leaders adopted the language of apoliticism to affirm their similarity with other groups and to demonstrate their respectability more generally. Similarly, the Jewish leadership's embrace of German patriotism hid their dissatisfaction with the political status quo. Utterances of love for the fatherland concealed their political motivations and provided them with the freedom to suggest new solutions to the conflicts taking place among Jews, governments, and non-Jewish society.

---

to diminish discrimination in public service and to promote Jewish education and respectability. It attempted to persuade nonsocialist parties to nominate Jews as candidates for political elections, and it used the courts to protect the Jewish community, its religious laws, and its members. Borut, *Wehrt Euch!*; Reinharz, *Fatherland or Promised Land*; Schorsch, *Jewish Reactions to German Anti-Semitism.*

[6]I am grateful to Evyatar Friesel's path-breaking articles for raising similar and additional concerns. Friesel, "The German-Jewish Encounter as a Historical Problem: A Reconsideration," *LBIYB* 41 (1996): 263–275; Friesel, "The Political and Ideological Development of the Centralverein before 1914." *LBIYB* 31 (1986): 121–146; Friesel, "A Response to the Observations of Chaim Schatzker and Abraham Margliot," *LBIYB* 33 (1988): 107–111.

[7]This was radically different than the "liberal decade" of 1867–1878, when 16 Jews (6 baptized) sat in the Reichstag, and 30 Jews (9 baptized) served in the various state parliaments. Michael Brenner has published one of the few studies of internal German-Jewish political parties. Michael Brenner, "The Jüdische Volkspartei: National-Jewish Communal Politics during the Weimar Period," *LBIYB* 35 (1990): 219–243.

[8]While dozens of Jewish physicians and scientists also defended Jewish rites, their actions are well documented and considered here only in part.

The 1886–1887 *Schächtfragen*

Before the late 1880s, most Jewish institutions tended to adhere to traditional defense tactics. They relied on non-Jewish authorities to intervene on the behalf of Jews, and they deflected attention by articulating concern for Jews outside of the German lands. Jewish leaders also responded to threats by remaining silent, offering apologetics, and enacting religious reforms. Even newly formed postemancipatory organizations were unable to break away from these inherited approaches. While founded in 1869 to defend German-speaking Jews from anti-Jewish actions, the German-Jewish Federation (DIGB), for example, quickly became reluctant to combat antisemitism publicly. By the mid-1870s, its bylaws prohibited any discussion of political issues at meetings and focused instead on social welfare and religious education as primary concerns. The formation of the Antisemitism Defense League similarly failed to mark a significant innovation in Jewish politics. Although the organization condemned Jew-hatred, its Jewish and non-Jewish membership represented the organization as a Christian group whose purpose was to strengthen Germany's Christian character. Its opposition to any form of Jewish separatism or difference precluded the possibility of upholding Jewish religious or cultural particularities.[9]

Jewish defense tactics began to change in the late 1880s when Jewish communal leaders from Berlin launched a national defense of kosher butchering in response to the attempt by animal protection societies to push for a ban on the slaughter of conscious animals. Two Berlin-based historical adversaries spearheaded these late-nineteenth-century resistance efforts. Esriel Hildesheimer and his supporters led one campaign; the Jewish executive community council of Berlin led the second. During the previous decades, these two entities had been at odds over the question of secession. Hildesheimer, the director of Berlin's Orthodox rabbinical seminary and the rabbi of its separatist Orthodox community, had pushed for the rights of individual Jews to secede from a state-recognized religious community without penalty.[10] Berlin's Jewish

[9]On the DIGB, see Shmuel Maayan, *Struggles for a System of Elections in the Union of German-Jewish Communities (Deutsch-Israelitischer Gemeindebund) in the Years 1911 and 1912* (Hebrew) (Givat-Haviva: Zvi Lurie Institute, 1982), esp. pp. 7–13; Schorsch, *Jewish Reactions to German Anti-Semitism*, pp. 23–52. On the Abwehr-Verein, see Barbara Suchy, "The Verein zur Abwehr des Antisemitismus (I) From its Beginnings to the First World War," *LBIYB* 28 (1983): 205–239.

[10]On Esriel Hildesheimer, see David Ellenson, *Rabbi Esriel Hildesheimer and the Creation of a Modern Jewish Orthodoxy* (Tuscaloosa: University of Alabama Press, 1990).

community council had opposed these efforts. To safeguard its authority, the Prussian Jewish leadership had encouraged the state to continue its policy of requiring all Jews to belong to a single, state-approved, local religious community. Now, ten years after the reversal of such a policy, the campaign critical of kosher butchering brought these two groups closer together. In 1886, both began to organize a national defense of kosher butchering that quickly departed from past political strategies and resulted in the cooperation of hundreds of smaller Jewish community councils located throughout Germany.

Although there is little evidence that Hildesheimer and the Berlin community council leadership collaborated on their first letters and petitions, their campaigns grew increasingly similar. First, both defense movements embraced analogous rhetoric in their campaigns. The campaigns drew from contemporaneous discourses of science and toleration to promote Jewry's religious particularism and kosher butchering's hygienic value. Despite the fact that some of these Jewish leaders were not religiously observant, their defense efforts emphasized the importance of religious freedom and the necessity of having kosher meat available to all German Jews. The campaigns emanating from Hildesheimer's circle and from the Berlin Jewish community council both insisted that the prohibition of kosher butchering would negatively affect the lives of all German Jews. As such, they drafted their petitions in "the interest of [their] religious lives," whether or not they observed the Jewish dietary laws at home.[11] Their rhetoric exaggerated the observance level of Jews in Germany at that time. It also reflected an unusual—and what would become a temporary—acceptance of German-Jewish religious particularity.[12] Such an impulse was evidenced in a petition submitted by the Jewish community of Elmshorn, which requested that "religion outweigh all other issues."[13]

As both camps emphasized the specifically Jewish character of the rite, they also continued to stress its scientific and compassionate nature. Inverting the claims of their opponents, supporters of kosher butchering persisted in asserting that the rite killed the animal quickly and caused it little pain. "It is not a *Schächtverbot* that is animal friendly," argued

[11]21 June 1886 letter to Germany's Jewish communities from the Jewish community council of Berlin CAHJP DA/648; 1886 counterpetition issued by the Jewish community council of Berlin CJA 75 Aer1 97 16–16rs; Vorstandes der jüdischen Gemeinde zu Berlin, *Vorstellung des Vorstandes der jüdischen Gemeinde zu Berlin zur Petition des Thierschutz-Vereins das Thierschlachten betreffend* (Berlin: Druck H. Baendel, 1886).

[12]December 1886 letter from Esriel Hildesheimer CAHJP GA II/721.

[13]1 January 1887 petition from the Jewish community of Elmshorn to the Reichstag CJA 75 A El 5 24.

Im Deutschen Reich editor Alphonse Levy. "Instead, *shehitah* is [animal friendly]; it strives to cause the animal a less painful death."[14] According to Levy and others, the removal of blood from the meat allowed it to remain healthier and fresher longer than that retrieved from animals stunned before slaughter. Their defenses, which relied heavily on recently published letters by non-Jewish professors of veterinary medicine and science, compared the supposedly rational stance of German Jews with the "blindness and fanaticism" of the animal protection movement.[15]

In addition to utilizing similar rhetoric, the two Berlin defense efforts shared a second characteristic; namely, their reliance on mass mailing, a political strategy employed by other European special interest groups at this time, including the German animal protection societies. In 1886 and 1887, Berlin Jewish leaders sent almost identical letters to hundreds of Jewish community councils, individual Jews, and Jewish and non-Jewish leaders from across Germany.[16] These letters alerted their readers to the existence, status, and danger of the animal protection campaigns; they also encouraged their readers to submit counterpetitions to the Reichstag, a model of which they almost always included.[17] These letter-writing campaigns generated hundreds of letters and petitions to the Reichstag and to Prussian ministries from Jewish communities throughout Germany.

The mass mailing reflected a third shift in strategy embraced by both Berlin-based defense campaigns: the attempt to overcome the social and political concerns that once had made coalition building among Jews difficult. As demonstrated in the earlier circumcision conflicts, Jewish community councils often were unwilling or unready to work in concert with one another. In Prussia, this trouble with network building had been exacerbated by the state's earlier prohibition of a Jewish federated body. Now, almost twenty years after emancipation and unification, the deliberations concerning kosher butchering encouraged Jewish councils to become involved in a single "Jewish" cause. The Berlin Jewish community council and the circle around Hildesheimer both encouraged Germany's fragmented Jewry to work together. They

---

[14]Alphonse Levy, "Das Schächtverbot in Sachsen," *IDR* 10 (1901): 528.

[15]1888 form letter sent by Esriel Hildesheimer to German-Jewish orthodox organizations CJA 75AEr196 3–6RS.

[16]Hildesheimer contacted fellow traditionalist rabbis; the Berlin community council communicated with other similar agencies.

[17]1886 letters between Hildesheimer and Orthodox rabbis throughout Germany CJA 75 Aer1 96; 21 June 1886 letter to Germany's Jewish communities from the Committee of the Association of German Jews in Berlin (Ausschuss) CAHJP DA/648; 1886 counterpetition issued by the Ausschuss CJA 75 Aer1 97 16–16rs; January 1 1887 petition from the Jewish community of Elmshorn CJA 75 A El 5 24.

warned their readers that a prohibition of kosher butchering would affect all Jewish communities and beseeched other councils to join their defense efforts. "This is not only an issue of local concern," wrote the Berlin council, "but also that of the rabbis of communities in Breslau, Danzig, Dresden, Königsberg, Magdeburg, and Stettin."[18] The leadership's emphasis on the communities in eastern Germany was a conscious one. Many of the Jewish communities of eastern Prussia and Saxony communities were more religiously observant than their Berlin coreligionists and therefore more affected by a potential *Schächtverbot*. Moreover, these communities were hesitant to align themselves with Berlin Jewry out of a concern with the capital city's perceived liberal and historically dominant nature.

As the Berlin council tried to overcome these historic divisions, Hildesheimer worked to heal the rift caused by the secessionist movement of the 1870s and early 1880s. He had come to Berlin in 1869 to serve as the rabbi of the separatist Orthodox community. Now he chided those communities who let internal religious squabbles cloud their better judgment. His letters urged his fellow observant coreligionists to act "unanimously and energetically."[19]

These efforts helped to forge a network of German-Jewish political activism and lay the groundwork for the creation of a Jewish public sphere. After Hildesheimer contacted Hanover's rabbinic council in 1887 concerning the animal protectionist campaign, local rabbis there sent a petition and an accompanying letter to the Reichstag. They mailed letters to their local Jewish lay leaders and began to communicate with other Jews outside Berlin and Hanover regarding the threat to kosher butchering. Jewish leaders in Hagen, Danzig, Hamburg, and Vienna who had received letters from Hanover's rabbinate then sent their own petitions, which incorporated large segments of Hildesheimer's original letter, to the Reichstag and to other Jewish community councils.[20] Similar results followed the Berlin community council campaign. These mass mailings helped to create a dense network of Jewish political activity where previously little had existed.

The Berlin-based defense campaigns did not depend solely on mass mailings. Instead, both resistance movements relied on other developing

---

[18]1886 counter-petition issued by the Ausschuss CJA 75 Aer1 97 16–16rs.

[19]March 1887 letter from Esriel Hildesheimer to Germany's Jewish communities CAHJP GA 11/166.

[20]Jewish community of Hagen's 1887 petition CAHJP GA II/166: 1887 petition from the Jewish community of Danzig CAHJP DA/648, 1887; 10 January 1887 from the Berlin Jewish community council GA II/166. An article in *Der Israelit* reported on this phenomenon in 1886. "Die Schechitah-Angelegenheit vor dem detuschen Reichstage," *Der Israelit* 45/46 (June 1886).

lessons of mass politics. They used a professionally edited press, producing over fifty leaflets, brochures, books, and articles in the defense of kosher butchering. In addition, they created new alliances or built on those already established. Hildesheimer and others made contact with non-Jewish scientists, slaughterhouse directors, veterinarians, and Protestant theologians requesting support in their attempt to thwart the animal protectionist campaign. The Berlin-based Jewish leadership asked that these authorities write statements of support for kosher butchering, and eventually, the Berlin Jewish community council, the Frankfurt-based Free Association for the Interests of Orthodox Judaism (Free Association), and German General Rabbinical Association published these letters individually and in collaborative anthologies.[21] These groups also departed from past political strategies because they sought out the animal protectionists whose policies they opposed. The Jewish defense campaigns tracked these supposedly "dangerous" non-Jewish organizations and published the names, occupations, and addresses of the animal protectionist leadership. They even publicized the dates and places where the organizations would next meet.[22] While there is no evidence concerning how many Jews responded to this call, Jewish organizations used this strategy regularly during the 1890s and early 1900s.[23]

The years 1886–1889 lay the groundwork for the kosher butchering defense strategies that would follow. Five years before the Central-verein existed, Jewish voluntary associations recognized the need to modernize their defense tactics. The responses of German-Jewish organizations and individuals as early as 1886 to the ritual questions, then, emphasizes that the Centralverein was not entirely original. Previously

[21]See Karl Damman, *Gutachten über das jüdische Schlachtverfahren* (Hannover: Verlag Ludwig Ey, 1886); *Gutachten über das jüdisch-rituelle Schlachtverfahren ("Schächten")* CAHJP AHW 127; Vorstande der Freien Vereinigung für die Interessen des orthodoxen Judenthums, *Auszüge aus den Gutachten der Hervorragendsten Physiologen und Veterinärärzte über das "Schächten"* (Frankfurt am Main: Buchdruckerei von Louis Golde, 1887). Despite the opposition it engendered from the animal protectionists, German-Jewish organizations continued to use these letters into the twentieth century.

[22]This was particularly evident in Esriel Hildesheimer's 1888 letters concerning the *Schächtfrage* CJA 75 Aer1 96.

[23]The archives, however, reveal few instances during the 1880s when Jews attended national or local animal protection society meetings and spoke in defense of *shehitah*. 25 March 1887 statement issued by Jacob Cohn CJA 75DCo1 27 21. This would occur more regularly during the 1890s. Otto Hartmann "Aus dem Rechenschaftsbericht für 1889/92," *Ibis* 9/10 (September-October 1892): 49–51; Otto Hartmann, *Bericht über die sechste Versamlung des Verbandes der Thierschutz-Vereine des Deutschen Reiches in Braunschweig* (Cologne: Thierschutz-Vereine des Deutschen Reiches, 1895); 1906 minutes of the TSV CJA 75Cve1 344, 153.

fragmented Jewish communities and associations united to defend kosher butchering. They demanded legal protection of their religious
practices and relied on the nascent tools of mass politics. The *Schächtfrage* of 1886–1889 was thus a watershed in the development of Jewish
defense strategies.[24]

Over the next ten years, the Berlin-based Jewish organizations accelerated their efforts to defend kosher butchering. As dozens of town
councils and a few state parliaments considered animal slaughter reforms, the Federation of Saxon Jewish Communities, the Committee for
the Defense Against Antisemitic Attacks (Comité), the German General
Rabbinical Association, the Free Association, and several local rabbis
joined the Berlin-based defense campaigns. Until the early 1900s, these
groups continued to rely on the strategies they had devised during the
late 1880s. Yet, in the early twentieth century their continued emphasis that religious obligations overrode state and local laws faced several
internal challenges. As the animal protection movements and their discourses radicalized, the campaigns to defend kosher butchering underwent a corresponding shift as well.

The Making of Modern Jewish Politics

During the first decade of the twentieth century, the campaigns defending kosher butchering again changed in character. These modifications were part of the larger historical phenomena described in
chapters 3 and 4, including the proliferation of special-interest politics, the radicalization of antisemitism, the evolving interpretations of
toleration, and the professionalization of the animal protection movement. Jewish organizations responded to the escalation of the anti-
kosher campaigns with matching intensity.[25] Their paradoxical defense
efforts, which demonstrated a richness not seen previously, included
new Jewish organizations and leaders and relied on novel political
forms and strategies. Yet, these campaigns were divisive. Organizations
increasingly bickered over how best to approach defense and who was
its rightful spokesman. They no longer unanimously presented kosher

[24]The *Schächtfragen* of 1886–1889 suggest that an interest in kosher butchering, and
not the Xanten ritual murder charge of 1891, marked a radical change in the development of Jewish defense strategies.

[25]As chapters 3 and 4 suggested, most slaughterhouse laws of the 1880s and early
1890s had exempted Jews from their purview.

butchering as a rite of religious significance or as a ritual that affected all Jews.

After the turn of the century, a growing number of Jewish organizations became involved in the defense of kosher butchering, including those associations that previously had barely invested in religious observance. In 1901, for example, after a decade of seemingly little interest in the kosher butchering question, the Centralverein announced its intention to protect the Jewish rite.[26] Two concomitant legal campaigns sparked its interest: the Prussian High Court's decision to uphold a town's right to implement a ban on kosher butchering and the publication of two antisemitic postcards that conflated kosher butchering with the blood libel charge.[27] The following year, the DIGB similarly broadcast its new role in safeguarding kosher butchering, despite its historic reluctance to publicly fight discrimination based on religious distinctions. For the DIGB, this turning point came about when the Jewish council of a small Rhine town asked the national organization for assistance in battling its recent prohibition of kosher butchering. Perhaps motivated by its loss of prominence in the Jewish national arena to the Centralverein and by the latter's involvement in deliberations the year before, the DIGB quickly heeded the call for help. Over the next year, it joined forces with the local town council to file a set of appeals with the regional authorities and to orchestrate a defense campaign throughout the Rhine region.[28]

The DIGB and the Centralverein also were likely to have been motivated to join the kosher butchering defense efforts because of their relatively recent desire to adopt a more inclusive character.[29] Both organizations were federated societies, with national offices in Berlin and member-organizations throughout Germany. At the turn of the century, the two groups had expressed an interest in attracting members from outside of their historic, liberal Berlin base. The campaigns

---

[26]In 1894, the Centralverein had joined the Comité zur Abwehr antisemitischer Angriffe (Comité) to raise funds for the defense of kosher butchering. The Comité also included the DIGB, Rabbinerverbandes in Deutschland (RD), and the Rabbinats der jüdischen Gemeinde zu Berlin (RB).

[27]See the letters exchanged between the Centralverein and the DIGB CJA 75CGE1 893 19–24 and the letters exchanged between the Prussian minister of interior and the Rabbinical Assembly CJA 75CGE1 893 24–24rs. Also see "Die Dewaldschen Ansichtspostkarten," *IDR* 9 (1901): 457–463.

[28]1902 petition (DIGB and Prussian Federation) CJA 75CGE1 893 8–19; June 1903 letters between the DIGB and the communities of Breslau, Oldenburg, Posen, West Prussia, Stuttgart, and Insterburg CJA 75CGE1 893 60–73.

[29]The Centralverein was based in Berlin; the DIGB had been based in Leipzig but moved to Berlin in 1882.

to safeguard kosher butchering might have offered such a solution. The defense efforts gained the sympathies of local community councils throughout Germany, particularly those in East Prussia, and among the Orthodox. By joining the defense efforts, the DIGB and Centralverein could have hoped to attract attention and respect from potential member-groups. Such a strategy had been successful when employed by other Berlin-based groups a decade earlier.

Unlike the DIGB and Centralverein, which slowly came to the public defense of kosher butchering, the Verband der deutschen Juden (Verband) participated in these efforts immediately upon its creation in 1904. Its involvement in the defense of kosher butchering similarly marked this second shift within Jewish politics. Although historians overlook the Verband in their studies of German-Jewish political behavior, the organization achieved a degree of prominence in its defense of the rite.[30] After its formation, the group coordinated the publication of letters defending kosher butchering and organized lobbying efforts at all levels of government. It also helped staff and fund committees whose sole purpose was to defend kosher butchering.[31] Its place in the defense of the Jewish ritual was illustrated clearly by the fact that until 1909, the *shehitah* commission met at the Verband headquarters in Berlin.

Created in May 1904 as the "Commission to Fight the Prohibition of *Shehitah*," the emergence of the *shehitah* commission similarly characterized a change in modern Jewish political defense. An umbrella organization whose sole purpose was to defend kosher butchering, the commission was one of the first national single-issue German-Jewish defense organizations of its kind. Based in Berlin, it was composed of board members of major Jewish organizations from across Germany, the rabbis of several large Liberal and Orthodox Berlin congregations, and other important Jewish leaders from elsewhere in Germany.[32]

[30]They do so because the Verband never acquired a mandate to speak in the name of German Jewry and because the Centralverein provided much of the Verband's start-up costs and staff and shared many members and lay-leaders with it. In his study of German-Jewish politics, for example, Ismar Schorsch described the Verband as an "illusion." Schorsch, *Jewish Reactions to German Anti-Semitism*, p. 150.

[31]9 May 1904 minutes of the Commission to "Fight the Prohibition of *Shehitah*" (commission) CJA 75CGE1 893 90–94; 10 May 1905 letter from the commission CAHJP AHW 943b; 29 May 1906 letter from the Berlin-based Jewish agencies to Germany's Jewish communities CAHJP BII 3; 7 July 1908 minutes of the commission CJA 75Cve1 340 1–6; July 1908 letters between the Verband and the Centralverein CJA 75Cve1 340 7–9; February 1909 letters between the Verband and the Centralverein 75Cve1 114–115; 24 February 1909 letter from Rabbi Bergmann to the Verband CJA 75Cve1 340 123.

[32]First housed in the Verband's headquarters, the organization became incorporated in 1908 with a leadership that served two year terms. Minutes of the 9 May 1904 meeting

Other similar associations surrounding kosher butchering defense soon followed. Separatist Orthodox groups in Frankfurt and Berlin created and oversaw separate agencies within a decade after the *shehitah* commission's formation. These different organizations bickered over issues of control but trained a generation of new Jewish leaders and shared a number of defense strategies.

Participation in organizations like the *shehitah* commission provided an opportunity for a new generation of Jewish leaders to learn and apply models of management and defense, as well as to further the political alliances created two decades earlier. These leaders did not necessarily originate in Berlin. Instead, the *Schächtfrage* introduced diverse Jewish activists into a rich network of defense efforts. Rabbi Jacob Cohn, a communal Orthodox rabbi in Kattowitz, and Benjamin Hirsch, a businessman in Halberstadt, both demonstrated this trend. Cohn became actively involved in the ritual questions in the late 1880s, when his local animal protection society endorsed a proposal to ban kosher butchering. Over the next few decades, he attended meetings of the Silesian regional animal protection society and heatedly debated the coordinator of the anti–kosher butchering petition drive. He lobbied his magistrate and town councilors for safeguards on the Jewish rite and defended the ritual in a variety of public forums.[33] Rabbi Cohn gradually began participating in defense at the national level as well. By the 1890s, he was attending national animal protection society meetings and taking part in regional and national campaigns for Jewish self-defense. These national activities soon catapulted him to a degree of political prominence. Cohn coordinated the writing of the counterpetition to the 1906 anti–kosher butchering campaign.[34] His defense activities may have encouraged him to assume the chair of the Association of Rabbis of Upper Silesia and led to his participation in the *shehitah* commission, the Verband,

---

of the Commission to "Fight the Prohibition of *Shehitah*" CJA 75CGE1 893 90–94; 10 May 1905 letter from the Commission to Protect *Shehitah* CAHJP AHW 943b; 29 May 1906 letter from the Berlin-based Jewish agencies to Germany's Jewish communities CAHJP BII 3; 7 July 1908 minutes of the major Jewish defense agencies CJA 75Cve1 340 1–6; July 1908 letters between the Verband and the Centralverein CJA 75Cve1 340 7–9; February 1909 letters between the Verband and the Centralverein 75Cve1 114–115; 24 February 1909 letter from Rabbi Bergmann to the Verband CJA 75Cve1 340 123.

[33]Otto Hartmann, ed., *Bericht über die siebente Versammlung des Verbandes der Thierschutz-Vereine des Deutschen Reiches.* Cohn previously had sent out letters to his congregants about kosher butchering but became more actively involved in the 1890s. 1883 letter from Jacob Cohn to his community members CJA 75DCo1 27 11. Also see Hartmann, ed., *Bericht über die neunte Versammlung*, pp. 61–62.

[34]1906 minutes of the TSV CJA 75 Cve1 344 153–158rs.

and the Centralverein.[35] He was considered so important to the defense efforts that, in 1914 when the Centralverein leadership issued a report on the prohibition of kosher butchering in Oppeln (Prussian Silesia), it reported that it had been strategizing with Cohn on how to overcome the local prohibition.[36] Like Cohn, Hirsch became part of this same network of defense. A member of the philanthropic brass works family that previously had married into the Hildesheimer clan, Hirsch worked tirelessly with a wide range of Orthodox and Liberal-leaning organizations in and out of Berlin to combat the threat against kosher butchering. It is possible that Hirsch participated in these activities because of his family's familial and philanthropic ties with Hildesheimer and his seminary or because Halberstadt's Jewish community felt threatened by a potential *Schächtverbot*.[37]

During the early twentieth century, Jewish community councils also began communicating with one another over kosher butchering defense, thus advancing the German-Jewish political network. During the 1880s and early 1890s, much of the kosher butchering defense came out of Berlin. Increasingly, however, Jewish community councils interacted with one another without the facilitation from the capital city's leadership. In 1904, after the Upper Austrian parliament called for the mandatory stunning of animals before slaughter, the Jewish community council of Vienna sent letters and questionnaires to their coreligionists in Berlin, Hamburg, Munich, Breslau, Fulda, Spandau, Halberstadt, Regensburg, Frankfurt, Cologne, Budapest, Prague, and Krakow. Their correspondence questioned what methods other Jewish communities used for *Niederlegen* (shackling). More important, they inquired as to whether these communities had met with opposition to kosher butchering, and what, if any, kinds of defense practices they had employed. This 1904 series of letters developed into a decade-long conversation among certain Jewish municipal leaders.[38] The Königsberg kosher butchering commission similarly engaged in contact

[35] 28 February 1906 letter from Horovitz to Cohn CJA 75Dco128 193–194; November 1907 letter from Cohn to the Verband CJA 75Dco128 237–238; November 1907 letters from the Commission CJA 75Cve1 344 220–223; 5 November 1907 minutes of the Commission CJA 75Dco1 28 233–234; 11 March 1914 letter from Munk to Cohn CJA 75Dco129 82.

[36] 21 February 1914 letter from the Centralverein to Rabbi Goldmann of Oppeln CJA 75Dco1 29 69.

[37] 5 April 1904 letter to the Centralverein from B. Hirsch 75CGe1893 79; 12 February 1906 letter to B. Hirsch from H. Hildesheimer CJA 75DCo128; 3 July 1906 letter to B. Hirsch from the Free Association CJA 75CVe1344 59; April 8 1904 letter to Centralverein from B. Hirsch CJA 75CGe1893 80; 15 December 1910 letter to Elb from B. Hirsch CJA 75CVe1344 425.

[38] 18 November 1904 letter (13366) to fifteen Jewish community councils from the Jewish community council of Vienna CAHJP A/W 1388 6 and the resulting correspondence

with other Jewish communities in Germany. Originally the commission oversaw issues pertaining to the licensing of *shohetim* and the inspection of kosher meat; by the turn of the century, however, it engaged in kosher butchering defense. It also distributed letters to Jewish communities to inquire about their best practices and, in so doing, launched a series of discussions concerning *Niederlegen* and stunning as well as the role of local communal agencies in national defense efforts.[39] While the Berlin-based agencies continued to be crucial in the self-defense campaigns, German-Jewish political networks existed outside of Berlin and extended beyond the political boundaries of the German state. Jews in Germany communicated with their coreligionists across Germany and in Vienna, Graz, Prague, and Aargau to defend the Jewish rite.[40]

Over time, these inquiries did more than advance the political network of Jews. Slowly, Jewish leaders cemented their relationships with one another despite differences of denominational affiliation, class, generation, or geographic location. Their letters took on a softer tone, imparting personal or financial advice, inquiring about weddings, births, or funerals, and extending well wishes after surgeries or vacations.[41] The defense of kosher butchering offered some Jewish leaders a social network as well as a political one.

As Jewish leaders took part in these emerging political and social networks, they shared defense strategies. Until 1916, Jewish leaders relied on overlapping justifications when they demanded the protection of kosher butchering. They drew on the expansive understandings of religious tolerance to portray Jews as deserving participants on the German political stage and to cast the German government as one that supported religious freedom. They promoted the religious significance

---

between the cities in 1904 and 1905 CAHJP A/W 1388 5, 1388 6, 1388 7, and 1389. Also see 1 January 1912 letter from Verein zur Förderung der Interessen der Synagogen-Gemeinde to the Jewish community of Königsberg CAHJP KN/II/E/III/3. Of course such discussions also could originate out of Berlin. Two years after the Viennese Jews sparked a political conversation concerning self-defense, the *shehitah* commission sent a similar inquiry to twenty-four Jewish community councils. Over a dozen responded, similarly launching a long-term political discourse among local and national Jewish leaders. July 1906 letter from the *shehitah* commission CAHJP KN/II/E/III/3.

[39] 10 February 1909 report from the Jewish community council of Königsberg CAHJP KN/II/E/III/.

[40] An analysis of the defenses of kosher butchering therefore refines the concern that too much of German political history is "prussocentric."

[41] See, e.g., 15 December 1910 letter to Elb from B. Hirsch CJA 75CVe1344 425. Hirsch Hildesheimer seemed to become increasingly fond of some of the men with whom he worked to defend kosher butchering. It became difficult to track with whom he was engaging in correspondence for he often included only the first name.

of the rite and affirmed the ways in which ritual behavior allegedly enhanced the public good.[42]

Emphasizing their own status as citizens, Jewish leaders positioned themselves as deserving of access to the constitution and its supposed freedoms. As such, they crafted their petitions on behalf of "Jewish citizens" or "German citizens of the Jewish faith."[43] Petitions and lobbying campaigns highlighted the constitution's supposed promise of non-discrimination, past public utterances of support, and previous court decisions upholding religious freedoms. A 1902 petition, for example, beseeched Prussia's ministers of interior, culture, and commerce and transportation to "help us protect our rights.... The State constitution guarantees Jewish citizens our religious freedom."[44] These calls for religious toleration frequently inverted the rhetoric of animal protectionists, blending concerns over cruelty with those over the violation of religious freedom. In 1906 Cohn made this case at the national meeting of animal protection societies in Nüremberg. "Let us be good to animals," Rabbi Cohn implored, "but let us also be good to mankind! We should protect the animal from cruelty, but we should also protect men from cruelty to one's conscience."[45] Jewish participants, like their non-Jewish compatriots, used toleration as one way to position themselves in the political debates of the era. They juxtaposed the "Liberal" character of governmental exemptions with the "illiberal" nature of the animal protectionist campaigns.[46]

The defense campaigns also championed the religious importance of kosher butchering. It made sense that religious character would serve as a cornerstone of the defense efforts. Many Jewish leaders invoked religious tolerance when they pleaded for the rite's protection. Moreover,

[42]As earlier chapters revealed, these were not new lines of thinking.

[43]Hirsch Hildesheimer, "Noch ein wort über das Schächten" (typewritten manuscript) 7 June 1906 CJA 75DCo128 85–100; November 9 minutes of the meeting of the *shehitah* commission CJA 75Ve1340 260–7.

[44]1902 petition (draft) from the DIGB and the Federation of Jewish communities of Prussia CJA 75CGe1893. Also see 1902 letter to the Prussian minister of interior from the Federation of Jewish communities of Prussia CJA 75CRA14 275.

[45]Minutes of the 1906 TSV meeting CJA 75Cve1 344 154.

[46]4 November 1906 statement issued by the West Prussian synagogue community council CJA 75CVe1 344 103–104; 29 May 1901 statement published by Erfurt's Jewish community council and Rabbinate CJA 75A Erl 96 67; 1900 letter from the rabbis of Berlin to Berlin's Jewish community council CJA 75Dco1 28 32; letter from Berlin Jewish community council to the community council of Königsberg CAHJP KN/II/E/III/3; 28 February 1906 letter to Jacob Cohn from Horwich CJA 75DCo128 193–4; 4 September 1907 petition/report to the magistrate of Rathenow from its Jewish community CJA 75CVe1344 182–192; July 1901 letter from the Rabbinerverband CJA 75CRa1 4 178; June 1902 letter from the Rabbinerverband CJA 75CGe1893 24. Also see Rabbiner

the campaigns had to contend with critics' countercharge that the rite lacked contemporary religious import and that it was no longer practiced in great numbers. As such, several discussants cast the rite as a mosaic imperative that had far-reaching consequences for all Jews.[47] After the Austrian parliament considered an amendment to ban the slaughter of conscious animals, Vienna's Jewish community council rejected the notion that contemporary scientific knowledge and practice had made kosher butchering superfluous. "Religious writings form the basis of the laws of kosher butchering...Because there is no doubt that the laws of kosher butchering originate in the Biblical commandments, the obligatory character of the rite has been preserved."[48] By describing the rite as "compulsory," "necessary," or "applicable to all," Jewish leaders in Vienna and elsewhere suggested that a prohibition of kosher butchering would force all Jews to go without kosher meat, an exaggerated claim. Petitions often cited an 1894 statement issued by two hundred German rabbis that a ban on kosher butchering "would affect *hundreds of thousands* of adherents of the Jewish faith," a problematic assertion because increasing numbers of Jews no longer observed the dietary laws.[49]

Finally, the kosher butchering campaigns acknowledged the ways in which ritual behavior supposedly improved the public good, thus undermining charges of Jewish particularism. Inverting the criticism lodged against the rite, this defense recast kosher butchering as superior to other methods. The defense campaigns relied heavily on scientific and medical literature to argue that meat from ritually slaughtered animals remained fresher longer and tasted better. Kosher meat also allegedly was free of contagion because blood carried the dreaded syphilis and tubercular pathogens.[50] These efforts also insisted on the humanity of

---

Verband, "Zur Schächtfrage" IW (21 February 1902): 115–116; 9 May 1904 minutes of the Commission CJA 75Cge1 893 90–94; 2 April 1914 petition from the Jewish community of Oppeln CJA 75Dco1 29 84–89.

[47]1888 letter and statement addressed from E. Hildesheimer to his congregants CJA 75AEr196; 21 June 1886 letter to Germany's Jewish communities from the Ausschuss CAHJP DA/648; Counter-petition issued by the Ausschuss CJA 75 Aer1 97 16–16rs. Also see 1 January 1887 petition from the Jewish community of Elmshorn CJA 75 A El 5 24; 22 January 1908 petition (draft) to the minister of culture from the Saxon Jewish Federation CJA 75CVe1344 321–322.

[48]23 March 1905 letter to the Jewish communities of Vienna from the rabbinate of Vienna CAHJP A/W 1388 #8.

[49]Rabbiner Verband in Deutschland, *Rabbinical Statement in Support of Shehitah* CAHJP CA 1657; emphasis is mine. Also see W. and M. L., "Das Tödten der Schlachtthiere," *IDR* 2(1901): 73–80.

[50]See, e.g., J. A. Dembo, *The Jewish Method of Slaughter Compared With Other Methods From the Humanitarian, Hygienic, and Economic Points of View*, trans. Trustees of

kosher butchering, suggesting that because kosher butchering was so rapid it supposedly caused the animals little pain. Supporters of the rite described slaughter combined with stunning as the most unmerciful form of killing. They asserted that stunning damaged the brain and nervous system, but did not result in death. In his study of kosher butchering, J. A. Dembo made that clear. He wrote:

> the charge is brought against the Jewish method of slaughtering that it is not ethical.... It seems to me more than strange that people should look for ethics in the slaughter-house when it is often not to be found outside the cruel place...On me and many persons I know, the spectacle of the blow struck on the animal's head, and particularly when it has to be repeated more than once, has a far more distressing effect. A cold shudder seizes me whenever I witness it.[51]

For Dembo and others, the suggestion implicit in their publications was transparent: Jews eat kosher meat not only because of their religious orientation but also because they are good, rational, moral individuals.[52] Inversely, a decision to ban such a method of slaughter would be contrary to German culture and ideals.

To effectively disseminate these arguments, the defense campaigns of the early twentieth century encouraged the adoption of novel political strategies or improved on the techniques activists already had embraced. These efforts went beyond conducting letter-writing campaigns. Organizations now proactively encouraged varying points of exchange between Jewish and non-Jewish activists. Jewish defense organizations distributed

---

J. A. Franklin (London: Kegan Paul, Trnech, Trübner, 1894); Kallner, "Einiges zur jüdischen Fleischhygiene," in *Die Hygiene der Juden im Anschluß an die Internationale Hygiene-Ausstellung Dresden 1911*, ed. Max Grunwald (Dresden: Verlag der Historischen Abteilung der Internationalen Hygiene-Ausstellung, 1911), pp. 284–291; Vorstande der Freien Vereinigung für die Interessen des orthodoxen Judenthums, *Gutachten der hervorragendsten Physiologen und Veterinärärzte über das "Schächten"* (Frankfurt am Main: Buchdruckerei von Louis Golde, 1894); M. Friedlander, "Sprechsaal," *AZDJ* 15 (1911): 180; Hirsch Hildesheimer, *Replik des Dr. Hirsch Hildesheimer auf das Druckwerk, welches der Buchdruckerei-Besitzer F. W. Glöss seiner Klage-Beantwortung entgegengestellt hat* (Berlin: H.S. Hermann, 189?). An examination of the medical literature can be found in Efron, *German Jews and Medicine*.

[51]Dembo, *The Jewish Method of Slaughter*, p. 14. Also see S. Meyer, "Der Kopfschlag oder der Genickstich nach dem Schächten," *DIZ* 2 (1912): 1–2.

[52]21 June 1886 letter to Germany's Jewish communities from the Ausschuss CAHJP DA/648; 23 November 1907 letter from Beneke, Pathologisches Institut der Universität Marburg CJA 75Dco128 235; Draft of April 1910 statement by Horowitz (Centralverein) CJA 75Cve1 340 356–357; 17 September 1908 letter to H. Hildesheimer from the *shehitah* commission and 1908 corresponding letter from Hildesheimer to Apfel CJA 75CVe1 nr 340 nr 24; 8 April 1909 letter from Leiger to Verbande CJA 75Ve1340 144, 148, 153, and 157.

questionnaires to non-Jewish agencies who they hoped would support them in their safeguarding efforts.[53] They continued to seek alliances with scientific and veterinary authorities, asking that these "experts" procure letters in support of the rite. They also worked with inventors with the hope to create new devices whose improvements would eliminate any grounds for criticism on the part of animal protectionists. The *shehitah* commission was especially active in subsidizing inventors to develop new methods of shackling.[54] One commission member, the Liberal Rabbi Vogelstein (Stettin) pushed his colleagues to support these specific subsidies and touted inventions, such as the one developed by Hugo Silberbach. "That was the perfect *Schächtmethode* of the present: painless…and swifter."[55]

A few other Jewish defense groups called for a different kind of interaction between Jewish advocates of kosher butchering and animal protectionists. The *shehitah* commission and the Bureau for the Protection of *Shehitah* (*Büro für Schächtschutz*) asked their members to join local animal protection societies. They hoped that Jews who attended the advocacy meetings and read the animal protectionist literature would understand the anti–kosher butchering campaign and would be well placed to argue passionately for the rite's defense. Jacob Cohn and Hirsch Hildesheimer, the son of Esriel Hildesheimer, both attended local and national animal protectionist meetings, while between 1906

---

[53]In 1907, the *shehitah* commission sent a detailed questionnaire to dozens of local slaughterhouse commissions to inquire about their best practices; the Saxon Jewish Federation acted similarly. These strategies involved obvious risks. A number of the commissions and agencies with whom these groups openly responded now rejected the Jewish rite in favor of stunning methods. The disadvantages of this strategy may explain why Jewish self-defense organizations abandoned this technique after World War I.

[54]12 May 1907 minutes of the *shehitah* commission CJA 75DCO128 222; 21 October 1907 letter to M. Philippson from Elb CJA 75CVe1344 195; "Schutzvorrichtung für zu schächtende Tiere hauptsächlichst 'Rinder'<hr>" (1912) CJA 75DCo129 49–50.

[55]27 April 1907 letter from Julius Bier to Cohn CJA 75Dco1 28 217; 24 June 1907 letter to the Verband CJA 75Cve1344 159–160; 1908 letter from L. Rosenak to the Bremen Jewish community CJA 75Cve1 344 389; Hugo Silberbach , *Neue! Niederlegerapparat Neu!* CJA 75Dco1 29 112–113; Schwarzenberg & Co., *Beschreibung!* CJA 75Dco1 29 116; Albert Währer, *Schlachtmaschine* (1900) CJA 75Aer1 96 65. "Neue Schlachtmethode," *Der Israelit* 46 (1905): 620. Also see *Apparat zum Festhalten des Kopfes beim rituellen Schlachten von Hornvieh*, CAHJP AHW 127; R. Stern, *Eine neue Methode zum Niederlegen des zum Schächten bestimmen* (Fulda: self-published, 1893); S. Goldberg, *Detusches Reichspatent für stossfreies Neiderlegen von Grossvieh jeder Art zu Schlacht- und Operationszwecken*, CJA 75 Cge1 893 95–96 and 21 April 1907 letter from the Verband to Robert Drucker CJA 75Cve1 350 14. Also see "Halberstadt, 2. Februar," *IDR* 2 (1905): 100–101; "Korrespondenzen, Oldenburg," *IDR* 10 (1906): 609.

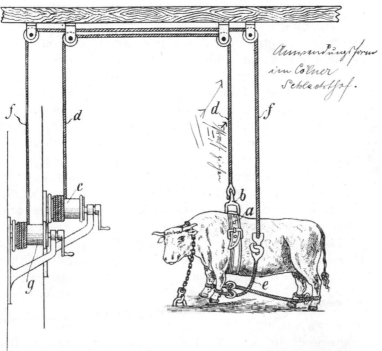

These 1914 images of Niederlegen apparatuses emphasize the humanity of their devices. *Sources*: Neue Synagoge Berlin-Centrum Judaicum Archiv, Berlin (CJA) 75DC01 29 109 and CJA 75DC01 29 115.

and 1910 Benjamin Hirsch reported every few months to the *shehitah* commission on the progress of his local association.

Jewish defense efforts continued to rely heavily on the press.[56] Defense agencies published testimonials (individually and in anthology form) in favor of the rite as well as a variety of leaflets and articles elaborating on the supposed threat to kosher butchering. As the campaigns against the ritual increasingly invoked antisemitic themes, the Jewish press correspondingly publicized the allegedly antisemitic character of the animal protection movement and the link between the anti–kosher butchering and blood libel campaigns. Between 1900 and 1910, Jewish newspapers published over sixty articles concerning the rite, as well as the transcripts of venomous debates over kosher butchering that took place locally, regionally, and nationally. *Im Deutschen Reich* editor Alphonse Levy and *Die Jüdische Presse* editor Hirsch Hildesheimer authored several editorials defending kosher butchering and spearheaded the publication of leaflets and books that specifically addressed the challenges to kosher butchering. Their other defense activities reinforced the link between the press and Jewish defense efforts. Both played significant roles in the *shehitah* commission and separately lobbied regional Prussian ministers on the community's behalf.[57]

The Centralverein's successful legal suits at the turn of the century encouraged a further adjustment in defense strategies; namely, the use of the legal system.[58] After it effectively sued an editor and book publisher for making antisemitic claims about kosher butchering, the Centralverein and other Jewish organizations continued to enter into two kinds of litigation. First, they sued or threatened to sue those in-

---

[56]An example of the call for infiltration can be seen in July 1906 letter from the *shehitah* commission to German-Jewish community councils CAHJP KN/II/E/III/3; H. Hildesheimer 26 July 1906 letter to the synagogue communities CAHJP KN/II/E/III/3.

[57]When the slaughterhouse director v. Schwartz published his study critical of *shehitah*, for example, nine articles and pamphlets dismissing Schwartz and his claims immediately followed. All of these studies rejected the possibility of the Jewish reading public positioning themselves in any way other than supporting kosher butchering. One writer explicitly questioned whether the Jewish supporters Schwarz mentioned were "apostates." See, e.g., Hirsch Hildesheimer, *Das Schächten. Vol. Separatabdruck aus "Blätter für höheres Schulwesen"* (Berlin: Verlag von Rosenbaum & Hart, 1905); *Das Schächten: Eine Vorläufige Auseinandersetzung* (Berlin: Druckerei u. Verlag, U-G, 1906); Noch Ein Wort Über Das Schächten (Typewritten Manuscript 7 June 1906) CJA 75DCo128 85–107; *Replik Des Dr. Hirsch Hildesheimer Auf Das Druckwerk, Welches Der Buchdruckerei-Besitzer F.W. Glöss Seiner Klage-Beantwortung Entegenestellt* CAHJP Inv/1417; Ehrentreu, "Der neuste Vorstoß der Schächtgegner," *DIZ* (26 May 1905) CJA 75DCo128 57–58.

[58]To do so, it relied on criminal law, specifically two articles of the constitution: article 130, which prohibited the inciting of class hatred, and article 166, which prohibited defaming any religious community.

dividuals who allegedly incited hatred against Jews by casting kosher butchering in an antisemitic light. Soon after slaughterhouse director Ernst von Schwartz published his critical study of kosher butchering, for example, Hirsch Hildesheimer and Benjamin Hirsch strategized over how to bring effective legal action against him. "His book," wrote Hildesheimer in a letter to Hirsch, "is filled with falsehoods and lies. We have a powerful case against him and should sue him for a fine." Recognizing that "no case would slow down Schwartz or the members of the animal protection society," Hildesheimer still thought it worthwhile to engage in a legal dispute. In his view, such action might deter other critics and would affect the national political arena.[59] Jewish agencies also used the courts to sue slaughterhouses, which barred Jews from conducting animal slaughter.[60] Prussian law ensured citizens entry to public institutions, and the Centralverein, Verband, and other groups insisted that this gave *shohetim* the right to practice their craft in municipal slaughterhouses without interference. Yet, unlike the body of law that concerned religious defamation, this argument was difficult to craft. Prussian slaughterhouse legislation also established that local authorities had jurisdiction over animal slaughtering practices, which meant that these authorities could mandate the stunning of animals before slaughter. Prussian law only prevented local municipalities from prohibiting *shohetim* from entering the slaughterhouse.

To support these legal campaigns, as well as their questionnaires, postcards, and publications, the defense organizations required substantial funding. Although some existing organizations, such as the Centralverein, were committed to help finance these endeavors, the costs of these campaigns were higher than individual associations could afford.[61] Jewish organizations launched a fourth effort—a series of fund-raising endeavors. They effectively used their letter and postcard campaigns to alert readers to the dangers of animal protection and to request funds. Articulating concern that the "animal protection society is willing to spend a great deal of money," they appealed to their readership to help cover the costs of a national defense.[62] Other fund-raising efforts

---

[59] 12 February 1906 letter to B. Hirsch from H. Hildesheimer CJA 75DCo128.

[60] In both cases, the court agreed that the publications had intended to provoke hatred against the Jews. 24 June 1912 letter from M. Loewenthal to M. Elb CJA 75Cve1 341 74–75.

[61] 9 May 1904 minutes of the Commission CJA 75CGE1893 90–94; 3 April 1906 minutes of the Centralverein LBA AR 3965 I 96–130; 16 July 1908 letter to the Verband from the DIGB CJA 75 CVE1340 12. Also see Derek J. Penslar, "Philanthropy, the 'Social Question' and Jewish Identity in Imperial Germany," *LBIYB* 38 (1993): 51–73.

[62] 1902 letter from the Rabbinerverbandes to the Jewish community of Königsberg CAHJP KN/II/E/III/3; 15 June 1902 letter from B. Hirsch to DIGB CJA 75CGE1893

included the sale of pamphlets and collections of letters defending kosher butchering. Yet, despite their best efforts, Jewish organizations frequently discovered that the costs of financing the protection of Jewish rites had escalated beyond their expectations. In the first eight months of 1906, for example, the *shehitah* commission met its fund-raising goal of 6,765 marks (approximately $1,691) from its letter-writing campaign as well as its sale of an anthology of letters supporting kosher butchering.[63] Two months later, commission leaders announced with some alarm that the intensification of the animal protection crusade necessitated a stronger defense campaign. They now estimated that to adequately safeguard kosher butchering, they needed to solicit more than double what they had already received, namely, some amount between 15,000–20,000 marks (approximately $3,750–5,000).[64]

Finally, Jewish communal councils and agencies continued to defend the rite by attempting to eliminate some of the problems critics identified in kosher butchering practices. They suggested new modifications to the practice, particularly improvements to *Niederlegen*. Worried that current shackling practices undermined efforts to safeguard kosher butchering, *shehitah* commission member Heinemann Vogelstein argued for its improvement. "We can not hide it [*Niederlegen*] away," the Liberal rabbi from Stettin warned.[65] Seven years later, Aron Kober of Breslau expressed a similar hope. The Orthodox Agudat Israel rabbi enthusiastically embraced a new shackling mechanism for his community, suggesting that its humane character might eliminate concerns about kosher butchering more generally.[66] Other agencies and community councils recommended new licensing regulations for *shohetim*.[67] In 1906, the Posen Jewish community council created stricter licensing laws to "create a new generation of exemplary *shohetim* who could not be accused of being cruel to animals." Inspecting their slaughterers yearly, the Posen council trained young community members in the tradition of *shehitah*, even subsidizing them so they would

---

12–13. Also see 2 November 1906 letter to the synagogue communities of Posen from the commission CJA 75Cve1 344 100; 2 September 1908 letter from the commission to German-Jewish community councils CJA 75CVE1340 18.

[63]19 August 1906 minutes of the *shehitah* commission CJA 75Dco128 131–132; Freie Veinigung für die Interessen des orthodoxen, *Bericht über die Geschäftsperiode 1912/1913*, vol. 24 (Frankfurt a.M.: Druckerei Louis Golde, 1914).

[64]November 1907 statement by the *shehitah* commission CJA 75CVE1344 220–3.

[65]12 May 1907 minutes of the *shehitah* commission CJA 75DCO128 222. Also see 16 December 1906 letter to B. Hirsch from the *shehitah* commission CJA 75CVe1344 130.

[66]22 June 1914 letter to Cohn from Aron Kober CJA 75DCo129 117.

[67]January 1912 letter to the community of Königsberg from the Vienna Jewish community CAHJP KN/II/E/III/3.

not be tempted to abandon their new profession.[68] The Jewish board of Königsberg similarly raised the standards of its licensing practice, demanding that the *shohetim* be better versed in veterinary science; this new process favored the German-born Jews of the town and not the Orthodox eastern European Jews, who complained that their *shohetim* would be penalized.[69] Königsberg's Jewish communal leaders divided over who should serve as the Jewish community's rightful spokesman and how best to defend the Jewish rite. Disagreement between native-born and immigrant Jewish leaders concerning issues of political strategy was not limited to Königsberg. Instead, this phenomenon affected Jewish defense throughout Germany.

Confessional Politics

As evidenced by the developments in Königsberg, turn-of-the-century Jewish leaders found it increasingly difficult to contend with the contradictions inherent in their campaigns.[70] Despite the richness of the efforts to safeguard kosher butchering during the decade preceding World War I, the campaigns were internally divided, sometimes to the point of their incapacitation.

A number of overlapping historical phenomena can explain this shift. First, the accusations from critics that few Jews actually practiced the Jewish dietary laws and that technological advancements negated the potential benefits of kosher butchering complicated kosher butchering defense. Both of these charges contained an element of truth. Greater numbers of Jews no longer observed the dietary laws; moreover, Jewish leaders recognized that new stunning and shackling techniques were improvements on those of the past, even if they did not believe that these methods were acceptable according to Jewish law or better than the Jewish method of slaughter. Nevertheless, these charges made it more difficult for Jewish leaders to insist that the religious significance of the rite necessitated exceptional treatment for Jews.[71]

[68] 30 October 1906 letter CJA 75Cve1 344 9.

[69] 20 April 1908 minutes of the Königsberg *shehitah*-commission CAHJP KN/II/E/III/3; 2 January 1912 memo CAHJP KN/II/E/III/e 285. Königsberg Jewish leaders reiterated these complaints during the Weimar era. 6 June 1921 letter from the Synagogue members "Chassidim" CAHJP KN/II/E/III/5.

[70] For a similar argument in another context, see the works by Jacob Borut. Borut, "'A New Spirit Among Our Brethren in Ashkenaz': German Jews Between Antisemitism and Modernity in the Late Nineteenth Century," (Hebrew), Ph.D. diss., Hebrew University, 1991; Borut, "The Rise of Jewish Defense Agitation."

[71] Minutes of the May 12 1907 meeting of the *shehitah* commission CJA 75DCo128 222.

Second, the escalating antisemitic nature of the anti–kosher butchering campaigns similarly encouraged Jewish leaders to be suspicious of tactics that exaggerated Jewish difference. The late nineteenth- and early twentieth centuries saw the radicalization of rhetoric opposing kosher butchering and the implementation of policies that responded to widespread images of Jewish cruelty and bloodthirstiness. Within that charged arena, many Jewish leaders expressed anxiety over the possibility of emphasizing their distinctiveness. Such wariness was exacerbated by the growing presence within Germany of an eastern European Jewish population with distinctive language, dress, and customs. The native Jewish leadership had distanced itself socially from the eastern European Jewish (*Ostjude*) population, which, among other things was more likely to depend on kosher butchers for its meat source. The discomfort with strategies promoting a Jewish reliance on kosher meat may also have been due to the concern that such a portrait would suggest a similarity among native Jews and their eastern European–born coreligionists.

Finally, the growing involvement in the defense efforts of increasingly diverse Jews from across the denominational and geographic spectrum campaigns also complicated organizational efforts to safeguard kosher butchering. Jewish discussants represented varying organizational memberships, religious communities, and regional contexts. As illustrated by the changes within the Königsberg *shehitah* commission, by the turn of the century, growing numbers of eastern European immigrants also became involved in kosher butchering defense. The sheer number of these Jewish activists involved increased the likelihood for internal conflict. As a result of these phenomena, over the course of the early twentieth century, the defense efforts became characterized by intense, internal squabbles.

Jewish leaders continued to debate the extent to which they ought to emphasize the religious significance of kosher butchering. As early as 1903, the Centralverein distanced itself from insisting on religious value as a strategy for defense. Only two years after it first became involved in the *Schächtfrage*, the agency issued a public statement that it had no interest in considering the religious character of kosher butchering. Instead, the Centralverein leadership asserted that it wished to defend the rite on two grounds: (1) the ritual's humanitarian and hygienic character and (2) the illegal discrimination against free religious practice that ensued whenever governments banned the rite.[72] Other national and local Jewish agencies eventually followed the Centralverein's lead.[73] By

[72]"Vereinsnachrichten," *IDR* 11 (1903): 678–683.

[73]In 1906, for example, two members of the Verband, Heinemann Vogelstein and Martin Philippson, demanded that references to *shehitah*'s solely religious character be

1910 there existed a clear divide. Mainstream defenses of kosher butchering coming out of Berlin distanced themselves from the religious character of kosher butchering and, ironically, from the Jews they were trying to protect. In contrast, Orthodox associations, as well as smaller federations and rural community councils, continued to emphasize the rite's religious importance.[74]

This tension was illustrated by the *shehitah* commission's inability to respond unanimously to the amendment proposed by Center Party deputy Adolf Gröber. The commission leadership was deeply divided over Gröber's description of kosher butchering as legally binding for all German Jews. The commission's board consisted of Jewish leaders representing disparate regions and denominational affiliations. Its religiously observant members, Hirsch Hildesheimer (Berlin), Esra Munk (Frankfurt), and Jacob Cohn (Kattowitz) championed Gröber's portrayal; representatives from the Centralverein, Verband, and DIGB ardently disagreed. Proclaiming that it was unwise to stress Jewish difference, Eugen Fuchs, the vice president of the Centralverein, ironically insisted that religion ought to stay out of politics. In his view, religious defenses "belonged only to the cultural sphere."[75] After weeks of in-fighting, a majority of commission leaders demanded that the rite be described as a ritual that held deep importance for some but was significantly healthy for all.[76] Not surprisingly, the Orthodox members of the commission objected to what they saw as the belittling of kosher butchering's religious significance. They suggested that the rite be described as "a Jewish ritual that is based in law and absolutely binding on traditional, torah-true Jews." Kosher butchering, Rabbi Munk reminded the committee members, "was not just a law for orthodox Jews,

---

deleted, 23 October 1906 minutes of the *shehitah* commission meeting CJA 75Dco1 28 209–213. Vogelstein was a Liberal rabbi in Stettin and a determined reformer. Dr. Martin Philippson was a former professor of history at the University of Brussels and served as the chair of the DIGB and the founder of the Verband.

[74]The Jewish community councils in Munich and Vienna and federations in Saxony and Bückeburg, Hagenburg, Stadthagen und Steinhude continued to insist on such a strategy. 22 January 1908 letter (accompanying draft of a petition) to Verband from Max Elb CJA 75CVe1344 320; 2 February 1908 letter to Elb from *shehitah* commission CJA 75CVe1344 328; March 1910 minutes of the Saxon Jewish Federation CJA 75Ve1 340 nr. 250–255; Vorstände der Synagogen-Gemeinden Bückeburg, Hagenburg, Stadthagen und Steinhude, *Petition to the Ministers of Fürstlich Schaumburg-Lippische* (Berlin: Druck von R. Boll, 1907); 23 March 1905 report issued by the Vienna Jewish community council CAHJP A/W 1388 8.

[75]12 May 1907 minutes of the *shehitah* commission meeting CJA 75Dco1 28 222–224.

[76]December 1909 statement by M. Loewenthal CJA 75Cve1 344 44–49; 20 November 1910 *shehitah* commission statement and minutes CJA 75Cve1 340 268–278.

but something that bound all Jews."[77] After the majority of the *shehitah* commission rejected these suggested changes, the Free Association submitted its own petition with much stronger language. Soon after that, it created its own kosher butchering defense agency.[78]

The controversy surrounding Gröber's bill highlights another challenge that defenders of kosher butchering faced: whether they were to demand laws protecting Jewish rituals or merely respond to attacks against them. Most Jewish leaders agreed that it was necessary to launch public campaigns when kosher butchering seemed threatened. However, they disagreed on whether they should promote laws ensuring the ritual's protection.[79] The Bavarian and Saxon Jewish federations, small Jewish community councils in Prussia, and many Orthodox leaders throughout Germany tended to demand the creation of legislation that would safeguard the rite whether or not it was endangered. In contrast, most (Liberal-leaning) Berlin-based organizations expressed concern that such a strategy would merely call attention to Jewish difference. Why, they asked, should the Jewish community willingly portray itself as a separate or particularistic unit? Centralverein executive board member and *Im Deutschen Reich* editor Levy voiced his opposition to a proactive strategy as soon as the Centralverein became involved in defending kosher butchering (1901). That year, Hirsch Hildesheimer began lobbying for individual city laws throughout Prussia that would explicitly protect religious freedoms. After Hildesheimer petitioned Prussia's minister of interior for the promulgation of such legislation, Levy angrily sent letters to members of the Centralverein board denouncing the younger Hildesheimer.[80] Insisting that the efforts to safeguard the rite assumed a different set of strategies than those employed by his Orthodox colleague, he argued that "as long as there was no prohibition, nothing good" could come out of such a proactive

[77]20 November 1910 minutes CJA 75CVe1 340 277–278.

[78]Ironically, the Reichstag later passed Gröber's bill with some significant modifications, but this debate would continue. April 1914 comments by Lowenthal on the Oppeln petition CJA 75DCO129 90.

[79]8 April 1904 letter from B. Hirsch to the Centralverein CJA 75Cge1 893 80; H. Hildesheimer 4 September 1906 letter CJA 75Dco1 28 144–146; 30 July 1906 letter from the Jewish members of the TSV (Offenbach) CJA 75CVe1 344 138; 14 November 1907 letter from H. Hildesheimer to Cohn CJA 75Dco1 28 237–238; 28 April 1909 minutes of the *shehitah* commission CJA 75CVe1 344 402–404; March 1910 minutes of the *shehitah* commission CJA 75CVe1 340 250–255; 11 October 1912 letter from Munk to Cohn CJA 75Dco1 29 30–38.

[80]1901 letters from Hildesheimer to the Prussian ministry of interior and from the Minister to Hildesheimer CJA 75Cra14.

campaign.[81] Over the next ten years, the Centralverein leadership made it clear that their involvement in kosher butchering defense was limited to those disputes in which there existed an explicit threat to German-Jewish freedoms.[82]

As the leadership of dozens of local, regional, and national Jewish agencies bickered over the appropriate political strategies for the defense of kosher butchering, they revealed other long-standing concerns over who, within the Jewish community, could serve as an authentic spokesman for German-speaking Jews. These struggles tapped into long-standing turf wars over the control of Jewish religious and cultural activities. By the turn of the century, Liberal acculturated Jews composed the leadership of most large-sized urban Jewish community councils and agencies. They worried that traditional factions would demand control in organizing the defense of kosher butchering. In their view, traditionalists might—and did—insist on representing Jewish interests when safeguarding kosher butchering because the traditionalists allegedly were "authentic" Jews who supposedly spoke to a higher standard of religious behavior. If successful, such action would not only rob the current leadership of their positions of prominence but also result in a defense campaign that publicly depicted Jews as religiously distinct. Traditional factions had parallel concerns. Increasingly robbed of their positions of control, they saw the defense of kosher butchering as an arena in which they legitimately could position themselves in places of leadership. Worried that a Liberal-led defense of kosher butchering would misrepresent traditionalist needs and desires, they continuously asserted their right to speak on German-Jewry's behalf.

Many of the participating organizations in the defense of kosher butchering were aware of this dilemma. Between 1907 and 1914, they bickered incessantly over whether it was possible for them to collaborate and defend kosher butchering together despite their differences.[83] Some Liberal and moderate groups were open to a potential partnership, but agreed to collaboration only if their denominational and Berlin-based

---

[81]22 September 1902 letter from A. Levy CJA 75Cra14 331. Interestingly, animal protection societies copied Hildesheimer's campaign in 1906 when they pushed for local prohibitions of the Jewish rite.

[82]The Centralverein leadership had been confident in the German constitution's protectionary powers before 1901. In 1898, its legal adviser, Martin Loevinson, remarked that defenses of *shehitah* should be limited to the courtroom. Martin Loevinson, "Bericht der Rechtschutzkommission," *IDR* 7/8 (1898): 287–312.

[83]Early mention of this tension can be found in 5 November 1907 minutes of the *shehitah* commission CJA 75Dco1 28 233–234. Local Jewish agencies faced the same issue. 23 March 1905 Memo from the Vienna Jewish community council CAHJP A/W 13888.

forces remained in control.[84] Traditional leaders, like Agudat Israel's E. Munk, similarly expressed a willingness to cooperate, but only if observant Jews organized the defense efforts. According to Munk, Liberal Jews represented a constituency of nonobservant Jews only; they supposedly were unable to speak on behalf of observant Jews or knowingly defend a religious practice. These discussions came to a head in 1913 when Meier Hildesheimer, also the son of Esriel Hildesheimer, suggested healing the rift between the Jewish agencies. Meier Hildesheimer promoted the creation of a new single organization to protect kosher butchering. Active in religious and secular politics, the rabbi of Berlin's Orthodox community strongly believed that a single agency would carry more weight with the German government. In a letter to a Berlin lawyer and Centralverein activist, Hildesheimer described his vision and rationale.

> Since the death of my brother [Hirsch Hildesheimer], we have done all sorts of work on *shehitah*. We have published letters, written brochures, attended meetings, and spoken at two animal protection association meetings and I have had to settle the writings and correspondence of my brother. The whole process has been unorganized. We want to consolidate our resources and create a single agency that will employ administrators and a secretary... the purpose of my earlier visit [to a number of liberal *shehitah* commission members] was solely to prevent later animosity.[85]

Even though the Verband and Centralverein leadership agreed with Hildesheimer's reading of the political landscape, they immediately rejected his proposal. They had no desire to be subsumed under a potentially Orthodox-led organization. The refusal of the Verband and Centralverein to collaborate with Hildesheimer enraged Orthodox leaders in Berlin and elsewhere. They created a new Orthodox-led defense agency, which they claimed had a mandate to represent all of German Jewry. Hildesheimer, Munk, and their followers housed this new agency, the *Büro für Schächtschutz*, in a building owned by Berlin's Orthodox Jewish community, thus making the agency's denominational affiliation abundantly clear.[86] Members of the Verband and the *shehitah* commis-

---

[84]9 November 1910 minutes of the *shehitah* commission CJA 75Cve1 344 260–267; 28 April1910 statement written by Horowitz CJA 75Cve1 340 356–357; 15 December 1910 letter from B. Hirsch to M. Elb CJA 75Cve1 344 425–426.

[85]M. Hildeshimer was the rabbi of Berlin's Orthodox community. 6 February 1913 letter to M. Horwitz from M. Hildesheimer CJA 75CVe1341 128. Also see 4 February 1913 letter from Verband to Horovitz CJA 75Cve1 341 126.

[86]1914 reports of the *Schächtburo* CAHJP DA 439; CAHJP D/Ba28/2; Büros für Schächtschutz, *Mitteilungen des Büros für Schächtschutz* (1914) CAHJP D/Ba28/212; 1916 reports of the *Schächtburo* CAHJP D/BA28/2 12; 3 November 1925 report to the Vienna Jewish community CAHJP A/W1392; August 1927 letters to Königsberg.

sion expressed outrage that their more observant coreligionists had circumvented their authority. Over the next two years, they bickered with one another over who was the rightful leader of defense. By the Weimar period, however, the Büro had emerged as the dominant player in kosher butchering defense politics.

While these conflicts were framed confessionally, bickering around other issues took place as well. One significant dispute centered on internal Berlin Jewish politics. The four Berlin-based groups active in the defense of kosher butchering—the Verband, Centralverein, DIGB, and the General Assembly of German Rabbis—all attempted to position themselves as spokesmen for German Jewry. Despite their unanimity in trying to wrest control away from their Orthodox coreligionists, they incessantly squabbled over who would emerge as the dominant Jewish agency within Berlin. In 1908, for example, the leaders of these Berlin-based groups temporarily ceased their collaborative efforts when they learned that the Verband was going to be listed as the first editor in a massive anthology of letters defending kosher butchering. Bitterly accusing the Verband of unrightfully accentuating its place in Jewish defense, the other organizations' leadership demanded that the Verband retreat from a prominent view within kosher butchering defense. The fact that the Orthodox rabbi, H. Hildesheimer, had drafted the list of participating organizations made little difference. Instead, after months of backbiting and threats, the organizations finally reached a compromise. They agreed that the Verband could be listed as the publisher, but only if other Jewish organizations were named prominently in the preface. Soon after the release of the anthology, the Berlin groups reconsidered the *shehitah* commission's organizational structure. Their modifications ensured that no one organization would dominate the commission.[87] This was not the last time that the groups would divide over issues of control. Instead, between 1908 and 1916 they continued to jostle for prominence.[88]

As Berlin-based groups squabbled, organizations outside the capital also vied for power. Although the Berlin Jewish leaders envisioned themselves as the most sophisticated and appropriate voices for Jewish self-defense, Jewish communal and regional leaders in other parts of Germany did not necessarily agree. In 1907, the Saxon Jewish Federation and the Berlin-based *shehitah* commission clashed over strategies

[87]The organizations finally agreed that the Verband could be listed as the publisher, with the other Jewish organizations prominently named in the preface. February 1909 letters between the Verband and the Centralverein CJA 75Cve1 114–115.

[88]1908 letter from E. Munk to the Verband CJA 75CVe1 340 15; 11 March 1909 letter from the Centralverein to Verband CJA 75Ve1340 141.

for responding to the Saxon prohibition on kosher butchering. Between 1892 and 1907, the Saxon Federation had restricted its crusade to Saxony's borders, a strategy that the Centralverein, DIGB, and *shehitah* commission endorsed. In 1907, however, the president of the Saxon Federation, Max Elb, suggested that they might be more successful in their campaign if they gained the sympathies of Germans living outside of Saxony. The newly formed *shehitah* commission quickly demanded that Elb reconsider his strategy. Anxious that such an expansionist stance would compromise their own authority, commission members also worried that Elb's new direction would raise an awareness of Jewish particularism and result in additional anti–kosher butchering agitation. In response to Elb's suggestion, the commission demanded that the federation continue to limit its operation to Saxony's borders. The federation president then manipulated the commission's anxieties for his association's benefit. He threatened to take his petition drive to the national arena unless the commission offered additional assistance. The Saxon Jewish community received additional financial and administrative assistance from the Berlin-based group, and Elb restricted his efforts to Saxony.[89]

Motivations

An analysis of the conflict between the Saxon Federation and the *shehitah* commission raises the question of why different groups of German Jews entered the public arena at this juncture. Clearly, more religiously observant participants in the debate were concerned that a restriction or prohibition of kosher butchering would result in a vegetarian diet or the payment of high taxes on meat imports. But why did Liberal members of the *shehitah* commission and other groups attempt a collaborative defense and demand the protection of a Jewish rite that many of them did not follow at home? Although few proponents articulated specific reasons for involvement, there were several issues that likely motivated Jewish leaders to participate in the defense of kosher butchering.

The rise and recasting of antisemitism during the late nineteenth and early twentieth centuries promoted a shift within German-Jewish

[89]21 October 1907 letter from Elb to M. Philippson CJA 75Cve1 344 195; 1908 petition of the Saxon Jewish Federation CJA 75Cve1 344 320. The Berlin-based leadership continued to clash with local community leaders in places as disparate as Oppeln, Munich, Vienna, and Breslau. 25 July 1905 letter to the Association of East Prussian Synagogue Communities from the DIGB CAHJP KN/II/E/III/3; January 1910 draft to

political behavior. Jewish leaders identified the proposed slaughter-house laws as part of the antisemitic shift, arguing that the *Schächtverbo-ten* were pretexts for revoking Jewish privileges more generally. Jewish leaders portrayed the animal sentimentalists as insidious and manipulative. They presented a clear message: Attacks against Jewish rituals composed a central aspect of modern antisemitic platforms.[90] Esriel Hildesheimer ridiculed Otto Hartmann, the national animal protection society president, for his allegedly antisemitic motives. "He is not concerned with cattle but with human beings," wrote Hildesheimer, "particularly with Jews."[91] Three years later, the Jewish community of Berlin revived its defense efforts when its leadership felt itself the object of antisemitic derision. In 1901 the Berlin Society for the Protection of Animals mailed a letter veiled with antisemitic threats to all registered Jews in Berlin. Members of Berlin's Jewish community council decried the antisemitic and scheming tone of the animal protectionist communication and vowed to double their efforts to protect the rite whether or not they ate kosher meat at home.[92] For them, the antisemitic nature of the anti–kosher butchering crusades necessitated their participation in the defense campaigns.

Certainly, the international trend among Jewish organizations to take part in self-defense encouraged interest in the safeguarding of kosher butchering. During the 1890s and early 1900s, Jewish leaders created what Evyatar Friesel has called "Jewish civil rights organizations."[93] These groups demanded Jewish civic and religious freedoms and articulated

---

Schneider from Breslauer CJA 75CVe1344 444; 1 January 1912 letter to the *shehitah* commission from the Jewish community council of Breslau KN/II/E/III/3. Despite Elb's difficult dealings with the commission in 1907, he remained a strong supporter of the Verband. Elb letter to the Chemnitz Jewish community CJA 75CVe1344 197.

[90]See, e.g., 2 April 1914 petition to the minister of interior, CJA 75Dco129 84–89; "Zur Schächtfrage," *JP* 30 (1886), p. 287; Rabbiner-Verband, "Zur Schächtfrage," *IW* 8 (1902): 115–116.

[91]E. Hildesheimer, 1888 *Letter and Statement* CJA 75AEr1 96 3 and 7. Also see Alliance Israélite Universelle, 1 December 1896 report CJA 75DCo128 24. Leopold Hamburger, *Herr Otto Hartmann in Cöln and sein Kampf gegen die Schlachtweise der Israeliten: Denverehr-lichen Mitgliedern der Tierschutzverein gewidmet von einem Collegen* (Frankfurt a.M.: Buch-druckerei von M. Slobotzky, 1889).

[92]1900 statement of the Berlin TSV CJA 75Aer196 68. An analysis of the letter can be found in Alphonse Levy, "Antisemitischer Thierschutz," *IDR* 10 (1900): 501–505. 1900 letter from the rabbis of Berlin to Berlin's Jewish community CJA 75Dco1 28 32. The authors of the letters included Hirsch Hildesheimer, as well as Liberal rabbis Drs. Maybaum, Weisse, Stier, Rosenzweig, Eschelbacher, and L. Blumethal. Also see letter from Berlin Jewish community council to the community council of Königsberg CAHJP KN/II/E/III/3.

[93]Friesel's article interestingly places the creation of these organizations into a comparative context and he examines the creation of the Alliance, the American Jewish

an awareness of problems facing Jews throughout the world. Nationally based and unconnected (in principle at least) to a religious position, they drew heavily from the lessons of mass politics to act against and remedy discrimination. The German-Jewish organizations that participated in the campaigns promoting kosher butchering not only shared a number of these characteristics but also frequently communicated and strategized with "civil rights organizations," such as the French Alliance Israélite Universelle and the Union of German-Austrian Jews.[94] While Jewish national groups tended to pursue their own foreign and domestic policies, they did work together on some issues. Central European Jewish organizations shared strategies over how to combat anti–kosher butchering campaigns in Germany, Austria, and Switzerland.[95] With the onset of World War I, they also increasingly collaborated on questions concerning minority rights.[96]

The Jews' interest in confessional politics, like the revival of antisemitism, was part of a larger change within the German political system. When Jews entered the national arena and demanded their specific rights as minority members of the state, they did so during a political watershed. The 1890s saw the dismissal of Bismarck, the defeat of the pro-governmental "cartel parties" (National Liberals and Conservatives), and the electoral successes of the Social Democratic Party (SPD) and other opposition parties. Late nineteenth- and early twentieth-century Germany witnessed the emergence of a dynamic popular politics characterized by high electoral participation, detailed political coverage, and the emergence of new interest-driven movements. As Jews engaged in special interest defense campaigns, so too did members of associations as diverse as the German Peace Society, the Evangelical League, the Pan-German League, and National Social Association. Politicized Catholics were particularly likely to do so. In their defense against attacks concerning clerical control over education, they similarly made

---

Committee, and the British Board of Deputies alongside the Centralverein. Friesel, "The Political and Ideological Development of the Centralverein." His analysis launched a significant amount of debate. Abraham Margaliot, "Remarks on the Political and Ideological Development of the Centralverein before 1914," *LBIYB* 33 (1988): 101–106; Chaim Schatzker, "Comments on Evyatar Friesel's Essay in Year Book 31," *LBIYB* 33 (1988): 97–99.

[94]2 April 1894 letter from the Jewish community council of Vienna CAHJP A/W 1388 #2; 1 December 1896 statement by the Alliance Israélite Universelle CJA 75Dco128 24; 1904 response to Jewish community council of Vienna from the Jewish community of Breslau CAHJP A/W 1388 7.

[95]28 September 1907 letter from Guggenheim (Zürich) CAHJP A/W 1389. While there existed a small movement to ban kosher butchering in England, the German defense organizations paid little attention to it until the Weimar period.

[96]Fink, *Defending the Rights of Others.*

claims for religious tolerance while asserting their place as deserving citizens within the German state. Jewish agencies learned from, and were encouraged by, the strategies, successes, and failures of these groups.[97]

Yet, the defenses of kosher butchering did not simply imitate other special interest groups. Instead, Jewish agencies served as subcultures within the larger political sphere. They launched confessionally oriented campaigns that, by their very nature, could not escape the question of Jewish difference. Despite the fact that many of the German-Jewish leaders did not embrace the religious rites they sought to defend, Jewish leaders responded to the animal protection appeals by justifying their own acculturation and that of other Jews. Their defenses emphasized their universality by highlighting the respectability of Jewish rites and simultaneously defending Jewish religious difference. These agencies emphasized the religious significance of the rite despite their differences in actual religious practice.

The defense campaigns not only were influenced by the political arena but also helped to shape it. The attempts to safeguard kosher butchering successfully encouraged dozens of slaughterhouse directors, state ministers, and local town authorities to reject proposed or existing legislation. In some cases they forced governments to consider the viability of religious tolerance in the modern age; in other settings they provided validation and a larger audience for Center Party attempts to force similar issues. In addition, the successes of the kosher butchering defenses changed the *Schächtfragen* more generally. As Jewish groups made inroads in safeguarding the Jewish rite, animal protection and antisemitic associations correspondingly shifted their operations. Soon after the incorporation of the *shehitah* commission, for example, the Association of Animal Protection Societies of the German Reich intensified its efforts and launched a costly nationwide petition campaign. It and similar groups quickly copied the programs operated by the Jewish agencies. They funded the publication of anthologies critical of kosher butchering, began tracking the Jewish operations, and communicated with a wide spectrum of special interest groups.

† † † † †

In the fall of 1906, the *shehitah* commission contacted Jewish community councils throughout Germany. Hoping to launch a successful countercampaign to a recent animal protectionist operation, it asked

[97]On Wilhelmine politics, see Margaret Lavinia Anderson, *Practicing Democracy: Elections and Political Culture in Imperial Germany* (Princeton, NJ: Princeton University Press, 2000); David Blackbourn, *Class, Religion, and Local Politics in Wilhelmine Germany: The Centre Party in Württemberg before 1914* (New Haven: Yale University Press, 1980), esp. pp. 23–60; Oded Heilbronner, *Catholicism, Political Culture, and the Countryside: A Social History of the Nazi Party in South Germany* (Ann Arbor: University of Michigan Press, 1998).

rabbis and Jewish leaders to provide them with detailed information concerning local slaughtering practices and the agitation being launched against them. Dozens of communities responded directly to the commission; other regional councils assumed the responsibility of contacting their local councils and submitting detailed reports.[98] The 1906 correspondence generated little new information but reflected the modern character of Jewish political behavior. The letter-writing exchange among Jewish community councils, agencies, and individual participants, like the petition campaigns they generated, involved all Jewish communities across denominational affiliation, size, or wealth. The flurry of correspondence helped to cement political and social relationships among diverse Jews.

This is not to suggest that no divides existed. Instead, the paradoxes inherent in the confessional campaigns tended to generate two models of defense: one Berlin-based and liberal leaning and the other willing to adopt the language of the religiously observant camp and located inside and outside of Germany's capital. Berlin-based groups tended to insist on control and the liberal spirit; local agencies wished to retain their authority.

Despite their divisions, for the duration of the Wilhelmine period, the two camps collaborated—albeit sometimes awkwardly—and, in so doing, developed a modern political form. The constant networking encouraged extant and new Jewish activists to share rhetoric and strategies of defense. Their organizations developed their missions, strategies, and membership base. They took part in the formulation of novel fundraising efforts, letter-writing and postcard campaigns, lobbying enterprises, and publication ventures. They entered into partnerships with scientists, veterinarians, slaughterhouse directors, and inventors. Most important, they also began working with an unlikely bedfellow, the Catholic Center Party.[99] With the help of these different alliances, Jewish leaders helped to prevent a national prohibition of kosher butchering, encouraged the repeal of dozens of local

[98]2 November 1906 letter to the Jewish community council of Posen from the *shehitah* commission CJA 75CVe1 344 100; 22 November 1906 letter to the *shehitah* commission from the Jewish community council of Posen CJA 75CVe1344 119; 30 November 1906 letter from the *shehitah* commission to the Jewish community of Posen CJA 75CVe1344 127; 1904 letter from Vienna's Jewish community council to German-Jewish community councils CAHJP A/W 1388 6; 1904 responses from the community councils of Frankfurt, Breslau, Danzig, Halberstadt, Lemberg, and Munich CAHJP A/W 1388 7. Many similar efforts followed.

[99]As early as the 1886–1887 Reichstag debates, Center Party leaders emerged as important alliances in the protection of Jewish ritual behavior. *Aus den Verhandlungen des Deutschen Reichstags über das Schächten (18. Mai 1887, 25. April 1899, und 9. Mai 1899)* (Berlin: n.p., 1909), pp. 3–4.

restrictions of kosher butchering, and advanced a national awareness of the cause.

The enthusiasm over the successes of kosher butchering defense came to a head twice during the years immediately preceding World War I: first, when the Reichstag approved Gröber's amendment in 1910 and, second, in 1914, when the Prussian Ministry of Trade overturned a set of Silesian prohibitions of the rite. During World War I, however, both sides of the debate paid little attention to kosher butchering. This disinterest continued until 1917, when the Bundesrat approved a set of policies that safeguarded the Jewish rite.

The 1917 Bundesrat intervention should have put an end to the decades-long *Schächtfragen*. Instead, that year ushered in a new series of conflicts that continued until the Nazi assumption of power in 1933. Chapter 6 turns to this set of disputes.

A "Renaissance" for the Ritual Questions?
The Ritual Debates of the Weimar Republic

In 1917 the German Bundesrat considered kosher butchering for the first time since the outbreak of World War I. In a controlled war economy, the German state had begun to regulate food production and distribution two years earlier. During the so-called turnip winter of 1916–1917, the nation faced escalating food prices and shortages. German civilians witnessed a dramatic diminution in the quantity and quality of their food, which resulted in the deterioration of health and morale. Food quickly became the focus of politics and conflict. Striking workers voiced the frustration of those who could not earn enough to buy necessary foodstuffs. Women and children attempted to procure food on the black market. On marches to government buildings, they and their male compatriots demanded access to additional foodstuffs. In response, the German government tightened its controls. It conducted searches of farms to find hidden reserves of food and implemented strict regulations concerning the retrieval, preparation, and distribution of food.[1]

Spurred by both these menacing conditions and his desire to implement political reforms, German Chancellor Bethmann-Hollweg requested that the Bundesrat reconsider slaughterhouse practices. Just months before the Kaiser demanded Bethmann-Hollweg's resignation, the chancellor asked that deputies deliberate two issues: (1) whether kosher butchering ought to be prohibited and (2) whether the practice of itinerant kosher and nonkosher animal slaughter should be permitted.[2]

[1] Richard Bessel, *Germany after the First World War* (Oxford: Clarendon Press, 2002 reprint); Belinda Davis, *Home Fires Burning: Food, Politics, and Everyday Life in World War I Berlin* (Chapel Hill: University of North Carolina Press, 2000).

[2] The archives hold no evidence of Hollweg's personal motivation in this matter.

Members of the Bundesrat agreed that it would be expedient for Germany's abattoirs to disallow both. Kosher butchering allegedly required more manpower and supposedly resulted in meat that spoiled quickly. These characteristics were problematic in a time of war. The military fronts—and not the slaughterhouse—required strong men, and meat needed to remain edible for as long as possible, especially if it was going to be sent to the men fighting the war. For all of these reasons, legislators banned the cut required by kosher butchering. However, they were unwilling to force Germany's Jews to comply with this order. Recognizing the religious significance of kosher butchering, deputies and the minister of interior formally exempted German Jews from the 1917 regulation. The Bundesrat and Ministry did not create a similar exemption for itinerant kosher slaughter. Deputies viewed itinerant kosher butchering as doubly undesirable and explicitly forbade it.[3]

The 1917 deliberations constituted a break in the *Schächtfragen*, ending a brief phase of disinterest in the Jewish rite. Between 1914 and 1916, few governmental agencies had paid attention to kosher butchering. Yet, Bethmann-Hollweg's mandate that the Bundesrat investigate the cut of kosher butchering and the practice of itinerant animal slaughter encouraged some animal protectionists and governmental leaders once again to express interest in the Jewish method of killing animals for food. The 1917 kosher butchering question differed from earlier disputes. During the imperial period, municipalities, regional agencies, and state governments had bickered incessantly over their jurisdiction to regulate Jewish ritual behavior. The Bundesrat's 1917 intervention insisted on the right of the Reich vis-à-vis individual states to control or protect Jewish rites. Moreover, the 1917 deliberations illuminated a fissure in Jewish self-defense. In their reaction to the Bundesrat's discussion, local and national German-Jewish organizations exhibited little of the political activity they had demonstrated in years past. Instead, they were quiet.[4]

Why the acquiescence? There are a number of explanations. Like their German compatriots, Germany's Jews were occupied with the hardships of war. Moreover, they were not inconvenienced dramatically by these 1917 orders. Much of German Jewry no longer observed religious dietary laws, and fewer benefited from the practice of itinerant

[3]Perhaps deputies worried that Jewish communities might employ illegal slaughterers to avoid rations or profit from additional unregulated slaughter. 2 March 1917 Bundesrat Session SHD MDI 16178 no. 33; Grünpeter, "Sind Die Schächtverbote Rechtsgültig?" *Central-Verein Zeitung* (*CVZ*) 20 (15 May 1931): 251–252. Also see earlier concerns in 19 June 1916 letter to the Jewish community of Hüttenbach CAHJP N 13/24, 1916.

[4]One exception can be found in Büro für Schächtschutz (Büro), *Mitteilungen des Büros für Schächtschutz* (Berlin) CAHJP D/Ba28/212.

slaughter.[5] It also is likely that Jewish organizations chose not to actively defend kosher butchering because, at this juncture, they had little interest in publicly safeguarding a practice that raised concerns with Jewish violence and financial noxiousness. Antisemitic opinion had become more commonly accepted as the war situation had worsened, evidenced by the Prussian War Ministry's 1916 census of Jewish participation in the war effort.[6] These events and the *volkisch* charges that inspired them occupied the attention of German-Jewish leaders and encouraged their unwillingness to respond to the 1917 Bundesrat deliberations. Such trepidation was not limited to the kosher butchering question. As David Engel has suggested elsewhere, during World War I, Jewish organizations were often reluctant to challenge instances of antisemitism.[7]

The 1917 Bundesrat intervention and the changes accompanying it should have put an end to the kosher butchering questions. Instead, the concluding years of World War I ushered in a new series of conflicts. In the years between defeat in the war and the dissolution of the Weimar Republic, kosher butchering served as a topic of interest in spoken and written debates. While circumcision remained a subject of fascination in publications, kosher butchering attracted attention from a widening group of participants in an expanding number of locations.[8] The most significant addition to the *Schächtfragen* was the National Socialist German Worker's party (NSDAP), whose members increasingly contributed to the disputes after the party's reorganization in 1925. Over the course of the late 1920s and early 1930s, the Nazis were active—and sometimes dominant—participants in the kosher butchering questions. Their involvement heralded a shift in the character of the debates and alarmed Germany's Jewish communities and their supporters.

[5]It is difficult to ascertain the percentage of German Jews that observed the Jewish dietary laws; historians estimate that it was approximately 15–20 percent of the entire population. Trude Mauer, "From Everyday Life to a State of Emergency: Jews in Weimar and Nazi Germany," in Kaplan, ed., *Jewish Daily Life in Germany, 1618–1945*, p. 277.

[6]The 1917 creation of the chauvinistic Fatherland party also highlighted the vulnerable position of German Jews.

[7]David Engel, "Patriotism as a Shield: The Liberal Defense Against Anti-Semitism in Germany During the First World War," *LBIYB* 31 (1986): 147–172.

[8]Medical, anthropological, and sexology journals continued to analyze the Jewish rite of circumcision, but few Jewish communities or governmental agencies devoted political attention to this rite. Felix Bryk, *Die Beschneidung bei Mann und Weib: ihre Geschichte, Psychologie, und Ethnologie* (Neubrandenburg: Verlag Gustav Feller, 1931); Julie Bender, "Zur Geschichte und Bedeutung der Beschneidung bei den Juden," *ZFS* (1922); Berndt Götz, "Das Zweigeschlechterwesen und die Beschneidung der Knaben und Mädchen," *Archiv für Frauenkunde* 17.1 (1931): 60–69; Henryk Leuchter, "Die prophylaktische Zirkumzision," *Dermatologische Wochenschrift* (10 May 1930); Erich Schlüssel "Hygienische Auswirkungen der Beschniedung," *Hygiene und Judentum: Eine Sammelschrift*, ed. Hans

The deliberations' expanded participatory base corresponded with significant changes in the character and content of the kosher butchering questions. Between 1919 and 1923, when the *Schächtfragen* attracted the narrowest band of participants, the disputes mostly concerned the economic implications of the rite. Animal protectionist pleas that kosher butchering constituted a form of cruelty largely went unheeded. Instead, during this period, most discussants repeated anxieties over the disproportionate rate at which Jews allegedly consumed meat and profited from the meat trade.

These concerns remained active during the debates of 1924–1933, when participants increasingly focused on Jewish ritual behavior. Several intersecting conversations took place. Some contributors expressed a general concern over extant slaughterhouse practices. Because they insisted that advancements in fastening and stunning methods did not clash with Jewish custom, their petitions differed from the earlier campaigns of the imperial period. These new crusades maintained that Jewish religious authorities would come to condone the new technologies. A second group argued against the universal enforcement of new stunning technologies. Pointing to the constitution's promise of religious and democratic freedoms, they claimed that the proposed (or enacted) slaughterhouse promulgations violated religious toleration. These discussants faced tremendous opposition from a widening group of participants who increasingly linked antisemitic images and rhetoric with the Jewish rite. This third group frequently demanded the explicit prohibition of kosher butchering and was not content with slaughterhouse reforms that would indirectly ban the rite.

Despite the popularity of these antisemitic views, between 1924 and 1929 local and state governments tended to heed calls for religious

---

Goslar (Dresden: Verlag Jac Sternlicht, 1930), pp. 23–25; Felix A. Theilhaber, *Die Beshneidung* (Berlin: Verlag von Louis Lamm, 1927). Circumcision also served as a topic of interest for a few psychoanalysts at the time and was the focus of a novel. Erich Ludendorff, *Die Vollendung des künstlichen Juden durch Zwangsbeschneidung* (Berlin: self-published, 1927). Ludwig Levy, "Ist das Kainszeichen die Beschneidung? Ein kritischer Beitrag zur Bibelexegese," in *Imago,* ed. Sigmund Freud (Leipzig und Wien: Internationaler Psychoanalytischer Verlag, 1919): pp. 290–293; Theodor Reik, "Das Kainszeichen: Ein psychoanalytischer Beitrag zur Bibelerklärung," in *Imago,* ed. Freud, pp. 31–42. With the exception of licensing issues, governments ceased to debate the rite's merits and regulatory agencies. The few spoken debates occurred almost entirely within the Jewish community and involved the growing funds required to support the rite and the possibility of circumcising children born to Jewish fathers and non-Jewish mothers. 12 November 1919 letter to the Jewish community of Mannheim from Hirschhorn CJA 75BKa124 239; 30 January 1920 letter to the Jewish community council of Baden from Mazer CJA 75BKa124 242; 8 February 1920 report from the *Konferenzrabbiner* (Freiburg) CJA 75Bka124 244. Also see materials concerning the funding of circumcisions in Vienna CAHJP A/W 1362.

protection rather than demands for Jewish compliance. This period witnessed an explosion in the number of local and state deliberations but experienced few bans on the rite. In contrast, the last phase of the disputes—between 1930 and 1933—saw an escalation of the kosher butchering question. During this period, an increasing number of local and state governments implemented slaughterhouse reforms that directly or indirectly prohibited the rite. Yet, the majority of local municipalities still rejected animal protectionist petitions. It was only in April 1933, less than three months after the Nazis seized power that the National Socialist government forbade kosher butchering throughout Germany.[9]

A Twisted Path

The 1933 prohibition of the rite by the National Socialists, like the *Schächtfragen*'s antisemitic component and the significant presence of the National Socialists within the deliberations, superficially suggests an inevitability of some kind: perhaps that the conflicts foreshadowed the Nazis' legislative restrictions or their genocidal atrocities. Such assumptions, while tempting in their simplicity, are unsuitable. As scholars have shown in other contexts, this kind of reading uses hindsight as the lens through which historical events are understood. It also presents a deeply flawed view of the disputes themselves.

The kosher butchering questions were neither linear nor direct; the early deliberations did not neatly or gradually develop into the vitriolic debates that followed. To adapt the famous terminology of Karl Schleunes, the *Schächtfragen* assumed a "twisted road" to the April 1933 ban.[10] The disputes met with successes and failures, which often mirrored the up- and downturns of the German economy. The deliberations were mildest during the years of relative economic stability (1924–1929) and fiercest after the depression of 1929. However, even within these phases, they experienced irregularities. The conflicts were vitriolic in regions affected by peasant agrarian activism while government leaders in tourist areas sometimes squashed the animal protectionist demands out of fear that Jewish self-defense efforts would deter visitors to their region. Instead of foreshadowing what was to come, the disputes were

[9]The prohibition was part of the Nazis' first set of economic restrictions on Jews. "Gesetz über das schlachten von Tieren vom 21 April 1933," *Reichsgesetzblatt* (21 April 1933): 203. It did not, however, put an end to kosher butchering practices.

[10]Karl A. Schleunes, *The Twisted Road to Auschwitz; Nazi Policy toward German Jews, 1933–1939* (Urbana: University of Illinois Press, 1970).

lodged firmly within a republic that witnessed painful political and economic changes and compromises.[11]

Likewise, the *Schächtfragen* suggest that German antisemitism and the Nazi rise to power were nonlinear developments. The deliberations, like the Republic in which they occurred, were shaped by liberal, tolerant, and reformist motivations, as well as by illiberal, antireformist, and intolerant impulses. On the one hand, the kosher butchering questions provided moderates and leftists with the opportunity to offer formulations and implement policies concerning democracy, reform, and the authority of the nation vis-à-vis the states. On the other hand, they also served as a laboratory for the development of antisemitic rhetoric and the growth of antisemitic political power. These contradictions continued to shape the deliberations through the early 1930s. While a greater number of governments passed bans on the rite during this phase, those in positions of power continued to clash over the extent to which they wished to translate anti-Jewish rhetoric into action.

Analogous inconsistencies were evident in the political maturation of the disputes' participants. The kosher butchering questions illuminate the complicated trajectory taken by the Nazis to positions of power and the significance of place and time to these different paths. Municipal animal protection campaigns offered the Nazis a platform and an opportunity for political participation; in some areas, the kosher butchering question provided local Nazis with an entry into the formal political sphere. However, Nazi successes and failures depended on several overlapping factors, including, but not limited to, economic conditions, the availability of foodstuffs, the religious and social environment, and local receptiveness to antisemitic rhetoric and to a Nazi presence.

The self-defense campaigns also paralleled economic and political fluctuations. The movement to safeguard kosher butchering underwent a renaissance during the republican era. New Jewish and gentile groups became actively involved in defense efforts and employed novel strategies to protect the rite. Yet, at the same time, Jewish self-defense no longer strove to be unified, democratic, and nondenominational (at least in name). Now, the Orthodox *Schächtbüro* and the Centralverein launched separate, dissimilar, competing campaigns to defend Jewish rites, while local community councils and synagogue boards clashed over issues of control. The *Schächtfragen* of this era highlight the vulnerability and complexity of the more than 1,600 Jewish communities of Weimar Germany.[12]

[11]Detlev J. K. Peukert, *The Weimar Republic: The Crisis of Classical Modernity*, trans. Richard Deveson (New York: Hill and Wang, 1987), p. xiii.

[12]Weimar Jewry lost 627 of its previous Jewish communities under the Versailles Treaty. After 1919, the Jewish communities of Posen, West Prussia, and Alsace-Lorraine had new national allegiances.

Historical irregularities punctuated the kosher butchering questions, just as they did the formation, middle years, and end of Germany's first republic. The *Schächtfragen* took place in three overlapping phases, each affected by changes in state and society. These phases between 1919 and 1924, 1924 and 1929, and 1930 and 1933 illuminate the republic's contradictory character; they also highlight the inconsistent nature of German antisemitism, Nazi political development, and Jewish self-defense.

Phase I: Limited Interest, 1919–1924

The kosher butchering disputes that occurred between 1919 and 1924 illustrate the strange nature and limitations of postwar German antisemitism. Even though antisemitic sentiment engulfed Germany following the country's devastating defeat in war, this phase witnessed a set of *Schächtfragen* that were—at least on paper—devoid of antisemitic sentiment. Instead, these deliberations revolved around rates of consumption, not the ways in which Jews slaughtered animals.

Between 1919 and 1924, punitive calls to reconsider kosher butchering went unheeded.[13] When Dresden's and Magdeburg's chapters of the Association of Animal Protection Societies of the Reich (Reichstierschutzverband) launched an anti–kosher butchering campaign in 1919, their petitions fell on deaf ears. Few outside this circle of animal advocates called for the prohibition of the rite; the majority of association members disapproved of the Magdeburg/Dresden proposal.[14] Instead, these initial disputes were over the relationship between kosher butchering and the paucity of available foodstuffs. The handful of town councils, local animal protectionists, and state ministers who took part in the early *Schächtfragen* expressed alarm that Jews slaughtered meat at a higher rate than the non-Jewish population and suggested reforms that would curb Jewish consumption of kosher meat. They typically did not call for a ban on the rite.

[13]An exception can be found in Würzburg. 13 April 1923 memo and letter to the Jewish community of Würzburg from the city council CAHJP WR 561; 3 November 1924 letter to German Jewish communities from the Würzburg Jewish community and responses CAHJP WR 561.

[14]"Das Schächten auf dem Verbandstag der Tierschutzvereine," *Frankfurter Israelit* (*FI*) (11 September 1919) CJA 75CVE1341 217; September 1919 report of the Büro CAHJP D/Ba28/212; and "Münchner Tierschutzverein," *Münchner Neueste Nachrichten* (*MNN*) 146 (1924): 3. Also see 28 May report by the Office for Legal Affairs (Vienna) CAHJP A/W 13924 and June 1923 memo to Rudolf Taussig from Vienna Jewish community council CAHJP A/W 1392. The Schächtburo and DIGB interpreted both events as attacks against the Jewish rite. 1919 letter from Munk to DIGB CAHJP AHW 568 b-2.

Evidence from a few states suggests that a disproportionate percentage of meat slaughtered at this time was killed by the Jewish method. In Hamburg, for example, 2 percent of the city's population was Jewish, but 12 percent of the city's animal slaughter took place without stunning the animals first. In Hesse, the rate was similar. Slaughterhouses there reported that 10 to 15 percent of their animal slaughter was conducted by the Jewish method. Yet, these numbers were misleading: They included the slaughter of conscious animals by non-Jews for the gentile population.[15] Moreover, Ministry reports from this era suggest that butchers across Germany used the "Jewish method of slaughter" with some regularity because of the method's low cost and technological simplicity. Kosher butchering required only a butcher, a knife, and some kind of fastening mechanism; it did not rely on costly stunning mechanisms, something that many butchers found appealing during the economic hardships of the postwar period. There were other factors as well. Jews who observed the Jewish dietary laws could not eat all of the meat an animal produced, a fact that had garnered much attention by animal protectionists before the war. Moreover, despite the growing number of Jews who no longer practiced *kashrut*, the eastern and central European Jewish immigrants who had made their way to Germany during and after the war frequently required kosher meat for their diet.

Governments in Hamburg, Hesse, and elsewhere issued ordinances that addressed concerns with Jewish consumption of kosher meat. Similar to some of the earlier slaughterhouse legislation of the *Kaiserreich*, these laws restricted the number of cattle *shohetim* could slaughter and when that slaughter could take place.[16] The purpose was to reduce

[15]Slaughterhouse officials in Hamburg estimated that *shohetim* conducted 52–65 percent of all slaughter done on conscious animals, whereas the number was only 11 percent in Leipzig. 11 June 1925 report from the Reich minister of interior BH ML 2437. The minister stated that between 52–65 percent of that amount was conducted by *shohetim*. However, Hamburg slaughterhouse commission member Neumann estimated that in the first eight weeks of 1925 49 percent of the animals slaughtered by *Schächten* were kosher, which was a 1 percent decrease from the previous year. 12 March 1924 letter from Neumann to Heidecker CAHJP AHW 568a; 29 March 1924 letter from Heidecker to local public health authorities CAHJP AHW 568a. In this way, the numbers differ slightly from those given by Trude Mauer for 1925. Mauer stated that 12 percent of the slaughter was done by *shehitah*. Mauer, "From Everyday Life to a State of Emergency," p. 277.

[16]6 October 1919 memo from Georg Sternber to the magistrate of Danzig CAHJP DA 439; 17 February 1922 Munich police regulations SM Pol. Dir. München 4644; 3 November 1924 letter to unnamed German Jewish communities from Würzburg government CAHJP WR 561 and the November 1924 responses of the communities of Nürnberg, Bamberg, and Munich CAHJP WR 561. Also see the 19 June 1916 letter to the Jewish community of Hüttenbach CAHJP N 13/24.

the amount of meat Jews slaughtered and ate.[17] In the few cases where these restrictions had no measurable effect, local governments temporarily limited the amount of cattle Jews could slaughter or denied Jews access to meat rations. After the Jewish community of Danzig, for example, failed to reduce its meat intake in October 1919, the city council ruled that the Jewish population would receive no red meat that week, only kosher margarine.[18] Danzig's councilors may have expressed frustration in the face of Jewish noncompliance, but they did not ban the rite nor propose a prohibition.

The councilors' weeklong reductions in the Jewish community's rations included no explicit antisemitic references.[19] Such an absence was surprising during a period engulfed by antisemitism. In his recollections of coming of age in Weimar Germany, Henry Buxhaum describes this time as a period when "the whole atmosphere of Jewish life inside Germany changed for the worse. You could taste antisemitism everywhere; the air of Germany was permeated by it."[20] The antisemitic rhetoric "tasted" by the young Buxhaum blamed Jews for Germany's defeat in war and for the internal revolutions that followed, reproached Jews for Germany's financial devastation, and accused eastern European Jewish immigrants (*Ostjuden*) of seizing the jobs of unemployed Germans. Antisemitism pervaded the written and spoken realms and shaped behavior on Germany's streets where paramilitary groups, ex-soldiers, and street thugs lashed out against Jewish bystanders.[21] Within this context, the Danzig council's decision to limit the amount of meat available to

[17]8 April 1921 report from the city council of Königsberg CAHJP Kn/II/E/III/5; 11 June 1925 report from the Reich minister of interior (Reichsminister) BH ML 2437; 29 March 1924 letter from Heidecker to the health authorities of Hamburg CAHJP 568a; March 1924 memo from Pfeiffer to Peter CAHJP 568a; 1924 response from Peter to the health authorities CAHJP 568a; 14 November 1924 report to the Reichsminister from the President of the Reich Health Office CAHJP 568a; Record of 14 October 1925 telephone conversation between Nathan and Heidecker CAHJP AHW 568a.

[18]6 October 1919 memo from Sternber to Danzig's magistrate CAHJP DA 439.

[19]This would shift over the course of 1924, as evidenced in the April and May 1924 letters between Heidecker and the Hamburg health authorities CAHJP AHW 568a.

[20]Henry Buxhaum, "Recollections," in *Jewish Life in Germany: Memoirs From Three Centuries*, ed. Monika Richarz, trans. Stella P. Rosenfeld and Sidney Rosenfeld (Bloomington: Indiana University Press, 1991), p. 303.

[21]In 1923, for example, mobs rioted in the Scheunenviertel area of Berlin, a neighborhood heavily populated by Eastern European immigrants. See Avraham Barkai, "Under the Lengthening Shadow of Antisemitism," in Michael A. Meyer, ed., *German-Jewish History in Modern Times*, vol. 4 (New York: Columbia University Press, 1998): pp. 46–55; Werner Bergmann and Juliane Wetzel, "'Der Miterlebende weiß nichts.' Alltagsantisemitismus als zeitgenössische Erfahrung und spätere Erinnerung (1919–1933)," in Wolfgang Benz, Arnold Paucker, and Peter Pulzer, eds., *Jüdisches Leben in der Weimarer Republik: Jews in the Weimar Republic* (Tübingen: Mohr Siebek, 1998), pp. 173–196; Anthony Kauders,

Jews is noteworthy. Why not prohibit the rite or at least inveigh against Jewish financial opportunism or deviancy?

In part, the answer may lie in the many worries that followed the war's defeat. Rather than concern themselves with a form of animal slaughter, those in positions of political responsibility focused on concluding the war's domestic front. Between 1918 and 1919, the German government had to bring millions of soldiers home and find them employment; care for Germany's many war victims; transform its economy into one geared for a time of peace; and consider its new relationship with the "lost communities" of Upper Silesia, Poznan, Pomerania, and Danzig. The Republic's leaders tried to maintain some kind of order as they created and implemented a new government and faced revolutions from the left and right. Moreover, as Germany's high inflation increased the prices on all goods and services, the Weimar government became devoted to procuring and moving goods. These chaotic conditions did not encourage either animal protection associations or local and state governments to fret over the Jewish method of animal slaughter. Governments were unconcerned with how food was processed as long as they could control its procurement, transport, and distribution.[22] In 1919 and 1923/4, when food supplies were especially low and inflation particularly high, local governments worried that kosher butchering somehow contributed to the low food supply. They may have investigated the weekly and sometimes daily trends within the slaughterhouses, but they did so without invoking the antisemitic rhetoric that had been or would be used during other "peaks" in the *Schächtfragen.*[23]

Antisemitism's absence from the immediate postwar kosher butchering debates can also be explained by looking to the political evolution of antisemitic factions within Germany. Before 1924, the antisemitic actors who later took part in the anti–kosher butchering campaigns were not

---

"Legally Citizens: Jewish Exclusion from the Weimar Polity," in Benz, Paucker, and Pulzer, eds., *Jüdisches Leben in der Weimarer Republik*, pp. 159–172.

[22]It is also possible that the democratic promises of this era contributed to the stifling of the anti-kosher butchering movement. The Weimar republic offered Jews certain autonomies and protections, including their freedom of religious association and right of self-administration.

[23]6 October 1919 memo from Sternberg CAHJP DA 439; 1921 letter from Sternberg to Jewish Community of Danzig CAHJP DA/439; 23 April 1922 letter from Bergmann and Lehrmann to the Jewish community of Königsberg; 4 November 1922 memo from the slaughterhouse commission of Königsberg to the Jewish community CAHJP KN/II/E/III/5. On food rationing, see Belinda Davis, *Home Fires Burning*. Generally, Jewish communities received rations that did not take into account the Jewish prohibition of certain parts of the calf for consumption.

yet politically empowered or organized. Between 1919 and 1923, these future participants were neither equipped to launch effective political movements nor necessarily even thinking in those terms. Antisemitic action was violent, chaotic, and disorganized.[24] During the Republic's first phase of the *Schächtfragen*, the precursor to the National Socialists, the German Workers' Party (DAP), constituted a small, fragmented group located mainly in Bavaria. It made no effort to ban kosher butchering and instead focused on its putsch of 1923. Once the followers of this and similar groups transitioned from rabble-rousers to sophisticated and well-funded political activists, the movement to ban kosher butchering would become increasingly successful. Such a transformation ebbed and flowed during the second phase of the kosher butchering questions between 1924 and 1929.

Phase II: Conflict, 1924–1929

Between 1924 and 1930, the governments of thirteen municipalities and seven states investigated the possibility of banning kosher butchering, as a dozen other municipalities and several remaining states considered the alleged dangers of the Jewish method of animal slaughter.[25] This second phase of the *Schächtfragen* commenced as the Weimar Republic entered a period of relative economic and political stabilization. By 1924, Germany had emerged from many political crises, including left-wing political insurgencies in Saxony and Thuringia and an attempted right-wing coup in Bavaria. The Weimar leadership had achieved success in its foreign policy and stopped the state's runaway inflation, albeit at an enormous cost. In addition to other changes, this period of relative stabilization brought with it greater access to goods and foodstuffs. The Republic's political stabilization did not prevent *Schächtfragen* from recurring; instead the greater availability of foodstuffs and relative stability in politics and the economy set the conditions for a new series of conflicts. Shaped by a developing antisemitic movement, an embrace of technology, and an enthusiasm over religious protection, the discussions

[24]Martin Broszat, *Hitler and the Collapse of Weimar Germany*, trans. V. R. Berghahn (Leamington Spa: Berg Publishers, 1987), esp. p. 43.

[25]Of these seven states only three dealt with this question in parliament: Hesse, Baden, and Bavaria. 11 July 1925 report to the regional governments from the Reich Minister CAHJP AHW 568a; Hans Albrecht "Kunst, Wissenschaft und Leben: Tierschutzbestrebungen der Gegenwart" (1925) CAHJP AHW 568 a 157. No national governmental body in Germany considered the possibility of a *Schächtverbot* until 1933.

concerning kosher butchering paradoxically attracted significant popular attention but failed to translate into bans on the rite.

After a half-decade of disinterest in Jewish ritual behavior per se, local animal protectionists across Germany launched campaigns to bring kosher butchering to local, state, and national attention. Opponents of the rite had become an effective political force. They had obtained the funds, expertise, and machinery necessary to launch successful political campaigns. They printed leaflets, posters, and monographs quickly and in great number. They lobbied at local, state, and national levels of governance and held rallies.[26] They created new partnerships and animal protectionist platforms that reflected a wide range of concerns.

Animal advocacy groups formed coalitions within and across cities and states to push for new slaughterhouse laws. Organizations, which before 1924 had paid no attention to kosher butchering, now joined other animal protectionists in their attempt to fight the injustices allegedly taking place in Germany's abattoirs. When the Association of Animal Protection Societies of the Reich launched a campaign for a Prussian ban on the slaughter of conscious animals, national associations, such as the Association for the Protection of Birds and Other Animals, Prussian regional groups, such as the Prussian Animal Protection Association, and regional societies based outside of Prussia, including the Lower Bavarian Animal Protection Society, joined the national group in its efforts.[27] The Munich Animal Protection Society was joined by

[26]This period witnessed the reemergence of dozens of publications defending and opposing kosher butchering. These texts included Berliner Tierschutzverein and Münchener Tierschutzverein, *Neues vom betaubungslosen Schächten: Mit einer Antwort auf die neuesten Schächtgutachten* (unpublished manuscript October 1927); Basel, "Beitrag zur Schächtfrage," *Sonderabdruck aus der "Berliner Tierärztlichen Wochenschrift*," 43 (1927): 655; Dexler, *Ueber das Bewegungsverhalten eines grosshirnlosen Schafes beim Schächten* (Hannover: H&M Schaper, 1928); Josef Weigl, "Das Schächten vom Standpunkt der Physiologie, Hygiene, u. Humanität," *DIZ* 7 (9 April 1926): 5–7; Jacob Levy, *Das neue Niederlegeverfahren bei der Schlachtung: Nachwort zur Umfrage der Tierschutzvereine vom Jahre 1927* (Berlin: Reichszentrale Schächtangelegenheiten, 1930); Reichszentrale Schächtangelgenheiten, *Das Neue Niederlegeverfahren bei der Schlachtung von Grosstieren* (Berlin: self-published, 1930). This phase also saw an increase of publications concerning circumcision.

[27]22 April 1925 letter from Buckeley to the Munich city council StM SUV 90; 23 June 1926 proceedings of the Bavarian parliament; 11 December 1926 letter from the Munich TSV to the Bavarian parliament BH ML 2437; "Schächtdebatte auf der Tierschutztagung," *DZ* 134 (11 June 1927) BH Gesandtschaft Darmstadt 1369; Tiernothilfe München, *Tierhelfer heraus!* StM Vereine 2223; 19 November 1929 statement of the Society Against Vivisection and Other Forms of Cruelty (Society Against Vivisection) StM SUV 90; Thimm, "Anträge," *Danziger Beobachter (DB)* (December 1930): CAHJP DA 652a. The Munich TSV also insisted that the issue resulted in a substantial increase in membership. "Münchner Tierschutzverein," *MNN* 146 (1924): 3.

seven animal rights societies to promote far-reaching abattoir reforms. Some of these groups were newly formed; others had previously been disinterested in kosher butchering or had objected to laws that violated religious freedoms.[28]

As animal protectionists increasingly collaborated with one another, they were also joined by small groups of National Socialists. The National Socialists had begun to identify kosher butchering as an important cause in 1925 when they began to shift from a group of rabble-rousers into a political party.[29] When Adolf Hitler left prison in 1924, it seemed unlikely that the National Socialists would succeed politically or serve in the vanguard of these particular animal protection campaigns. The country had not only entered a period of relative stability but the party was penniless and disorganized. After the failed putsch, the Nazis labored to attract followers from all regions and social groups and worked to construct a party program and bureaucracy. The campaign against kosher butchering lent the National Socialists an agenda and political allies across Germany. Members of the NSDAP were attracted to the campaign's charge of Jewish deviance and cruelty and its call for curbing Jewish religious rights. Almost immediately after their reorganization, National Socialists in Munich began to participate in the kosher butchering question there, among their many activities. The kosher butchering deliberations in Munich took place at the same time that the Nazis employed political and violent street tactics to "protect" the city's culture from its Jews, and the Nazis spoke out against the rite in slaughterhouse commission meetings and at the town council hall.[30]

[28]The bird protection movement previously had been uninterested in kosher butchering; anti-vivisectionists had expressed discomfort with creating legislation that affected the Jewish community. Not all animal protectionist groups participated in these disputes. A portion of the *Naturschutz* movement only became involved in anti-kosher butchering causes in the early 1930s. In addition, the Association of Animal Protection Societies of the Reich (RTSV) had not closed itself off to Jewish members. At a national meeting, its members purposely arranged a discussion concerning kosher butchering for a day that did not conflict with a Jewish holiday. 15–18 April 1925 agenda and minutes of the RTSV StM Verereine 2223.

[29]22 April 1925 letter from Buckeley to the Munich city council StM SUV 90; 5 October 1926 letter and petition from the NSDAP to the Munich city council StM SUV 90. The National Socialist presence in the kosher butchering disputes quickly became known, evidenced by a group of kosher butchers who tried to prevent the formation of a National Socialist group in Bonn.

[30]31 March 1926 letter from the Munich TSV to the Munich city council StM SUV 90; 30 April 1926 letter from Klein to the Munich TSV StM SUV 90; 2 May 1926 letter from the Jewish community to the Munich council; 30 April 1926 letter from *shohetim* to Munich Jewish community council StM SUV 90; 2 May 1926 letter from the Jewish community to the slaughterhouse directors StM SUV 90; 4 June 1926 letter from the

By April 1925, Munich-based observers identified the Nazis as a driving force behind the petitions.[31] That same month, a group of National Socialists began lobbying the Bavarian parliament to pass a similar ban.[32]

The National Socialists were not the only right-wing presence within the mid-1920s disputes. Other radical chauvinist and nationalist parties also latched on to the animal protectionist campaign, which, in turn, lent them some visibility in the political arena. Between 1924 and 1930, parties such as the Business and Agriculture Party (Wirtschaft und Bauernpartei) and the German People's Freedom Party (Deusches-völkische Freiheitspartei) worked with the NSDAP, local animal protectionists, veterinarians, and slaughterhouse directors in championing a prohibition.

In their overlapping campaigns for new slaughterhouse legislation, these radical groups and their moderate collaborators emphasized concerns over Jewish deviancy and animal protection. "The majority of people who consider Schächten, find it unnecessarily cruel," one governmental official cried.[33] "Without consciousness," another Schächtverbot advocate insisted, "there is no feeling of pain."[34] These critics of the rite promoted new stunning and fastening technologies. Still interested in the consumption rates of Jews,[35] some questioned whether the technological advancements might be permissible according to Jewish law; others lauded these new technologies while concomitantly resurrecting charges of Jewish otherness, cruelty, and financial noxiousness.[36]

Germany's relative economic stability encouraged the invention and greater use of technological advancements in the stunning and fastening

---

slaughterhouse commission to the Jewish community StM SUV 90; 28 October 1927 letter from slaughterhouse director Schmidt StM SUV 90.

[31] 22 April 1925 letter from Buckeley to the Munich council and response StM SUV 90; 5 October 1926 letter and petition from the NSDAP to the Munich town council StM SUV 90.

[32] 22 April 1925 proposal to the Bavarian parliament by Glaser, Drexel, and Party BH Mwi 1267.

[33] 20 March 1928 minutes of the Bavarian ministerial meeting BH MWi 1267.

[34] L. (Leo?) Teitz, "Schmerzemfindung und Bewusstsein" CAHJP D/BA28/212.

[35] State ministers in Saxony, Mecklenburg-Schwerin, Waldeck, Lippe, and Schaumburg Lippe issued such restrictions. 11 July 1925 report to the state governments from the Reich minister of the interior CAHJP AHW 568a; 22 February 1924 letter from the Director of the Hamburg slaughterhouse commission to its members CAHJP AHW 568a 161; 27 March 1924 letter to butchers from Hamburg's slaughterhouse commission AHW 568a 160; 21 March 1928 order from the Prussian minister for agriculture, lands, and forests CJA 75Ael279 14.

[36] Discussants drew from these different charges interchangeably, depending on their location and context.

of animals. Increasingly after 1924, animal protectionists touted the use of electricity as a new means of stunning animals into states of unconsciousness. Slaughterers now could apply electric shocks to cattle with machines that channeled electricity through electrodes attached to the animal's head. Dozens of slaughterhouse officials, veterinarians, and animal protectionists championed this form of stunning as humane, efficient, and effortless, albeit expensive.[37] They made similar claims concerning newly invented fastening techniques, which either held animals in varying positions or relied on different materials or design for their construction.[38]

The proponents tended to make one of two arguments concerning these new technologies. In a dramatic departure from the petitions during the *Kaiserreich*, one group suggested that the equipments' newness made them permissible under Jewish law. As such, these petitions did not request the prohibition of kosher butchering per se. Instead, they demanded that animals be unconscious when slaughtered. Advocates asserted that stunning by electricity caused animals no muscle cramps, which meant that cattle did not move when killed.[39] At a meeting in 1928, Bavaria's state ministers unanimously advocated this view. They agreed that a ban on the slaughter of conscious animals was desirable and wondered how to persuade the Jewish community to permit the consumption of meat from electrically stunned animals. "Jewry is united in its stand against the *Schächtverbot*," one participant declared, "but Jewry's position on electrical stunning is not as final. Most Bavarian Jews would agree to electrical stunning, if it was legally prescribed."[40]

---

[37]Max Müller, "Neue Wege zum humanen Schlachten: das elektrische Betäubungsverfahren," *AFZ* (28 September 1927): 421–426; Max Müller, "Tierschutz und Schlachtfrage," *Tierärztliche Rundschau* (*TR*) 5 (29 January 1933): 1–15; November 1927 report concerning the electric form of stunning by Weinberger for the minister of interior BH MWi 1267; 20 March 1928 minutes of the ministerial meeting BH MWi 1267. Studies from the late 1920s revealed that the higher the voltage, the longer the animal remained unconscious.

[38]4 June 1926 letter from Munich's slaughterhouse commission to its Jewish community CAHJP A/157.

[39]November 1927 report by Weinberger; Max Müller, "Das elektrische Betäuben der Schlachttiere," *Monatsschrift für Schlachthoftechnik und veterinäre Nahrungsmittelhygiene* 27 (10 November 1927): 446; 9 December 1927 letter from the Bavarian minister for education and culture to the minister of interior BH ML 2437. These discourses would reemerge a number of years later when the Jewish community of England faced a similar challenge.

[40]20 March 1928 minutes of the ministerial meeting BH MWi 1267. Jewish communal leaders in Bavaria and elsewhere argued otherwise. Their defenses of kosher butchering maintained that the new method resulted in meat with a sandpaper quality and odd taste and that it exposed the animal to pain. 23 August 1926 letter to Funk from Horovitz CAHJP A/W 1392; 24 November 1927 statement by the Bavarian Conference of Rabbis

Participants made similar arguments concerning the new fastening technologies, many of which the Jewish community did approve.[41] The suggestion that these forms of stunning and fastening might be permissible was politically expedient, implying an endorsement of the Jewish community's right to observe Jewish law. Such insinuation certainly was absent in the second set of overlapping campaigns, which charged that the Jewish community's refusal to abandon kosher butchering reflected Jewry's deviant nature.

The second set of anti–kosher butchering campaigns invoked the antisemitic rhetoric that had continued to engulf Weimar Germany and, like the campaigns themselves, drew from the propagandistic tactics and ideological traditions that had roots in fin-de-siècle Europe. The culture of the *Schächtfragen* permitted, if not encouraged, participants to revive radically antisemitic views within mainstream political arenas.[42] Claims of Jewish cultural and political corruption had found significant currency at the war's end and with the creation of the Weimar Republic.[43] Charges of Jewish corruption and treachery took many forms: claims that Jews monopolized German state and society; accusations that Jews were simultaneously responsible for leftist revolutionary agitation and for a wide range of capitalist monopolies; and anxieties that eastern European Jewish immigrants caused the problems faced by Germans in everyday life, especially the growing unemployment, high rates of inflation, and housing shortages. In Weimar Germany, groups other than those on the extreme right commonly utilized antisemitic discourse in their programs. The conservative German National People's Party (DNVP), for example, candidly affirmed its antisemitism in electoral propaganda; even the German People's Party (DVP), which sidestepped the use of openly antisemitic slogans and ideologies in its propaganda, tacitly ignored when others utilized anti-Jewish tactics and claims in political debate.[44]

The campaigns against kosher butchering used this antisemitic vitriol. Anti-Jewish forces asserted that the rite threatened German culture,

---

BH ML 2437; 22 December 1927 letter from the minister of interior to the minister presidents BH ML 2437; Max Junack, "die Literarische Umschau vom 5 Juli 1931" LBA RSC AR 2112 (B 30/7); "Rückwirkungen der elektrischen Betäubung? Eigenartige Beobachtungen beim Schweinfleisch," *AFZ* (1 October 1931) CAHJP AHW 568b.

[41]Some suggested that *shohetim* stun their animals before they used the new fastening mechanisms, a request that clearly violated Jewish tradition. 4 June 1926 letter from the Munich slaughterhouse commission to the munich Jewish community CAHJP A/157.

[42]16 May 1925 letter from Einhauser to the mayor of Munich StM SUV 90.

[43]Avraham Barkai, "Under the Lengthening Shadow of Antisemitism," in Meyer, ed., *German-Jewish History in Modern Times*, vol. 4, pp. 46–55.

[44]Winkler, "Die deutsche Gesellschaft."

posed an economic menace, and illustrated Jewish brutality. Critics described the ritual as outside of—if not hostile to—German culture. The rite, they insisted, was "Asiatic," allegedly constituting a "foreign world, an angry, sick fantasy."[45] "The Jews," wrote one author, "are somewhat 'special' in the European states in which they live, although this is only in a negative way."[46] Critics, such as this anonymous journalist, located Jewish deviancy in Jewry's refusal to accept new stunning mechanisms and laws. They also found Jewish difference in Jewry's persistent disregard of how few German Jews actually practiced the rite in juxtaposition to the large number of eastern European Jewish immigrants, now settled in Germany, who would require kosher meat for their diets.

Anxieties concerning the *Ostjuden* and traditional Jewish factions appeared in the anti-kosher butchering campaigns. During 1925, at the peak of Jewish immigration into Germany and two years after the Bavarian government had expelled eastern European immigrants from Munich and Nuremberg, the governor of Upper Bavaria insisted that permitting the Jewish community an exemption from new slaughterhouse regulations would be harmful for the majority. Such deviation was "not in the public interest."[47] The following year, an NSDAP deputy complained that a failure to implement the *Schächtverbot* in Bavaria "protected the *Ostjuden*."[48] Bavarian ministers later also suggested that local Jews would accept the stunning mechanisms if they could be freed from foreign influence. "The main opposition to the stunning of animals before slaughter comes from Jewish circles outside of Bavaria," offered one minister.[49] A participant in the Baden deliberations similarly warned

---

[45]J. B., "Asiatische Gebräuche im Schlachthof: Metzger und Auffsichtsbeamte gegen die Tierquälerei," *Völkischer Beobachter* (*VB*) 17 (1927) StM SUV 90 and Theodor Fritsch, "Um das Schächtverbot," *Hammer* 603 (1 August 1927): 383. Also see "Der Tierschutzverband und die Schächtfrage," *Völkischer Kurier* (*VK*) 111 (24 April 1925); "Eine Zuschrift zur Forderung des Schächt-Verbotes," *VK* 136 (19 May 1925); 18 October 1927 letter from Schmidt to the Upper Bavarian government StM SUV 90; "Endlich ein Schächtverbot!" *Hammer* 665 (1 March 1930): 122; "Gegen das Schächten," *Hammer* 559 (1 June 1927): 300.

[46]"Rituelle Tierquälerei," *Landwirtschaftliche Beilage: Neue Völkische Rundschau* 6.11 (16 May 1924): 2.

[47]1 July 1925 letter from the government of Upper Bavaria to the Munich police authorities SM Pol Dir. München 4644. The Weimar state had 90,000 eastern European Jews, one-fifth of the total Jewish population. The *Ostjude* population tended to fluctuate; many immigrants left Germany for other destinations while some returned to their homelands. On the improvement of the German Jewish image of the *Ostjuden* during the Weimar period, see Michael Brenner, *The Renaissance of Jewish Culture in Weimar Germany* (New Haven: Yale University Press, 1996), esp. pp. 142–152.

[48]11 February 1926 proceedings of the Bavarian Landtag (parliament) BH ML 2437.

[49]20 March 1928 minutes of the Bavarian ministerial meeting BH MWi 1267.

against allowing observant Jews to practice their rites. If the state government took "the feelings of the orthodox into consideration," he argued, Jews would fashion German culture and politics according to their own wishes.[50] Another commentator warned of Jewish religious and cultural domination, asking, "Do we want our German cultural realm to be made subservient to the Jews?"[51]

These claims of Jewish domination drew from an additional anxiety; namely, the right-wing obsession with the role of Jews in the economy. Petitions and propaganda bewailed not only the high amount of Jewish meat consumption but also the predominance of Jews in the cattle trade, particularly in southern Germany, and in the banking industry.[52] In his introduction of the Bavarian animal protectionist amendment, one National Socialist deputy awkwardly launched into a tirade concerning the "gross pain" animals experienced when slaughtered by the Jewish method and the growing monopoly Jews supposedly had in finance.[53] Four years later, NSDAP deputy Herbert Kraft articulated the same sentiments on the floor of Baden's parliament. He argued the Jews' practice of kosher butchering reinforced and illuminated their economic danger.[54] These two deputies were not alone. Between 1924 and 1929, the Hessian, Bavarian, and Prussian Ministers of the Interior, Justice, and Agriculture, Lands, and Forests expressed concerns that the practice allowed Jews to manipulate financial markets and circumvent existing meat allowances.[55]

[50]"Beginn der Landwirtschaftsdebbate (38 Sitzung)," *Karlsruhe Zeitung* (*KZ*) (March 13 1930)· BH Gesandtschaft Karlsruhe 1413. Also see comments by Fiehler in the 5 August 1925 minutes of the Munich Hauptausschusses StM SUV 90; "Rituelle Tierquälerei," *Landwirtschaftliche Beilage: Neue Völkische Rundschau* 6.11 (16 May 1924): 2. For some, this Jewish influence manifested itself in the decision by German Social Democrats to protect the Jewish rite. Because Social Democrats in Northern European countries tended to favor bans on kosher butchering, these participants insisted that Jewry had magically swayed German socialists from voting against what they normally would approve. "Gegen das Schächten," *Hammer* 559 (1 June 1927): 300; "Beginn der Landwirtschaftsdebatte (38 Sitzung)," *KZ* (March 13 1930) BH Gesandtschaft Karlsruhe 1413.

[51]Manfred Kyber, *Tierschutz und Kultur* (Stuttgart: Walter Seifert Verlag, 1925).

[52]Fritsch echoed this concern in his complaint that veterinarians and scientists only defended *shehitah* if the Jewish community paid them to do so. Theodor Fritsch "Um das Schächtverbot."

[53]11 February 1926 proceedings of the Bavarian Landtag BH ML 2437.

[54]March 13 1930 transcript of Baden's parliamentary debates concerning kosher butchering BH Gesandtschaft Karlsruhe 1413.

[55]21 March 1928 order from the Prussian minister of agriculture, lands, and forests CJA 75Ael279 14; "Der neue Schächt-Erlaß," *Jüdische Zeitung* (*JZ*) (1 February 1929): CAHJP A/159.

Agitation against the Jewish rite became even more venomous in the campaign's charge of Jewish brutality. During a period when violent attacks against Jews continued on a frequent basis, critics lambasted the rite for its aggressive and rough character. The Jewish method, one slaughterhouse director complained, is "a particularly brutal form of animal cruelty."[56] It was, according to a second writer, "a certain kind of rough cruelty."[57] Animals slaughtered by the Jewish method ostensibly "waited many minutes to die, wild eyes rolling with terror and pain."[58] Some of these critics avoided explicit references to Jewish brutality per se, but emphasized the gruesome nature of the rite and the intensity of the animal's pain. For many, the fact that many Jews no longer observed the dietary laws exaggerated the pointlessness of kosher butchering and, thus, the futility of the animal's pain.[59]

Others emphasized that Jews enjoyed the killing process, a charge that hundreds of antisemitic publications and periodicals launched more generally during the 1920s and early 1930s.[60] Consider the antisemitic writer Theodor Fritsch's portrait of the *shohet*, gleeful in his brutality. "The *shohet* binds the animal in chains, violently throwing him down. The Jewish animal slaughterer then takes his sharp knife in his hand, stands a bit to the side, and watches."[61] Describing Jews as a "blood thirsty, parasitic people," these antagonists warned that Jewish cruelty endangered people as well as animals.[62] "The inhuman cruelty

[56]Carl Klein, *Sind geschächtete Tier sofort nach dem Schächtschnitt bewußtlos?* (Berlin: Berliner Tierschutz-Verein, 1927), p. 16.

[57]"Rituelle Tierquälerei." Also see Berliner Tierschutzverein and Münchener Tierschutzverein, *Neues vom betaubungslosen Schächten*; 16 June 1929 proposal concerning animal protection submitted by Werner to Hessian Landtag BH Gesandtschaft Darmstadt 1369; 3 December 1929 proposal for the Baden Landtag BH Gesandtschaft Karlsruhe 1413.

[58]Fritsch, "Um das Schächtverbot," p. 383.

[59]Kyber, *Tierschutz Und Kultur;* Münchener Tierschutzverein, *Gegen das betäubungslose Schächten* (Munich: self-published, 1926), esp. p. 6; Rudolf Einhauser, "Die Notwendigkeit des Tierschutzes," *VB* 58 (11 March 1927); "Die bemitleidenserten Opfer," *VB* 18 (23 January 1930); 27 November 1930 report and letter from the Society Against Vivisection StM SUV 90. More moderate rhetoric is evident in the collection of letters sent to the Munich city council in 1925 from city residents who supported a ban. See April 1925 letters StM SUV 90.

[60]In 1929, Julius Streicher's antisemitic periodical, *Der Stürmer*, accused the Jewish community of ritually murdering a boy in Manau (Lower Franconia). Although the antisemites were charged with inciting hatred against the Jewish community, the court case provided them with a public forum to lodge additional complaints against the Jews.

[61]Fritsch, "Um das Schächtverbot," p. 381.

[62]"Kämpfe gegen Jüdische Vorrechte im Ausland," *Hammer* 660 (15 December 1929): 636 "Schächtung?" *Hammer* 579 (1 August 1926): 387; "Wider das Schächten," *Hammer* 577 (1 July 1926): 331; "Gegen das Schächten," *Hammer* 599 (1 June 1927): 300; Fritsch, "Um das Schächtverbot"; R.G. "Ist Schächten Tierquälerei?" *Hammer* 619

of kosher butchering," wrote one author "illustrates that the Jews demonstrate brutality against animals just as they do against humans." In his view, kosher butchering was akin to ritual murder, a form of killing that supposedly had resumed in Bulgaria and Russia.[63]

These understandings of kosher butchering's cruelty were widespread even outside of the animal protectionist campaigns. In his acclaimed novel, *The Magic Mountain* (1924), Thomas Mann also painted the Jewish rite in bloody strokes. Leo Naphta, Mann's protagonist for conservative politics and religion, was the son of a *shohet*. As a youngster, Naphta observed his beloved father joyously "catch the spurting steaming blood" of the animals he brutally slaughtered. Rather than use the stunning mechanisms employed by Christian butchers to lessen the animals' pain, the elder Naphta killed animals according to the Jewish method. His father's blood-centered piety—which later caused the man's undoing and horrific, bloody death—encouraged Naphta to assume a fundamental relationship among purity, blood, and brutality. "The idea of piety became bound up with cruelty," writes Mann, "just as the sight and smell of spurting blood was bound up in his mind with the idea of what is holy and spiritual."[64] Mann's portrait of Naphta has encouraged his critics to level charges of antisemitism against him, at least in his early writings. To be sure, an illogical and popular belief in Jewish cruelty may have shaped Mann's portrait. Yet, the novelist's portrayal of Jewish ritual behavior was analogous to that embraced by many non-Jews who viewed the rite as something bloody and violent but also religiously significant and thus deserving of protection.

Between 1924 and 1930, a wide range of discussants resisted the animal protectionist demands for a ban on kosher butchering but,

---

(1 April 1928): 181; "Der Tierschutzverband und die Schächtfrage," *VK* 111 (24 April 1925). On the journal, *Hammer*, see Alexander Volland, "Theodor Fritsch (1852–1933) und die Zeitschrift 'Hammer'" (Inaugural dissertation zur Erlangung des Doktorgrades der Medizin der Johannes Gutenberg-Universität Mainz dem Fachbereich Medizin vorgelegt. Medizinhistorischen Institut der Johannes Gutenberg-Universität Mainz, 1993).

[63]Wakowsky, "Zu Schächtfrage Und Freimaurerei," *Hammer* 607 (1 October 1927): 507. Wakowsky's contemporary, Benjamin Segel, warned his readers against the assumption that blood libel charges inspired antisemitism: "It is not ritual murder mania that promotes Jew-hatred, but Jew-hatred that promotes ritual murder frenzy." Benjamin Segal, "Die Ritualmord-Wahn in Wandel der Zeiten," *Jüdisches Wochenblatt* 14 (1929): 114 LBA Karl. D. Darmstaedter Collection AR 15 III.6.

[64]Thomas Mann, *The Magic Mountain*, trans. John E. Woods (New York: Vintage Books, 1995), p. 433. My appreciation to Stephen Kern for discussing this section of the novel with me. On Naphta, see Herbert Lehnert, "Leo Naphta und sein Autor (Thomas Mann)," *Orbis Litterarum* 37.1 (1982): 47–69.

like Naphta, offered an inconsistent formulation that simultaneously expressed discomfort with and appreciation of the rite.[65] These contributors did not favor the Jewish method of animal slaughter over the non-Jewish practice.[66] Instead, many uttered their dissatisfaction with the method, identified its cruelty as an issue of concern, but promoted the safeguarding of the rite. At the eighth annual national meeting of German animal protection societies, one Darmstadt town councilor argued against a potential ban but agreed that the ritual forced animals to experience "unnecessary brutality."[67] The majority of Munich councilors during this period seemed to concur. In their almost yearly considerations of petitions submitted by the National Socialists, the city leaders portrayed the rite as "bloody," painful," and "in need of improvement." At the same time, they were unwilling to implement a prohibition of the rite and, like their Darmstadt contemporaries, recognized the religious significance that the ritual held within Judaism.[68]

These awkward defenses of kosher butchering, which laid the foundation for the future disputes of the early 1930s, offered three overlapping issues of concern. First, proponents of the Jewish rite argued that the animal protectionist campaigns interfered with the religious freedom of Jews. In their view, the constitution ensured the Jewish community its religious freedoms; because the ban on kosher butchering forced the transgression of Jewish tradition, it was unacceptable.[69] Second,

[65]At first, the Munich TSV expected non-Jewish defenses to insist on the ritual's superiority to current methods. 11 December 1926 letter from the Munich TSV to the Bavarian parliament BH ML 2437.

[66]The exception, of course, lay with the scientists and veterinarians who, in promoting the ritual's humanitarian character, supported the Jewish community's right to practice kosher butchering. The number of these authorities dwindled in the mid-1920s, but they continued to be an important source for the Jewish community's defense efforts. Büro für Schächtangelegenheiten, *Zur Frage der Betäubenden Wirkung des Schächtschnitts* (Berlin: self-published, 1927); Büro für Schächtangelegenheiten, *Zweite Reiche Neuer Gutachten zur Frage der betaubenden Wirkung des Schächtschnitts* (Berlin, self-published, 1929); Max Junack, "Die Literarische Umschau vom 5 Juli 1931" LBA RSC AR 2112 (B 30/7).

[67]11 June 1927 minutes of the RTSV BH Gesandtschaft Darmstadt 1369.

[68]14 May 1925 minutes of the Munich senate StM SuV 90; 16 May 1925 letter to Scharnagl from Einhauser StM SUV 90; 7 August 1925 minutes of the Munich administrative committee StM SUV 90; 5 August 1926 minutes of the Munich administrative committee StM SUV 90; November 1927 report by Weinberger BH MWi 1267; July 1927 letter from the Bad Reichenhall city council to the Munich city council StM SUV 90; 6 October 1927 report by Munich slaughterhouse director Schmidt StM SUV 90.

[69]Comments of Haecker in minutes of June 1927 RTSV meeting BH Gesandtschaft Darmstadt 1369; 15 April 1924 letter from Peter to Heidecker CAHJP AHW 568a; "Zur Schächtfrage: Die Reden der sozialdemokratischen Abgeordneten Frohme und Liebknecht für das Schächten in deutschen Reichstag," *DIZ* 19 (7 October 1926): 3–4; 1925 report from Bavarian minister of interior to the minister of agriculture, lands, and forests BH ML 2437.

these discussants bemoaned the disputes' antisemitic character. Rejecting the permissibility of antisemitic discourse, defenders of the rite dismissed the "National Socialist petitions" as a vehicle for spreading hatred. Third, some discussants took part in the *Schächtfragen* because of their interest in protecting the authority of the nation vis-à-vis individual states. Even if they personally endorsed laws mandating the use of stunning mechanisms in animal slaughter, these mostly gentile participants condemned state governments that wished to create promulgations that would override religious freedoms. They believed that only the national government had the jurisdiction to make those kinds of policies. In Bavaria, the minister of the interior, Karl Stützel, argued that a ban on kosher butchering would be preferable but that it needed to come from a national mandate. "Religious freedom," he wrote, "is an assurance of national law, not state dictum."[70]

Between 1924 and 1929, critics and supporters of kosher butchering offered these competing (and sometimes overlapping) arguments in the press, at association meetings, and in a wide venue of political arenas. Despite the growth of the anti–kosher butchering movement and its effective incorporation of antisemitic language and imagery, the campaigns failed to materialize into any significant bans. Of the nearly twenty city councils that considered prohibitions, only a few enacted promulgations concerning the rite. These laws established kosher butchering oversight committees, mandated the adoption of new animal fastening techniques, and set meat allowances. They did not prohibit kosher butchering at this time.[71] Similarly, while seven state governments investigated the possibility of enacting a ban on the rite, only the Bavarian parliament passed legislation mandating the use of stunning mechanisms in all of its slaughterhouses.

Even the Bavarian anti–kosher butchering movement witnessed significant political failures during the late 1920s, illustrating that antisemitic

[70]5 November 1926 letter from the Bavarian minister of interior to the minister presidents BH ML 2437. Also see 13 June 1925 letter from the minister of interior to the minister of agriculture, lands, and forests BH ML 2437; 15 March 1930 letter from Fischer to the minister of the state of the exterior BH Gesandtschaft Karlsruhe 1413; comments by Jung in minutes of June 1927 RTSV meeting BH Gesandtschaft Darmstadt 1369; 21 March 1928 memo from the Prussian minister for agriculture, lands and forests CJA 75AE1279 14. As we shall see, the BVP seemed to vacillate between its support and disapproval of the ban.

[71]A few examples of these restrictions include 27 July 1927 letter from the chair of the butchers association in Main to its Jewish community CAHJP D/BA28/212; 2 June 1926 letter to the Jewish community of Regensburg from the meat-handlers association CAHJP A/157; "Der neue Schächt-Erlaß," *JZ* (1 February 1929): CAHJP 1 A/159. The 11 July 1925 report to the regional governments set out the local promulgations passed in late 1924 and 1925 CAHJP AHW 568a.

thought did not translate neatly into law. Bavaria's parliament first passed a version of the animal protection ban in 1926 but state ministers took four years to implement the petition. Between 1926 and 1930, state leaders debated the permissibility of the prohibition. For four years, reformist and antireformist forces battled over whether religious toleration mandated the protection of kosher butchering and whether the state or nation had the jurisdiction to make such a determination.

The Bavarian *Schächtverbot*, 1924–1930

Despite the proliferation of antisemitic sentiment in Bavaria and the successes of its Nazi movement, its anti–kosher butchering movements failed to translate into a municipal or state ban until 1930. The Bavarian government did not succeed in implementing this proposal because of several factors: the ambivalence of several well-placed governmental leaders toward the animal protection campaign, the economic challenges posed by the technologies and the animal advocacy movement, the inconsistent political influence of the Nazis in Bavaria and elsewhere, and the Bavarian leadership's political struggles with the national government in Berlin. These explanations illuminate the inconsistencies within the deliberations and highlight the ways in which place and context influenced the disputes.

In the few Bavarian city council debates and in the more frequent parliamentary and ministerial disputes, a majority of governmental representatives expressed ambivalence. Despite the presence of impassioned National Socialist and Conservative supporters of a prohibition, a larger number of discussants articulated unease with its permissibility. Similar to concomitant debates in other states, some policy makers worried about the impact of a ban on the Jewish community. "This will negatively affect the Jewish community," insisted Bavaria's minister of the interior. "I am not in favor of it." Karl Stützel and others also hesitated over the proposed prohibition because they wondered whether the religious freedoms promised by the national constitution protected kosher butchering and if state or city governments had the authority to create laws banning the rite.[72] According to Franz Goldenberger, Bavaria's minister of culture and education, "We [ministers] need to better understand

[72] 13 June 1925 letter from the minister of interior to the minister of agriculture, lands, and forests BH ML 2437; 5 November 1926 letter from the Bavarian minister of interior to the minister presidents BH ML 2437; 2 January 1927 letter from the Bavarian minister of justice to that of the interior BH MWi 1267; 9 December 1927 letter from the Bavarian minister of education and culture to other ministers BH MWi 1267; 19 April 1928 letter

religious protections," namely both their boundaries and who held jurisdiction over them.[73]

These latter questions were particularly pressing. Strains between the second largest state in the Republic and national interests long had plagued the Weimar Republic, and participants were aware that a state ban on the rite would defy earlier national promulgations.[74] The kosher butchering debates in Bavaria took place at a time when the German national government under Gustav Stresemann had expressed serious frustrations over the fragile state of Jewish affairs in Bavaria. Immediately before Stresemann's celebratory and much-desired admission into the League of Nations, Bavarian Nazi papers had published a series of stinging antisemitic attacks and the Bavarian Landtag had voted for a *Schächtverbot*.[75] Neither Stresemann nor the foreign office were able to quiet the Nazi press, but they castigated the Bavarian government for allowing such antisemitism to occur when Stresemann was attempting to negotiate for the rights of German-speaking minorities outside of Germany. Perhaps this rebuke encouraged state ministries to delay the ban in order to appease Stresemann and his fellow cabinet members.[76]

Economic factors also played a significant role in the ban's temporary failure. Electric stunning was costly, and economic conditions, while improved, had not entirely recovered. Slaughterhouses required considerable renovations to attain the high voltage requirements necessary for the new method. In 1925, one year after Bavarian animal protectionists launched their campaign, few slaughterhouses were equipped to stun animals electrically for more than a minute, an insufficient period of time. Despite their general enthusiasm toward these new stunning mechanisms, many directors encouraged some kind of moderation or an increase in funding. Faced with complaints that mandatory stunning laws would bankrupt local slaughterhouses, city and state governments had to determine whether they wished to supply

---

from the minister of interior to Buttmann and Drexel BH ML 2437. Similar debates took place in Prussia, Baden, Saxony, Mecklenburg-Schwerin, Lippe, and Schaumburg Lippe. Ministries in Hesse, Braunschweig, Bremen, and Weldek consistently issued much stronger statements against the rite, although they did not ban it.

[73]9 December 1927 letter from the minister of education and culture to the other ministers BH MWi 1267.

[74]These tensions were not new to the Weimar republic. Bavaria had been one of the last states to join the newly formed empire in 1871 in part because of its reluctance to surrender to Prussian influence and control.

[75]Although it was responsible for the protection of minority rights, the council did not impose a minorities obligation as a condition of Germany's admission to the League.

[76]A sophisticated analysis of Germany's activities on the League Council can be found in Fink, *Defending the Rights of Others*, esp. pp. 295–335.

municipal commissions with additional funds for the transition to new forms of stunning. By necessity, such budget rearrangements would divert monies from another part of the city or state budget.[77] Bavarian ministers shared a second financial concern regarding the animal protection campaign. Bavaria was the home to several popular spas for Jews and non-Jews, and state officials worried that the Bavarian travel industry would be affected negatively by a ban. England's *Jewish Chronicle*, for example, had called for a boycott of travel to Bavaria, even though no Jewish group in Germany supported any such restriction on their travel. Nevertheless, the state's minister of finance, Hans Schmelzle, commenced an investigation into the economic implications a ban on kosher butchering might have on Bavarian tourism.[78]

A final set of issues may have been at play as well, namely, the increased tensions between the National Socialists and the dominant Bavarian People's Party (BVP). Beginning in May 1919, Bavaria had been dominated by the right-leaning BVP. A conservative Catholic party, it—like the NSDAP—was hostile to the national government in Berlin. Before 1924 it mildly tolerated the Nazis, assuming that it could manipulate the radical group. After 1924, the BVP and NSDAP moved apart. Support for the National Socialist Party had increased in Bavaria, particularly among young Protestant men who resented the Catholic Church's influence and the BVP's dominance. As the Nazis became more active in local and state party politics—often through the kosher butchering deliberations—a number of BVP politicians expressed concern with the National Socialist presence in the political arena.[79] Perhaps this discomfort contributed to the consistent rejection of the proposed *Schächtverboten* by BVP members until 1930.[80]

[77]After 1928, several slaughterhouses in Bavaria had gained the availability and funding to stun animals for the necessary period of time, usually three to six minutes. Max Müller, "Neue Wege zum humanen Schlachten"; Max Müller, "Das Elektrische Betäuben der Schlachttiere," *Monatsschrift für Schlachtoftecknik und veterinäre Nahrungsmittelhygiene* 27 (10 November 1927): 446; Weinberger, November 1927 report BH MWi 1267; 18 January 1928 letter from the government of Unterfranken and Aschaffenburg to the slaughterhouse commission of Munich StM SUV 90; H. Kuppelmayr, "Der Tierschutz im Münchener Schlacht- und Viehhof," *Erlösung dem Tiere: Kampfblatt für vivisektionslose Kultur* 3/4 (1930): ALM SUV 91. Also see the less-glowing review in Max Junack, "Die Literarische Umschau vom 5 Juli 1931" LBA RSC AR 2112 (B 30/7).

[78]31 March 1930 letter to the Bavarian minister of interior from the minister of finance BH MWi 1267.

[79]Staunch constitutionalists and Catholic, many BVP leaders were wary of the mass politics the Nazis embraced.

[80]20 March 1928 minutes of the ministerial meeting BH: MWi 1267. When the BVP supported the ban in 1930, the government finally implemented the petition.

Whatever the reason for the reluctance, between 1926 and 1929 state ministers and parliamentary deputies negotiated over the wording and content of the animal protectionist petition. During this time, Bavarian Jews continued to practice kosher butchering as they had done in the past. In the fall of 1929, however, Bavarian ministers finally agreed to a compromise: They would move forward on the ban and see if the national government intervened. Much to the consternation of Bavaria's Jews, in 1930 the Bavarian parliament approved the revised ban and this time state ministers willingly enacted the ban.[81]

The state's prohibition on kosher butchering reflected a shift in the kosher butchering disputes. As Weimar Germany entered a new phase of its political, economic, and social history—what Detlev Peukert has called a period of "total crisis"—the *Schächtfragen* underwent a parallel development.[82] Beginning in 1930, the animal protectionist campaigns escalated, now taking place in dozens of cities and in a greater number of states.

Phase III: Crisis, 1930–1933

Between 1930 and 1933, more than half of the German states engaged with the possibility of banning kosher butchering. By January 1933, six had outlawed the rite and over eighty cities and towns took part in local

"Schächtverbot in Bayern? Gesetzliche Regelung Der Schächtfrage Bleibt Sache Des Reiches," *CVZ* 29 (16 July 1926): 383.

[81] 23 June 1926 proceedings of the Bavarian Landtag BH MWi 1267; 8 July 1926 Proceedings of the Bavarian Landtag BH MWi 1267; 11 December 1926 letter from the Munich TSV to the Bavarian Landtag BH ML 2437; 4 February 1927 proceedings of the Bavarian Landtag BH ML 2437; 20 March 1928 minutes of the Bavarian ministerial meeting BH MWi 1267; 4 March 1929 letter from the minister of education and culture to the Bavarian Jewish community council BH MWi 1267; 8 June 1929 announcement of the Bavarian Landtag BH ML 2437; 19 November 1929 petition from the Munich TSV and the Society Against Vivisection StM SUV 90; Bayerischer Israelitischer Gemeinden, *Rituelles Schlachten und Betäubung: Eingabe des Verbandes Bayerischer israelitischer Gemeinden an den Bayerischen Landtag vom 14. Mai 1929* (Munich: B. Heller, 1929); "Der Betäubungszwang für Schlachtvieh," *MNN* 22 (23 January 1930): 3; "Schlachtvieh Betäubungszwang: Annhame des Gesetzes im Landtagsausschuß," *MNN* 23 (24 January 1930). 2; "Die Annahme des Schächtgesetzes," *Bayerischer Kurier und Münchener Fremdenblatt* (*BK*) 24 (24 January 1930): 3; Aus dem Verfassungs-Auschuß," *Bayerische Staatszeitung und Bayerische Staatsanzeiger* 19 (24 January 1930): 14; "Das Schächtverbot vom Bayrischen Landtag angenommen," *IF* 6 (6 February 1930).

[82] Peukert, *Weimar Republic*.

disputes. Observers reported that whether or not a ban existed, it had become increasingly difficult for *shohetim* across Germany to practice their trade. According to a report published by the Reich Central Office for the Protection of Kosher Butchering one month before the Nazis banned the rite, Jews found it almost impossible to buy fresh kosher meat anywhere in Germany.[83]

The kosher butchering conflicts of the early 1930s shared several commonalties with those that preceded them. The character of the participants was generally unchanged. The right-leaning sponsorship of the bills to ban kosher butchering remained consistent. Just as before, animal protectionists, *volkisch* nationalists, and Conservative and right-wing politicians championed a ban. Dissenting voices continued to come mostly from the left, center, and a wide range of Jewish communal leaders.

Participants employed rhetoric similar to that invoked during the late 1920s. During both phases of the disputes, animal protectionist campaigns touted new technologies. Earlier supporters had promoted the use of electricity for stunning animals; after 1930, they publicized a newly developed chemical mix.[84] Moderate discussants continued to suggest that the newness of these technologies opened up the possibility for their acceptance under Jewish law. When the Jewish community rejected these new stunning techniques, many of these participants looked to this denunciation as proof of Jewry's social and political deviance. Others made stronger allegations of Jewish otherness. Radical participants persisted in cautioning against the danger Jews—and not the Jewish rite per se—posed to state and society. Invoking claims of Jewish blood-thirst, economic menace, and cultural corruption, they implored others to approve a kosher butchering ban to stem a wave of Jewish corruption.[85]

Defenders of the rite remained concerned with the presence of the far right in these campaigns and rejected the anti–kosher butchering

[83]Reichsszentrale, "Aus dem Tätigkeitsbericht der Reichszentrale" (March 1932) LBA RSC AR 2112 (B 30/7). Similar suggestions can be found in 19 March 1933 memo from Fischer to the Bavarian minister of interior BH Gesandtschaft Darmstadt 1369.

[84]1927 Bavarian ministerial report concerning stunning methods BH ML 2437; Proposal concerning the slaughter of animals (no. 67) to the Baden Landtag BH Gesandtschaft Karlsruhe 1413. Also see "Der Stand der Schächtfrage Interview mit Rabbiner Dr. Munk in Berlin," *Der Israelit* (29 January 1931): 4–5.

[85]Antisemitic publications and pogrom-like disturbances of this era reinforced these antisemitic images of Jewish danger. 1929 ushered in a new phase of violence. Michael Burleigh, *The Third Reich: A New History* (New York: Hill and Wang: 200), p. 122; Henry Buxhaum, "Recollections."

movement because of the discussants' supposed manipulation of the campaign to further their chauvinistic and antisemitic agenda. Deeply distressed that the proposals did "not protect animals but attack[ed] Jews," Center Party and Communist deputies in Hesse charged that National Socialists merely used the anti–kosher butchering movement to "spread hate."[86] Such concern did not imply public support. As before, the majority of non-Jewish opponents of the ban quietly conceded that the rite involved some kind of cruelty to animals but rejected the prohibition because of its unconstitutionality. One group of discussants rejected local bans because they believed that the jurisdiction to create a *Schächtverbot* lay in the nation rather than the state or city.[87] When Baden's parliament deliberated a proposed ban, for example, DVP deputy Wilhelm Mattes voted against the prohibition, stating that "there should be a *Schächtverbot* for—*and passed by*—the entire Reich."[88] In dramatic contrast, others rejected the prohibition because of its violation of religious freedom, a much-valued liberty promised by the constitution. The Hessian SPD deputy Glen, contended bleakly that a ban would result in "terrible consequences…an interference with religious practices."[89] For Glen and others, religious freedom was one of the democratic underpinnings of the state. To do away with religious freedom would imply a willingness to abandon the democratic nature of the republic.

Because the disputes of 1930–1933 were similar to those that had preceded them, it is surprising that the campaigns of the early 1930s translated into active debates and sometimes into local or state promulgations while the previous ones had not. An answer to this inconsistency can be found in the historical and political rearrangements of the final phase of the Weimar Republic. The *Schächtfragen*, one contemporary observer commented, were "part of the political situation."[90]

[86]Zur Schächtfrage," *DZ* (8 October 1932): BH Gesandtschaft Darmstadt 1369. In Danzig, such antisemitic agitation even concerned a few members of the German National People's Party, who later voted in favor of the prohibition. 2 February 1931 letter to Strunk from Danzig's Jewish community council CAHJP DA 652.

[87]"Beginn der Landwirtschaftsdebbate"; 15 March 1930 letter from Fischer to the Bavarian minister of the state of the exterior BH Gesandtschaft Karlsruhe 1413; "Verbot des Schachtens der Schlachttiere," *Frankfurter Zeitung* 13.3 (1930): BH Gesandtschaft Karlsruhe 1413.

[88]Emphasis is mine. DVP deputy Mattes in 29 April 1931 proceedings of the Baden Landtag BH Gesandtschaft Karlsruhe 1413. Also see, "Beginn der Landwirtschaftsdebbate."

[89]"Zur Schächtfrage," *DZ* (8 October 1932): BH Gesandtschaft Darmstadt 1369.

[90]2 February 1931 letter to Strunk from Danzig Centralverein (draft) CAHJP DA 652a.

The Escalation of the Disputes

Between 1930 and 1933, the anti–kosher butchering campaigns intensified as the Weimar Republic experienced grave economic and political threats. The crash of the U.S. stock market in 1929 sent the German economy in a downward spiral, encouraging a new set of charges concerning the relationship of kosher butchering to the dwindling food supply and providing the context in which the coalition government of that time dissolved. The National Socialists drew from and fed into this economic and political discontent. In the course of the late 1920s and early 1930s, they transformed themselves into a viable political organization and gradually experienced successes within the kosher butchering disputes. These conditions alone, however, did not push the *Schächtfragen* forward, as evidenced by the number of local and state measures that failed in 1930 and 1931. Instead, the coup d'etat against the Prussian state government in July 1932 and the assumption of power by the Nazis in 1933 gradually created the conditions in which a national ban on kosher butchering could be accepted by a growing number of political leaders.

The world depression of 1929 sparked some of the conditions that altered the kosher butchering debate. Among other things, the economic crisis resulted in material deprivation and in a corresponding rise of antisemitism. In the beginning of the 1930s, the supply of goods and foodstuffs fell steadily. Between 1929 and 1930 the index for capital goods production dropped from 103 to 81; between 1931 and 1932 the same index sank from 61 to 46, a rate that was below half of its prewar level.[91] Many Germans were unable to purchase the few goods that were available. The depression had caused wages to fall and, more important, led to tremendous unemployment: 21.9 percent in 1931 and 29.9 percent in 1932.[92] German residents could no longer afford to buy the same quantities of foodstuffs that they had purchased during the years of relative stability, a problem exaggerated by the agricultural downturn occurring throughout Germany but particularly affecting East Elbian farming.[93] The depression led to agitation among peasants and urban townsfolk alike.

Within this context, proponents of bans on kosher butchering shifted their focus to the relationship of kosher butchering with the limited food supply. Their complaints were twofold: (1) that Jews

[91]Peukert, *Weimar Republic*, pp. 251–252.

[92]For men aged between 18 and 30, unemployment was above the average. Unemployment among women also was high although less so than among men. Broszat, *Hitler and the Collapse of Weimar Germany*, p. 11; Peukert, *Weimar Republic*, pp. 250–255.

[93]On the concomitant agricultural crises, see Peukert, *Weimar Republic*, p. 121.

contributed to the paucity of foodstuffs because they consumed large quantities of meat and (2) that Jews exacerbated current conditions because of their manipulation of the meat trade. The former argument had its roots in earlier debates, reviving the old arguments of Jews' excessive meat consumption and of the cruel and pointless nature of killing animals. According to a National Socialist sponsored petition submitted to the Danzig senate, of the 900 Jews in Danzig only 20 percent observed Jewish dietary laws, but many more ate the meat killed by kosher slaughterers.[94]

As participants inveighed against the Jewish tendency to rely heavily on kosher meat for their diet, they also accused Jews of treachery within the valuable meat trade. Petitions to local and state government officials articulated concern that Jews would supply meat and other foodstuffs to their coreligionists rather than to fellow citizens in need. They encouraged governments not simply to ban kosher butchering but also to implement laws that would regulate the import and export of kosher meat. In Thuringia, for example, National Socialists warned that Jews exported much needed meat to Bavaria, where kosher butchering was illegal, rather than keeping that meat for Thuringian citizens. They questioned the patriotism of those Jews who would choose to slaughter animals for their Bavarian coreligionists instead of reserving the cattle for their Thuringian neighbors. "We do not want there to be excessive ritually slaughtered meat for export," the district authority of Meiningen warned its local Jewish community. There was only to be enough produced locally.[95] In Danzig, too, butchers expressed the concern that a ban on kosher butchering might allow Jews to import their meat from Poland, thus undercutting the local Danzig economy.[96] Even several op-

---

[94]1931 Danzig petition to the town council CAHJP DA 652 a. On the Danzig petition see "Um ein Schächt-Verbot: Der jüdische Standpunkt" (7 January 1931) CAHJP DA 652 a. Other discussants raised similar concerns. 27 November 1930 report by the the Society Against Vivisection and Other Forms of Cruelty (Munich) StM SUV 90; "Betäubung der Schlachttiere," *MNN* 20 (21 January 1930); Max Müller, *Warum humanes Schlachten: Eine Stellungnahme gegen das betäubungslose Verbluten und für den gesetzlichen Betäubungszwang beim Schlachten der Tiere* (Kirchhain, Brücke-Verlag Kurt Schmersow, 1931).

[95]12 February 1931 letter from the district office in Thüringen to the Jewish community of Meiningen and the Jewish communal response CAHJP A/159; 17 February 1931 letter to Drs. Bamberger (Bad Kissingen), Bruer (Aschaffenburg), Ephraim (Burgpreppach), Hanover (Wurzburg), Salomon (Bayreuth), Stein (Schweinfurt), Wohlgemuth (Kitzingen), Katten (Bamberg) from the Jewish Community of Munich CAHJP a/159; "Thüringer Schächtgesetz," *AFZ* (22 January 1931) CAHJP D 652/a; A.L., "Thierschutzvereine und Schächtfrage," *CVZ* (17 April 1931). Similar concerns were expressed in 27 November 1930 report and letter from the Society Against Vivisection StM SUV 90.

[96]23 December 1930 letter to Fabian from Zander CAHJP DA 652b; "Um ein Schächt-Verbot: Der jüdische Standpunkt" (7 January 1931) CAHJP DA 652 a.

ponents of the kosher butchering bans expressed concern with Jewish economic control, complaining that a reduction in Jewish purchases of kosher meat would threaten the viability of local economies.[97] A few state governments responded to these and other charges, and by 1933 some states forbade the export and import of kosher meat.[98]

Local and regional contexts shaped these concerns. The threat of importing meat from Poland, for example, struck a deep chord with Danzig and German nationalists because Danzig had been involved in a trade war with Poland. Poland had discriminated against the city-state in favor of the new Polish port of Gdynia, which had a negative impact on Danzig's economy.[99] Similarly, concerns over Jewish malevolence in the meat industry attracted attention in regions where Jewish populations lived in rural areas and were involved in food-related industries. Bavaria, Baden, Hesse, and Württemberg, which witnessed vitriolic conflicts over the rite, had a high percentage of Jews who made a living in trading cattle, wine, or grain. Many of these Jews also owned farms that produced their own food or cattle feed. The site of rural antisemitic activism, these regional governments were sympathetic toward passing bans on kosher butchering, even though such laws interfered with the rights of their Jewish populations.[100]

The National Socialists used these frustrations and other anxieties exacerbated by the depression to launch successful kosher butchering disputes. The Nazis had become better organized over the course of the 1920s, moving slowly from what Oded Heilbronner has called the "peripheries" of German politics to the "center."[101] Though failing to

[97]They also complained about the high cost of stunning techniques. "Obermeistertagung bayerischer Fleischermeister: die Erhebung der Schlachtsteuer—gegen das Schächtverbot," *Bayreuther Tagblatt* 277 (27 November 1930): 2; 12 January 1931 letter to the senate of Danzig CAHJP DA 652 a.

[98]2 June report of the veterinary authorities of Munich StM SUV 90; 22 June 1933 letter to Engel from P., Hamburg CAHJP AHW 568 b.

[99]Herbert S. Levine, *Hitler's Free City: A History of the Nazi Party in Danzig, 1925–1939* (Chicago: University of Chicago Press, 1970), p. 16–17. With the exception of Danzig, state governments expressed anxiety over Jews trading with Jews in other German states not with Jews in other countries.

[100]Many rural Jews were likely to observe the laws of *kashrut*, although as Jacob Borut has shown the west German countryside saw a diminution in the observance level of Jews. Jacob Borut, "'Bin ich doch ein Israelit, ehre ich auch den Bischof mit,' Village and Small-Town Jews within the Social Spheres of Western German Communities during the Weimar period," in Benz, Paucker, and Pulzer, eds., *Jüdisches Leben in der Weimarer Republik*, pp. 126–127. On rural protests, see Jonathan Osmond, *Rural Protest in the Weimar Republic: The Free Peasantry in the Rhineland and Bavaria* (New York: St. Martin's Press, 1993).

[101]Heilbronner, "From Antisemitic Peripheries to Antisemitic Centres."

receive a significant majority in the Reichstag, they slowly coalesced as a political unit and encouraged the movement of some groups further to the political right. Specific historical events hastened this shift. The world depression, combined with their involvement in a campaign against the 1929 reparations redistribution plan (Young Plan), catapulted the Nazis and other right-leaning groups into a state of greater popularity. In the face of scarcities and emotional upheaval, the unemployed had radicalized, joining parties on the right and left that promised revolutionary change.[102] The NSDAP recruited members from this group and from the millions of Germans who envisioned themselves as being "between" the social classes. In 1930, the Nazis won 107 seats in the Reichstag, becoming the second largest party, a huge increase over their previous 12 seats. In July 1932 their numbers climbed to 230 seats.[103] They also gained seats in the state parliaments of Anhalt, Brunswick, Mecklenburg, Oldenburg, and Thuringia, all of which would hold rancorous disputes over kosher butchering during the early 1930s.

Between 1930 and 1933, the Nazis repeatedly introduced petitions for slaughterhouse reform in dozens of cities and several states. Increasingly they worked with a wide continuum of conservative and right-wing politicians who also championed these animal protection proposals. Members of the German State Party, the conservative German National People's Party (DNVP), and the more fringe Agarian League of Farmers (Reichslandbund) and Christian National Peasant/Rural Party cosponsored dozens of local petitions to mandate the stunning of animals before slaughter.[104] Their efforts were most successful when they also received support from the left and right liberal parties, as evidenced in Thuringia and Bavaria where some members of the DVP and SPD voted for the ban.[105] If the petitions failed, however, they reintroduced them, often unchanged. In Hesse, for example, National Socialist deputies and their coalition of supporters submitted petitions for a ban in 1929,

[102]Broszat, *Hitler and the Collapse of Weimar Germany*, p. 12.

[103]Out of thirty parties that ran for seats in 1932, they received 32 percent of the vote. In the elections of November of 1932, however, they declined to 196 seats.

[104]Although only the Deuschsvölkischen Freiheitspartei had cosponsored a *Schächtverbot* in the late 1920s, the period after 1930 saw much more participation from other groups. The German State Party was formed in 1930 fusing the bourgeois German Democratic People's Party (DDP) with the antisemitic Young German Order.

[105]"Thüringer Schächtgesetz," *AFZ* (22 January 1931) CAHJP D 652/a. Similar complaints were uttered in Braunschweig and Bavaria. M. Junack, "Zu der Frage, ob Schlachtrinder durch Elektrizität betäubt werden können," *Die Literarische Umschau* (5 July 1931); "Zur Schächtfrage: Die Reden der sozialdemokratischen Abgeordneten Frohme und Liebknecht für das Schächten in deutschen Reichstag," *DIZ* 19 (7 October 1926): 3–4.

in 1931, and again in March, September, and October 1932. Hessian state ministers finally crafted a ban in March 1933, one month before the Nazis created a national prohibition.[106]

The growing acceptability of these anti–kosher butchering campaigns in Hesse and elsewhere took place only with certain significant shifts in German politics, all of which have been the subject of exhaustive historical research. The 1930 resignation of the Great Coalition cabinet, the 1932 coup d'etat in Prussia, and the gradual assumption of national power by the Nazis slowly changed the nature of the kosher butchering disputes. With the dissolution of the Great Coalition cabinet in 1930, the national government altered in character at the very moment that the Bavarian prohibition challenged its authority over kosher butchering. The Great Coalition, which had governed Germany between 1928 and 1930, had unraveled in the aftermath of the depression. Unable to resolve domestic issues, the coalition dissolved, making the way for a right-leaning cabinet.[107] The Brüning administration, weak and ruling largely by decree, tacitly ignored the Bavarian government's handling of the kosher butchering question and ignored that the new slaughterhouse law defied national jurisdiction. The cabinet continued to remain silent when other states and municipalities passed similar laws, thus allowing for the gradual abandonment of the 1917 Bundesrat decisions.[108] This abdication process, however, was slow, evidenced by the majority of states and municipalities that, between 1930 and 1932, rejected bans on kosher butchering.

The dissolution of the Great Coalition also allowed for other significant political changes, which, in turn, encouraged the radicalization of the *Schächtfragen*. The new chancellor, Franz von Papen's, ouster of the

[106]2 March 1932 memo from Fischer to the Bavarian minister of interior BH Gesandtschaft Darmstadt 1369; 16 September 1932 memo from Fischer to the Bavarian minister of interior BH Gesandtschaft Darmstadt 1369; "Zur Schächtfrage," *DZ* (8 October 1932) BH Gesandtschaft Darmstadt 1369; 12 October 1932 memo from Fischer to the minister of exterior BH Gesandtschaft Darmstadt 1369; Hessische Gesamtministerium, "Verordnung über das Betäuben von Schlachttieren in Hessen," BH Gesandtschaft Darmstadt 1369; 20 March 1933 Darmstadt regulations BH Gesandtschaft Darmstadt 1369.

[107]The right liberal DVP represented employers and, as such, hoped to cut benefits and taxes. The SPD represented unions; they wished to see the passage of emergency taxes and the increase of unemployment benefits. The difficulties of the Great Coalition were complicated by the large debts the government owed.

[108]Der Betäubungszwang für Schlachtvieh," *MNN* 22 (23 January 1930): 3; "Schlachtvieh Betäubungszwang: Annhame des Gesetzes im Landtagsausschuß," *MNN* 23 (24 January 1930). 2; "Die Annahme des Schächtgesetzes," *BK* 24 (24 January 1930): 3; "Bayerischer Landtag: Das bayerische Schächtgesetz," 14 *Neue Freie Volkszeitung* (24 January 1930) StM SUV 90; "Bayerischer Landtag. Aus dem Verfassungs-Auschuß," *Bayerische Staatszeitung und Bayerische Staatsanzeiger* 19 (24 January 1930): 14; 28 February 1930 letter to its members from the Munich TSV StM Vereine 2223; October 1930 ministerial order (Bavaria)

Prussian Social Democratic government in July 1932 had a transformative affect on German politics and, as such, influenced the kosher butchering disputes. Shaped by long-standing tensions between the national government and the largest state in the Reich, the takeover followed a rancorous transit workers' strike in Berlin and the corresponding events of Bloody Sunday, when street fighting in Altona between Communist and Nazi paramilitary groups resulted in the deaths of eighteen civilians. Three days after the urban unrest, Papen executed his coup d'etat. His government appointed a Reich commissioner as Prussian interior minister and combined the offices of German chancellor and Prussian minister-president. Now, the Reich would oversee the administration of Germany's largest state.[109] Moreover, after the coup d'etat, the Nazis gradually assumed positions in the Prussian police while conservative civil servants replaced Social Democratic and left liberal police presidents and regional administrators. The archival evidence leaves no clear trail between the 1932 coup and the increasing frequency with which state governments and municipalities outside of Prussia began to debate animal protectionist petitions after the summer 1932.[110] However, there may be significant connections. Prussian animal protectionists might have felt emboldened to push again for a ban on kosher butchering even if their earlier petitions had not succeeded. Despite the failure of the 1930 anti–kosher butchering campaign in Berlin, for example, its supporters resumed their campaigns soon after the coup.[111]

CAHJP A/159. Local bans took place in Zwickau, Hirschberg, Gotha, and Osthheim. They were rejected in Quakenbrück, Berlin, Leipzig, Königsberg, Cologne, Muhlhausen i. Thür, Soest, Ratibor, Schweidnitz, Rosock, and Ulm. "Ruhiger Tag im Stadtrat: Um Die Besetzung des Fürsorgeauschusses—Und wieder das Schächtverbot," *Bayreuther Tagblatt* 128 (3 June 1930): 3; 12 January 1931 letter from Thüringen district department to the Jewish community of Meiningen; A. L. "Thierschutzvereine und Schächtfrage," *CVZ* (17 April 1931); "Schächtverbot in Gotha," *CVZ* (13 February 1931); Reichsszentrale für Schächtangelegenheiten, "Aus dem Tätigkeitsbericht der Reichszentrale" (March 1932) LBA RSC AR 2112 (B 30/7).

[109]While the takeover took place in July 1932, supporters of the Braun government brought suit against the Reich for the coup d'etat. The case was tried at Leipzig in October 1932. On Bloody Sunday, see Anthony McElligott, *Contested City: Municipal Politics and the Rise of Nazism in Altona, 1917–1937* (Ann Arbor: University of Michigan Press, 1998). Also see Broszat, *Hitler and the Collapse of Weimar Germany*, pp. 119–122.

[110]See, e.g., "Darmstadt," *FZ* 15.9 (15 September 1932): BH Gesandtschaft Darmstadt 1369; announcement in *DZ* 277 (15 September 1932): BH Gesandtschaft Darmstadt 1369; 16 September 1932 memo from Fischer to the Bavarian minister of interior BH Gesandtschaft Darmstadt 1369.

[111]Reichsszentrale, "Aus dem Tätigkeitsbericht der Reichszentrale." It would be interesting to discover whether local police charged greater numbers of *shohetim* with animal cruelty after 1932.

The summer of 1932 provided a further break within the kosher butchering disputes; animal protectionists in Berlin and elsewhere vigorously resumed their campaigns, often petitioning governmental agencies on a monthly or twice-monthly basis. The existence of these renewed *Schächtfragen*, however, did not necessarily dictate their passage. Instead, between July 1932 and April 1933, dozens of municipal governments and several state ministries and parliaments rejected the proposed bans.[112] Despite their unease with the rite, these participants framed their defense of kosher butchering as rejections of the Nazi Party and as statements in support of national governance and social progress. The rejections of the anti–kosher butchering campaigns were significant. Until April 1933, the majority of discussants in positions of power preferred not to position themselves with the Nazi camp in these disputes.

Jewish communal defense of the rite saw a parallel development. Gravely concerned by the Nazi presence and influence in the kosher butchering disputes, Jewish leaders described the campaigns against the rite as pure "matters of agitation."[113] Between 1919 and 1933, they worked diligently to safeguard kosher butchering. Whether or not they observed the dietary laws or could procure meat in their town or state, Jewish participants crafted a rich but also a contradictory set of responses to the new threat.

Jewish Self-Defense

The campaigns to defend kosher butchering mirrored the inconsistencies of the emerging *Schächtfragen* as well as the internal divisions within Weimar Jewry. Efforts to safeguard kosher butchering began in 1919, when a group of local and national Jewish agencies expressed frustration with their leaders' reluctance to defend the rite, and continued through 1933, only ceasing with the onset of war in 1939. The safeguarding efforts drew from political strategies and rhetoric of the imperial campaigns but also introduced new techniques. Despite the richness of these efforts, the campaigns failed to unite German Jewry around a single issue. Participating organizations initiated

[112]Participatory states were more likely to implement prohibitions than cities—a phenomenon due perhaps to the fact that the simultaneous passage of state and local bans was unnecessary.

[113]2 February 1931 letter to Strunk from Danzig Centralverein (draft) CAHJP DA 652a; Also see Verein zur Abwehr des Antisemitismus, "Schächten," in *Abwehr ABC* (Berlin: Verein zur Abwehr des Antisemitismus, 1920): 105–106.

competing campaigns to defend Jewish rites, which sometimes had the adverse effect of exaggerating differences among German Jews. The fragility of the defense efforts does not imply that the Jews of Weimar disregarded signs pointing to their own destruction. Instead, it suggests that communal leaders had a real interest in power. They used the defenses of kosher butchering as one means of acquiring that much-desired authority.[114]

Attempts to safeguard the Jewish rite commenced within a few months after the war's defeat. In January 1919, the Centralverein and the Bureau for Kosher Butchering Defense (Büro) began to revitalize earlier efforts to defend kosher butchering. The Centralverein initiated the campaign immediately after the slaughterhouse directors Carl Klein and Hermann Ramdohr released a short film in the winter of 1919 documenting the alleged brutality of kosher butchering. The film was not the first attempt by Ramdohr to push for new slaughterhouse laws. Indeed, the Centralverein had tracked the anti–kosher butchering efforts of the Leipzig slaughterhouse director earlier in the century when he had helped found the Association for the Advancement of Humane Slaughter in 1906 and when he edited an anthology of letters criticizing the rite. Now, immediately after the creation of the Weimar Republic, the Centralverein leadership charged Klein and Ramdohr with deceiving their audience. According to the organization's press releases and letters, the film captured a non-Jewish butcher using a (forbidden) blunt knife to cut only half of the animal's neck. In February 1919, the Centralverein mailed letters to its member organizations beseeching them to "make the untruths of the film be known."[115] Seven months later, it and the Büro responded to

---

[114]Early understandings of Jewish political behavior in Weimar can be found in Hannah Arendt, *The Origins of Totalitarianism* (San Diego: Harcourt Brace Jovanovich, 1968), esp. p. 24; and Gershom Scholem, "On the Social Psychology of the Jews in Germany, 1900–1933," in *Jews and Germans from 1860–1933: The Problematic Symbiosis*, ed. David Bronsen (Heidelberg: Winter, 1979), pp. 9–32. Recent explorations into Jewish political participation, voting patterns, and associational life have portrayed the political Jewish renaissance of the Weimar Republic in bold strokes. Their emphases have been threefold: (1) an investigation into Jewry's attachment to Liberalism, (2) the partisan struggles over the character of local Jewish communities, and (3) a comparison of the defense campaigns launched by the Centralverein and the Zionist Organization in Germany (ZVFD). An early example of this revisionism can be seen in Donald Niewyk, *The Jews in Weimar Germany* (Baton Rouge: University of Louisiana Press, 1980). A more recent example can be found in Martin Liepach, *Das Wahlverhalten der jüdischen Bevölkerung. Zur politischen Orientierung der Juden in der Weimarer Republik* (Tübingen: Mohr Siebeck, 1996).

[115]25 February 1919 (# 131) letter to member organizations from the Centralverein CAHJP WR 561; February 1919 press releases by the Centralverein CAHJP WR 561. The Büro had responded to a similar film made in 1914. Büro, *Mitteilungen des Büros für Schächtschutz: Lenneper Film* CAHJP DA 439.

the National Animal Protection Society's attempt to initiate a national campaign against the rite. The animal protection attempt failed, but the movement to safeguard kosher butchering had begun in earnest.[116]

As kosher butchering defense efforts gradually intensified over the course of the 1920s and early 1930s, other organizations joined the Büro and Centralverein in their efforts to protect the rite. Increasingly after 1923, the Society to Combat Antisemitism, the Jewish federations of Prussia and Bavaria, and several local Jewish synagogue communities headed additional efforts to protect the rite.[117] Several of the organizations that had been fundamental in earlier campaigns now were absent. The Berlin-based *shehitah* coalition had dissolved during World War I, making room for the Büro. The defense efforts no longer witnessed the participation of the Verband or the DIGB. The former no longer existed, while the latter had lost its energy and authority.

In their initiatives for active defense, the participating organizations drew on the political strategies and rhetoric of the imperial period. They attempted to counter the anti–kosher butchering movement with rational arguments and emphasized the Nazi and antisemitic presence within the campaigns to ban the rite. Consistently referring to the animal protection proposals as "Nazi petitions," Jewish communal leaders implied that no politician who supported the Republic would choose to side with these radical extremists.[118]

The safeguarding of religious freedom was at the center of this defense operation. Unlike past campaigns, Jewish leaders no longer needed to create a tradition of religious freedom. Now, they could invoke the freedom of belief and conscience guaranteed by the Weimar constitution, as well as the 1917 Bundesrat order.[119] Proponents made one

[116]September 1919 report of the Büro CAHJP D/Ba28/212; September 1919 letter to member organizations from the Centralverein CAHJP WR 561; "Das Schächten auf dem Verbandstag der Tierschutzvereine," *FI* 36 (11 September 1919): CJA 75Cve1341 217; "Die Schächtfrage," *JR* (7 October 1919) CJA 75CVe1341 218; "Schächten auf dem Berbandstag der Tierschutzvereine," *Neue Jüdische Presse* 41/42 (8 October 1919): CJA 75CVe1341 219.

[117]The archival evidence suggests that the Zionists continued to be disinterested in kosher butchering.

[118]24 April 1925 letter from the Jewish community of Munich to Munich's mayor StM SUV 90; April 3 1930 letter to Jewish community rabbis from the Büro CJA 75Ael2796; March 4 1930 letter to rabbis from Büro CJA 75Ael2796; 12 January 1931 letter to the Danzig senate from the Jewish community council there CAHJP DA 652 a; 2 January 1931 report of the Danzig Synagogue community CAHJP DA 652a; E. Munk, "Um die Schächtfreiheit" *CVZ* 5 (30 January 1931): 50; 2 February 1931 letter to Strunk from Danzig CV (draft) CAHJP DA 652a; 21 January 1932 letter from the Reichszentrale to Nathan CAHJP A/W 568b; A.L. "Thierschutzvereine und Schächtfrage."

[119]In 1930, Jewish community councils and organizations submitted 128 counterpetitions to the Bavarian parliament requesting their religious freedoms. 12 February 1930

of two arguments concerning religious freedom. The majority argued that kosher butchering constituted a "religious dictate of Judaism" and that by hindering this "institution of Judaism," the proposed laws violated the constitution's promise of free religious practice.[120] Some promoted this line of defense while portraying the rite as something affecting all Jews. In its 1931 campaign against a local *Schächtverbot*, for example, the Danzig synagogue community warned that the petition "would have severe and disastrous consequences on one fundamental component of our Jewish religion: that we eat [kosher] meat and slaughter cattle ritually....As members of the Jewish community of Danzig we request your support: invoke the freedom of belief and consciousness."[121] Others were less likely to endorse this universalistic view. Possibly concerned that such a rhetorical turn would paint Jews as unable to assimilate, the spokesmen of the Centralverein claimed that governments needed to overturn the bans because of their unconstitutionality. In their view, even though "only a small percentage" of German Jews would be affected directly by a prohibition, the proposed slaughterhouse laws threatened to destabilize the progressive premises of the Weimar constitution.[122]

The Centralverein spokesmen and their colleagues also revived the decades-old argument that scientific evidence had established the rite's humanity. Similar to earlier defense efforts, the Weimar campaigns asserted that kosher butchering could be rapid and painless, as demonstrated by exhaustive studies of the animals' corneal reflexes

---

letter from the Bavarian Rabbinical assembly CAHJP A/159; "Betäubung der Schlachttiere," *MNN* 20 (21 January 1930) StM SUV 90. Some of these petitions can be found in StM SUV 90. Also see E. Munk, *Leitsätze für den Bericht über die Schächtfrage* CAHJP D/BA28/212; "Um die Schächtfreiheit" *CVZ* 5 (30 January 1931): 50. Also see 23 April 1926 Munich Jewish community declaration CAHJP DA/219; 29 April 1925 letter from the Munich Jewish community StM SUV 90; Minutes of the 28 February 1928 meeting of the Königsberg shehitah commission CAHJP KN/II/E/III/5; January 1931 report of the Danzig Synagogue community (handwritten notes suggests it was sent to seven individuals including Strunk) CAHJP DA 652a.

[120]Munk, *Leitsätze für den Bericht über die Schächtfrage.* Also see Bayerischer Israelitische Gemeinden, *Zur Schächtfrage: Vorstellung des verbandes Bayerischer Israelitscher Gemeinden und der Bayer-Rabbinerkonferenz an den bayerischen Landtag vom 10 Mai 1926* (Munich: Verlag B. Heller, 1926).

[121]January 1931 report of the Danzig Synagogue community CAHJP DA 652a. Also see similar language in *Zur Schächtfrage* and 14 January 1932 memo from the Vienna Jewish community to the Ministers of Education and Interior CAHJP A/W1392.

[122]They argued that liberal Jews "recognized the significance of *shehitah* even if they do not practice it." "Der Tierarzt als Theologe: Unbefugter Versuch einer Interpretation religiös-jüdischer Angelegenheiten," *DIZ* 22 (18 November 1926): 3. Also see Grünpeter, "Sind die Schächtverbote rechtsgültig," *CVZ* (15 Mai 1931): 251; S. Lichtenstaedter,

and muscle movements during and after slaughter.[123] Animals, these discussants argued, did not live long after the cut of slaughter but died almost instantly.[124] This argument dismissed the critics, insisting that "hundreds of men of science...particularly university professors and a Nobel prize winner" had verified the humanity and worthiness of kosher butchering.[125] In 1928, members of the Königsberg *shehitah* commission had used similar language when rejecting the animal protectionist claims. "Lay people will see it one way, but experts know" otherwise, they argued.[126]

Participants complemented this approach of establishing the rite's religious and scientific worth with expressing sensitivity to issues concerning kosher butchering and the economy. Reversing their opponents' complaints, Jewish communal leaders maintained that a prohibition on the rite would economically devastate communities and families. In Munich, one Jewish leader bemoaned that the families of seven slaughterhouse employees would face financial ruin; his contemporary in Berlin warned of the potential impact a ban on kosher butchering would have on 170 practitioners of the rite.[127] Jewish defense campaigns similarly responded to charges concerning Jewish consumption. In their petition and lobbying efforts, participants insisted that Jews ate less meat than animal protectionists had claimed. At the same time, they tried to explain away the amount of cattle Jews butchered: They tended to eat only cattle, poultry, and veal (rather than pigs) and could consume only a portion of the meat from the animal. In 1928, Dr. J. Jakobovits, head of the Königsberg *shehitah* commission, met with his local slaughterhouse director to convey these messages. Jakobovits also assured him of the Jewish community's vigilance in maintaining

---

"Sind die Schächtverbote rechtsgültig?" *CVZ* (21 August 1931): 414. By 1931 these premises had become hollow.

[123]According to one letter writer, the "answers" concerning the animal's pain during slaughter "are not grounded in psychology but strong advanced science and experiments." 2 February 1931 letter to Strunk from Zander CAHJP DA 652 a.

[124]Dexler, *Über das Bewegungsverhalten eines grosshirnlosen Schafes beim Schächten*; S. Lieben, "Über das Verhalten des Blutdruckes in den Hirngefäßen nach durschneidung des Halses," *Sonnderabdruck aus Monatshefte für praktische Tierheilkunde* 31: 481–496.

[125]23 April 1926 Munich Jewish community declaration CAHJP DA/219.

[126]20 February 1928 minutes of the Königsberg *shehitah* commission CAHJP KN/II/E/III/5. Also see 12 January 1931 letter to the town council from the Jewish community of Danzig CAHJP DA 652a and January 1931 report of the Danzig Synagogue community CAHJP DA 652a.

[127]28 April 1925 letter from Fränkel to the city council StM SUV 90; 26 June 1929 memo and draft sent to Ismar Freund CAHP P2/L/22. Also see "Schächtverbot in Bayern—und seine Folgen!" CAHJP DA 652a; January 1931 report of the Danzig Synagogue community CAHJP DA 652a.

a low consumption rate as well as observing the laws set forth by the abattoir commission.[128]

National and local Jewish communal agencies translated these arguments into action by drawing from extant and novel forms of political behavior. They continued to meet individually with non-Jewish politicians and to launch letter writing, postcard, and petition campaigns. The Büro, which later changed its name to the Reich Central Office for Matters Concerning Kosher Butchering (Reichszentrale), initiated seven such efforts between 1923 and 1933. Each effort was twofold. The Büro's head, Rabbi Esra Munk, contacted individual policy makers at all levels of government; he also wrote to local Jewish community councils and rabbis throughout Germany, asking them to participate in a letter-writing campaign and to help defray the costs of kosher butchering defense.[129] Dozens of Jewish organizations responded and lobbied their local slaughterhouse commissions, city governments, regional administrators, and state deputies to vote against a ban. Soon after local kosher butchering debates began in Munich in 1925, for example, the local Jewish community council sent over two dozen letters to local politicians within a single month.[130] These letters and petitions often borrowed

[128]30 March 1928 letter to the synagogue community of Königsberg from Jakobovits CAHJP KN/II/E/III/5. Also see 1921 letter to the Jewish community of Danzig from Sternberg CAHJP DA 439; 25 February 1923 letter from Königsberg community to Munich and 1 March 1923 response CAHJP KN/II/E/III/5; June 1932 letter from Reichszentrale to German Jewish communities CAHJP DA 652b.

[129]These campaigns took place in 1923, 1925, 1927, 1928, 1930, 1932, and 1933. 1923 letter and report from the Büro CAHJP KN/II/E/III/5; 11 August 1927 letter to the Jewish community of Königsberg from the Büro CAHJP KN/II/E/III/5; 23 February 1928 letter to Rabbis and Jewish communal leaders CAHJP A/159; 1 September 1932 letter from the Reichszentrale to the Jewish community of Hamburg CAHJP 568 b-#75; 17 November 1932 letter to member Jewish communities. CJA 75AEl279; 25 January 1933 letter to member rabbis CAHJP DA 652/b. Fund-raising requests can be found in 15 September 1931 letter from the Reichszentrale to Centralverein members in Dazing CAHJP DA 652a; 24 April 1931 letter from the Reichszentrale to the Jewish community of Danzig CAHJP DA 652a; 25 August 1932 letter from the Reichszentrale CAHJP DA 652b; 24 June 1931 letter from the Reichszentrale to the Hamburg Jewish community CAHJP A/W 568b; 24 April 1931 letter to German rabbis from the Reichszentrale A/W 568b; 22 December 1932 letter from the Reichszentrale to Synagogue communities CAHJP DA 652b; 24 August 1932 letter from the Reichzentrale to the Hamburg Jewish community CAHJP AHW 568b and to Danzig DA 652b; 28 March 1932 letter from Reichszentrale CAHJP A/159; 9 June 1932 notice from the Reichszentrale CAHJP DA 652b.

[130]See, e.g., 28 April 1925 letter from Fränkel to the Munich city council StM SUV 90; 24 April 1925 letter from the Munich Jewish community to Schnarnagl StM SUV 90; 29 April 1925 letter from the Jewish community of Munich to the city council; 3 May 1925 letters from the Munich Jewish community to the city council StM SUV 90; 21 May 1925 letter from the Munich Jewish community to the slaughterhouse commission StM

heavily from the materials distributed by the Büro or, in other cases, the Centralverein.[131] At other times, their campaigns were unscripted by Berlin, reflecting local issues and disputes.[132] When Danzig Jewry faced a potential ban in 1930, its community leaders dispatched a dozen letters to local politicians, targeting those with whom they had some kind of social relationship even if it was a superficial one.[133] Their letters specifically responded to anxieties that the Jewish community might import meat from Poland.[134]

In addition to lobbying local, national, and regional politicians, Jewish communal agencies continued to rely heavily on the press to influence Jewish and non-Jewish circles. Just as they had done during the *Kaiserreich*, discussants wrote letters to editors, sent sympathetic articles to prominent leaders, and published dozens of articles, monographs, and letters defending the rite.[135] They distributed responses to particularly vexing animal

---

SUV 90; *Vorstellung des Verbandes Bayerischer Israelitischer Gemeinden und der Bayerischen Rabbinerkonferenz vom 10 Mai 1926.*

[131]Templates included 25 February 1919 letter to the Jewish communities of Germany from the Centralverein (#131) CAHJP WR 561 (Würzburg); 15 March 1928 letter from the Büro to German rabbis CAHJP D/BA 28/212; 23 February 1928 from the Büro CAHJP A/159s. See the different styles of letters in 30 March 1928 letter from the Königsberg Jewish community CAHJP KN/II/E/III/5; 11 February 1930 letter from the Bayreuth Jewish community to the Government of Oberfranken CAHJP a/159; 14 January 1932 memo from the Vienna Jewish community to the Ministers of Education and Interior CAHJP A/W1392.

[132]Record of telephone conversation between Nathan and Heidecker 14 October 1925 CAHJP AHW 568a; 1929 minutes of telephone conversation between Harmann and Jewish community council leaders of Vienna (unnamed) CAHJP A/W 1392; 2 February 1931 letter to Strunk from Danzig Centralverein (draft) CAHJP DA 652a.

[133]One Jewish community leader contacted a city senator that he had met a few weeks earlier. The letter writer, Zander, reminded councilor Strunk that the two had "taken a cure" at the same time and had spoken about the pending ban. 2 February 1931 letter to Strunk from Danzig Centralverein (draft) CAHJP DA 652a. The 5 January–3 February 1931 letters between members of the local chapter of the Centralverein, the Jewish community council, and city councilors are instructive. CAHJP DA 652a.

[134]2 January 1931 report of the Danzig Jewish community CAHJP DA 652 a. Similarly, Jewish leaders in Munich commented on local antisemitic disturbances. 2 May 1926 letter from the Jewish community to the Munich council; 2 May 1926 letter from the Jewish community to the slaughterhouse directors StM SUV 90.

[135]The weekly *CV Zeitung*, which published several articles defending the rite, had a circulation of 65,000 and its monthly edition was sent gratis to 30,000 non-Jewish "opinion makers." The Reichszentrale also sent its publication to Jewish communities throughout Germany. 15 September 1931 letter and publications list from the Reichszentrale to Jewish community of Danzig CAHJP DA 652 a; March 1932 publication and cost list of the Reichszentrale CAHJP A/W 568b.

protectionist publications.[136] The Centralverein's *Deutsche Israelitische Zeitung* (DIZ) and Munich rabbi Max Eschelbacher, for example, separately confronted the publications of Munich professor and veterinarian Max Müller. The DIZ publicly challenged Müller to respond to a specific set of questions regarding his views of the rite, while Eschelbacher published his retort in monograph form.[137] Three years later, the Büro published a lengthy pamphlet in response to the Berlin animal protection association's *Jewish Votes Against Slaughter Without Stunning.*[138]

Jewish defense efforts similarly released scientific statements in support of the rite. In 1926 the Bavarian Jewish Federation reprinted letters from the pre- and postwar periods that touted the rite's superiority over methods that slaughtered unconscious animals; the following year, the Büro published a similar collection, which they reissued yearly until 1932.[139] These agencies distributed lengthy scientific articles and pamphlets, including texts as diverse as Jacob Levy's *New Fastening Mechanisms for Slaughter* and an article that reported on the poor quality of the meat that came from a pig stunned before slaughter.[140]

Participants also introduced novel strategies to safeguard the rite. One such tactic was the introduction of competitions to improve kosher

[136]In addition to the discussions below, see September 1919 report of the Büro; (Reichszentrale, *Jüdische Kronzeugen* (n.d.) LBA RSC AR 2112 (B 30/7); Vorstand und Rabbinat der Israelitischen Kultusgemeinde München, *Die Besprechung der Eingabe des Münchener Tierschutzvereins an den Landtag im Bayerischen Kurier vom 20 April 1926 gibt zu flogender Erklärung Anlass,* CAHJP D/BA28/212; "Der Tierarzt als Theologe: Unbefugter Versuch einer Interpretation religiös-jüdischer Angelgenhciten," *DIZ* 22 (18 November 1926): 1–3; Max Eschelbacher, *Erwiderung auf die Ausführungen des Herrn Prof. Dr. M. Müller (München) in den Münchener Neuesten Nachrichten und der Deutschen Schlachthof-Zeitung* (Düsseldorf: Druck von Itzkowski, 1927); Büro Für Schächtangelegenheiten, *Zur Frage* and *Zweite Reiche Neuer Gutachten;* Jewish community of Vienna's report on animal protection in Judaism (1929) CAHJP A/W 1392; Verein zur Abwehr des Antisemitismus, "Schächten," in *Abwehr ABC,* p. 105. A useful document is the March 1932 publication and cost list of the Reichszentrale CAHJP A/W 568b.

[137]They refuted Müller's assertion that kosher butchering shared links with ancient human sacrifice practices. They also contested his claims of electric stunning's superiority, its supposed permissibility, and the possibility that only a small percentage of Jews would be affected by a ban on the rite. "Der Tierarzt als Theologe: Unbefugter Versuch einer Interpretation religiös-jüdischer Angelegenheiten," *DIZ* 22 (18 November 1926): 1–3; Eschelbacher, *Erwiderung.* Müller's earlier works can be found in: Max Müller, *Die Schächtfrage* (Berlin: Berliner TSV, 1927); Max Müller, "Der Betäubungszwang bei Schlachttieren" *MNN* 4 (31 July 1927): 206; Max Müller, "Das elektrische Betäuben der Schlachttiere."

[138]Reichszentrale "Jüdische Kronzeugen" LBA RSC AR 2112 (B 30/7).

[139]Bay. Isr. Gemeinden, *Zur Schächtfrage;* Büro, *Zur Frage and Zweite Reiche Neuer Gutachten.*

[140]Jacob Levy, *Das neue Niederlegeverfahren bei der Schlachtung;* "Rückwirkungen der elektrischen Betäubung? Eigenartige Beobachtungen beim Schweinfleisch," *AFZ* (1 October 1931): CAHJP AHW 568b.

butchering. In 1925, the Büro, Rabbinical Assembly, and Kashrut Commission (Berlin) publicly recognized that the Jewish community had to engage with the problems concerning the fastening of animals or it would never thwart attempts to ban kosher butchering. Hoping to make kosher butchering "faster and more painless," these organizations hosted a contest under the direction of Rabbi Leo Baeck to create an improved *Niederlegen* mechanism.[141] The cities of Berlin, Frankfurt, Hamburg, Munich, Breslau, and Danzig took part in these competitions, and the sponsoring agencies simultaneously worked with German inventors to create "simple, painless, fast" mechanisms that "even the weakest of men could use."[142] This competition was significant. It paved the way for future attempts to fund and coordinate experiments concerning animal fastening and stunning.[143] Moreover, it illustrated the discomfort of many Jewish communal leaders with extant slaughtering practices. Such unease was also reflected in their attempts to refute the charges of disproportionately high meat consumption among Jews.[144] After 1929, the Büro tried to determine the actual rate of Jewish meat consumption and slaughter in order to rebut criticisms of the rite. To do so, the organization sent out annual questionnaires to Jewish communities in Germany, warning them of the shift in the animal protection campaign and asking them to determine how many animals they slaughtered and how much meat they ate.[145]

[141]13 November 1925 letter from the Kashruth commission of Berlin to the Jewish community of Vienna CAHJP A/W 1392; Report 2161 (1925) of the Rabbinerverband CAHJP A/W 1392.

[142]Reichszentrale für Schächtangelgenheiten, *Das neue Niederlegenverfahren.* Also see 22 December 1927 letter from the minister of interior to the minister presidents BH ML 2437; 15 March 1928 letter from the Büro to German rabbis CAHJP D/BA 28/212; "Der Stand Der Schächtfrage"; 2 February 1931 letter to Strunk from Danzig Centralverein (draft) CAHJP DA 652; Jacob Levy, *Das neue Niederlegeverfahren bei der Schlachtung; Endlich eine praktische Erfindung! Neuheit! Trunk'sche Sicherheitskette zum Niederhalten des Kopfes vom Schlachttieren* (Frankfurt a/M, 1919) CAHJP DA 439; Bloch, *Mitteilung* CAHJP WR 565.

[143]November 1927 report BH MWi 1267; 24 November 1927 statement by the Jewish Federation of Bavaria; 29 January 1929 letter to Nathan from Münk CAHJP AHW 568b 2; Report of Bavarian Rabbinical Assembly BH ML 2437; 4 January 1932 letter from the Reichszentrale to Nathan CAHJP A/W 568b.

[144]"Anregung für die Synagogenemeinden zur Feststellung und Begründung der Mindestzahl zuzulassender Schächtungen," (1929) CJA 75Ael279 15; 4 February and 14 March 1929 letters, memos, and questionnaires from the Büro and responses CJA 75Ael279; 26 January 1931 letter from the Jewish community of Bamberg CAHJP D/De4/18; June 1932 letter from Reichszentrale to German Jewish communities and Danzig's Response CAHJP DA 652b; 17 November 1932 letter form the Reichszentrale to Jewish communities and responses CJA 75Ael2792.

[145]17 November 1932 letter from the Reichszentrale CJA 75Ael2792. Earlier correspondence can be found in 4 February 1929 letter, memo, and questionnaire from the

As the Büro's work suggests, the defense campaigns mirrored trends within Weimar Jewry. First, the safeguarding efforts reflected other initiatives for active defense. Similar to the political activities of the Centralverein at this time, the kosher butchering campaigns relied on the written word to convince those in positions of power of Jewry's respectability and worthiness. Likewise, just as Jewish self-defense focused on safeguarding equal rights, the kosher butchering campaigns promoted the freedoms guaranteed by the Weimar constitution. Moreover, the efforts to protect the rite radicalized at the same moment that Jewish self-defense shifted in character. Jewish defense activity underwent a transformation in 1929 when communal organizations increasingly acknowledged that antisemitism had taken a dangerous form. They began to focus on the prevention of a takeover of government and concentrated on providing support to parties loyal to the Republic.[146] The campaigns to defend kosher butchering emulated this trend in part. They too adopted a feverish quality after the onset of the depression. Explicitly framing their campaign in opposition to that of the Nazis, supporters of the rite stepped up their lobbying efforts and increasingly placed economic concerns at the center of their literature and propaganda.

Furthermore, much like Weimar Jewry, the defense initiatives were fragmented.[147] Between 1919 and 1933, German Jews took advantage of an elaborate associational life with new cultural institutions, social services, and educational agencies. At the same time, these institutions experienced fierce divisions over questions of leadership and definition. The growing influence of Zionism, the influx of *Ostjuden*, and heightened German political debates over the direction of the Republic exaggerated these struggles. Similar to the confessional debates of imperial Germany,

---

Büro to Jewish communities CJA 75Ae1279 16; Some of the responses can be found in CJA 75Ae1279; 26 January 1931 letter from the Jewish community of Bamberg to the Jewish community of Demmesdorf-Scheßlitz CAHJP D/De4/18; June 1932 letter from Reichszentrale to German Jewish communities CAHJP DA 652b. If they did not respond, the Büro sent out a follow-up letter, explaining that they needed to take "immediate defensive measures."

[146]Sibylle Morgenthaler, "Countering the Pre-1933 Nazi Boycott against the Jews," *LBIYB* 36 (1991): 127–149; Arnold Paucker, *Der jüdische Abwehrkampf gegen Antisemitismus und Nationalsozialismus in den letzten Jahren der Weimarer Republik* (Hamburg: Leibniz-Verlag, 1968).

[147]On Weimar Jewry, see Brenner, *Renaissance of Jewish Culture in Weimar Germany,* and the outstanding articles in Benz, Paucker, and Pulzer, eds., *Jüdisches Leben in der Weimarer Republik.* The synopses in the recent volumes on German Jewry complement each other nicely. See Meyer, ed., *German-Jewish History in Modern Times,* vol. 4, pp. 7–194; Mauer, "From Everyday Life to a State of Emergency."

Jewish organizations continued to disagree over whether Jews constituted a religiously or ethnically defined community.[148] They now disputed their allegiances as well, looking in opposite directions either to Germany or to Zion. Given these intense ideological and cultural divides, it is not surprising that Jewish agencies and communities bitterly debated who had the authority to serve as German Jewry's spokesman.

The kosher butchering defense efforts demonstrated similar intensity and division. The campaigns lent the Jewish communities of Germany a decidedly political character. They reinforced political networks among Jews and provided an issue around which diverse communities and agencies could mobilize. They also offered an opportunity to enhance existing political strategies and develop new ones. Yet German Jewry remained on the defensive, poised to defend Jewish rites, if not proactively championing them. Within that context, attempts to safeguard the rite were bifurcated between and among local and national agencies. The Büro and Centralverein separately organized national defenses. The former organization, which was overseen by the Adas Jisroel separatist community in Berlin, was the dominant actor in kosher butchering defense; in contrast, the much larger Centralverein consistently published defenses of the rite but only sporadically took part in political initiatives.[149] While they participated in Centralverein- or Büro-led defense efforts, the Jewish federations of Bavaria and Prussia also organized their own campaigns. Similarly, individual Jewish community councils, rabbinates, and *shehitah* commissions also participated in national safeguarding operations and in their own municipal defenses. The fragmented character of these efforts does not imply passivity on the part of Weimar Jewry but instead highlights the real interest Jewish organizations had in power and control.

When divisions took place, they did so at all levels of governance. Local Jewish agencies and institutions debated who would coordinate the initiatives to safeguard the rite: the Jewish community council, rabbinate,

---

[148]The divisions within these camps were not always clear. While it could be assumed that Zionists supported the *volkisch* faction and that Liberals backed the other, there were complications. Zionists tended to disengage themselves publicly from politics outside of the local Jewish community or the Zionist platform. Moreover, many Orthodox sided with the ethnic camp, despite the fact that they disagreed over Zionist agendas. Traditional Jews clashed with the Liberal leaderships' understanding of religious orientation and defined religious character in expansive *volkisch* terms. Despite the murky nature of these clashes, they would have important implications on Jewish communal governance and self-defense.

[149]During the Weimar Republic, it was the largest Jewish organization with 60,000 registered members organized into 555 local chapters and 21 state federations.

kashrut/shehitah commission, or the local chapter of the Centralverein.[150] In 1928 Königsberg, for example, the *shehitah* commission expressed deep frustration with the extant defense efforts. Complaining that neither the local Jewish community council nor the Büro effectively combated attacks against the rite, it insisted that it be involved in future defense campaigns.[151] In Hamburg, local synagogue boards and Jewish community councilors disputed questions of leadership. Each insisted that its agency oversee defense efforts, a debate the continued through 1932.[152] Hamburg's Jewish community also clashed with the Prussian Jewish Federation over questions of ownership. In 1928, the federation chided the local Jewish council for attempting to organize a defense of its own. Insisting that it represented more than two-thirds of all German Jews, the federation demanded the right to lead the initiative.[153] Unfortunately for the federation, the Büro disagreed. It maintained that its organization, which was funded in part by the federation, ought to coordinate future efforts. In so doing, it, like the federation, usurped Hamburg's control.[154]

While these organizations contested places of authority and visibility, they did not challenge the content or strategies of other defense efforts. Debates over the possibility of proactive political behavior were now pointless. The campaigns against the Jewish rite were unrelenting and it would have been difficult to envision ways to promote the ritual without responding to charges already lodged against it. Moreover, with a few exceptions, the majority of defense initiatives cast Jewish rites as religiously significant and humanitarian. The confessional disputes did not seem to share the concern over religious particularity that shaped the defense campaigns of the *Kaiserreich.* Nor did they mirror the calls by Jewish leaders for restraint.

[150]There were many exceptions. In Danzig, the synagogue community and local Centralverein chapter worked well together. 21 December 1930 letter to Zander and the Danzig Centralverein CAHJP Da/2070; 2 February 1931 letter from the Centralverein to the Jewish community of Danzig CAHJP DA 652a.

[151]Minutes of the 28 February 1928 meeting of the Königsberg *shehitah* commission CAHJP KN/II/E/III/5; also see 1928 letters between the Königsberg *shehitah* commission and the Büro CAHJP KN/II/E/III/5. Similar frustrations were evident in the February 1928 exchange between the Büro and the Jewish community of Regensburg CAHJP A/159.

[152]19 June 1924 letter to Herman Samson from the Hamburg Jewish community CAHJP AHW 568; 30 August 1932 letter from the Jewish community of Hamburg to the Reichszentrale and responses CAHJP AHW 568b.

[153]31 January 1928 letter from the Prussian Jewish Federation to the Jewish community of Hamburg and response CAHJP AHW 568b.

[154]March 1928 letters between the Prussian Jewish Federation and the Büro CJA 75AE1279.

The initiatives for active defense illustrated the same kinds of irregularities exhibited in the *Schächtfragen*, in Weimar Jewish life, and in the Republic more generally. On the one hand, the movement to safeguard kosher butchering offered German Jews a rich tapestry of political strategies, organizations, opportunities, and programs. On the other hand, Jewish self-defense was fragmented, with individual organizations and actors each positioning themselves in places of authority and power. However, despite these contradictions, the campaigns to defend the rite occupied an important place in Weimar Jewish politics. They did not fall within the Zionist/Assimilationist or German/Ostjuden binaries that so frequently characterized Jewish life. Moreover, without expressing fear of an antisemitic backlash, these campaigns put Jews in the political arena and demanded that the Republic support their presence.

✝✝✝✝✝

In October 1931, Dr. Feiber was handed an anonymous pamphlet while he walked down the streets of Hamburg, his town of residence. The receipt of such a leaflet was hardly unusual. Diverse groups flooded Germany's streets with propagandist materials concerning a wide range of political and social issues. This leaflet, however, immediately caught Feiber's eye. Addressed to the "Working People of Hamburg," the pamphlet called for a ban on kosher butchering. Feiber immediately contacted the president of Hamburg's Jewish community council to inquire about the impending attack on kosher butchering and the defense efforts planned. He implored the Jewish community to act quickly. "Today the majority may side with the Liberals [on the kosher butchering question]," he wrote, "but they [the National Socialists] may win and then make us intoxicated from their slogans of animal protection."[155]

Many Jewish and non-Jewish participants shared Feiber's alarm. Since 1919, interest in kosher butchering had escalated. While the immediate postwar attention to the rite had been limited to the relationship of kosher butchering with the availability of foodstuffs, after 1924 a wide range of participants looked to questions explicitly concerning Jewish ritual behavior. Many embraced new technologies for animal slaughter; others linked the rite with charges of Jewish cultural corruption, bloodthirstiness, and economic noxiousness. Proponents of the Jewish community's right to practice kosher butchering without interference intensified their defense initiatives as the flow of the deliberations quickened. The initiatives had been steady between 1919 and 1923, but they escalated in 1924 and again in 1930. When Feiber contacted his

[155] 14 October 1931 letter to Nathan from Feiber and responses A/W 568b.

Jewish community council, it and similar Jewish agencies throughout Germany had been actively involved in defending the ritual for over two years. The Hamburg defense initiatives expressed alarm at the Nazi and antisemitic presence within the deliberations. Their pre-1929 efforts had focused on promoting religious freedom and on the humanitarian character of the rite. By the time Feiber became involved in kosher butchering defense, participants increasingly concentrated on ways to defeat the Nazis, protect the Republic, and promote an image of Jewish economic health.

The disputes in Hamburg and elsewhere reflect the paradoxical nature of the Weimar Republic. The paradox, according to German historian Detlev Peukert, was "an integral feature" of the Republic whose formation, middle years, and termination were moments of painful compromises.[156] Anti-reformist *and* reformist impulses split the deliberations concerning kosher butchering, just as they did the Republic. Municipal and statewide animal protection campaigns offered the Nazis a platform and opportunity for political participation, but also encouraged their opponents to enter the debates only to thwart the Nazis' progress. The self-defense campaigns imitated economic and political fluctuations as well. They underwent a renaissance but also saw tremendous fragmentation and division. The disputes, then, did not neatly lead to the Nazi rise to power. Instead, they were very much a part of the Weimar Republic in which they occurred.

The kosher butchering disputes between 1919 and 1933 offer a fruitful case study for an analysis of the crisis of Weimar democracy. A key aspect of protecting Weimar democracy was the safeguarding of religious freedoms. For much of the 1920s, Jews continued to practice the Jewish method of animal slaughter despite growing opposition to the Jewish rite. By 1930, certain historical phenomena had shifted the terms and implications of the *Schächtfragen*. The Nazis successfully manipulated the space allotted for the anti–kosher butchering campaign by the crisis of Weimar democracy. The movement between 1930 and 1933 toward a ban on kosher butchering fundamentally changed the character of conversations concerning the rite and, more important, signaled a shift in thought and policy concerning toleration.

[156] Peukert, *Weimar Republic*, p. xiii.

Epilogue

On April 21, 1933, the Nazi government promulgated Germany's first national law mandating the stunning of all animals into a state of unconsciousness before slaughter. Beginning on May 1, German Jews within the Reich's borders could no longer legally slaughter animals using the Jewish method.[1] The Nazi ban remained in place until 1946 when the allies repealed all National Socialist legislation, including the prohibition on kosher butchering.[2]

The 1933 slaughterhouse reforms were part of a series of anti-Jewish legislation intended to "stabilize" the economy and exclude Jews from a variety of professional and social arenas. They followed an April 7 law,

---

[1]Gesetz über das Schlachten von Tieren vom 21 April 1933 (Reichsgesetz—Berlin)," *Reichsgesetzblatt* 39 (21 April 1933): 203. The law, however, did include one important exception. Until July 14, 1937, the Jews in Upper Silesia were permitted to practice kosher butchering because of the international minority protection in force in that province.

[2]Eugene Kelly Jr., Office of Military Government, "Order Concerning the Slaughter of Cattle Pursuant to Jewish Religious Customs" 27 October 1945 ALM 133/2. Kosher butchering re-emerged as an issue of concern after World War II. As individual state parliaments and city councils addressed the Jewish right to practice kosher butchering, these nascent mutterings of concern developed into an organized campaign. In 1951, a number of Bavarian animal protection societies pushed the Munich city council to reinstate the 1933 ban. When the council endorsed the prohibition, the societies turned to the Bavarian diet with a similar request. A national campaign soon followed. See, American Jewish Committee, *Munich City Council Votes Ban on Shechita* (New York: self published, 21 June 1951); "Neuer Tierschutz in Bayern," *Allgemeine Wochenzeitung der Juden in Deutschland* (6 July 1951): 11+; "Animal Protection Petitions," Orthodox Jewish Archives (AJA) Collection of Rabbi Michael Munk; 16 December 1954 report to the police authorities from the city veterinary authorities ALM 133/2. The campaign continued through the twentieth century, shifting its focus to include the Muslim method of slaughter.

which provided for the dismissal of "non-Aryans" from the civil service, and preceded the establishment of a quota limiting the number of Jewish university students and school pupils.[3] The abattoir legislation deviated from these other restrictions in one important way. The quota and the "Law for the Restoration of the Professional Civil Service" included exemptions for certain groups of Jews. Veterans and those who had lost a father or brother on the front could retain their civil service job or attend university, at least temporarily.[4] Yet, no matter how valiantly they had fought on the front, Jewish men could no longer practice kosher butchering. The era of granting exemptions to Jewish communities on the basis of religious toleration had ended. "Kosher butchering," commented one Munich authority "should only be done in the Zionist state of Palestine."[5]

Despite the existence of a Nazi ban on kosher butchering, two separate conversations concerning the rite took place after April 1933. On the one side, Nazi legislators and propagandists remained interested in kosher butchering. They discussed the repercussions for illegal kosher slaughter, further restrictions on available kosher meat, and possible propagandist tactics that would feature the Jewish rite. On the other side, German Jews responded to the meat shortages prompted by the 1933 ban and other subsequent restrictions. Jewish communal leaders contemplated how to distribute available kosher meat and reply to the current food scarcities. Rabbinical authorities simultaneously investigated permissible deviations from Jewish law, specifically whether to allow the stunning of animals before slaughter or the transgression of Jewish dietary laws.

Local and state administrators further exaggerated the painful effect of the April 1933 legislation on observant Jews by punishing those who practiced clandestine *shehitah* and by restricting Jewry's access to kosher meat. Governmental leaders recognized that illegal slaughter would and did take place. Worried that Jews would transgress German law, local and state administrators fined illegal kosher slaughterers and their Jewish communities. In some cases, German authorities also interned these

---

[3]While the number of Jewish civil servants was fairly small (approximately 5000), approximately 4000 physicians, 3500 lawyers, and thousands of students were affected. The abattoir legislation also followed the failed national economic boycott of Jews, which took place on April 1. Avraham Barkai, "Exclusion and Persecution: 1933–1938," in Meyer, ed., *German-Jewish History in Modern Times* vol. 4, pp. 201–203. Also see Marion A. Kaplan, *Between Dignity and Despair: Jewish Life in Nazi Germany* (New York: Oxford University, 1988), pp. 17–49.

[4]These exemptions remained in place until Hindenburg's death.

[5]2 June 1933 letter from the veterinary authorities to the Munich city council StM SUV 90.

shohetim in the newly built concentration camps, which had opened one month before the passage of the slaughterhouse laws.

German administrators concomitantly limited Jewry's access to kosher meat. Some city or state governors taxed kosher meat highly or rationed it; others forbade Jews from importing meat or meat products. Baden's state government, for example, prohibited Jews from importing kosher meat, and Munich's veterinary authorities championed similar legislation.[6] The national government acted likewise. In December 1935, three months after the passage of the The Law for the Protection of German Blood and German Honor and The Reich Citizenship Law (the Nuremberg laws), it ceased part of its barter program with Denmark. This affected the amount of kosher meat that came into Germany. The following year, the Ministry for Food rejected the Jewish community's petition to reinstitute the barter agreement, thus making it impossible for Jews to legally obtain kosher meat from Germany's northern neighbor.[7] All the while, Nazi propaganda continued to focus on Jewish rites as proof of Jewish blood-thirst and economic danger. A year after the ban, the Nazi newspaper, *Der Stürmer* devoted an entire issue to ritual murder, which contained essays and cartoons that linked the Jewish method of animal slaughter with the supposed practice of Jews killing humans for ritualistic purposes. It also included graphic photographs from Carl Klein's interwar book that had championed a ban on kosher butchering.[8] Josef Goebbels' 1940 propaganda film, *The Eternal Jew,* similarly evoked the horror of kosher butchering with its scene of a demonic looking *shohet* killing a steer according to the Jewish method.[9]

German Jews also continued to engage with issues relating to kosher butchering as they responded to the meat scarcities prompted by the 1933 ban and other subsequent checks on meat consumption. Until

[6] 2 June 1933 letter; *IF* (December 23 1933); 22 September 1933 Munich regulations StM SUV 90; 1933 letter to community members from the Rabbi of Nuremberg CAHJP D/Ba28/212.

[7] August 20 1936 memo from J.C. Hyman to Paul Baerwald, Felix Warburg, and Jonah Wise Joint Distribution Committee Archives (JDC) collection 1933/1944 656; October 12 1936 letter from Joint Distribution Committee executive director to its chairman, Bernhard Kahn JDC collection 1933/1944 656. Moreover, because the Nazi government now forbade Jews from receiving foreign currency, Jews who wished to procure kosher meat had to obtain it as a present from abroad. "JDC's Contributions for the Purchase of Kosher Meat for Germany" JDC collection 1933/1944 656; Gerhardt Neumann, *Der Morgen* 13.6 (1937): 261.

[8] *Der Stürmer* special issue (May 1934) LBA Centralverein AR 3965 (location B 28/4) II. no 24–38. The May 1939 issue also concerned charges of ritual murder.

[9] Rolf Giesen, *Nazi Propaganda Films: a History and Filmography* (Jefferson, N.C.: McFarland & Co., 2003); Richard Taylor, *Film Propaganda: Soviet Russia and Nazi Germany* (London: I.B.Tauris, 1998) pp. 174–187; Alon Confino, "Fantasies about the Jews: Cultural

November 1938, when the Nazis disbanded the Reich Central Office for Matters Concerning Kosher Butchering (Reichszentrale), German-Jewish communities bickered over how best to distribute the limited kosher meat that was available. The Reichszentrale formally coordinated the import and allocation of kosher meat, although several local Jewish community councils responded to the Reichszentrale disapprovingly. They tended to criticize the Reichszentrale's high prices and distribution choices, and demanded their right to take part in discussions over meat allocations. In June 1933, for example, the chairman of Hamburg's Jewish community, Dr. Max Plaut, publicly complained about the Central Office's "monopoly on meat" and unsuccessfully sought permission to distribute meat to Jews in Hamburg. According to Plaut, the Berlin-based office was insensitive to the special needs of Jewish communities outside the capital city. He then demanded access to the deliberations concerning meat rationing.[10] Plaut and his colleagues also reached out to Jewish agencies in the United States, France, and England for assistance. The Joint Distribution Committee (JDC) offered to help provide observant German Jews with kosher food but expressed their unwillingness to secure the large sums of money necessary to purchase the required amount of meat. By 1938, a separate Jewish organization, the Kosher Meat Fund for Jewish Institutions in Germany, joined the ongoing efforts of the JDC and the international Agudat Israel to help abate the crisis.[11]

As Plaut and others sought ways to negotiate higher meat allotments and lower prices, German Jews exhibited other responses to the increased scarcity and cost of meat and meat products. Some Jewish community councils coordinated soup kitchens or extended financial assistance to families. A few families procured kosher meat clandestinely. Until the

---

Reflections on the Holocaust," *History & Memory* 17.1&2 (2005) 296–322; Jeffrey Herf, "The "Jewish War": Goebbels and the Antisemitic Campaigns of the Nazi Propaganda Ministry," *Holocaust and Genocide Studies* 19.1 (2005) 51–80. A worthwhile, but somewhat problematic, analysis of the film can be found in Baruch Gitlis, *"Redemption" of Ahasuerus: The "Eternal Jew" in Nazi Film* (New York: Holmfirth Books, 1991). Ironically, by 1937 it was difficult for the Germans to find a kosher slaughterer. The Munich archives holds letters from 1937, 1938 and 1939 written among Munich and Frankfurt slaughterhouse authorities, veterinary authorities, and city governments concerning this issue StM SUV 203/2 and ALM 133/2.

[10]28 June 1933 report by Plaut concerning the import of kosher meat CAHJP AHW 568b; June 1933 letters between Plaut and the Reichszentrale CAHJP AHW 568b.

[11]April 11 1935 letter from Kahn to Hyman JDC collection 1933/1944 656; June 28 1936 letter from Kahn to Hyman JDC collection 1933/1944 656; September 28 1936 memo from Morrissey to Emanuel JDC collection 1933/1944 656; October 1938 letter from Bublick and Rosenberg to member list JDC collection 1933/1944 656.

late 1930s, illegal kosher slaughtering took place, although some Jewish community leaders officially prohibited their butchers from doing so.[12] Other Jewish leaders encouraged community members to adapt their diets to a meatless existence. Jewish newspapers offered vegetarian recipes and suggestions for meat substitutes. Jewish women who observed the dietary laws increasingly adjusted their families' diet to these changes. They would stuff cabbage with rice instead of meat and serve oatmeal as part of the main meal in order to fill their family members' stomachs. When, in 1935, the League of Jewish Women released a cookbook featuring vegetarian recipes, the publisher issued four printings in its first year alone.[13] Not everyone, of course, observed the Jewish dietary laws. Many Jews had ceased to follow the laws of *kashrut* decades earlier. Others abandoned the dietary laws during the 1930s, which prompted several rabbis to comment mournfully on the ways in which the Nazi assumption to power precipitated violations of Jewish law.

Concerned by the growing number of Jews who transgressed the dietary laws and by the threat of malnutrition, rabbis increasingly debated whether they ought to permit the stunning of animals before slaughter. The majority of German rabbis consistently ruled against the permission of stunning techniques, but a large number allowed for deviation. A local Hamburg rabbi, for example, permitted patients at the Israelite Hospital in Hamburg to eat anything except pork. Other accounts suggest that a few Bavarian rabbis condoned the consumption of meat from anesthetized animals, while others permitted the feeding of nonkosher meat to children or to the sick.[14]

Once the war started, many of these conversations and adjustments became pointless. The Nazis granted Jews ridiculously small food allotments, which made survival itself difficult. Deportations of German-born Jews to the extermination camps began in 1941. By 1942, Jews who remained in Germany could no longer legally procure the foodstuffs necessary for their existence. The Nazis forbade Jews from obtaining any meat or meat products, whether kosher or not. Jews also could not

[12] 15 May 1933 letter to community members from the Rabbi of Nürnberg CAHJP D/Ba28/212; 29 October 1937 letter between the police-president of Frankfurt to the slaughterhouse director of Munich ALM 133/2; Trude Maurer, "Housing and Housekeeping," in Kaplan, ed., *Jewish Daily Life in Germany*, p. 278.

[13] Kaplan, *Between Dignity and Despair*, p. 34.

[14] 4 May 1933 letter from the Reichszentrale special commission to German rabbis CAHJP AHW 568 b; 28 June 1933 report concerning the import of kosher meat by Dr. Plaut CAHJP AHW 568b; "Rabbinical declaration," *Israelit* 75 (March 29 1934): 1; Jeremiah J. Berman, *Shehitah: A Study in the Cultural and Social Life of the Jewish People* (New York: Bloch Publishing, 1941) p. 269; Maurer, "Housing and Housekeeping," in Kaplan, ed., *Jewish Daily Life in Germany, 1618–1945*, p. 279.

purchase milk, eggs, and wheat products. If Jews managed to obtain food packages from outside of Germany, the Nazi government subtracted their contents from their fixed rations.[15]

Although circumcision occupied a less visible space within public debate during the early Nazi era, concomitant discussions concerning that rite shared similar characteristics with those regarding kosher butchering. During the early 1930s, German Jews and gentiles separately paid attention to circumcision. The Nazi propaganda machine under Goebbels looked to circumcision as evidence of Jewish cruelty and separateness. The 1937 volume that linked kosher butchering with ritual murder similarly suggested that circumcision played a key role in the killing of Christian children for Jewish ritualistic purposes. Drawing on Bernardin Freimut's charge, *Der Stürmer* accused Jews of using "the blood of the slaughtered" for circumcision.[16] A physical marker of Jewish distinction, the Nazis also used the rite as a way to identify Jewish males who could otherwise pass within the gentile community.[17] Jews simultaneously worried that circumcision posed a real risk to Jewish men. During the 1930s and early 1940s, many Jewish parents questioned whether they wished to mark their children as Jews during such a vulnerable time.[18]

The discussions that took place during the Nazi Reich differed dramatically from those disputes that preceded them. During the Nazi regime, Jews and gentiles engaged separately, if at all, with ritual behavior. Between 1843 and 1933, a wide range of Jewish and gentile groups participated in political dialogue with one another. As Jewish leaders, local governments, regional administrations, state regimes, and associational activists took part in discussions investigating the two rites, they used and interacted with diverse political structures. In so doing, they contributed to the creation of several overlapping public spheres. They created new organizations and developed new political techniques. They relied heavily on the press. Their publications created communities of readers and disseminated language and imagery, which brought these individuals together and pushed them apart. Their political interactions helped to create new generations of political actors.

---

[15]Kaplan, *Between Dignity and Despair*, pp. 145–172. Also see Maurer, "Housing and Housekeeping," in Kaplan, ed., *Jewish Daily Life in Germany, 1618–1945,* p. 281.

[16]*Der Stuermer* 14 (April 1937).

[17]See, for example, Joan Ringelheim, "The Split between Gender and the Holocaust," *Women in the Holocaust,* Dalia Ofer and Lenore J. Weitzman, eds. (New Haven: Yale University Press, 1998), p. 345; Kaplan, *Between Dignity and Despair*, p. 207.

[18]The *mohel* registry of Heinrich Glaser suggested a drop in the number of circumcisions that took place in 1938, although it is not clear whether that would have been the natural outcome of the drop in birthrate and the increase in emigration. *Mohel* book (1913–1938) of Heinrich Glaser, LBA AR 143 no. 11: Kaplan, *Between Dignity and Despair*, p. 207.

They also created coalitions that united groups that previously had not worked together within the public sphere. During the late nineteenth and early twentieth centuries, suffragists joined with animal protectionists; Catholic politicians collaborated with Jewish leaders; and Orthodox Jews fought alongside their reform coreligionists for the right to practice their rituals without interference. This is not to suggest that these political collaborations were consistent or without conflict. To the contrary, they were inconsistent and uneven. However, they provided an opportunity for dialogue and political activism in ways that often were unique.

The pre-1933 conflicts concerning Jewish ritual behavior differed from the Nazi discussions in a second significant way. The deliberations that followed the Nazi assumption to power were typified by a heightened racialized, eliminationist antisemitism on the part of the gentile discussants and by Jewish communal despondency.[19] Before the Nazi assumption to power, two competing frames of reference drove the ritual questions: a radicalizing antisemitism and an expansive understanding of toleration.

Antisemitism certainly played a central role in the nineteenth- and early twentieth-century deliberations concerning Jewish rites. Antisemitic organizations and individuals frequently participated in the debates. During the imperial period, antisemitic political parties took part in the disputes, while antisemitic actors often utilized discourses of apoliticism and animal protectionism to position themselves with other groups in the political arena and to insist on their own political prestige. During the Weimar Republic, this impulse was exaggerated. After 1924, the Nazis served as active, and sometimes dominant, participants in the kosher butchering questions. They spoke against the rite in slaughterhouse commission meetings, town council halls, and parliamentary rooms. By 1925, they began lobbying several states to pass bans on kosher butchering and sought collaboration with other chauvinistic and nationalist groups.

Over the course of the Kaiserreich and the Weimar Republic, participants in the ritual questions drew from propagandistic tactics and ideological traditions in order to push for governmental intervention in Jewish ritual behavior. They charged Jews with brutality, blood-thirst, financial noxiousness, and political and social deviance. During the imperial period, the mainstream political arenas did not encourage discussants to voice radically antisemitic views. By the mid-1920s, however, the antisemitic rhetoric that had engulfed Weimar Germany characterized

---

[19]My cursory reading of the archival material resulted in finding no case in which the Jewish community invoked its [fictive] right to religious freedom in its petitions to government.

the ritual questions of that era. Participants were permitted to launch militantly chauvinistic views concerning Jews and their behavior within public arenas. Ironically, despite the radicalization of their discourse and the significant presence of antisemitic actors within the disputes, the ritual questions did not translate into legislative policy until three years before the Nazis came to power. Even then, a significant number of cities and states voted against laws that would violate Jewish religious freedoms.

Before 1933, the concern over religious toleration frequently posed a barrier many participants were unwilling to cross. At their core, the discussions concerning kosher butchering and circumcision questioned the appropriateness of government to force the violation of, or change in, Jewish religious practice. The ways in which discussants positioned themselves in this debate shifted as understandings of toleration and the disputes themselves evolved. Before German unification, discussants used toleration as a way to request that the state acknowledge religious diversity within its borders and, on occasion, extend civic rights to religious minorities. When Rabbi Schwarz of Hürben called for tolerance, he hoped the state would remove itself from the previously autonomous realm of Jewish religious autonomy. Ten years later, his coreligionists offered different views of toleration. Unification and emancipation had complicated this pre-emancipatory model. Between 1867 and 1880, supporters of Jewish rites tended to portray toleration as a form of accommodation. They were unlikely to insist that toleration extended to rituals that threatened public health or deviated from acceptable cultural norms. By the turn of the century, those who defined toleration broadly argued that governments ought to exempt Jewish communities from current laws. In their view, the safeguarding of religious values and beliefs was paramount, even if such protection posed some other kind of risk. By the interwar period, two competing notions of religious toleration characterized the disputes. One group invoked toleration only when discussing which governmental agency had the authority to implement policies that would ensure or violate religious freedoms. Others championed religious toleration as a fundamental democratic right promised by the Weimar Republic's constitution. In their view, any impulse that would force the transgression of religious freedom would undermine the state.

Clearly, a variety of motivations and contexts, not merely anti-Jewish animus or toleration, encouraged a wide segment of the population to become interested in Jewish ritual behavior. New and old forms of anti-Jewish animus or religious tolerance informed the disputes. So too did concerns for the well-being of children and of animals, economic considerations, anxieties relating to health and hygiene, political aspirations, religious motivations, and appreciation for technology and its advancements. Between 1843 and 1933, the two ritualized markings of difference became a central focus of political struggles among Jews and gentiles because they offered these diverse groups ways to welcome, resist, or reconcile themselves to change. Important touchstones of identity during an extended period of Jewish communal reorganization and German nation building, circumcision and kosher butchering enjoyed tremendous symbolic power over a long period of time.

Bibliography

Consulted Archives and Special Library Collections

American Jewish Archives, Cincinnati (AJA)
Archiv der Landeshauptstadt München, Munich (ALM)
Bayerisches Hauptstaatsarchiv, Munich (BH)
Central Archives for the History of the Jewish People, Jerusalem (CAHJP)
Central Zionist Archives, Jerusalem
Friedenwald Library, Jerusalem
Joint Distribution Committee Archives, New York City (JDC)
Leo Baeck Institute, New York (LBA)
New York Public Library (Judaica Collection), New York City
Neue Synagoge Berlin-Centrum Judaicum Archiv, Berlin (CJA)
Orthodox Jewish Archives, New York City (OJA)
Sächsischen Hauptstaatsarchiv, Dresden (SHD)
Staatsarchiv München, Munich (SM)
Stadtarchiv München, Munich (StM)
Stadtarchiv Nürnberg, Nuremberg

Newspapers and Journals

Der Abolitionist
Allgemeine Encyclopädie der Wissenschaften und Künste
Allgemeine Fleischer Zeitung (*AFZ*)
Allgemeine Medicinische Central Zeitung
Allgemeine Zeitung des Judenthums (*AZDJ*)
Archive für Anthropologie
Archiv für Frauenkunde und Konstitutionsforschung

Archives of Pediatrics

Bayerische Staatszeitung und Bayerische Staatsanzeiger

Bayerischer Kurier und Münchener Fremdenblatt

Bayreuther Tagblatt

Berliner Tageblatt

Berliner Thierschutz-Verein (*BTV*)

Breslauer Zeitung

Central Verein Zeitung: Blätter für Deutschtum und Judentum (*CVZ*)

Danziger Beobachter (*DB*)

Danziger Intelligenz-Blatt

Darmstädter Zeitung (*DZ*)

Dermatologische Wochenschrift

Deutsche Aerzte-Zeitung

Deutsche Israelitische Zeitung (*DIZ*)

Deutsche Tageszeitung (*DT*)

Deutsche Thierschutz-Zeitung (*Ibis*)

Deutsches Volksblatt (*DV*)

Dr. Bloch's Oesterrerichische Wochenschrift: Zentralorgan für die gesamten Inte-
    ressen des Judentums

Dresdener Anzeiger (*DA*)

Dresdener Nachrichten (*DN*)

Dresdener Neueste Nachrichten (*DNN*)

Frankfurter Israelit (*FI*)

Frankfurter Zeitung (*FZ*)

Hammer: Blätter für deutschen Sinn (*Hammer*)

Im Deutschen Reich (*IDR*)

Die Irrenpflege: Monatsblatt zur Hebung, Belehrung und Unterhaltung des Irren-
    pflegepersonals

Der Israelit

Israelitisches Familienblatt (*IF*)

Israelitisches Gemeindeblatt: Verbreitetste jüdische Zeitung Westdeutschlands (*IG*)

Israelitische Wochenschrift: Zeitschrift für die Gesamtinteressen des Judentums (*IW*)

Janus: Archives Internationales Pour L'Histoire de la Médicine et la Géographie

Jewish Social Studies (*JSS*)

Jewish Studies Quarterly (*JSQ*)

Journal of the American Pediatrics Association

Journal of Modern History (*JMH*)

Journal of Social History

Der jüdische Kantor: Kultusbeamten-Zeitung (*JK*)

Die jüdische Presse (*JP*)

Jüdische Rundschau (*JR*)

Jüdische Volkszeitung (*JV*)

Jüdisches Wochenblatt

Jüdische Zeitung (*JZ*)

Karlsruhe Zeitung (*KZ*)

The Lancet
Die Laubhütte: illustrirtes israelitisches Familienblatt
Lehrerheim: Unabhängiges Organ für die Interessen der jüdischen Lehrer
Leipziger Neueste Nachrichten (*LNN*)
Leipziger Volks-Zeitung
Leo Baeck International Yearbook (*LBIYB*)
Die Literarische Umschau
London Journal
Mittheilungen des Aertzlichen Vereines in Wien
Mitteilungen der Fleischerei-Berufsgenossenschaften
Mitteilungen aus dem Verein zur Abwehr des Antisemitismus
Monatsschrift für Geschichte und Wissenschaft des Judenthums
Münchener Gemeinde Zeitung (*MGZ*)
Münchner-Augsburger Abendzeitung (*MAA*)
Münchner neueste Nachrichten und Handels-Zeitung, Alpine und Sports Zeitung,
    Theater- und Kunst Chronik (*MNN*)
Nathanael, Zeitschrift für die Arbeit der evangelischen Kirche an Israel
National Zeitung
Neue freie Presse (*NFP*)
Neue freie Volkszeitung
Neue kirchliche Zeitschrift
New York Times
Norddeutsche Allgemeine Zeitung (*NAZ*)
Der Orient
Pediatrics
Der Protestant
Das Recht der Tiere: Zeitschrift des Verbandes westdeutscher Tierschutzvereine
    (*Das Recht der Tiere*)
Rheydter Zeitung
Rundschau auf dem Gebiete der gesamten Fleischbeschau und Trichinenbeschau
    (*RdG*)
Rundschau für Fleischbeschau (*RF*)
Schlesische Zeitung
Staatsbürger Zeitung
Der Stuermer
Süddeutsche Monatshefte
Tages-Zeitung, Potsdam
Tierärztliche Rundschau (*TR*)
Die Umschau: Forschung, Entwicklung, Technologie
Der Urquell: Eine Monatschrift für Volkskunde
Verhandlungen der Berliner Gesellschaft für Anthropologie, Ethnologie, und
    Urgeschichte
Völkischer Beobachter (*VB*)
Völkischer Kurier (*VK*)
Volks-Zeitung: Organ für Jedermann aus dem Volke

Vorwärts
Zeitschrift für Bahnartze
Zeitschrift für die religiösen Interessen des Judenthums
Zeitschrift für Sexualwissenschaft (*ZFS*)

Published Sources

Abrams, Lynn. *Bismarck and the German Empire, 1871–1917.* London: Routledge, 1995.

Abwehr ABC. Berlin: Verein zur Abwehr des Antisemitismus, 1920.

Albert, Phyllis Cohen. *The Modernization of French Jewry: Consistory and Community in the Nineteenth Century.* Hanover, NH: Brandeis University Press/University Press of New England, 1977.

Alderman, Geoffrey. "Power, Authority and Status in British Jewry: The Chief Rabbinate and Shechita." In *Outsiders and Outcasts: Essays in Honour of William J. Fishman.* Ed. Geoffrey Alderman and Colin Holmes, 12–31. London: Duckworth, 1993.

Alexander, Carl. *Die hygienische Bedeutung der Beschneidung.* Breslau: Druck von Th. Schatzky, 1902.

Alt, Konrad. "Etwas vom "Weltbund zur Bekämpfung der Vivisection." *Die Irrenpflege: Monatsblatt zur Hebung, Belehrung und Unterhaltung des Irrenpflegepersonals* 6 (1899): 133–136.

Andersen, Arne. "Heimatschutz: Die bürgerliche Naturschutzbewegung." In *Besiegte Natur: Geschichte der Umwelt im 19. und 20. Jahrhundert.* Ed. Franz-Joseph Brüggermeister and Thomas Rommelspacher, 143–156. Munich: C.H. Beck, 1987.

Anderson, Benedict. *Imagined Communities: Reflections on the Origin and Spread of Nationalism.* Rev. ed. (London: Verso, 1991).

Anderson, Margaret Lavinia. "Piety and Politics: Recent Works on German Catholicism." *Journal of Modern History* 63 (1991): 681–716.

——. *Practicing Democracy: Elections and Political Culture in Imperial Germany.* Princeton, NJ: Princeton University Press, 2000.

——. *Windthorst: A Political Biography.* Oxford: Oxford University Press, 1981.

Andree, Christian. *Rudolf Virchow als Prähistoriker.* Köln and Wien: Böhlau, 1976.

Andree, Richard. "Die Beschneidung." *Archive für Anthropologie* 8 (188?): 53–78.

——. *Zur Volkskunde der Juden.* Bielefeld/Leipzig: Verlag von Velhagen & Klasing, 1881.

Angress, Werner T. "Prussia's Army and the Jewish Reserve Officer Controversy Before World War I." *Leo Baeck Institute Yearbook* 17 (1972): 19–42.

Antisemiten-Spiegel: Die antisemiten im Lichte des Christenthums, des Rechtes und der Moral. Danzig: Verlag und Druck vom A.W. Kafemann, 1892.

Applegate, Celia. *A Nation of Provincials: The German Idea of Heimat.* Berkeley: University of California Press, 1990.

Arendt, Hannah. *The Origins of Totalitarianism.* San Diego: Harcourt Brace Jovanovich, 1968.

Ascher, Maurice. *Sexuelle Fragen vom Standpunkte des Judentums.* Frankfurt a.M.: A.J. Hofmann, Verlag, 1922.

Ascherson, P. "Üngeborenen Mangel der Vorhaut bei beschnitten Völkern." *Verhandlungen der Berliner Gesellschaft für Anthropologie* (1888): 126–130.

Aschheim, Steven E. *Brothers and Strangers: The East European Jew in German and German Jewish Consciousness, 1800–1922.* Madison: University of Wisconsin Press, 1982.

Auer, Herbert. "Hayum Schwarz, der letzte Rabbiner in Hürben." In *Geschichte und Kultur der Juden in Schwaben.* Vol. 2. Ed. Peter Fassl, 65–81. Stuttgart: Jan Thorbecke Verlag, 2000.

Auerbach, Benjamin Hirsch. *Berith Abraham oder die Beschneidungsfeier und die dabei stattfindenden Gebete und Gesänge.* Frankfurt a.M.: Verlag von J. Kauffmann, 1880.

Aus den Verhandlungen des Deutschen Reichstags über das Schächten (18. Mai 1887, 25. April 1899 und 9. Mai 1899). Berlin: n.p., 1909.

Austensen, R. "Austria and the 'Struggle of Supremacy in Germany' 1848–1864." *Journal of Modern History* 52 (1980): 195–225.

Baader, Benjamin Maria. *Gender, Judaism, and Bourgeois Culture in Germany, 1800–1870.* Bloomington: Indiana University Press, 2005.

Back, W. *Schächten oder Betäuben?—eine Bedürfnisfrage. Ein Beitrag zum Erlaß eines Reichsschlachtgesetzes.* Straßburg: Akademische Buchhandlung, 1911.

Balz, Theodor Friedrich. *Die schädlichen Folgen der Beschneidung: Ein Sendschreiben an die hocherwürdige Versammlung der Herren Rabbiner in Frankfurt a.M.* Berlin: privately published, 1845.

Bamberger, Simon. *Die Beschneidung: Eine populäre Darstellung ihrer Bedeutung und Vollziehung.* Wandsbek: Verlag von A. Goldschmidt-Hamburg, 1913.

——. "Die Hygiene der Beschneidung." In *Die Hygiene der Juden im Anschluß an die Internationale Hygiene-Ausstellung Dresden 1911.* Ed. Max Grunwald. Dresden: Verlag der historischen Abteilung der Internationalen Hygiene-Ausstellung, 1912.

Baraz, Daniel. *Medieval Cruelty: Changing Perceptions, Late Antiquity to the Early Modern Period.* Ithaca: Cornell University Press, 2003.

Barclay, David E. *Frederick William IV and the Prussian Monarchy, 1840–1861.* Oxford: Oxford University Press, 1995.

Baron, Salo W. "Ghetto and Emancipation." In *The Menorah Treasury: Harvest of Half a Century.* Ed. Leo W. Schwarz, 50–63. Philadelphia: Jewish Publication Society of America, 1964.

Baum, Moritz. *Der theoretisch-praktische Mohel.* 2nd ed. Frankfurt a.M.: Buchdruckerei von M. Glohotzlyn, 1884.

Bauman, Zygmunt. *Modernity and Ambivalence.* Cambridge: Polity Press, 1991.

Baumann, Hermann. "Jünglingweihe: Missionare beschneiden ihre Zöglinge." *Die Umschau* 22 (1932): 426–429.

Bauwerker, Carl. *Das rituelle Schächten der Israeliten im Lichte der Wissenschaft. Ein Vortrag Gehalten im wissenschaftlich-literarischen Verein zu Kaiserslautern am. 5 Dezember 1881.* Kaiserslautern: Verlag von Aug. Gotthold's Buchhandlung, 1882.

Bayerischer Israelitischer Gemeinden. *Rituelles Schlachten und Betäubung: Eingabe des Verbandes Bayerischer israelitischer Gemeinden an den Bayerischen Landtag vom 14. Mai 1929.* Munich: Verlag B. Heller, 1929.

——. *Zur Schächtfrage: Vorstellung des verbandes Bayerischer Israelitscher Gemeinden und der Bayer-Rabbinerkonferenz an den bayerischen Landtag vom 10 Mai 1926*. Munich: Verlag B. Heller, 1926.

Bell, Catherine. *Ritual: Perspectives and Dimensions*. New York: Oxford University Press, 1997.

——. *Ritual Theory, Ritual Practice*. New York: Oxford University Press, 1992.

Ben-Avner, Yehudah. "Antisemitism in the Weimar Republic as Seen in the Jewish Newspapers." (Hebrew) *Sinai* 107 (1991): 265–283.

Bender, Julie. "Zur Geschichte und Bedeutung der Beschneidung bei den Juden." *Zeitschrift für Sexualwissenschaft* (8 November 1922): 229–230.

Bentham, Jeremy. "An Introduction to the Principles of Morals and Legislation (1789)." In *The Collected Works of Jeremy Bentham*. Ed. J. H. Burns and H. L. A. Hart, 11–12. Vol. 2. London: Athlone Press, 1968–1984.

Benz, Wolfgang, Arnold Paucker, and Peter Pulzer, eds. *Jüdisches Leben in der Weimarer Republik: Jews in the Weimar Republic*. Tübingen: Mohr Siebek, 1998.

Berger, Peter. *The Sacred Canopy*. Garden City, NY, 1967.

Bergson, Joseph. *Die Beschneidung vom historischen, kritischen und medicinischen Standpunkt mit Bezug auf die neuesten Debatten und Reformvorschläge*. Berlin: Verlag von Th. Scherk, 1844.

Bering, Dietz. *The Stigma of Names: Antisemitism in German Daily Life, 1812–1933*. Trans. Neville Plaice. Ann Arbor: University of Michigan Press, 1992.

Beringer, Hans, ed. *Lesebüchlein des Berliner Tierschutz-Vereins (zur Bekämpfung der Tierquälereien im Deutschen Reich)*. 5 vols. Berlin: Deutscher Verlag, 1910.

Berkovits, Berel. "Challenge to Shehitah in Europe." *Judaism* (Fall 1990): 470–487.

Berkovitz, Jay R. *Rites and Passages: The Beginnings of Modern Jewish Culture in France, 1650–1860*. Philadelphia: University of Pennsylvania Press, 2004.

Berman, Jeremiah J. *Shehitah: A Study in the Cultural and Social Life of the Jewish People*. New York: Bloch, 1941.

Bernstein, Michael André. *Foregone Conclusions: Against Apocalyptic History*. Berkeley: University of California Press, 1994.

Bernstein, Reiner. "Zwischen Emanzipation und Antisemitismus: Die Publizisktik der deutschen Juden am Beispiel der "C.V.-Zeitung," Organ des Centralvereins deutscher Staatsbürger jüdischen Glaubens, 1924–1933." Ph.D. diss. Freien Universität Berlin, 1969.

Bessel, Richard. *Germany after the First World War*. Reprint ed. Oxford: Clarendon Press, 2002.

Birnbaum, Pierre, and Ira Katznelson. "Emancipation and the Liberal Offer." *Paths of Emancipation: Jews States, and Citizenship*. Ed. Pierre Birnbaum and Ira Katznelson, 3–36. Princeton, NJ: Princeton University Press, 1995.

Blackbourn, David. *Class, Religion, and Local Politics in Wilhelmine Germany: The Centre Party in Württemberg before 1914*. New Haven: Yale University Press, 1980.

——. *The Long Nineteenth Century: A History of Germany, 1780–1918*. New York: Oxford University Press, 1998.

——. *Marpingen: Apparitions of the Virgin Mary in Nineteenth-Century Germany*. New York: Alfred A. Knopf, 1994.

Blackbourn, David, and Geoff Eley. *The Peculiarities of German History, Bourgeois Society and Politics in Nineteenth Century Germany.* New York: Oxford University Press, 1984.

Bleich, Judith. "Jacob Ettlinger, His Life and Works: The Emergence of Modern Orthodoxy in Germany." Ph.D. diss. New York University, 1974.

Blumenthal, Hermann. *Die besten jüdischen Anekdoten: Perlen des Humors.* Wien: Rudolf Lechner und Sohn, 1924.

Borut, Jacob. "'A New Spirit Among Our Brethren in Ashkenaz': German Jews Between Antisemitism and Modernity in the Late Nineteenth Century" (Hebrew). Ph.D. diss. Hebrew University, 1991.

———. "The Rise of Jewish Defense Agitation in Germany, 1890–1895: A Pre-History of the C.V.?" *Leo Baeck Institute Yearbook* 36 (1991): 59–96.

———. *"Wehrt Euch!" Founding of the Centralverein deutscher Staatsbürger Jüdischen Glaubens* (Hebrew). Jerusalem: Dinur Center, 1996.

Brantz, Dorothee Ingeborg. "Slaughter in the City: The Establishment of Public Abattoirs in Paris and Berlin, 1780—1914 (France, Germany)." Ph.D. diss. University of Chicago, 2003.

———. "Stunning Bodies: Animal Slaughter, Judaism, and the Meaning of Humanity in Imperial Germany." *Central European History* 35 (June 2002): 167–194.

Brecher, Gideon. *Die Beschneidung der Israeliten, von der historischen, praktisch-operativen und ritualen Seite zunächst für den Selbstunterricht.* Wien: Gedruckt bei Franz Edl. v. Schmid und J.J. Busch, 1845.

Brenner, Michael. "The Jüdische Volkspartei: National-Jewish Communal Politics during the Weimar Period." *Leo Baeck Institute Yearbook* 35 (1990): 219–243.

———. *The Renaissance of Jewish Culture in Weimar Germany.* New Haven: Yale University Press, 1996.

Breslauer, Walter. "Der Verband der deutschen Juden (1904–1922)." *Bulletin des Leo Baeck Instituts* 28.7 (1964): 345–379.

Breuer, Mordechai. *Modernity Within Tradition: The Social History of Orthodox Jewry in Imperial Germany.* Trans. Elizabeth Petuchowski. New York: Columbia University Press, 1992.

Breuilly, John. *Austria, Prussia and Germany, 1806–1871.* London: Longman, 2002.

———. "Nation and Nationalism in Modern German History." *The Historical Journal* 33.3 (1990): 659–675.

Broers, Michael. *Europe after Napoleon: Revolution, Reaction, and Romanticism, 1814–1848.* Manchester: Manchester University Press, 1996.

Broszat, Martin. *Hitler and the Collapse of Weimar Germany.* Trans. V. R. Berghahn. Leamington Spa: Berg Publishers, 1987.

Brubaker, Rogers. *Citizenship and Nationhood in France and Germany.* Cambridge: Harvard University Press, 1992.

Bryk, Felix. *Die Beschneidung bei Mann und Weib: ihre Geschichte, Psychologie, und Ethnologie.* Neubrandenburg: Verlag Gustav Feller, 1931.

Budd, Michael Anton. *The Sculpture Machine: Physical Culture and Body Politics in the Age of Empire.* New York: New York University Press, 1997.

Burleigh, Michael. *The Third Reich: A New History.* New York: Hill and Wang, 2000.

Büro für Schächtangelegenheiten. *Zur Frage Der betäubenden Wirkung des Schächtschnitts.* Berlin: self-published, 1927.

———. *Zweite Reiche neuer Gutachten zur Frage der betaubenden Wirkung des Schächtschnitts.* Berlin: self-published, 1929.

Buxhaum, Henry. "Recollections." In *Jewish Life in Germany: Memoirs From Three Centuries.* Ed. Monika Richarz. Trans. Stella P. Rosenfeld and Sidney Rosenfeld, 301–306. Bloomington: Indiana University Press, 1991.

Cahn, Michael. *Die Einrichtungen des Koscher-Fleisch-Verkaufs unter besonderer Berucksichtigung der Zeichnungs und Stempelungs-Methoden.* Frankfurt: A.J. Hofmann, 1901.

Caron, Vicki. *Between France and Germany: The Jews of Alsace-Lorraine, 1871–1918.* Stanford, CA: Stanford University Press, 1988.

Carson, Gerald. *Men, Beasts, and Gods: A History of Cruelty and Kindness to Animals.* New York: Scribner, 1972.

Cary, Noel D. *The Path to Christian Democracy: German Catholics and the Party System from Windthorst to Adenauer.* Cambridge: Harvard University Press, 1996.

Cassirer and Danziger, eds. *Für Schnorrer und Kitzinim: Sammlung gediegener jüdischer Witze und Anekdoten.* Berlin: Verlag von Cassirer & Danziger, 1889.

Chewrath, Mohalim. *Statuten.* Frankfurt a.M.: self-published, 1907.

Clark, Christopher. "The Politics of Revival: Pietists, Aristocrats, and the State Church in Early Nineteenth-Century Prussia." In *Between Reform, Reaction, and Resistance: Studies in the History of German Conservatism from 1789 to 1945,* 31–60. Ed. Larry Eugene Jones and James Retallack. Providence, RI: Berg, 1993.

Cohen, Shaye. "The Origins of the Matrilineal Principle in Jewish Law." *AJS Review* 10 (1985): 19–54.

———. "Why Aren't Jewish Women Circumcised?" *Gender & History* 9.3 (1997): 560–578.

———. *Why Aren't Jewish Women Circumcised? Gender and Covenant in Judaism.* Berkeley: University of California Press, 2005.

Confino, Alon. "Fantasies about the Jews: Cultural Reflections on the Holocaust." *History & Memory* 17 (2005): 296–322.

Cooper, Samuel. "The Laws of Mixture: An Anthropological Study in Halakha." In *Judaism Viewed from Within and from Without: Anthropological Studies.* Ed. Harvey E. Goldberg, 55–74. Albany: State University of New York Press, 1987.

Craig, Gordon A. *Germany, 1866–1945.* New York: Oxford University Press, 1978.

Curtius, Lorenz. *Der politische Antisemitismus vom 1907–1911.* München: Kommissions-Verlag des National-Vereins für das liberale Deutschland, 1911.

Dammann, Karl. *Gutachten über das jüdische Schlachtverfahren.* Hannover: Verlag von Ludwig Ey, 1886.

Danziger, Meier. *Der theoretische und praktische Schächter nach dem Ohel Jisrael des Rabbi J. Weil.* 5th ed. Brilon: Druck u. Verlag der M. Friedländer'schen Buchdruckerei u. Buchhandlung, 1858.

Darby, Robert. *A Surgical Temptation: The Demonization of the Foreskin and the Rise of Circumcision in Britain.* Chicago: University of Chicago Press, 2005.

Davis, Belinda. *Home Fires Burning: Food, Politics, and Everyday Life in World War I Berlin.* Chapel Hill: University of North Carolina Press, 2000.

Dawson, William Harbutt. *Municipal Life and Government in Germany.* 2nd ed. London: Longmans, Green, 1916.

Dembo, Isaak Aleksandrovich. *The Jewish Method of Slaughter Compared With Other Methods From the Humanitarian, Hygienic, and Economic Points of View.* Trans. Trustees of J.A. Franklin. London: Kegan Paul, Trnech, Trübner, 1894.

Dessauer, Julius. *Brit Olam Der ewige Bund: Die Beschneidung, vom rituallen, operativen und sanitären Standpunkte nach den besten Quellen.* Budapest: n.p., 1879.

——., ed. *Der jüdische Humorist.* Vol. 2. Budapest: Selbstverlag von Julius Dessauer, 1890–1899?

Dexler, Hermann. *Ueber das Bewegungsverhalten eines grosshirnlosen Schafes beim Schächten.* Hannover: H&M Schaper, 1928.

Dominick III, Raymond H. *The Environmental Movement in Germany: Prophet and Pioneers, 1871–1971.* Bloomington: University of Indiana Press, 1992.

Douglas, Mary. *Purity and Danger. An Analysis of Concepts of Pollution and Taboo.* New York: Frederick A. Praeger, 1966.

Dresser, Madge. "Minority Rites: The Strange History of Circumcision in English Thought." *Jewish Culture and History* 1.1 (1998): 72–87.

Duden, Barbara. *The Woman Beneath the Skin: A Doctor's Patients in Eighteenth-Century Germany.* Trans. Thomas Dunlap. Cambridge: Harvard University Press, 1991.

Durkheim, Emile. *The Elementary Forms of the Religious Life.* Trans. Joseph Ward Swain. New York: Free Press, 1965.

Ebstein, Wilhelm. *Die Medizin im Alten Testament.* Stuttgart: Verlag von Ferdinand Enke, 1901.

Efron, John M. *Medicine and the German Jews: A History.* New Haven: Yale University Press, 2001.

Ehrmann, H. *Thier-Schutz und Menschen-Trutz: Sämmtliche für und gegen das Schächten geltend gemachten Momente kritisch beleuchtet nebst einer Sammlung aller älteren und neueren Gutachten hervorragender Fachgelehrten.* Frankfurt a.M.: Verlag von J. Kauffmann, 1885.

Eilberg-Schwartz, Howard. *The Savage in Judaism: An Anthropology of Israelite Religion and Ancient Judaism.* Bloomington: Indiana University Press, 1990.

Eisen, Arnold M. *Rethinking Modern Judaism: Ritual, Commandment, Community.* Chicago: University of Chicago Press, 1998.

Eley, Geoff. *From Unification to Nazism: Reinterpreting the German Past.* Boston: Unwin Hyman, 1986.

——. *Reshaping the German Right: Radical Nationalism and Political Change after Bismarck.* 2nd ed. Ann Arbor: University of Michigan Press, 1991.

——. "Bismarckian Germany." In *Modern Germany Reconsidered, 1870–1945.* Ed. Gordon Martel, 1–32. London: Routledge, 1992.

——. "What Are the Contexts for German Antisemitism? Some Thoughts on the Origins of Nazism, 1800–1945." *Studies in Contemporary Jewry* 8 (1997): 100–132.

Elias, Nobert. *The Civilizing Process.* Trans. Edmund Jephcott. New York: Urizen Books, 1978.

Ellenson, David. "Accommodation, Resistance, and the Halakhic Process: A Case Study of Two Responsa by Rabbi Marcus Horovitz." In *Jewish Civilization: Essays and Studies.* Ed. Robert A. Brauner, 83–100. Philadelphia: Reconstructionist Rabbinical College, 1981.

——. *Rabbi Esriel Hildesheimer and the Creation of a Modern Jewish Orthodoxy.* Tuscaloosa: University of Alabama Press, 1990.

——. "Tzedakah and Fundraising: A Nineteenth-Century Response." *Judaism* 45.4 (1996): 490–496.

Endelman, Todd M. "The Legitimization of the Diaspora Experience in Recent Jewish Historiography." *Modern Judaism* 11.2 (1991): 195–209.

Engel, David. "Patriotism as a Shield: The Liberal Defense Against Anti-Semitism in Germany During the First World War." *Leo Baeck Institute Yearbook* 31 (1986): 147–172.

Engelbert, Hermann. *Das Schächten und die Bouterole: Denkschrift für den hohen Großen Rath des Kantons St. Gallen zur Beleutchtung des diesbezüglichen regierungsräthlichen Antrags und mit Zugrundlegung der neuesten mitagedruckten Gutachten.* St. Gallen: Zollikofer'sche Buchdruckerei, 1876.

Eschelbacher, Max. *Erwiderung auf die Ausführungen des Herrn Prof. Dr. M. Müller (München) in den Münchener Neuesten Nachrichten und der Deutschen Schlachthof-Zeitung.* Düsseldorf: Druck von Itzkowski & Co., 1927.

Evans, Richard J. *Death in Hamburg.* Oxford: Oxford University Press, 1987.

——. "Introduction: Wilhelm II's Germany and the Historians." In *Society and Politics in Wilhelmine Germany.* Ed. Richard J. Evans, 11–39. London: Barnes and Noble, 1978.

——. *Rethinking German History: Nineteenth Century Germany and the Origins of the Third Reich.* London: HarperCollins Academic, 1987.

——. *Rituals of Retribution: Capital Punishment in Germany 1600–1987.* Oxford: Oxford University Press, 1996.

Ferguson, Moira. *Animal Advocacy and Englishwomen, 1780–1900.* Ann Arbor: University of Michigan Press, 1998.

Ferziger, Adam Adam S. *Exclusion and Hierarchy: Orthodoxy, Nonobservance, and the Emergence of Modern Jewish Identity.* Philadelphia: University of Pennsylvania Press, 2005.

Fink, Carole. *Defending the Rights of Others: The Great Powers, the Jews, and International Minority Protection, 1878–1938.* Cambridge: Cambridge University Press, 2004.

Fitzpatrick, Martin. "Toleration and the Enlightenment Movement." In *Toleration in Enlightenment Europe.* Ed. Ole Peter Grell and Roy Porter, 213–230. Cambridge: Cambridge University Press, 2000.

Foucault, Michel. *The History of Sexuality: An Introduction.* Trans. Robert Hurley. Vol. 1. New York: Vintage Books, 1990.

Fout, John C., ed., *Forbidden History: The State, Society, and the Regulation of Sexuality in Modern Europe.* Chicago: University of Chicago Press, 1992.

Frank, Friedrich. *Die Ritualmord von der Gerichtshöfen der Wahrheit und der Gerichtigkeit.* Regensburg: GJ Manz, 1901.

——. *Die Schächtfrage vor der Bayerischen Volksvertretung.* Würzburg: Buchdruckerei von Leo Woerl., 1894.

Frankel, Jonathan. *The Damascus Affair: "Ritual Murder," Politics, and the Jews in 1840.* Cambridge: Cambridge University Press, 1997.

Frankel, Zacharias. "Ueber manch durch den Fortschritt der Medicin im Judenthum bedingte Reformen." *Zeitschrift für die religiösen Interessen des Judenthums* 2 (1845): 300–301.

Freie Vereinigung für die Interessen des orthodoxen Judenthums. *Auszüge aus den Gutachten der hervorragendsten Physiologen und Veterinärärzte über das "Schächten".* Frankfurt am Main: Buchdruckerei von Louis Golde, 1887.

———. *Bericht über die Geschäftsperiode 1912/1913.* Frankfurt a.M.: Druckerei Louis Golde, 1914.

———. *Gutachten der hervorragendsten Physiologen und Veterinärärzte uber das "Schächten".* Frankfurt am Main: Buchdruckerei von Louis Golde, 1894.

———. *Mitteilungen an die Vereinsmitglieder.* Vols. 15–20. Frankfurt a.M.: Buchdruckerei Louis Golde, 1902–1908.

Freimut, Bernardin. *Die Jüdischen Blutmorde von ihrem ersten Erscheinen der Geschichte bis auf unsere Zeit.* Münster: A. Russell's Verlag, 1895.

Frevert, Ute. *Krankheit als politisches Problem 1770–1880: Soziale Unterschichten in Preußen zwischen medizinischer Polizei und staatlicher Sozialversicherung.* Göttingen: Vandenhoeck & Ruprecht, 1984.

———. "Professional Medicine and the Working Classes in Imperial Germany." *Journal of Contemporary History* 20 (1985): 637–658.

Friedmann, Amos. *Leitfaden zur Erlernung der wesentlichsten Vorschriften über Schechitah und Bedikah mit einem Anhange.* Dettensee, Hohenzollern: Selbstverlag des Verfassers, 1894.

———. *Vollständiges Handuch für Shehitah und Bedika nach dem Ohel Jizchak.* Budapest: Ignatz Schwarz, 1911.

Friedreich, JB. *Ueber die jüdische Beschneidung in historischer, operativer, und sanitätspolizeilicher Beziehung.* Ansbach: Verlag der Dollfusschen Buchhandlung, 1844.

Friesel, Evyatar. "The German-Jewish Encounter as a Historical Problem: A Reconsideration." *Leo Baeck Institute Yearbook* 41 (1996): 263–275.

———. "The Political and Ideological Development of the Centralverein before 1914." *Leo Baeck Institute Yearbook* 31 (1986): 121–146.

———. "A Response to the Observations of Chaim Schatzker and Abraham Margliot." *Leo Baeck Institute Yearbook* 33 (1988): 107–111.

Fritsch, Theodor. *Handbuch der Judenfrage die wichtigsten Tatsachen zur Beurteliung des judischen Volkes.* 1st ed. Hamburg: Hanseatische Druck- und Verlangsanstalt, 1907.

Froelich, Ernst. *Das Schächten—ein mosaischer Ritualgebrauch? Beitrag zur Lösung der Schächtfrage.* Potsdam: self-published, 1899.

Fuchs, Eduard. *Die Juden in der Karikatur: Ein Beitrag zur Kulturgeschichte.* Munich: Albert Langen, 1921.

Gall, Lothar, ed. *Stadt und Bürgertum im 19. Jahrhundert.* Munich: Oldenbourg, 1990.

Garner, Robert. *Political Animals: Animal Protection Politics in Britain and the United States.* New York: St. Martins Press, 1998.

Gelbart, Heinrich S. *Lekach tauw, ein Handbuch für praktische Schächter.* Labes: Druck von A. Straube, 1899.

Geller, Jay. "(G)Nos(E)Ology: The Cultural Construction of the Other." In *People of the Body: Jews and Judaism from an Embodied Perspective*. Ed. Howard Eilberg-Schwartz, 243–282. New York: State University of New York Press, 1992.

——. "A Paleontological View of Freud's Study of Religion: Unearthing the Leitfossil Circumcision." *Modern Judaism* 13 (1993): 49–70.

Giesen, Rolf. *Nazi Propaganda Films: a History and Filmography*. Jefferson, NC: McFarland & Co., 2003.

Gilman, Sander L. *The Case of Sigmund Freud: Medicine and Identity at the Fin De Siécle*. Baltimore: The Johns Hopkins University Press, 1993.

——. *Franz Kafka: The Jewish Patient*. New York and London: Routledge, 1996.

——. *Freud, Race, and Gender*. Princeton, New Jersey: Princeton University Press, 1993.

——. "The Indelibility of Circumcision." *Koroth* 9.11–12 (1991): 806–817.

——. *The Jew's Body*. New York: Routledge, 1991.

Gitlis, Baruch. *"Redemption" of Ahasuerus: The "Eternal Jew" in Nazi Film*. New York: Holmfirth books, 1991.

Glassberg, Abraham, ed. *Die Beschneidung in ihrer geschichtlichen, ethnographischen, religiösen und medicinischen Bedeutung: Zum ersten Male umfassend dargestellt*. Berlin: Verlag von C. Boas Nachf., 1896.

Glick, Leonard B. *Marked in Your Flesh: Circumcision from Ancient Judea to Modern America*. Oxford: Oxford University Press, 2005.

Gollaher, David L. *Circumcision: A History of the World's Most Controversial Surgery*. New York: Basic Books, 2000.

——. "From Ritual to Science: The Medical Transformation of Circumcision in America." *Journal of Social History* 28 (1994): 5–36.

Goody, Jack. "Religion and Ritual: The Definitional Problem." *British Journal of Sociology* 12 (1961): 142–164.

Goslar, Hans, ed. *Hygiene und Judentum: Eine Sammelschrift*. Dresden: Verlag Jac. Sternlicht, 1930.

Götz, Berndt. "Das Zweigeschlechterwesen und die Beschneidung der Knaben und Mädchen." *Archiv für Frauenkunde und Konstitutionsforschung* 17.1 (1931): 60–69.

Gotzmann, Andreas. *Jüdisches Recht im kulturellen Prozess: Die Wahrnehmung der Halacha im Deutschland des 19. Jahrhunderts*. Tübingen: M. Siebeck, 1997.

——. "Reconsidering Judaism as a Religion: The Religious Emancipation Period," *Jewish Studies Quarterly* 7 (2000): 352–366.

Graetz, Michael. "Jewry in the modern period: the role of the 'rising class' in the politicization of Jews in Europe." *Assimilation and Community: the Jews in Nineteenth-century Europe*. Ed. Jonathan Frankel and Steven Zipperstein, 156–176. Cambridge: Cambridge University Press, 1992.

Grandin, Temple. "Humanitarian Aspects of Shehitah in the United States." *Judaism* (1990): 436–446.

Greive, Hermann. "Religious Dissent and Tolerance in the 1840s." *Revolution and Evolution: 1848 in German-Jewish History*. Ed. Werner E. Mosse, Arnold Paucker, and Reinhard Rürup, 337–352. Tübingen: J.C.B. Mohr, 1981.

Grell, Ole Peter, and Roy Porter. "Toleration in Enlightenment Europe." In *Toleration in Enlightenment Europe*. Ed. Ole Peter Grell and Roy Porter, 1–22. Cambridge: Cambridge University Press, 2000.

Gross, Michael B. *The War Against Catholicism: Liberalism and the Anti-Catholic Imagination in Nineteenth-Century Germany*. Ann Arbor: University of Michigan Press, 2004.

Großherzoglich Badischen Oberrat der Israeliten, Baden. *Dienstvorschriften für Mohelim*. Karlsruhe: Buchdruckerei von Malsch & Vogel, 1897.

Grünwald, Josef. *Die rituelle Circumcision (Beschneidung) operativ und rituell bearbeitet*. Frankfurt, a.M.: Verlag von J. Kauffmann, 1892.

Grunwald, Max. "Die Hygiene der Bibel." In *Die Hygiene der Juden im Anschluß an die Internationale Hygiene-Ausstellung Dresden 1911*. Ed. Max Grunwald, 175–188. Dresden: Verlag der Historischen Abteilung der Internationalen Hygiene-Ausstellung, 1911.

Grutzhaendler, Joseph. *De la Milah (Circoncision) son Histoire, son Importance Hygiénique sa Technique Opératoire*. Paris: M. Schifrine, 1914.

Habermas, Jürgen. *The Structural Transformation of the Public Sphere: An Inquiry into a Category of Bourgeois Society*. Trans. Thomas Burger with the assistance of Frederick Lawrence. 3rd ed. Cambridge: MIT Press, 1992.

Hamburger, Leopold. *Herr Otto Hartmann in Cöln and sein Kampf gegen die Schlachtweise der Israeliten*. Frankfurt a.M.: Buchdruckerei von M. Slobotzky, 1889.

Hamerow, Theodore S. *Restoration, Revolution, Reaction: Economics and Politics in Germany 1815–1871*. Princeton, NJ: Princeton University Press, 1958.

——. *The Social Foundations of German Unification 1858–1871*. 2 vols. Princeton, NJ: Princeton University Press, 1969–1972.

Harris, James F. *The People Speak! Anti-Semitism and Emancipation in Nineteenth-Century Bavaria*. Ann Arbor: University of Michigan Press, 1994.

Hart, Mitchell. "Moses the Microbiologist: Judaism and Social Hygiene in the Work of Alfred Nossig." *Jewish Social Studies* 2.1 (1995): 72–97.

Hartmann, Otto, ed. *Bericht über die sechste Versammlung des Verbandes der Thierschutz-Vereine des Deutschen Reiches in Braunschweig*. Vol. 6. Köln: Thierschutz-Vereine des Deutschen Reiches, 1895.

——. *Bericht über die siebente Versammlung des Verbandes der Thierschutz-Vereine des Deutschen Reiches in Hamburg*. Vol. 7. Köln: Thierschutz-Vereine des Deutschen Reiches, 1898.

——. *Bericht über die achte Versammlung des Verbandes der Thierschutz-Vereine des Deutschen Reiches in Kassel*. Vol. 8. Köln: Thierschutz-Vereine des Deutschen Reiches, 1901.

——. *Bericht über die neunte Versammlung des Verbandes der Tierschutz-Vereine des Deutschen Reiches in Leipzig*. Vol. 9. Köln: Tierschutz-Vereine des deutschen Reiches, 1904.

——. *Bericht über die zehnte Versammlung des Verbandes der Tierschutz-Vereine des Deutschen Reiches in Nürnberg*. Vol. 10. Köln: Druck von Jacob Pohl, 1906.

——. *Bericht über die elfte Versammlung des Verbandes der Tierschutz-Vereine des Deutschen Reiches in Düsseldorf*. Vol. 11. Köln: Druck von Jacob Pohl, 1908.

——. *Bericht über die Vierzehnte Versammlung des Verbandes der Tierschutz-Vereine des Deutschen Reiches in Stuttgart*. Vol. 14. Köln: Jacob Pohl, 1914.

Heilbronner, Oded. *Catholicism, Political Culture, and the Countryside: A Social History of the Nazi Party in South Germany.* Ann Arbor: University of Michigan Press, 1998.

Heinemann, Jeremias, ed. *Sammlung der die religiöse und bürgerliche Verfassung der Juden in den Königl. Preuß. Staaten betreffenden Gesetze, Verordnungen, Gutachten, Berichte und Erkenntnisse.* Hildesheim: Verlag Dr. H. A. Gerstenberg, 1976.

Herf, Jeffrey. "The 'Jewish War': Goebbels and the Antisemitic Campaigns of the Nazi Propaganda Ministry." *Holocaust and Genocide Studies* 19.1 (2005): 51–80.

Herzig, Arno. "The Process of Emancipation from the Congress of Vienna to the Revolution of 1848/1849." *Leo Baeck Institute Yearbook* 37 (1992): 61–69.

Herzog, Dagmar. *Intimacy and Exclusion: Religious Politics in Pre-Revolutionary Baden.* Princeton, NJ: Princeton University Press, 1996.

Hildesheimer, Hirsch. *Das Schächten. Vol. Separatabdruck aus "Blätter für höheres Schulwesen."* Berlin: Verlag von Rosenbaum & Hart, 1905.

——. *Das Schächten: Eine vorläufige Auseinandersetzung.* Berlin: Druckerei u. Verlag, U-G, 1906.

——. *Replik des Dr. Hirsch Hildesheimer auf das Druckwerk, welches der Buchdruckerei-Besitzer F. W. Glöss seiner Klage-Beantwortung entgegengestellt hat.* Berlin: H.S. Hermann, 189?

Hillker, Georg. *Der Lehrer, die Schule und die Tierschutzsache.* Paderborn: Druck und Verlag der Bonifacius-Druckerei, 1898.

Hirsch, Samson Raphael. "Milah." In *Jewish Symbolism.* Ed. Samson Raphael Hirsch, 65–111. New York: Philipp Feldheim, 1984.

Hoffman, Lawrence A. *Covenant of Blood: Circumcision and Gender in Rabbinic Judaism.* Chicago: University of Chicago Press, 1996.

Hoffmann, Christhard. "The German-Jewish Encounter and German Historical Culture." *Leo Baeck Institute Yearbook* 41 (1996): 277–290.

——. "Political Culture and Violence Against Minorities: The Antisemitic Riots in Pomerania and West Prussia." Trans. A. D. Moses. In *Exclusionary Violence: Antisemitic Riots in Modern German History.* Ed. Christhard Hoffmann, Werner Bergmann, and Helmut Walser Smith, 67–92. Ann Arbor: University of Michigan Press, 2002.

Hohendahl, Peter Uwe. *Building a National Literature: The Case of Germany, 1830–1870.* Ithaca: Cornell University Press, 1989.

Holborn, Hajo. *A History of Modern Germany.* Vol. 2. Princeton: Princeton University Press, 1982.

Holdheim, Samuel. *Ueber die Beschneidung zunächst in religiös-dogmatischer Beziehung.* Schwerin: Verlag der E. Kürschner'schen Buchhandlung (M. Marcus), 1844.

Homa, Bernard. *Metzitzah.* London: self-published, 1960.

Horovitz, Markus. *Frankfurter Rabbinen: Ein Beitrag zur Geschichte der israelitischen Gemeinde in Frankfurt a.M.* Hildeshim and New York: Georg Olm Verlag, 1972.

Hübinger, Gangolf. "Confessionalism." In *Imperial Germany: A Historiographical Companion.* Ed. Roger Chickering. Westport, CT: Greenwood Press, 1996.

Huerkamp, Claudia. "Ärzte und Professionalisierung in Deutschland: Überlegungen zum Wandel des Arztberufs im 19. Jahrhundert." *Geschichte und Gesellschaft* 6 (1980): 349–366.

Hull, Isabel V. *Absolute Destruction: Military Culture and the Practices of War in Imperial Germany.* Ithaca: Cornell University Press, 2005.

Hunt, J.C. "Peasants, Grain Tariffs, and Meat Quotas." *Central European History* 7 (1974): 311–331.

Hyman, Paula E. *The Emancipation of the Jews of Alsace.* New Haven: Yale University Press, 1991.

Ilgen, Theodor. "Organisation der staatlichen Verwaltung und der Selbstverwaltung." In *Die Rheinprovinz 1815–1915: Hundert Jahre preußischer Herrschaft am Rhein.* Ed. Joseph Hansen, 87–148. Vol. 1. Bonn; A. Marcus & E. Webers Verlag, 1917.

Israelitische Religionsgemeinde. *Denkschrift betreffend die von der Israelitischen Religions-Gesellschaft in Offenbach gewünschte Anstellung eines zweiten Schächters sowie auch das Verhältniß dieser Gesellschaft zur Israelitischen Religions-Gemeinde im Allgemeinen.* Offenbach a.M.: Druck von Kohler & Teller, 1864.

Itzkowitz, David C. "The Jews of Europe and the Limits of Religious Freedom." In *Freedom and Religion in the Nineteenth Century.* Ed. Richard Helmstadter, 150–171. Stanford, CA: Stanford University Press, 1997.

Jaffé, Julius. *Die Rituelle Circumcision im Lichte der antiseptischen Chirurgie mit Berücksichtigung der religiösen Vorschriften.* Leipzig: Gustav Fock, 1886.

Johlson, Josef. *Ueber die Beschneidung in historischer und dogmatischer Hinsicht; Ein Wort zu seiner Zeit. Den Denkenden in Israel zur Prüfung vorgelegt von Bar Amithai.* Frankfurt am Main: J.E. Hermann'sche Buchandlung, 1843.

John, Michael. "Constitution, Administration, and the Law." In *Imperial Germany: A Historiographical Companion.* Ed. Roger Chickering. Westport, CT: Greenwood Press, 1996. 185–214.

Judd, Robin. *German Jewish Rituals, Bodies, and Citizenship.* Ph.D. diss. University of Michigan, 2000.

——. "Samuel Holdheim and the German Circumcision Debates." *Re-Defining Judaism in an Age of Emancipation:Comparative Perspectives on Samuel Holdheim (1806–1860).* Ed. Christian Weise, 127–142. Leiden: Brill, 2007.

Junack, M. "Zu der Frage, ob Schlachtrinder durch Elektrizität betäubt werden können." *Die Literarische Umschau* (5 July 1931)

Kaelter, Robert. *Geschichte der jüdischen Gemeinde zu Potsdam.* Trans. Julius H. Schopes and Hermann Simon. 1903. Reprint. Berlin: Edition Hentrich, 1993.

Kallner, Josef. "Schächtvorschriften und Volkshygiene." In *Hygiene und Judentum: Eine Sammelschrift.* Ed. Hans Goslar, 36–41. Dresden: Verlag Jac. Sternlicht, 1930.

Kant, Immanuel. "Grundlegung zur Metaphysik der Sitten (1785)." In *Kant's gesammelte Schriften.,* Ed. Georg Reimer, 385–464. Vol. 4. Berlin: Georg Reimer, 1902–1903.

Kaplan, Marion A. *Between Dignity and Despair: Jewish Life in Nazi Germany.* New York: Oxford University, 1988.

——. "Friendship on the Margins: Jewish Social Relations in Imperial Germany." *Central European History* 34.4 (2001): 471–501.

——., ed. *Jewish Daily Life in Germany, 1618–1945.* Oxford: Oxford University Press, 2005.

——. "Redefining Judaism in Imperial Germany: Practices, Mentalities, and Community," *Jewish Social Studies* 9.1 (2002): 1–33.

Kaplan, Mordechai M. *Judaism as a Civilization: Towards a Reconstruction of American-Jewish Life.* New York: Macmillan, 1934.

——. *The Meaning of God in Modern Jewish Religion.* New York: Reconstructionist Press, 1962.

Kater, Michael H. "Professionalization and Socialization of Physicians in Wilhelmine and Weimar Germany." *Journal of Contemporary History* 20 (1985): 677–701.

Katz, Jacob. "Berthold Auerbach's Anticipation of the German-Jewish Tragedy." *Hebrew Union College Annual* 53 (1982): 215–240.

——. "The Controversy over Brit Milah during the first half of the 19th Century," In *Jewish Law in Conflict* (Hebrew). Ed. Jacob Katz, 123–149. Jerusalem: Magnes Press, 1992.

——. *Exclusiveness and Tolerance.* Reprint ed. Westport, CT: Greenwood Press, 1980.

——. Die Halacha unter dem Druck der modernen Verhältnisse." In *Judentum im deutschen Sprachraum.* Ed. Karl E. Grözinger, 309–324. Frankfurt am Main: Suhrkamp, 1991.

——. "The Metsitsah Controversy." In *Jewish Law in Conflict* (Hebrew). Ed. Jacob Katz, 150–183. Jerusalem: Magnes Press, 1992.

——. *Out of the Ghetto: The Social Background of Jewish Emancipation.* New York: Schocken Books, 1973.

——. "Religion as a Uniting and Dividing Force in Modern Jewish History." In *The Role of Religion in Modern Jewish History.* Ed. Jacob Katz, 1–15. Cambridge: Association for Jewish Studies, 1975.

——. *Tradition and Crisis.* Translated by Bernard Dov Cooperman. New York: Schocken Books, 1993.

Kayserling, Meyer. *Die rituelle Schlachtfrage oder ist Schächten Thierquäelerei?* Aargau: Druck und Verlag von H. R. Sauerländer, 1867.

Keane, John. "Despotism and Democracy: The Origins and Development of the Distinction between Civil Society and the State 1750–1850." In *Civil Society and the State.* Ed. John Keane, 35–72. London: Verso, 1988..

Keller, A. *Das Schächten der Israeliten, Referat gehalten an einer Versammlung von Thierschutzfreunden am 2 April 1890.* Aargau: Ph. Wirz-Schriften, 1890.

Kertzer, David I. *The Popes Against the Jews: The Vatican's Role in the Rise of Modern Anti-Semitism.* New York: Alfred A. Knopf, 2001.

Kieval, Hillel J. "Representation and Knowledge in Medieval and Modern Accounts of Jewish Ritual Murder." *Jewish Social Studies* 1 (1995): 52–72.

Klein, Carl. *Sind geschächtete Tiere sofort nach dem Schächtschnitt bewußtlos?* Berlin: Berliner Tierschutzverein, 1927.

Klenk, Philipp. *Tierschutz in Schule und Gemeinde. Neue Ausgabe von 1907.* Berlin: Berliner Tierschutz-Verein, 1907.

Kohn, P.J., ed. *Rabbinischer Humor aus alter und neuer Zeit.* Berlin: Verlag Louis Lamm, 1915.

Koltun-Fromm, Ken. *Moses Hess and Modern Jewish Identity.* Bloomington: Indiana University Press, 2001.

Komite zur Abwehrantisemitischer Angriffe, *Gutachten über das jüdische-rituelle Schlachtverfahren ("Schächten")*. Berlin: Verlag von Emil Apolant, 1894.

Koshar, Rudy. *Social Life, Local Politics, and Nazism: Marburg, 1880–1935*. Chapel Hill: University of North Carolina Press, 1986.

Krabbe, Wolfgang R. *Die deutsche Stadt im 19. und 20. Jahrhundert*. Göttingen: Vandenhoeck & Ruprecht, 1989.

Krauthammer, Pascal. *Das Schächtverbot in der Schweiz 1854–2000: Die Schächtfrage zwischen Tierschutz, Politik, und Fremdenfeindlichkeit*. Zürich: Schulthess, 2000.

Krohn, Helga. *Die Juden in Hamburg 1800–1850: Ihre soziale, kulturelle und politische Entwicklung während der Emanzipationszeit*. Hamburg: Europäische Verlasanstalt, 1967.

Kyber, Manfred. *Tierschutz und Kultur*. Stuttgart: Walter Seifert Verlag, 1925.

Ladd, Brian. *Urban Planning and Civic Order in Germany, 1860–1914*. Cambridge: Harvard University Press, 1990.

Lamberti, Marjorie. *Jewish Activism in Imperial Germany: The Struggle for Civil Equality*. New Haven: Yale University Press, 1978.

——. "Liberals, Socialists and the Defence against Antisemitism in the Wilhelminian Period." *Leo Baeck Institute Yearbook* 25 (1980): 147–162.

Landau, Wolff. "Antrag an die zweite Synode," *Referat über die der ersten israelitischen Synode zu Leipzig überreichten Anträg*. Ed. Wolff Landau, 195–217. Berlin: Louis Gerschel Verlagsbuchhandlung, 1871.

Landsberg, Wilhelm. *Das Rituelle Schächten der israeliten im Lichte der Wahrheit*. Kaiserlautern: Verlag von Eugen Crufins, 1882.

Langewiesche, Dieter. *Liberalismus in Deutschland*. Frankfurt am Main: Suhrkamp Verlag, 1988.

Lässig, Simone. "Emancipation and Embourgeoisement: The Jews, the State, and the Middle Classes in Saxony and Anhalt-Dessau." In *Saxony in German History: Culture, Society, and Politics, 1830–1933*. Ed. James Retallack, 99–118. Ann Arbor: University of Michigan Press, 2000.

Lehnert, Herbert. "Leo Naphta und sein Autor (Thomas Mann)." *Orbis Litterarum* 37.1 (1982): 47–69.

Lenger, Friedrich. "Bürgertum und Stadtverwaltung in Rheinischen Grossstädten des 19. Jahrhunderts: zu einem vernachlässigten Aspekt bürgerlicher Herrschaft." In *Stadt und Bürgertum im 19. Jahrhundert*. Ed. Lothar Gall, 97–169. Munich: R. Oldenbourg, 1990.

Levine, Herbert S. *Hitler's Free City: A History of the Nazi Party in Danzig, 1925–1939*. Chicago: University of Chicago Press, 1970.

Levit, Eugen. *Die Circumcision der Israeliten*. Wien: Druck und Commissions-Verlag von Carl Gerold's Sohn, 1874.

Levy, Jacob. *Das neue Niederlegeverfahren bei der Schlachtung: Nachwort zur Umfrage der Tierschutzvereine vom Jahre 1927*. Berlin: Reichszentrale Schächtangelegenheiten, 1930.

Levy, Ludwig. "Ist das Kainszeichen die Beschneidung? Ein kritischer Beitrag zur Bibelexegese." In *Imago: Zeitschrift für Anwendung der Psychoanalyse auf die Geisteswissenschaften*. Ed. Sigmund Freud. Leipzig und Wien: Internationaler Psychoanalytischer Verlag, 1919. 290–293.

Levy, Richard S. *The Downfall of the Anti-Semitic Political Parties in Imperial Germany*. New Haven: Yale University Press, 1975.

Liberles, Robert. *Religious Conflict in Social Context: The Resurgence of Orthodox Judaism in Frankfurt Am Main, 1838–1877*. Westport, CT: Greenwood Press, 1985.

———. "Emancipation and the Structure of the Jewish Community in the Nineteenth Century." *Leo Baeck Institute Yearbook* 31 (1986): 51–67.

———. "The So-Called Quiet Years of German Jewry 1849–1869: A Reconsideration." *Leo Baeck Institute Yearbook* 41 (1996): 65–74.

Liepach, Martin. *Das Wahlverhalten der jüdischen Bevölkerung. Zur politischen Orientierung der Juden in der Weimarer Republik*. Tübingen: Mohr Siebeck, 1996.

Loeb, Heinrich. "Circumcision und Syphilis-Prophylaxe." *Sonderabdruck aus der "Monatsschrift für Harnkrankeiten und Sexuelle Hygiene"*. Vol. 6. Leipzig: Verlag der Monatsschrift für Harnkrankheiten und Sexuelle Hygiene, W. Malende, 1904. 1–6.

Löffler, Gustav. *Die Beschneidung im Lichte der Medizin: Vier Vorträge von Dr. med. Gustav Löffler gehalten im "Mohelim-Verein" zu Frankfurt a.M*. Frankfurt a.M.: Buchdruckerei Louis Golde, 1912.

Löw, Albert. *Thierschutz im Judenthume nach Bibel und Talmud*. Budapest: Buchdruckerei F. Buschmann, 1890.

Löwenstein, Ludwig. *Die Beschneidung im Lichte der heutigen medicinischen Wissenschaft, mit Berücksichtigung ihrer geschichtlichen und unter Würdigung ihrer religiösen Bedeutung*. Trier: Commissionsverlag von Heinr. Stephanus, 1897.

Lowenstein, Steven M., ed. *The Mechanics of Change: Essays in the Social History of German Jewry*. Atlanta, Georgia: Scholars Press, 1992.

Ludendorff, Erich. *Die Vollendung des künstlichen Juden durch Zwangsbeschneidung*. Berlin: self published, 1927.

Maayan, Shmuel. *Struggles for a System of Elections in the Union of German-Jewish Communities (Deutsch-Israelitischer Gemeindebund) in the Years 1911 and 1912* (Hebrew). Givat-Haviva: The Zvi Lurie Institute, 1982.

Maehle, Andreas-Holger, and Ulrich Tröhler. "Animal Experimentation from Antiquity to the End of the Eighteenth Century: Attitudes and Arguments." In *Vivisection in Historical Perspective*. Ed. Nicolaas A. Rupke, 14–47. London: Routledge, 1987.

Mann, Thomas. *The Magic Mountain*. Trans. John E. Woods. New York: Vintage Books, 1995.

Marcus, Ivan G. *Rituals of Childhood*. New Haven: Yale University Press, 1996.

Margaliot, Abraham. "Remarks on the Political and Ideological Development of the Centralverein before 1914." *Leo Baeck Institute Yearbook* 33 (1988): 101–106.

Martin, M. H. G. *De la circoncision avec un novel appareil inventé par l'auteur poru faire la circoncision*. Paris: Adrien Delahaye, 1870.

Mayersohn. *De la Circoncision et Spécialement de la Circoncision Rituelle*. Paris: Henri Jouve, 1905.

McElligott, Anthony. *Contested City: Municipal Politics and the Rise of Nazism in Altona, 1917–1937*. Ann Arbor: University of Michigan Press, 1998.

Melton, James Van Horn. "The Emergence of 'Society' in Eighteenth- and Ninteenth-Century Germany." In *Language, History and Class*. Ed. Penelope J. Corfield, 131–149. Oxford/Cambridge: Basil Blackwell, 1991.

Mendelsohn, Ezra. *On Modern Jewish Politics.* New York: Oxford University Press, 1993.

Mendes-Flohr, Paul. *German Jews: A Dual Identity.* New Haven: Yale University Press, 1999.

Meyer, Michael A. "Alienated Intellectuals in the Camp of Religious Reform: The Frankfurt Reformfreunde, 1842–1845." *AJS Review* 6 (1981): 61–86.

——. "Berit Mila Within the History of the Reform Movement." In *Berit Mila in the Reform Context.* Ed. Lewis M. Barth, 141–151. Berit Mila Board of Reform Judaism, 1990.

——., ed. *German-Jewish History in Modern Times.* Vol. 2, *Emancipation and Acculturation 1780–1871.* New York: Columbia University Press, 1997.

——., ed. *German-Jewish History in Modern Times.* Vol. 3, *Integration in Dispute 1871–1918.* New York: Columbia University Press, 1997.

——., ed. *German-Jewish History in Modern Times.* Vol. 4, *Renewal and Destruction, 1918–1945.* New York: Columbia University Press, 1998.

——. "German-Jewish Social Thought in the Mid-Nineteenth Century—A Comment." In *Revolution and Evolution: 1848 in German-Jewish History.* Ed. Arnold Paucker, Werner E. Mosse, and Reinhard Rürup, 329–335. Tübingen: J.C.B. Mohr, 1981.

——. *Response to Modernity: A History of the Reform Movement in Judaism.* New York and Oxford: Oxford University Press, 1988.

Mittermaier, Carl. *Das Schlachten geschildert und erlätert auf Grund zahlreicher neuerer Gutachten.* Heidelberg: Carl Winter's Universitätsbuchhandlung, 1902.

Moeller, Robert. "Peasants and Tarrifs in the Kaiserreich." *Agricultural History* 55 (1981): 370–384.

Morgenthaler, Sibylle. "Countering the Pre-1933 Nazi Boycott against the Jews." *Leo Baeck Institute Yearbook* 36 (1991): 127–149.

Mosse, George. *German Jews beyond Judaism.* Cincinnati: Hebrew Union College Press, 1985.

Mosse, Werner E. "From 'Schutzjuden' to 'Deutsche Staatsbürger Jüdischen Glaubens': The Long and Bumpy Road of Jewish Emancipation in Germany." In *Paths of Emancipation: Jews, States, and Citizenship.* Ed. Pierre Birnbaum and Ira Katznelson, 59–93. Princeton, NJ: Princeton University Press, 1995.

Muir, Edward. *Ritual in Early Modern Europe.* Cambridge: Cambridge University Press, 1997.

Müller, Max. "Das Elektrische Betäuben der Schlachttiere." *Monatsschrift für Schlachthoftechnik und veterinäre Nahrungsmittelhygiene* 27 (10 November 1927): 446.

——. *Die Schächtfrage.* Berlin: Berliner Tierschutzverein, 1927.

——. *Warum humanes Schlachten: Eine Stellungnahme gegen das betäubungslose Verbluten und für den gesetzlichen Betäubungszwang beim Schlachten der Tiere.* Kirchhain: Brücke-Verlag Kurt Schmersow, 1931.

Münz, P. "Ueber die Vortheile der rituellen Beschneidung." *Münchener Medicinische Wochenschrift* 9 (1898): 244–266.

Neuman, R. P. "Masturbation, Madness, and the Modern Concepts of Childhood and Adolescence." *Journal of Social History* 8 (1975): 1–27.

Niewyk, Donald. *The Jews in Weimar Germany*. Baton Rouge: University of Louisiana Press, 1980.

Nipperdey, Thomas. "Interessenverbände und Parteien in Deutschland vor dem Ersten Weltkrieg." In *Moderne Deutsche Geschichte*. Ed. Hans-Ulrich Wehler, 369–388. Cologne: Keipenheur u. Witsch, 1966.

——. "Verein als soziale Struktur in Deutschland im späten 18. und frühen 19. Jahrhundert. Eine Fallstudie zur Modernisierung I." In *Gesellschaft, Kultur, Theorie: Gesammelte Aufsätze zur neueren Geschichte*. Ed. Thomas Nipperdey, 174–205. Göttingen: Vandenhoeck und Ruprecht, 1976.

Nossig, Alfred. *Die Sozialhygiene der Juden und des altorientalischen Völkerkreises*. Stuttgart, Leipzig, Berlin and Wien: Deutsche Verlags-Anstalt, 1894.

Osmond, Jonathan. *Rural Protest in the Weimar Republic: The Free Peasantry in the Rhineland and Bavaria*. New York: St. Martin's Press, 1993

Palmowksi, Jan. "The Politics of the 'Unpolitical German': Liberalism in German Local Government, 1860–1880." *The Historical Journal* 42.3 (1999): 675–705.

Paucker, Arnold. *Der jüdische Abwehrkampf gegen Antisemitismus und Nationalsozialismus in den letzten Jahren der Weimarer Republik*. Hamburg: Leibniz-Verlag, 1968.

Penslar, Derek J. "Philanthropy, the 'Social Question' and Jewish Identity in Imperial Germany." *Leo Baeck Institute Yearbook* 38 (1993): 51–73.

——. *Shylock's Children: Economics and Jewish Identity in Modern Europe*. Berkeley: University of California Press, 2001.

Petuchowski, Jakob J. "Abraham Geiger and Samuel Holdheim: Their Differences in Germany and Repercussions in America." *Leo Baeck Institute Yearbook* 22 (1977): 139–159.

Peukert, Detlev J. K. *The Weimar Republic: The Crisis of Classical Modernity*. Trans. Richard Deveson. New York: Hill and Wang, 1987.

Philippson, Johanna. "Ludwig Philippson und die Allgemeine Zeitung des Judentums." In *Studien zur Frühgeschichte der Emanzipation*. Ed. Hans Liebeschütz and Arnold Paucker, 243–291. Tübingen: Schriftenreihe wissenschaftlicher Abhandlungen des Leo Baeck Instituts, 1977.

Philipson, David. *The Reform Movement in Judaism*. Rev. ed. New York: Ktav Publishing House, 1967.

Pickus, Keith H. "German Jewish Identity in the Kaiserreich: Observations and Methodological Concerns." *Jewish History* 9.2 (1995): 73–91.

Ploss, Hermann Heinrich. "Geschichtliches und Ethnologisches über Knabenbeschneidung." *Deutsches Archiv für Geschichte der Medicin und medicinische Geographie* 8.3 (1885): 312–343.

Pott, R[ichard?]. "Ueber die Gefahren der rituellen Beschneidung." *Münchener medizinische Wochenschrift* (1898): 100–113.

Preuss, Julius. *Biblical and Talmudic Medicine*. Trans. Fred Rosner. 2nd ed. Northvale, NJ: Jason Aronson, 1993.

Preyer. *Die Schächtfrage: Widerlegung des von Herrn Magistrats-Vice-Director Preyer in der Ausschuss-Sitzung des Wiener Thierschutz-Vereines vom 9. December 1899*. Wien: Verlag des israelitischen Cultusgemeinde (Druck von Ignaz Spitz), 1900.

Pucher, S. *Mitgefühl mit den Thieren eine heilige Pflicht der jüdischen Religion: ein Wort an seine Glaubensgenossen.* Mitau: J.F. Steffenhagen und Sohn, 1876.

Pulzer, Peter. "Jewish Participation in Wilhelmine Politics." In *Jews and Germans from 1860 to 1933: The Problematic Symbiosis.* Ed. David Bronsen, 78–99. Heidelberg: Carl Winter Universitätsverlag, 1979.

———. *Jews and the German State: The Political History of a Minority, 1848–1933.* Oxford: Blackwell, 1992.

———. *The Rise of Political Anti-semitism in Germany and Austria.* Rev. ed. Cambridge: Harvard University Press, 1988.

Rabbinowicz, Israel Michal. *Die thalmudischen Principien des Schächtens und die Medicin des Thalmuds.* Trans. S. Trier. Paris: self-published, 1881.

Rahden, Till van. "Ideologie und Gewalt: Neuerscheinungen über den Antisemitismus in der deutschen Geschichte des 19. und freuehen 20. Jahrhunderts." *Neue Politische Literatur* 41 (1996): 11–29.

———. "Intermarriage, the New Woman, and the Situational Ethnicity of Breslau Jews, 1870s to 1920s." *Leo Baeck Institute Yearbook* 46 (2001): 125–150.

———. "Words and Actions: Rethinking the Social History of German Antisemitism, Breslau, 1870–1914." *German History* 18.4 (2000): 413–438.

Ramdohr, Hermann. *Kritische Betrachtungen, Wünsche und Anregungen.* Leipzig: Franz Wagner, 1928.

———., ed. *Leipziger Flugschriften-Sammlung zur Betäubungsfrage der Schlachttiere.* 9 vols. Leipzig: Haberland, 1907.

Reichszentrale Schächtangelgenheiten. *Das Neue Niederlegeverfahren bei der Schlachtung von Grosstieren.* Berlin: self-published, 1930.

Reik, Theodor. "Das Kainszeichen: Ein psychoanalytischer Beitrag zur bibelkerlärung." In *Imago: Zeitschrift für Anwendung der Psychoanalyse auf die Geisteswissenschaften.* Ed. Sigmund Freud, 31–42. Leipzig und Wien: Internationaler Psychoanalytischer Verlag, 1919.

Reinharz, Jehuda. *Fatherland or Promised Land: The Dilemma of the German Jew, 1893–1914.* Ann Arbor: University of Michigan Press, 1975.

Remondino, P. C. *History of Circumcision from the Earliest Times to the Present: Moral and Physical Reasons for Its Performance, with a History of Eunuchism, Hermaphrodism, etc., and Of the Different Operations Practiced upon the Prepuce.* Philadelphia: F.A. Davis, 1891.

Reulecke, Jürgen, ed. *Die deutsche Stadt im Industriezeitalter.* Wuppertal: Peter Hammer, 1978.

Ritter, Gerhard A. "Parlament, Parteien und Ineressenverbände 1890–1914." In *Das kaiserliche Deutschland.* Ed. Michael Stürmer, 340–377. Düsseldorf: Droste Verlag, 1970.

Ritvo, Harriet. *The Animal Estate: The English and other Creatures in the Victorian Age.* Cambridge: Harvard University Press, 1987.

Roberts, Mary Louise. *Civilization Without Sexes: Reconstructing Gender in Postwar France, 1917–1927.* Chicago: University of Chicago Press, 1994.

Rohling, August. *Die Polemik und das Menschenopfer: Eine wissenschaftliche Antwort ohne Polemik für die Rabbiner und ihre Genossen.* Paderborn: Druck und Verlag der Bonifacins-Druckerei, 1883.

Rohrbacher, Stefan, and Michael Schmidt. *Judenbilder: Kulturgeschichte antijüdicher Mythen und antisemitischer Vorurteile.* Reinbeck bei Hamburg: Rowohlt Taschenbuch Verlag, 1991.

Rosenberg, Hans. *Grosse Depression und Bismarckzeit: Wirtschaftsablauf, Gesellschaft und Politik in Mitteleuropa.* Berlin: de Gruyter, 1967.

Rosenzweig, David. *Zur Beschneidungsfrage: ein Beitrag zur öffentlichen Gesundheitspflege.* 2nd ed. Schweidnitz: Verlag von C. F. Weigmann, 1889.

Ross, Ronald. "Enforcing the Kulturkampf in the Bismarckian State and the Limits of Coercion in Imperial Germany." *Journal of Modern History* 56 (1984): 456–482.

——. *The Failure of Bismarck's Kulturkampf: Catholicism and State Power in Imperial Germany, 1871–1887.* Washington, DC: Catholic University of America Press, 1998.

——. "The Kulturkampf and the Limitations of Power in Bismarck's Germany." *Journal of Ecclesistical History* 46.4 (1995): 669–688.

Rothbarth, E. *50 Jahre Kieler Tierschutzverein.* Kiel: CHR Haase & Co., 1922.

Rozenblit, Marsha L. "Jewish Identity and the Modern Rabbi: The Cases of Isak Noa Mannheimer, Adolf Jellinek, and Moritz Güdemann in Nineteenth-Century Vienna." *Leo Baeck Institute Yearbook* 35 (1990): 103–131.

Rund, Moritz, ed. *Perlen jüdischen Humors: Eine Sammlung von Scherzen und kleinen Erzählungen aus dem jüdischen Volksleben.* Berlin: Verlag von Max Schildberger, 1914.

Rürup, Reinhard. "Emancipation and Crisis: The 'Jewish Question' in Germany, 1850–1890." *Leo Baeck Institute Yearbook* 20 (1975): 13–25.

——. *Emanzipation und Antisemitismus.* Göttingen: Vandenhoeck & Ruprecht, 1975.

——. "Jewish Emancipation and Bourgeois Society." *Leo Baeck Institute Yearbook* 14 (1969): 67–91.

——. "The Tortuous and Thorny Path to Legal Equality 'Jew Laws' and Emancipatory Legislation in Germany from the Late Eighteenth Century." *Leo Baeck Institute Yearbook* 31 (1986): 3–49.

Ruthner, Clemens. "Vampirism as Political Theory: Voltaire to Alfred Rosenberg and Elfriede Jelinek." In *Visions of the Fantastic: Selected Essays from the Fifteenth International Conference on the Fantastic in the Arts,* ed. Allienne R. Becker, 3–11. Westport, CT: Greenwood Press, 1996.

Salomon, M.G. *Die Beschneidung: historisch und medizinisch Beleuchtet.* Braunschweig: Friedrich Vieweg und Sohn, 1844.

Schieder, Theodor. *Das deutsche Kaiserreich von 1871 als Nationalstaat.* Cologne: Westdeutscher Verlag, 1961.

Schilling Gustave (pseudo. Ben Rabbi). *Die Lehre von der Beschneidung der Israeliten, in ihrer mosaischen Reinheit dargestellt und entwickelt.* Stuttgart: Hallberger'sche Verlhagshandlung, 1844.

Schleunes, Karl A. *The Twisted Road to Auschwitz; Nazi Policy toward German Jews, 1933–1939.* Urbana: University of Illinois Press, 1970.

Schlich, Thomas. "Medicalization and Secularization: The Jewish Ritual Bath as a Problem of Hygiene (Germany 1820s-1840s)." *Social History of Medicine* 8:3 (1995): 423–442.

Schlüssel, Erich. "Hygienische Auswirkungen der Beschneidung." In *Hygiene und Judentum: Eine Sammelschrift.* Ed. Hans Goslar, 23–25. Dresden: Verlag Jac. Sternlicht, 1930.

Schmidt, Hans D. "The Terms of Emancipation: The Public Debate in Germany and its Effects on the Mentality and Ideas of German Jewry." *Leo Baeck Institute Yearbook* 1 (1956): 28–45.

Schmidtmann, A., ed. *Tierschutz-Kalender 1913.* Berlin: Berliner Tierschutzverein und Deutschen Lehrer-Tierschutzverein, 1913.

Scholem, Gershom. "On the Social Psychology of the Jews in Germany, 1900–1933." In *Jews and Germans from 1860–1933: The Problematic Symbiosis.* Ed. David Bronsen, 9–32. Heidelberg: Winter, 1979.

Schorsch, Ismar. *Jewish Reactions to German Anti-Semitism.* New York: Columbia University Press, 1972.

———. "Scholarship in the Service of Reform." In *From Text to Context: The Turn to History in Modern Judaism.* Ed. Ismar Schorsch, 302–333. Hanover, NH: Brandeis University Press/University of New England Press, 1994.

Schroeder, Paul W. *The Transformation of European Politics, 1763–1848.* New York: Oxford University Press, 1994.

Schwanthaler, J. "Der Gevatter erwartet das Kind." In *Professor M. Oppenheim's Bilder aus dem Altjüdischen Familien-Leben.* Ed. J. Schwanthaler, 1. Frankfurt a.M.: Verlag von Heinrich Keller, 1876.

Schwantje, Magnus. *Die Beziehungen der Tierschutzbewegung zu andern ethischen Bestrebungen.* Berlin: Gesellschaft zur Förderung der Tierschutzes und verwandter Bestrebungen, 1909.

Schwartz, Ernst von. *Das betäubungslose Schächten der Israeliten: Vom Standpunkt des 20. Jahrhunderts auf Grund von Schächt-Tatsachen geschildert und erläutert.* Konstanz am Bodensee: Verlag von Ersnt Ackermann, 1905.

———. "Das Schächten." *Süddeutsche Monatshefte.* (April 1910): 514–523.

Seehaus, Otto. *Tierschutz und Tierquälerei.* Berlin: Otto Bremer, 1896.

Sheehan, James J. "Liberalism and the City in Nineteenth-Century Germany." *Past & Present* 51 (1971): 116–137.

Silverman, Dan. *Reluctant Union: Alsace-Lorraine and Imperial Germany, 1871–1918.* University Park: Pennsylvania State University Press, 1972.

Shorter, Edward. *A History of Women's Bodies.* New York: Basic Books, 1982.

Simon. *Die rituelle Schlachtmethode der Juden vom Standpunkt der Kritik und der Geschichte.* Frankfurt a.M.: Verlag von J. Kauffmann, 1893.

Smith, Helmut Walser. *The Butcher's Tale: Murder and Anti-Semitism in a German Town.* New York: W.W. Norton, 2002.

———. *German Nationalism and Religious Conflict: Culture, Ideology, Politics, 1870–1914.* Princeton, NJ: Princeton University Press, 1995.

Sorabji, Richard. *Animal Minds and Human Morals: the Origins of the Western Debate.* Ithaca: Cornell University Press, 1993.

Sorkin, David. *The Transformation of German Jewry 1780–1840.* New York: Oxford University Press, 1987.

——. "Jews, the Enlightenment and Religious Toleration—Some Reflections." *Leo Baeck Institute Yearbook* 37 (1992): 3–16.

Sperber, Jonathan. *Popular Catholicism in Nineteenth-Century Germany.* Princeton, NJ: Princeton University Press, 1984.

Steinschneider, Moritz. *Die Beschneidung: der Araber und Muhamedaner mit Rücksicht auf die Neueste Beschneidungsliteratur.* Wien: Gedruckt bei Franz Edlen von Schmid und J. J. Busch, 1845.

Steintrager, James A. *Cruel Delight: Enlightenment Culture and the Inhuman.* Bloomington: Indiana University Press, 2004.

Stern, Fritz. *The Politics of Cultural Despair.* Paperback ed. Berkeley: University of California Press, 1961.

Stern, R. *Eine neue Methode zum Niederlegen des zum Schächten bestimmen.* Fulda: self-published, 1893.

Strack, Hermann Leberecht. *Der Blutaberglaube in der Menschenheit, Blutmorde, und Blutritus.* Munich: CH Beck, 1892.

Suchy, Barbara. "The Verein zur Abwehr des Antisemitismus (I) From Its Beginnings to the First World War." *Leo Baeck Institute Yearbook* 28 (1983): 205–239.

Tal, Uriel. *Christians and Jews in Germany: Religion, Politics, and Ideology in the Second Reich, 1870–1914.* Trans. Noah Jonathan Jacobs. Ithaca: Cornell University Press, 1975.

Taylor, Richard. *Film Propaganda: Soviet Russia and Nazi Germany.* London: I.B. Tauris, 1998.

Theilhaber, Felix A. *Die Beschneidung.* Berlin: Louis Lamm, 1927.

Toury, Jacob. *Die politischen Orientierungen der Juden in Deutschland: von Jena bis Weimar.* Tübingen: J.C.B. Mohr, 1966.

Trevor-Roper, Hugh. "Toleration and Religion after 1688." *From Persecution to Toleration: The Glorious Revolution and Religion in England.* Ed. Ole Peter Grell, Jonathan Irvine Israel, and Nicholas Tyacke, 389–408. Oxford: Clarendon Press, 1991.

Trier, Salomon Abraham, ed. *Rabbinische Gutachten über die Beschneidung.* Frankfurt am Main: Druck der J.F. Bach'schen Buch- und Stenidruckerei, 1844.

Tröhler, Ulrich, and Andreas-Holger Maehle. "Anti-vivisection in Nineteenth-century Germany and Switzerland: Motives and Methods." In *Vivisection in Historical Perspective.* Ed. Nicolaas A. Rupke, 149–187. London: Routledge, 1987.

Trommler, Frank. "The Creation of a Culture of *Sachlichkeit.*" In *Society, Culture, and the State in Germany 1870–1930.* Ed. Geoff Eley. Ann Arbor: University of Michigan Press, 1996.

Trzeciakoskki, Lech. *The Kulturkampf in Prussian Poland.* Translated by Katarzyna Kretkowska. New York: Columbia University Press, 1990.

Turner, Victor. *The Forest of Symbols: Aspects of Ndembu Ritual.* Ithaca: Cornell University Press, 1967.

——. *The Ritual Process: Structure and Anti-Structure.* Ithaca: Cornell University Press, 1969.

Verein zur Abwehr des Antisemitismus. *Ergänzung zum Antisemiten-Spiegel: Die Antisemiten im Lichte des Christenthums, des Rechtes und der Wissenschaft.* Berlin: Hoffschläger Buchdruckerei u. Verlag (F. Sommer), 1903.

Vereins gegen Thierquälerei zu Königsberg. *4 & 5 Bericht über die Thätigkeit des Vereins gegen Thierqualerei zu Königsberg in den Jahren 1873 und 1874.* Königsberg: Ostpreußische Zeitungs- und Verlags-Druckerei, 1875.

Vick, Brian E. *Defining Germany: The 1848 Frankfurt Parliamentarians and National Identity.* Cambridge: Harvard University Press, 2002.

Volkov, Shulamit. "The Ambivalence of Bildung: Jews and Other Germans." In *The German-Jewish Dialogue Reconsidered: A Symposium in Honor of George L. Mosse.* Ed. Klaus L. Berghahn, 81–97. New York: Peter Lang, 1996.

——. "Antisemitism as a Cultural Code: Reflections on the History and Historiography of Antisemitism in Imperial Germany." *Leo Baeck Institute Yearbook* 23 (1978): 25–46.

——. "Die Erfindung einer Tradition: Zur Enstehung des modernen Judentums in Deutschland." *Historische Zeitschrift* 253 (1991): 603–628.

Volland, Alexander "Theodor Fritsch (1852–1933) und die Zeitschrift 'Hammer.'" Inaugural dissertation zur Erlangung des Doktorgrades der Medizin der Johannes Gutenberg-Universität Mainz dem Fachbereich Medizin vorgelegt. Medizinhistorischen Institut der Johannes Gutenberg-Universität Mainz, 1993.

Vorstandes der jüdischen Gemeinde zu Berlin. *Vorstellung des Vorstandes der jüdischen Gemeinde zu Berlin zur Petition des Thierschutz-Vereins das Thierschlachten betreffend.* Berlin: Druck H. Baendel, 1886.

Vorstände der Synagogen-Gemeinden Bückeburg, Hagenburg, Stadthagen und Steinhude. *Petition.* Berlin: Druck von R. Boll, 1907.

Walzer, Michael. *On Toleration.* New Haven: Yale University Press, 1997.

Wassertrilling, Hermann. *Torat ha'brit.* Militsch: Selbstverlage des Herausgebers, 1869.

Weeks, Jeffrey. *Sex, Politics, and Society: The Regulation of Sexuality since 1800.* 2nd ed. London: Longman, 1989.

——. *Sexuality and Its Discontents: Meanings, Myths, and Modern Sexualities.* London: Routledge, 1989.

Weindling, Paul. *Health, Race and German Politics Between National Unification and Nazism, 1870–1945.* Cambridge: Cambridge University Press, 1989.

Wertheimer, Jack. *Unwelcome Strangers: East European Jews in Imperial Germany.* New York: Oxford University Press, 1987.

Wolfers, Philipp. *Brit Kodesh: die Beschneidung der Juden.* Lemford: Friedrich Ernst Huth, 1831.

Wolff, Eberhard. "Medizinische Kompetenz und talmudische Autorität: jüdische Ärzte und Rabbiner als ungleiche Partner in der Debatte um die Beschneidungsreform zwischen 1830 und 1850." In *Judentum und Aufklärung; jüdisches Selbstverständnis in der bürgerlichen Öffentlichkeit.* Ed. Arno Herzig, Hans-Otto Horch, and Robert Jütte, 119–149. Göttingen: Vandenhoeck & Ruprecht, 2002.

Wolff, Salomon Alexander. *Dreinundzwanzig Sätze über die Beschneidung und den jüdisch-confessionell Charakter.* Leipzig: Albert Fritsch, 1869.

Zagler, J. J. *Pflichten gegen der Thiere.* Munich: self-published 1844.

Zagorin, Perez. *How the Idea of Religious Toleration Came to the West.* Princeton, NJ: Princeton University Press, 2003.

Zerbel, Miriam. *Tierschutz im Kaiserreich: Ein Beitrag zur Geschichte des Vereinswesens.* Frankfurt Am Main: Peter Lang, 1993.

Zeydner, H. "Kainszeichen, Keniter und Beschneidung." *Zeitschrift für die alltestamentliche Wissenschaft* 18.1 (1898): 120–125.

Zimmels, H. J. *Magicians, Theologians, and Doctors: Studies in Folk-medicine and Folklore as Reflected in the Rabbinical Responsa (12th–19th Centuries).* London: Edward Goldston & Son, 1952.

Zunz, Leopold. *Gutachten über die Beschneidung.* Frankfurt am Main: Druck der J.J. Bach'schen Buch- und Steindruckerei, 1844.

Index